Historical Conceptions
of Psychology

To Edna Heidbreder, who first aroused our interest in systematic psychology and who has continued to teach us to approach history systematically, this book is dedicated with the admiration and the gratitude of her friends and colleagues in the Cheiron Society.

Historical Conceptions of Psychology

Edited by

MARY HENLE
JULIAN JAYNES
JOHN J. SULLIVAN

SPRINGER PUBLISHING COMPANY, INC.

NEW YORK

SPRINGER PUBLISHING COMPANY, Inc.
200 Park Avenue South, New York, N.Y. 10003

Library of Congress Catalog Card Number: 73-80600

International Standard Book Number: (Hard) 0-8261-1430-X
(Soft) 0-8261-1431-8

Acknowledgments

The articles appearing on the following pages of this book are reprinted by permission of the *Journal of the History of the Behavioral Sciences:* pp. 63-73 (1970, *6*, 131-139); pp. 83-97 (1972, *8*, 168-180); pp.116-128 (1972, *8*, 86-102); pp. 150-165 (1971, *7*, 323-336).

The following articles are reproduced from the *American Psychologist* with the permission of the American Psychological Association and the authors: pp. 13-18 (1967, *22*, 435-443); pp. 74-82 (1969, *24*, 1006-1011); pp. 220-229 (1968, *23*, 149-157); pp. 230-245 (1968, *23*, 434-446).

The article on pp. 3-12 is reprinted from *Science, 136*, 760-764, June 1, 1962, by permission of the publisher and the author. Copyright 1962 by the American Association for the Advancement of Science.

The article on pp. 98-115 is a reprint of R. J. Herrnstein's Introduction to *Behavior: An Introduction to Comparative Psychology* by John B. Watson. Copyright © 1967 by Holt, Rinehart and Winston, Inc. Reprinted by permission of Holt, Rinehart and Winston, Inc.

The article on pp. 166-179 is reprinted with permission from the *Journal of the History of Ideas*, April 1970, 219-234.

The article on pp. 276-285 is from *Schools of Psychology: A Symposium,* edited by David L. Krantz. Copyright © 1969. By permission of Appleton-Century-Crofts, Educational Division, Meredith Corporation.

The article on pp. 286-288 is from the *British Journal of Psychology,* 1963, *54*, 199-200, and is reprinted by permission of The British Psychological Society.

Printed in U.S.A.

LIST OF CONTRIBUTORS

Richard A. Bagg, University of New Hampshire

Geraldine Jonçich Clifford, Ph.D., Associate Professor of Education, University of California, Berkeley

Solomon Diamond, Ph.D., Professor of Psychology, California State University, Los Angeles

Rand B. Evans, Ph.D., Associate Professor of Psychology, University of New Hampshire

Fritz Heider, Ph.D., University Distinguished Professor Emeritus, University of Kansas

Edna Heidbreder, Ph.D., Professor Emeritus of Psychology, Wellesley College

Harry Helson, Ph.D., Professor Emeritus of Psychology, State University of Kansas

Mary Henle, Ph.D., Professor of Psychology, Graduate Faculty, New School for Social Research

Richard J. Herrnstein, Ph.D., Professor of Psychology, Harvard University

Ernest R. Hilgard, Ph.D., Professor Emeritus, Stanford University

Julian Jaynes, Research Psychologist, Princeton University

David L. Krantz, Ph.D., Associate Professor, Lake Forest College

Thomas S. Kuhn, Ph.D., Professor of the History of Science, Princeton University

Robert B. MacLeod, Ph.D., Late Susan Linn Sage Professor of Psychology, Cornell University

Leo J. Postman, Ph.D., Professor of Psychology, University of California, Berkeley

John J. Sullivan, Ph.D., Professor of Psychology, School of Education, New York University

Robert I. Watson, Ph.D., Professor of Psychology, University of New Hampshire

Robert M. Young, Ph.D., Fellow of King's College, Cambridge University

CONTENTS

OF THEORIES AND THEORISTS: OCCASIONAL PAPERS BY EDNA HEIDBREDER

SOURCES IN THE HISTORY OF PSYCHOLOGY

Introduction:
The Study of the
History of Psychology

Julian Jaynes

Why study the history of psychology?

To most historians of science the question is not very interesting. The answer is quite obvious: the historical study of man's Promethean attempt to understand himself on this planet is a fascinating adventure that needs no rationale. It is the view from the mountain tops, the surveying of man's most profound problem against the huge panorama of his history, the place where the grandeur is, where the findings, theories, changing importances, and intellectual heroics of every age — including the present one — are woven into exciting patterns. Why study the history of psychology? Because it *is* psychology, all of it, and psychology cannot be studied seriously apart from its history.

One way to see this is in the everyday nature of contemporary research. Throughout his research, each scientist is actually an historian in his own specialty. Every journal article he writes describing new results necessarily begins with the immediate history of the problem. And it is only that context of history, of what has led up to that particular research, that can give significance and meaning to new findings. And so it is with his specialty. Its meaning, its significance within psychology, depends upon its relation to the larger ongoing history of which it is a part.

This first answer to our question merely touches the surface, for if we probe deeper we come upon more profound reasons which are not so apparent. There is, for example, a kind of truth in the history of a science which transcends the science itself. The history of a science as a kind of metascience is rarely seen by the individual scientist confined to his own specialty, for the very historical contexts that bestow significance on any discovery or specialty reach back in time to prior contexts, which in turn have been generated by still prior causation.

As we examine these matters, we are struck by a remarkable fact: the paths of these questions and contexts through time are not necessarily linear or logical. They diverge and come together, expanding and contracting, on the basis of many variables, only a few of which are what we generally think of in terms of reasoning out the world. The purpose of history is to discover and understand this historical structure which lies at the very foundation of the logical surface of science and to which present discovery is relative. Why study the history of psychology? For itself alone.

Neither science nor the individuals who perform its rites of discovery are outside historical causation. Psychologists, in particular, are as deeply embedded in textures of personal and chance situational causation as the very subjects they study. We can see what to do only by seeing what has been done. We can discover in the present only what we have conjectured in the past. We can recognize in front of us only what past scientific perception has trained us to see. And just as an individual, on the basis of his past history, selects out of his environment a particular phenomenon to attend to and to label as important, so an entire science, utilizing instruments of perception, moves about through its problems and its vital aspects with the same dependence on its history. And just as an individual, to be free, must verbalize the past that has resulted in his present, so an entire science must remain in dialogue with its past and analyze its hidden biases and omissions if it is not to wither away into dried-up specialties and unfulfilling evasions. Why study the past of psychology? Because it is the only way to understand the present.

Most of what I have said so far pertains to all the sciences. But there are reasons applicable to psychology alone, for current psychology is wedded to its history with much stronger ties than any other science. As a laboratory investigation, psychology is only a century old; as a body of insights, observations, and hypotheses, it is the oldest science in the world. Moreover, its history is not a musty attic of intellectual bric-a-brac and mildewed curiosa, as are often found in the history of chemistry or neurology, for example. It is instead a continuing discussion of the perennial and enduring problems of human and animal nature. It attempts the same questions again and again, even by the same routes. Current work on the nature-nurture problem, on emotion and intellect, on thought and language, on the problem of consciousness — all are simply the most recent voices in discussions which have been reverberating through history for more than two thousand years. Why study the history of psychology? It is relevant to present research, a fact that is not true of other sciences.

Another particular reason is the recently complicated and often bewildering growth of psychology. The oldest science in the world has suddenly expanded its factual content and the ranks of its scholars at a rate exceeding all other sciences. No other science, in no other century, has moved with such swiftness, confusion, and vigor. This is seen in the number of persons in professional societies, the expansion of academic departments and the demands upon them by students, the proliferation of specialist journals, the tumultuous diversity of research papers, the special jargons and schismatic methods, the huge conventions now too cumbersome to fulfill their original purposes, and the influence of psychology on the entire fabric of our times. What geology was to the early nineteenth century, biology to the late nineteenth century, and physics to the first half of the twentieth century, so psychology is very much the central major science of the latter half of the twentieth century. How did all this happen? The need for proper study of this phenomenal growth and its deep causes, rational and irrational, is obvious and urgent.

The urgency stems from the fragmentation by specialization that has accompanied this astonishing growth. Psychology has not only been expanding, it has also been separating. How can we understand it all? One problem has led to another, moving psychology to newer subsciences at an ever-increasing rate. And with each new field, thousands of research titles soon make their appearance. Psychology has diverged beyond the scope of any one specialist, shattering into brilliant fragments by its own progress and causing areas to lose touch with each other in their very successes. All about us, research pushes into research, often evading the larger questions with which it began.

As a result, psychology is at a critical stage in its development, and I would suggest that only its history can fit together all this divergence. The increasing multiplicity of psychology is not logical, but historical, like a jigsaw puzzle that cannot be fitted together in space, but only in time.

Why study the history of psychology? For all the reasons I have mentioned: to discover the historical structure under the logical surface of science, to understand the present, to be relevant to real questions, to liberate ourselves from the persuasions of fashions, to comprehend psychology as a whole, but also because it is the only way to understand a field of such divergence and conflicting emphases, which is at the same time the central science of our era.

And now a coda which concerns this volume and its publication at this time. A further reason for studying the history of psychology is the existence of a growing literature and interest in the subject itself. Ten years ago there was little in the field except several major textbooks, often written more for students than for professionals. But during the past decade the study of the history of psychology has grown into a science of considerable depth and exactness. This growth has been characterized by monographs on particular areas, topics, and men, setting old ideas into new reliefs and opening new perspectives which in some cases have changed the direction of contemporary research. A new journal, *The Journal of the History of the Behavioral Sciences,* has quickly become the major window opening upon these intellectual vistas. A new division in the American Psychological Association has been inaugurated for the exclusive study of the history of psychology. The National Science Foundation has been supporting a summer institute on the subject every few years. And in 1969 came the founding of a new interdisciplinary association, *Cheiron: The International Society for the History of the Behavioral and Social Sciences,* under whose auspices this book is being presented.

In part, the following papers are a selection of those presented at the four annual meetings of Cheiron held so far. Also included are articles from other sources, which we felt exemplified the standards and interests of current work. The contributions have been organized both to suggest the wide spectrum of the approach to the subject and to provide a series of collateral readings for courses in the area. It is hoped that they will prove harbingers of a new and more profound history of psychology in the years to come.

APPROACHES
TO HISTORY

Historical Structure of Scientific Discovery

Thomas S. Kuhn

My object in this article is to isolate and illuminate one small part of what I take to be a continuing historiographic revolution in the study of science.[1] The structure of scientific discovery is my particular topic, and I can best approach it by pointing out that the subject itself may well seem extraordinarily odd. Both scientists and, until quite recently, historians have ordinarily viewed discovery as the sort of event which, though it may have preconditions and surely has consequences, is itself without internal structure. Rather than being seen as a complex development extended both in space and time, discovering something has usually seemed to be a unitary event, one which, like seeing something, happens to an individual at a specifiable time and place.

This view of the nature of discovery has, I suspect, deep roots in the nature of the scientific community. One of the few historical elements recurrent in the textbooks from which the prospective scientist learns his field is the attribution of particular natural phenomena to the historical personages who first discovered them. As a result of this and other aspects of their training, discovery becomes for many scientists an important goal. To make a discovery is to achieve one of the closest approximations to a property right that the scientific career affords. Professional prestige is often closely associated with these acquisitions.[2] Small wonder, then, that acrimonious disputes about priority and independence in discovery have often marred the normally placid tenor of scientific communication. Even less wonder that many historians of science have seen the individual discovery as an appropriate unit with which to measure scientific progress and have devoted much time and skill to determining what man made which discovery at what point in time. If the study of discovery has a surprise to offer, it is only that, despite the immense energy and ingenuity expended upon it, neither polemic nor painstaking scholarship has often succeeded in pinpointing the time and place at which a given discovery could properly be said to have "been made."

SOME DISCOVERIES PREDICTABLE, SOME NOT

That failure, both of argument and of research, suggests the thesis that I now wish to develop. Many scientific discoveries, particularly the most

3

interesting and important, are not the sort of event about which the questions "Where?" and, more particularly, "When?" can appropriately be asked. Even if all conceivable data were at hand, those questions would not regularly possess answers. That we are persistently driven to ask them nonetheless is symptomatic of a fundamental inappropriateness in our image of discovery. That inappropriateness is here my main concern, but I approach it by considering first the historical problem presented by the attempt to date and to place a major class of fundamental discoveries.

The troublesome class consists of those discoveries — including oxygen, the electric current, x-rays, and the electron — which could not be predicted from accepted theory in advance and which therefore caught the assembled profession by surprise. That kind of discovery will shortly be my exclusive concern, but it will help first to note that there is another sort and one which presents very few of the same problems. Into this second class of discoveries fall the neutrino, radiowaves, and the elements which filled empty places in the periodic table. The existence of all these objects had been predicted from theory before they were discovered, and the men who made the discoveries therefore knew from the start what to look for. That foreknowledge did not make their task less demanding or less interesting, but it did provide criteria which told them when their goal had been reached.[3] As a result, there have been few priority debates over discoveries of this second sort, and only a paucity of data can prevent the historian from ascribing them to a particular time and place. Those facts help to isolate the difficulties we encounter as we return to the troublesome discoveries of the first class. In the cases that most concern us here, there are no benchmarks to inform either the scientist or the historian when the job of discovery has been done.

OXYGEN AS AN EXAMPLE

As an illustration of this fundamental problem and its consequences, consider first the discovery of oxygen. Because it has repeatedly been studied, often with exemplary care and skill, that discovery is unlikely to offer any purely factual surprises. Therefore it is particularly well suited to clarify points of principle.[4] At least three scientists — Carl Scheele, Joseph Priestley, and Antoine Lavoisier — have a legitimate claim to this discovery, and polemicists have occasionally entered the same claim for Pierre Bayen.[5] Scheele's work, though it was almost certainly completed before the relevant researches of Priestley and Lavoisier, was not made public until their work was well known.[6] Therefore it had no apparent causal role, and I shall simplify my story by omitting it.[7] Instead, I pick up the main route to the discovery of oxygen with the work of Bayen, who, sometime before March 1774, discovered that red precipitate of mercury (HgO) could, by heating, be made to yield a gas. That aeriform product

Bayen identified as fixed air (CO_2), a substance made familiar to most pneumatic chemists by the earlier work of Joseph Black.[8] A variety of other substances were known to yield the same gas.

At the beginning of August 1774, a few months after Bayen's work had appeared, Joseph Priestley repeated the experiment, though probably independently. Priestley, however, observed that the gaseous product would support combustion and therefore changed the identification. For him, the gas obtained on heating red precipitate was nitrous air (N_2O), a substance that he had himself discovered more than two years before.[9] Later in the same month Priestley made a trip to Paris and there informed Lavoisier of the new reaction. The latter repeated the experiment, both in November 1774 and in February 1775. However, because he used tests somewhat more elaborate than Priestley's, Lavoisier again changed the identification. For him, as of May 1775, the gas released by red precipitate was neither fixed air nor nitrous air. Instead, it was "[atmospheric] air itself entire without alteration . . . even to the point that . . . it comes out more pure." [10] Meanwhile, however, Priestley had also been at work, and, before the beginning of March 1775, he too had concluded that the gas must be "common air." To this point all of the men who had produced a gas from red precipitate of mercury had identified it with some previously known species.[11]

The remainder of this story of discovery is briefly told. During March 1775 Priestley discovered that his gas was in several respects very much "better" than common air, and he therefore re-identified the gas once more, this time calling it "dephlogisticated air," that is, atmospheric air deprived of its normal complement of phlogiston. This conclusion Priestley published in the *Philosophical Transactions,* and it was apparently that publication which led Lavoisier to reexamine his own results.[12] The reexamination began during February 1776, and within a year led Lavoisier to the conclusion that the gas was actually a separable component of the atmospheric air which both he and Priestley had previously thought of as homogeneous. With this point reached, with the gas recognized as an irreducibly distinct species, we may conclude that the discovery of oxygen had been completed.

However, to return to my initial question, when shall we say that oxygen was discovered and what criteria shall we use in answering that question? If discovering oxygen is simply holding an impure sample in one's hands, then the gas had been "discovered" in antiquity by the first man who ever bottled atmospheric air. Undoubtedly, for an experimental criterion, we must at least require a relatively pure sample like that obtained by Priestley in August 1774. But during 1774 Priestley was unaware that he had discovered anything except a new way to produce a relatively familiar species. Throughout that year his "discovery" is scarcely distinguishable from the one made earlier by Bayen, and neither case is quite distinct from that of the Reverend Stephen Hales who had obtained the same gas more than forty years before.[13] Apparently to discover something one must also be aware of the discovery and know as well what it is that one has discovered.

But, that being the case, how much must one know? Had Priestley come close enough when he identified the gas as nitrous air? If not, was either he or Lavoisier significantly closer when he changed the identification to common air? And what are we to say about Priestley's next identification, the one made in March 1775? Dephlogisticated air is still not oxygen or even, for the phlogistic chemist, a quite unexpected sort of gas. Rather, it is a particularly pure atmospheric air. Presumably, then, we wait for Lavoisier's work in 1776 and 1777, work which led him not merely to isolate the gas but to see what it was. Yet even that decision can be questioned, for in 1777 and to the end of his life Lavoisier insisted that oxygen was an atomic "principle of acidity" and that oxygen *gas* was formed only when that "principle" united with caloric, the matter of heat.[14] Shall we therefore say that oxygen had not yet been discovered in 1777? Some may be tempted to do so. But the principle of acidity was not banished from chemistry until after 1810 and caloric lingered on until the 1860s. Oxygen had, however, become a standard chemical substance long before either of those dates. Furthermore, what is perhaps the key point, it would probably have gained that status on the basis of Priestley's work alone, without benefit of Lavoisier's still partial reinterpretation.

I conclude that we need a new vocabulary and new concepts for analyzing events like the discovery of oxygen. Though undoubtedly correct, the sentence "Oxygen was discovered" misleads by suggesting that discovering something is a single simple act unequivocally attributable, if only we knew enough, to an individual and an instant in time. When the discovery is unexpected, however, the latter attribution is always impossible and the former often is as well. Ignoring Scheele, we can, for example, safely say that oxygen had not been discovered before 1774; probably we would also insist that it had been discovered by 1777 or shortly thereafter. But within those limits, any attempt to date the discovery or to attribute it to an individual must inevitably be arbitrary. Furthermore, it must be arbitrary just because discovering a new sort of phenomenon is necessarily a complex process which involves recognizing both *that* something is and *what* it is. Observation and conceptualization, fact and the assimilation of fact to theory, are inseparably linked in the discovery of scientific novelty. Inevitably, that process extends over time and may often involve a number of people. Only for discoveries in my second category — those whose nature is known in advance — can discovering *that* and discovering *what* occur together and in an instant.

URANUS AND X-RAYS

Two last, simpler, and far briefer examples will simultaneously show how typical the case of oxygen is and also prepare the way for a somewhat more precise conclusion. On the night of March 13, 1781, the astronomer William Herschel made the following entry in his journal: "In the quartile near Zeta Tauri . . . is a curious either nebulous star or perhaps a comet." [15] That entry is generally said to record the discovery of the planet Uranus, but it cannot quite have done that. Between 1690 and Herschel's observation in 1781 the same object had been seen and recorded at least 17 times by men who took it to be a star. Herschel differed from them only in supposing that, because in his telescope it appeared especially large, it might actually be a *comet*! Two additional observations on March 17 and 19 confirmed that suspicion by showing that the object he had observed moved among the stars. As a result, astronomers throughout Europe were informed of the discovery, and the mathematicians among them began to compute the new comet's orbit. Only several months later, after all those attempts had repeatedly failed to square with observation, did the astronomer Lexell suggest that the object observed by Herschel might be a planet. And only when additional computations, using a planet's rather than a comet's orbit, proved reconcilable with observation, was that suggestion generally accepted. At what point during 1781 do we want to say that the planet Uranus was discovered? And are we entirely and unequivocally clear that it was Herschel rather than Lexell who discovered it?

Or consider still more briefly the story of the discovery of x-rays, a story which opens on the day in 1895 when the physicist Roentgen interrupted a well-precedented investigation of cathode rays because he noticed that a barium platinocyanide screen far from his shielded apparatus glowed when the discharge was in process.[16] Additional investigations — they required seven hectic weeks during which Roentgen rarely left the laboratory — indicated that the cause of the glow traveled in straight lines from the cathode ray tube, that the radiation cast shadows, that it could not be deflected by a magnet, and much else besides. Before announcing his discovery, Roentgen had convinced himself that his effect was not due to cathode rays themselves but to a new form of radiation with at least some similarity to light. Once again the question suggests itself: When shall we say that x-rays were actually discovered? Not, in any case, at the first instant, when all that had been noted was a glowing screen. At least one other investigator had seen that glow and, to his subsequent chagrin, discovered nothing at all. Nor, it is almost as clear, can the moment of discovery be pushed back to a point during the last week of investigation. By that time Roentgen was exploring the properties of the new radiation he had *already* discovered. We may have to settle for the remark that x-rays emerged in Würzburg between November 8 and December 28, 1895.

AWARENESS OF ANOMALY

The characteristics shared by these examples are, I think, common to all the episodes by which unanticipated novelties become subjects for scientific attention. I therefore conclude these brief remarks by discussing three such common characteristics, which may help to provide a framework for further study of the extended episodes we customarily call "discoveries."

In the first place, notice that all three of our discoveries — oxygen, Uranus, and x-rays — began with the experimental or observational isolation of an anomaly, that is, with nature's failure to conform entirely to expectation. Notice, further, that the process by which that anomaly was educed displays simultaneously the apparently incompatible characteristics of the inevitable and the accidental. In the case of x-rays, the anomalous glow which provided Roentgen's first clue was clearly the result of an accidental disposition of his apparatus. But by 1895 cathode rays were a normal subject for research all over Europe, research that regularly juxtaposed cathode-ray tubes with sensitive screens and films; as a result, Roentgen's accident was almost certain to occur elsewhere, as in fact it had. Those remarks, however, should make Roentgen's case look very much like those of Herschel and Priestley. Herschel first observed his oversized and thus anomalous star in the course of a prolonged survey of the northern heavens. That survey was, except for the magnification provided by Herschel's instruments, precisely of the sort that had repeatedly been carried through before and that had occasionally resulted in prior observations of Uranus. And Priestley, too — when he isolated the gas that behaved almost but not quite like nitrous air and then almost but not quite like common air — was seeing something unintended and wrong in the outcome of a sort of experiment for which there was much European precedent and which had more than once before led to the production of the new gas.

These features suggest the existence of two normal requisites for the beginning of an episode of discovery. The first, which throughout this paper I have largely taken for granted, is the individual skill, wit, or genius to recognize that something has gone wrong in ways that may prove consequential. Not any and every scientist would have noted that no unrecorded star should be so large, that the screen ought not have glowed, that nitrous air should not have supported life. But that requisite presupposes another which is less frequently taken for granted. Whatever the level of genius available to observe them, anomalies do not emerge from the normal course of scientific research until both instruments and concepts have developed sufficiently to make their emergence likely and to make the anomaly which results recognizable as a violation of expectation.[17] To say that an unexpected discovery begins only when something goes wrong is to say that it begins only when scientists know well both how their instruments and how nature should behave. What distinguished Priestley, who saw an anomaly, from Hales, who did not, is largely the considerable articulation of pneumatic techniques and expectations that had come into being during the four decades which separate their two isolations of oxygen.[18] The very number of claimants indicates that after 1770 the discovery could not have been postponed for long.

MAKING THE ANOMALY BEHAVE

The role of anomaly is the first of the characteristics shared by our three examples. A second can be considered more briefly, for it has provided the main theme for the body of my text. Though awareness of anomaly marks the beginning of a discovery, it marks only the beginning. What necessarily follows, if anything at all is to be discovered, is a more or less extended period during which the individual and often many members of his group struggle to make the anomaly lawlike. Invariably that period demands additional observation or experimentation as well as repeated cogitation. While it continues, scientists repeatedly revise their expectations, usually their instrumental standards, and sometimes their most fundamental theories as well. In this sense discoveries have a proper internal history, prehistory, and a posthistory. Furthermore, within the rather vaguely delimited interval of internal history, there is no single moment or day which the historian, however complete his data, can identify as the point at which the discovery was made. Often, when several individuals are involved, it is even impossible unequivocally to identify any one of them as the discoverer.

ADJUSTMENT, ADAPTATION, AND ASSIMILATION

Finally, turning to the third of these selected common characteristics, note briefly what happens as the period of discovery draws to a close. A full discussion of that question would require additional evidence and a separate paper, for I have had little to say about the aftermath of discovery in the body of my text. Nevertheless, the topic must not be entirely neglected, for it is in part a corollary of what has already been said.

Discoveries are often described as mere additions or increments to the growing stockpile of scientific knowledge, and that description has helped make the unit-discovery seem a significant measure of progress. I suggest, however, that it is fully appropriate only to those discoveries which, like the elements that filled missing places in the periodic table, were anticipated and sought in advance and which therefore demanded no adjustment, adaptation, and assimilation from the profession. Though the sorts of discoveries we have here been examining are undoubtedly additions to scientific knowledge, they are also something more. In a sense that I can now develop only in part, they also react back upon what has previously been known, providing a new view of some previously familiar objects and simultaneously changing the way in which even some traditional parts of science are practiced. Those in whose area of special competence the new phenomenon falls often see both the world and their work differently as they emerge from the extended struggle with anomaly which constitutes that phenomenon's discovery.

William Herschel, for example, when he increased by one the time-honored number of planetary bodies, taught astronomers to see new things when they looked at the familiar heavens even with instruments more traditional than his own. That change in the vision of astronomers must be a principal reason why, in the half-century after the discovery of Uranus, 20 additional circumsolar bodies were added to the traditional seven.[19] A similar transformation is even clearer in the aftermath of Roentgen's work. In the first place, established techniques for cathode ray research had to be changed, for scientists found they had failed to control a relevant variable. Those changes included both the redesign of old apparatus and revised ways of asking old questions. In addition, those scientists most concerned experienced the same transformation of vision that we have just noted in the aftermath of the discovery of Uranus. X-rays were the first new sort of radiation discovered since infrared and ultraviolet at the beginning of the century. But within less than a decade after Roentgen's work, four more were disclosed by the new scientific sensitivity (for example, to fogged photographic plates) and by some of the new instrumental techniques that had resulted from Roentgen's work and its assimilation.[20]

Very often these transformations in the established techniques of scientific practice prove even more important than the incremental knowledge provided by the discovery itself. That could at least be argued in the cases of Uranus and of x-rays; in the case of my third example, oxygen, it is categorically clear. Like the work of Herschel and Roentgen, that of Priestley and Lavoisier taught scientists to view old situations in new ways. Therefore, as we might anticipate, oxygen was not the only new chemical species to be identified in the aftermath of their work. But, in the case of oxygen, the readjustments demanded by assimilation were so profound that they played an integral and essential role — though they were not by themselves the cause — in the gigantic upheaval of chemical theory and practice which has since been known as the "chemical revolution." I do not suggest that every unanticipated discovery has consequences for science so deep and so far-reaching as those which followed the discovery of oxygen. But I do suggest that every such discovery demands, from those most concerned, the sorts of readjustment that, when they are more obvious, we equate with scientific revolution. It is, I believe, just because they demand readjustments like these, that the process of discovery is necessarily and inevitably one that shows structure and therefore extends in time.

REFERENCES AND NOTES

1. The larger revolution is discussed in my book, *The Structure of Scientific Revolutions* (Chicago: University of Chicago Press, 1962). The central ideas in this paper have been abstracted from that source, particularly from its third chapter, "Anomaly and the emergence of scientific discoveries."

2. For a brilliant discussion of these points, see R. K. Merton, "Priorities in scientific discovery: A chapter in the sociology of science," *Am. Sociol. Rev.*, 22, 635 (1957). Also very relevant, though it did not appear until this article had been prepared, is F. Reif, "The competitive world of the pure scientist," *Science, 134,* 1957 (1961).

3. Not all discoveries fall so neatly as the preceding into one or the other of my two classes. For example, Anderson's work on the positron was done in complete ignorance of Dirac's electron theory from which the new particle's existence had already been very nearly predicted. On the other hand, the immediately succeeding work by Blackett and Occhialini made full use of Dirac's theory, and therefore exploited experiment more fully and constructed a more forceful case for the positron's existence than Anderson had been able to do. On this subject see N. R. Hanson, "Discovering the positron," *Brit. J. Phil. Sci., 12,* 194 (1961); *12,* 299 (1962). Hanson suggests several of the points developed here. I am much indebted to Professor Hanson for a preprint of this material.

4. I have developed a less familiar example from the same viewpoint in "The caloric theory of adiabatic compression," *Isis, 49,* 132 (1958). A closely similar analysis of the emergence of a new theory is included in the early pages of my essay "Conservation of energy as an example of simultaneous discovery," in *Critical Problems in the History of Science,* M. Clagett, Ed. (Univ. of Wisconsin Press, Madison, 1959), pp. 321-356. Reference to these papers may add depth and detail to the following discussion.

5. The still classic discussion of the discovery of oxygen is A. N. Meldrum, *The Eighteenth Century Revolution in Science—The First Phase* (Calcutta, 1930), chap. 5. A more convenient and generally quite reliable discussion is included in J. B. Conant, *The Overthrow of the Phlogiston Theory: The Chemical Revolution of 1775-1789,* "Harvard Case Histories in Experimental Science, Case 2" (Harvard Univ. Press, Cambridge, 1950). A more recent and indispensable review, which includes an account of the development of the priority controversy, is M. Daumas, *Lavoisier, théoricien et expérimentateur* (Paris, 1955), chaps. 2 and 3. H. Guerlac has added much significant detail to our knowledge of the early relations between Priestley and Lavoisier in his "Joseph Priestley's first papers on gases and their reception in France," *J. Hist. Med., 12,* 1 (1957), and in his very recent monograph, *Lavoisier — The Crucial Year* (Cornell Univ. Press, Ithaca, 1961). For Scheele see J. R. Partington, *A Short History of Chemistry* (London, 2nd ed., 1951), pp. 104-109.

6. For the dating of Scheele's work, see A. E. Nordenskiöld, Carl Wilhelm Scheele, *Nachgelassene Briefe und Aufzeichnungen* (Stockholm, 1892).

7. U. Bocklund ["A lost letter from Scheele to Lavoisier," *Lychnos* (1957-58), pp. 39-62] argues that Scheele communicated his discovery of oxygen to Lavoisier in a letter of Sept. 30, 1774. Certainly the letter is important, and it clearly demonstrates that Scheele was ahead of both Priestley and Lavoisier at the time it was written. But I think the letter is not quite so candid as Bocklund supposes, and I fail to see how Lavoisier could have drawn the discovery of oxygen from it. Scheele describes a procedure for reconstituting common air, not for producing a new gas, and that, as we shall see, is almost the same information that Lavoisier received from Priestley at about the same time. In any case, there is no evidence that Lavoisier performed the sort of experiment that Scheele suggested.

8. P. Bayen, "Essai d'expériences chymiques, faites sur quelques précipités de mercure, dans la vue de découvrir leur nature, Seconde partie," *Observations sur la physique* (1774), vol. 3, pp. 280-295, particularly pp. 289-291.

9. J. B. Conant (see 5, pp 34-40).

10. A useful translation of the full text is available in Conant (see 5). For this description of the gas see p. 23.

11. For simplicity I use the term *red precipitate* throughout. Actually, Bayen used the precipitate; Priestley used both the precipitate and the oxide produced by direct calcination of mercury; and Lavoisier used only the latter. The difference is not without importance, for it was not unequivocally clear to chemists that the two substances were identical.

12. There has been some doubt about Priestley's having influenced Lavoisier's thinking at this point; but, when the latter returned to experimenting with the gas in February 1776, he recorded in his notebooks that he had obtained "l'air dephlogistique de M. Priestley" [M. Daumas (see 5, p. 36)].

13. J. R. Partington (see 5, p. 91).

14. For the traditional elements in Lavoisier's interpretations of chemical reactions, see H. Metzger, *La philosophie de la matière chez Lavoisier* (Paris, 1935), and Daumas (see 5, chap 7).

15. P. Doig, *A Concise History of Astronomy* (Chapman, London, 1950), pp. 115-116.

16. L. W. Taylor, *Physics, the Pioneer Science* (Houghton Mifflin, Boston, 1941), p. 790.

17. Though the point cannot be argued here, the conditions which make the emergence of anomaly likely and those which make anomaly recognizable are to a very great extent the same. That fact may help us understand the extraordinarily large amount of simultaneous discovery in the sciences.

18. A useful sketch of the development of pneumatic chemistry is included in Partington (see 5, chap. 6).

19. R. Wolf, *Geschichte der Astronomie* (Munich, 1877), pp. 513-515, 683-693. The prephotographic discoveries of the asteroids is often seen as an effect of the invention of Bode's law. But that law cannot be the full explanation and may not even have played a large part. Piazzi's discovery of Ceres, in 1801, was made in ignorance of the current speculation about a missing planet in the "hole" between Mars and Jupiter. Instead, like Herschel, Piazzi was engaged on a star survey. More important, Bode's law was old by 1800 (R. Wolf, *ibid.*, p. 683), but only one man before that date seems to have thought it worth while to look for another planet. Finally, Bode's law, by itself, could only suggest the utility of looking for additional planets; it did not tell astronomers where to look. Clearly, however, the drive to look for additional planets dates from Herschel's work on Uranus.

20. For a-, β-, and γ-radiation, discovery of which dates from 1896, see Taylor *16*, pp. 800-804). For the fourth new form of radiation, N-rays, see D. J. S. Price, *Science Since Babylon* (Yale Univ. Press, New Haven, 1961), pp. 84-89. That N-rays were ultimately the source of a scientific scandal does not make them less revealing of the scientific community's state of mind.

Psychology:
A Prescriptive Science

ROBERT I. WATSON

In a recent analysis of the dynamics of the history of the older, more mature sciences, Kuhn (1962, 1963) holds that each of them has reached the level of guidance by a paradigm. In one of its meanings a paradigm is a contentual model, universally accepted by practitioners of a science at a particular temporal period in its development. With this agreement among its practitioners, the paradigm defines the science in which it operates. In a science where a paradigm prevails, one recognizes that a particular paradigm concerns chemistry, astronomy, physics, or the biological science. Illustrative in astronomy is the Ptolemaic paradigm which gave way to the Copernican paradigm; in physics, the Aristotelian paradigm gave way to the Newtonian dynamic paradigm which, in the relatively recent past, was superseded by the paradigm provided by Einstein and Bohr. The great events of science which occur when a new paradigm emerges Kuhn calls a revolution.

Kuhn holds the historical sequence to be as follows: As scientists go about the tasks of normal science, eventually an anomaly, i.e., a research finding which does not fit the prevailing paradigm, is obtained. A normal science problem that ought to be solvable by the prevailing procedures refuses to fit into the paradigm, or a piece of equipment designed for normal research fails to perform in the anticipated manner. Failures in science to find the results predicted in most instances are the result of lack of skill of the scientist. They do not call into question the rules of the game, i.e., the paradigm, that the scientist is following. Reiterated efforts generally bear out this commitment to the accepted paradigm that Kuhn calls a dogmatism. Only repeated failure by increasing numbers of scientists results in questioning the paradigm, which, in turn, results in a "crisis" (Kuhn, 1963). The state of Ptolemaic astronomy was a recognized scandal before Copernicus proposed a basic change; Galileo's contribution arose from recognized difficulties with medieval views; Lavoisier's new chemistry was the product of anomalies created both by the proliferation of new gases found and the first quantitative studies of weight relations. When the revealed anomaly can no longer be ignored, there begin the extraordinary investigations that lead to a scientific revolution. After sufficient acceptance of this anomaly is achieved from the other workers in the field, a new paradigm takes the place of the one overthrown and a period of normal science begins. Since a paradigm is sufficiently open-ended, it provides a host of still unsolved problems. In this period of normal science the task of the scientist is to fill out the details of the paradigm to determine what facts, perhaps already known, may be related to the theory, to determine what facts are significant for it, to extend to other situations, and in general to articulate the paradigm. In short, it would appear that the activities of normal science are a form of "working through" in a manner somewhat akin to that task which occupies so much time in psychoanalytic psychotherapy.

When a new anomaly appears and is given support, the cycle then repeats.

The bulk of Kuhn's monograph is taken up with a historical account of the events leading up to scientific revolutions, the nature of these revolutions, and the paradigmatic developments thereafter, with many familiar facts of the history of astronomy, physics, and chemistry cast in this particular perspective. It is here that the persuasiveness of his point of view is to be found. The test of the correctness of Kuhn's views rests upon the fit of his data with the available historical materials. Kuhn uses the key concept of paradigm in several degrees of breadth other than contentually defining, and it is difficult to know precisely what differentiates each of the usages. Fortunately, I can leave to the specialist in the history of the physical sciences the evaluation of the correctness of his reading the details of their history and the various meanings of paradigm, for I am more concerned with what can be drawn from what he has to say about other sciences that he contends lack a contentually defining paradigm.

In all of its meanings, a paradigm has a guidance function. It functions as an intellectual framework, it tells with what sort of entities the scientific universe is populated and how these entities behave, and informs its followers what questions may legitimately be asked about nature.

What are the consequences in those sciences that lack a defining paradigm? Foremost is a noticeable lack of unity within a science, indications of which Kuhn acknowledges as one of the sources for his paradigmatic concept, which arose in part from his being puzzled about "the number and extent of the overt disagreements between social scientists about the nature of legitimate scientific methods and problems" (1962, p. x) as compared to the relative lack of such disagreement among natural scientists.

That psychology lacks this universal agreement about the nature of our contentual model that is a paradigm, in my opinion, is all too readily documented.[1] In psychology there is still debate over fundamentals. In research, findings stir little argument, but the overall framework is still very much contested. There is still disagreement about what is included in the science of psychology. In part, at least, it is because we lack a paradigm that one psychologist can attack others who do not agree with him as being "nonscientific" or "not a psychologist," or both. Schools of psychology still have their adherents, despite wishful thinking. And an even more telling illustration, because it is less controversial, is the presence of national differences in psychology to such an extent that in the United States there is an all too common dismissal of work in psychology in other countries as quaint, odd, or irrelevant. National differences, negligible in such paradigmatic sciences as physics and chemistry, assume great importance in psychology. A provincialism in psychology in the United States is the consequence — provincialism on a giant scale, to be sure, but still a provincialism, which would and could not be present if a paradigm prevailed.

Before its first paradigm had served to unify it and while still in "the preparadigmatic stage," each physical science was guided by "something resembling a paradigm," says Kuhn. Since it was outside his scope, Kuhn said hardly more than this about the matter.

Psychology has not experienced anything comparable to what atomic theory has done for chemistry, what the principle of organic evolution has done for biology, what laws of motion have done for physics. Either psychology's first paradigm has not been discovered or it has not yet been recognized for what it is. Although the presence of an unrecognized paradigm is not ruled out completely, it would seem plausible to proceed on the assumption that psychology has not yet had its initial paradigmatic revolution. The present task is to answer the question: If psychology lacks a paradigm, what serves to take its place?

It would seem that it follows from Kuhn's position that whatever provides the guidance could not have the all-embracing unifying effect of defining the field in question, since if it did so, a paradigm would exist. What seems to be required is some form of trends or themes, numerous enough to deal with the complexity of psychology and yet not so numerous as to render each of them only narrowly meaningful. Those which I have isolated follow:

THE PRESCRIPTIONS OF PSYCHOLOGY ARRANGED IN CONTRASTING PAIRS

Conscious mentalism-Unconscious mentalism (emphasis on awareness of mental structure or activity — unawareness)

Contentual objectivism-Contentual subjectivism (psychological data viewed as behavior of individual — as mental structure or activity of individual)

Determinism-Indeterminism (human events completely explicable in terms of antecedents — not completely so explicable)

Empiricism-Rationalism (major, if not exclusive, source of knowledge is experience — is reason)

Functionalism-Structuralism (psychological categories are activities — are contents)

Inductivism-Deductivism (investigations begun with facts or observations — with assumed established truths)

Mechanism-Vitalism (activities of living beings completely explicable by physicochemical constituents — not so explicable)

Methodological objectivism-Methodological subjectivism (use of methods open to verification by another competent observer — not so open)

Molecularism-Molarism (psychological data most aptly described in terms of relatively small units — relatively large units)

Monism-Dualism (fundamental principle or entity in universe is of one kind — is of two kinds, mind and matter)

Naturalism-Supernaturalism (nature requires for its operation and explanation only principles found within it — requires transcendent guidance as well)

Nomotheticism-Idiographicism (emphasis upon discovering general laws — upon explaining particular events or individuals)

Peripheralism-Centralism (stress upon psychological events taking place at periphery of body — within the body)

Purism-Utilitarianism (seeking of knowledge for its own sake — for its usefulness in other activities)

Quantitativism-Qualitativism (stress upon knowledge which is countable or measurable — upon that which is different in kind or essence)

Rationalism-Irrationalism (emphasis upon data supposed to follow dictates of good sense and intellect — intrusion or domination of emotive and conative factors upon intellectual processes)

Staticism-Developmentalism (emphasis upon cross-sectional view — upon changes with time)

Staticism-Dynamicism (emphasis upon enduring aspects — upon change and factors making for change)

The overall function of these themes is orientative or attitudinal; they tell us how the psychologist-scientist must or should behave. In short, they have a directive function. They help to direct the psychologist-scientist in the way he selects a problem, formulates it, and carries it out.

The other essential characteristic is that of being capable of being traced historically over some appreciable period of time. On both counts, the term *prescription* seems to have these connotations.[2] It is defined in the dictionaries as the act of prescribing, directing, or dictating with an additional overtone of implying long usage, of being hallowed by custom, extending over time.[3]

It is for the reason of persisting over relatively long periods of time that prescriptions can be of historical moment. In fact, in choosing the particular prescriptions with which I deal, the presence of historical continuity over at least most of the modern period was a major decisive factor. If an instance of some conception serving a directive function was of relatively short temporal dimension, it was not considered a prescription. It is for this reason that some prominent trends in psychology today do not appear as prescriptions. Physicalism and operationalism are very much part of the current *Zeitgeist* in psychology; but because they are relatively new on the psychological scene, they are not considered prescriptions. Instead, they serve as challenges to utilize the prescriptions for their explanation. It is characteristic of prescriptions that modern, more specifically formulated versions of the more general historically rooted ones may appear. Empiricism-rationalism have modern descendants in environmentalism-nativism.

To arrive at a reasonably complete and appropriate categorization of the prescriptions, I carried out two separable, although actually intertwined, steps. I considered the present scene, for example, in a paper on national trends in psychology in the United States (1965), in order to ascertain what seemed to characterize psychology today, and then turned to the very beginning of the modern period in the history of psychology in the seventeenth century to see if these themes were then discernible in recognizable form. In the 300-page manuscript that I have so far prepared, I can say that I find encouraging indications of the historical roots of these prescriptions somewhere in the contributions of Bacon, Descartes, Hobbes, Spinoza, Leibniz, Locke, and Newton, and in those of the lesser figures of the seventeenth century.

Turning to its directive-orientative function, it will be remembered that this theory of prescriptions is more than a classificatory system, more than a convenient means for a particular historian to order his account. These prescriptions were and are part of the intellectual equipment of psychologists. Psychologists are always facing problems, novel and otherwise. They do so with habits of thought, methodological and contentual, which they have taken from the past. This applies today with just as much force as it ever did in the past. In short, they are dynamic because psychologists accept, reject, and combine prescriptions, thus thinking in certain ways and not in others.

In the above list, prescriptions have been presented in one of the ways they function — as contrasting or opposing trends.[4] At some point in their history, most of these prescription pairings have been considered as opposed, even irreconcilable — for example, naturalism as opposed to supernaturalism, and empiricism as opposed to rationalism.

A summarization, such as the list gives, inevitably distorts its subject matter. Especially pertinent here is the false impression of tidiness this arrangement of antithetical isolated pairs gives. Consider the dichotomy, mechanism-vitalism. Does this oppositional way of presenting them exhaust the matter? By no means — mechanism bears relation to molecularism, and molecularism may come in conflict with supernaturalism, which in turn, relates to certain forms of dualism.

Prescriptions are by no means simple, dominant, isolated themes moving monolithically through history. In a recent analysis of the history of mathematical concepts in psychology, George Miller (1964) warns expressly against this kind of oversimplification. His treatment of what he calls the "varieties of mathematical psychology" (p. 1), that I consider to bear considerable relation to the quantitativistic prescription, is further subdivided into several categories and subcategories. As he indicates, a more extensive treatment would require still others.

Their oppositional character does lead to explication of another characteristic of prescriptions. At a time, past or present, when both of the opposed prescriptions had or have supporters, it is possible to make some sort of an estimate of their relative strength; in other words, we may speak of dominant and counterdominant prescriptions. Rationalism dominated in seventeenth-century England; Locke was nearly alone in advocating empiricism. Nomotheticism dominates today in the United States; an idiographic prescription is sufficiently viable to make itself heard in protest against the prevailing state of affairs. Hence, idiography is counterdominant.

The presence of dominant and counterdominant prescriptions helps us to see how competitions and conflict may result. Whether purism or utilitarianism dominates in American psychology today, I would be hard put to say, but we can be sure of one thing: both prescriptions have sufficient protagonists to make for a prominent conflict. Dominance may shift with time; at one time supernaturalism dominated decisively, there followed centuries of conflict, and today naturalism dominates almost completely.

Although important, their oppositional nature is not always present. Empiricism-rationalism has been presented as a contrasting pair, yet at least to the satisfaction of some psychologists and philosophers of science, they have been reconciled today at a higher level of synthesis. Induction and deduction were also considered antithetical once. In actual practice today, the scientist often sees them as aspects of an integrated method that permits him to weave them together. Sometimes prescriptions, rather than being contradictory, are contrary; there may be gradations, or relationships of degree, as seems to be the case with methodological subjectivity-objectivity.

Reinforcing its directive character is the fact that prescriptions sometimes are "prejudgments," presuppositions or preconceptions that are acted upon without examination, that are taken for granted.[5] Some prescriptions are characterized by their being tacit presuppositions taken as a matter of course and even operating without explicit verbalization. What psychologist today says to himself that the problem he is considering is one about which I must decide whether I should or should not quantify; instead he immediately starts to cast the problem in quantitative terms without further ado. Similarly, most psychologists are monists. That many psychologists would react to being called monists with a sense of incredulity and even resentment nicely illustrates my point. We think monistically without using the term. Similarly, we are apt to follow empiricistic and naturalistic prescriptions without much thought to the fact that we do so. But there was a time when the issues of quantitativeness-qualitativeness, of monism-dualism, of empiricism-rationalism, and of naturalism-supernaturalism were very much explicit issues, occupying the center of the psychological stage. Often their implicit character seems to have come about when one became so dominant that the other no longer stirred argument. Sometimes no clean-cut agreed-on solution was verbalized; instead, they were allowed to slide into implicitness. A shift of interest, rather than resolution with a clear-cut superiority of one over the other, seems characteristic. Old prescriptions never die, they just fade away. Naturally, at some times and to some extent, a prescription became less relevant to psychology, but these are matters of degree.

Much of psychology's early history is, of course, a part of philosophy. Many of these prescriptions had their roots in philosophical issues, and are even still stated in what is current philosophical terminology, as in monism-dualism and empiricism-rationalism, to mention the two most obvious. I do not hesitate to use philosophical terminology because psychology cannot be completely divorced from philosophy either in its history or in its present functioning. This state of affairs is cause for neither congratulation nor commiseration. Psychology is not the more scientific by trying to brush this sometimes embarrassing fact under the rug, as do some of our colleagues who teach and preach psychology as if it had no philosophically based commitments. They are psychology's Monsieur Jourdains, who deny that they talk philosophical prose. Denying there is need to consider philosophical questions does not solve the problem. The very denial is one form of philosophical solution.

Since they were originally philosophical issues, it will be convenient to refer to some prescriptions as "contentual" problems. To bring home this point, the areas of philosophy in which certain of the prescriptions fall might be identified. Rationalism and empiricism have their origins in epistemology, monism and dualism in ontology (nature of reality), and molarism and molecularism in cosmology (structure of reality).

A major task in the history of psychology is to trace how the field individuated from the philosophical matrix. In this process, the prescriptions that served as major guidelines in the emergence of psychology as a separate discipline originally had a philosophical character, which took on a general scientific character with the emergence of the physical sciences in general, and of psychological science in particular. It is in this sense that they can be referred to as philosophically contentual in character. Moreover, consideration by psychologists and others in the sciences transformed them, sometimes in such ways that only by tracing their history can one see the relation to their parentage.

Often the traditional terminology used herewith — for example, its dualistic and mentalistic locus — has had to give way to objectivistic and monistic terminology. Confused and confusing though these terms might be, they still referred to something relevant to psychology. As they are formulated, psychologists may be repelled by the "old-fashioned" air of the statement of many of the prescriptions. Justification is found in the fact that these are the terms in psychology's long history until a short fifty years ago.

The lack of a paradigm has meant that psychology looked to other scientific fields for guidance. It is characteristic of prescriptions that borrowing from other fields has taken place. Psychology's heritage from philosophy could be viewed in this manner. But there are other forms of borrowing which have entered into prescription formation. There has been noteworthy borrowing from biology, physiology in particular, signalized by Wundt's calling his work "physiological psychology" in deference to the methodological inspiration it was to him. But physics, highest in the hierarchy of the sciences, has just as often served as the model science. Psychology has had its dream of being a changeling prince. The rejected child of drab philosophy and lowborn physiology, it has sometimes persuaded itself that actually it was the child of highborn physics. It identified with the aspiration of the physical sciences, and, consequently, acquired an idealized version of the parental image as a super-ego, especially concerning scientific morality, i.e., the "right" way for a scientist to behave.

Psychologists looked to these other sciences for methodological guidance.[6] This methodological cast is particularly evident in the prescriptions concerned with nomothetic law, inductivism-deductivism, quantitativism-qualitativism, methodological objectivism and subjectivism, and determinism-indeterminism. It follows that these prescriptions apply in varying degrees to other sciences. So, too, does the puristic-utilitarian prescription, and working through the naturalistic-supernaturalistic problem.

Some of the contentual prescriptions have counterparts in other sciences. Salient to all biological sciences are developmentalism-staticism, functionalism-structuralism, mechanism in its various guises, and molecularism-molarism. It is also at least possible that many of these prescriptions would be found to have counterparts in other nonscientific areas of knowledge, such as literature, religion, and politics. After all, man's reflective life, as the "Great Ideas" of Adler and Hutchins and their cohorts show, has much more interpenetration into the various compartmentalizations of knowledge than is customarily recognized. But to explore this further would be to extend discussion beyond the scope of the paper.

In the preparadigmatic stage of a science, a scientist may also become an adherent to a school — that is to say, he may accept a set of interlocking prescriptions espoused by a group of scientists generally with an acknowledged leader. Functionalism, behaviorism, Gestalt psychology, and psychoanalysis are representative.

The orientative character of prescriptions is also present in a school. As Marx and Hillix (1963) recognize, each school seems to follow a directive: you should be primarily concerned with the study of the functions of behavior in adapting to the environment and the formulation of mathematical functions relating behavior to antecedent variables: *functionalism;* you ought to study the stimulus-response connections through strict methodological objectivism: *behaviorism;* you can arrive at useful formulations of psychological principles through consideration of molar units of both stimulus and response, i.e., configurations or fields:

Gestalt; you should be concerned with the interplay and conflict of the environment and native constituents of the disturbed personality with special attention to its unconscious aspect: *psychoanalysis.*

Salience or nonsalience of particular prescriptions characterize schools. Behaviorism is both contentually objectivistic and environmentalistic (empirical). However, the former is salient; the latter is nonsalient. Contentual objectivism is central and indispensable; environmentalism is not crucial to its central thesis. Behaviorism would still be behaviorism even if all behaviorists were nativistic in orientation.

In broad strokes based on salient prescriptions, functionalism is functionalistic, empiricistic, quantitativistic, and molecularistic. Behaviorism has, as salient orientative prescriptions, contentual objectivism and molecularism. Gestalt psychology may be said to make salient molarism, subjectivism, and nativism. The salient directive prescriptions of psychoanalysis seem to be dynamicism, irrationalism, unconscious mentalism, and developmentalism.

The differing patterns of salient prescriptions of the schools serves also to make more intelligible their differing research emphases upon particular contentual problems — the functionalists with their empiricistic salience upon learning; the behaviorists with their peripheralism upon motor activity (including learning); Gestalt psychology with its molarism and nativism upon perception; and psychoanalysis with its dynamicism and irrationalism upon motivation.

There is an even broader level of prescriptions, that of national trends exemplified by the Symposium on National Trends at the XVIIth International Congress to which reference already has been made (Watson, 1965). Here greater diversity than that of the schools is expected. Instead of patterns, it is most meaningful to couch their discussion in terms of dominance and counterdominance.

Immersion in the current scene, as a participant-observer, adds immeasurably to the already complicated task of the historian who is apt therefore to approach the present with a great deal of trepidation. What will be hazarded is an inclusive, broad, and therefore crude overall characterization of the current scene of psychology in the United States. It will serve as another exercise in the application of the prescriptive approach. Although couched in terms of a somewhat different array of prescriptions than is now being used, for reasons explained earlier, I will quote from the concluding passage of my paper on this Symposium:

It has been seen that national trends in modern American psychology follow certain dominant prescriptions. Determinism, naturalism, physicalism, and monism, although very much operative, are judged to incite relatively little opposition. Functionalism, operationalism, quantification, hypothetico-deductivism, environmentalism, and nomotheticism are likewise dominant, but there are counterprescriptions which tend to oppose them. As for the schools of psychology, psychoanalysis, very obviously, and Gestalt psychology, less firmly, still stand apart. Serving as counterprescriptions to those dominant in psychology are those calling for increased complexity in theorizing, for an increased attention to philosophical matters, for general acceptance of phenomenology, for increased attention to existential psychology, and in a somewhat amorphous way almost all of the areas of personality theory call for counterprescriptions of one sort or another (p. 137).

It is important to note that most national prescriptive trends have been stated in terms of dominance and counterdominance, which reflects diversity, not integration. Indeed, the highest level of integration in psychology is still that of the schools, not that of the nation. Different patterns of dominance and counterdominance are present in different countries. For the sake of brevity, but at the risk of oversimplification, methodological and contentual objectivity, particularly in the form of operationalism, prevails in the United States, while methodological and contentual subjectivity, especially in the form of phenomenalism, does so in large segments of continental Europe.

It follows that patterns of dominant prescriptions characterize a given temporal period and geographical area. When we wish to emphasize the then current intertwined pattern of dominant prescriptions as having a massive cumulative effect, we refer to the *Zeitgeist*. The *Zeitgeist* in itself is empty of content until we describe that which we assign to a particular *Zeitgeist*. The strands that enter into the *Zeitgeist* include the dominant prescriptions of that time. So the *Zeitgeist* and prescriptive concepts are considered complementary. One of the puzzling facets of the *Zeitgeist* theory is just how to account for differential reaction to the same climate of opinion. The prescriptive approach may be helpful in this connection. Plato and Aristotle, Hobbes and Spinoza, Hume and Rousseau, each experienced the same *Zeitgeist* but also had idiosyncratic, nondominant prescriptive allegiances.

What I have said about prescriptions by no means exhausts this complexity. Prescriptive trends fall and rise again, combine, separate, and recombine, carry a broader or narrower scope of meaning, and enter into different alliances with other prescriptions, change from implicitness to explicitness and back again, and concern with different psychological content and its related theories. Beyond this, I hesitate to go, except to say I am confident there are probably other, as yet unrecognized ramifications. Prescriptions endure, whereas the psychological facts, theories, and areas which influenced their acceptance are ephemeral and ever-changing.

If I have stressed the directing and guiding phase of the effect of prescriptions on a scientist's thinking, it is not because of blindness to the other side of the coin, the originality of the scientist. A scientist not only is guided by, but also exploits, both paradigms and prescriptions. He does so in terms of his originality, and of other factors that make for individuality.

My enthusiasm for prescriptions may have left you wondering whether this is all that I can see in the history of psychology. Let me reassure you at this point. The usual contentual topics of psychology, most broadly summarized as sensation, learning, motivation, and personality and the hypotheses, laws, and theories to which their investigations give rise, are still considered very much a part of its history. As differentiated from philosophically oriented contentual prescriptions, it is these and related contentual topics which show that a concern for psychology is the subject matter of historical investigation. These contentual topics are the vehicles with which all historians of psychology must work. Even here there is another point about prescriptions that I might mention. There seems to be some historical evidence of an affinity between certain prescriptions and certain contentual topics, e.g., dynamicism with motivation, developmentalism with child and comparative psychology, personalism, idiographicism, and irrationalism with personality, and empiricism with learning. Individual psychologists who have been strongly influenced by particular prescriptions are apt to reflect them in their work. Although the evidence has not yet been sought, it is quite plausible to believe that, reciprocally, choice of problem area may influence allegiance to certain prescriptions. In similar vein, I suspect that prescriptions tend to cluster in nonrandom fashion. Offhand, acceptance of supernaturalism seems to have an affinity for teleology, indeterminism, and qualitativism; naturalism, for mechanism, determinism, and quantitativism; nomothesis, for determinism; rationalism, for deduction; empiricism for induction.

To return to extraprescriptive aspects of psychology, the methods of psychologists — observation and experiment — cannot be neglected in a historical account. Psychologists' use of these methods is an integral part of that history. However, certain prescriptions, particularly those identified earlier as methodological in nature, allow casting considerable historical material in the way that has been sketched.

Any adequate history of psychology must reconsider the personality characteristics of individual psychologists and the extrapsychological influences, such as social circumstance, which have been brought to bear upon each psychologist. Can one imagine that Hobbes' psychological views were independent of his detestation of organized religion, adoration of a strong central government, and fear of the consequence of political disorders?

I would like to summarize briefly some of the functions that I consider prescriptions to serve. They provide classification and summarization through a conceptual framework which can be applied historically. Prescriptions provide principles of systematization which are related to, and yet to some extent are independent of, the particular contentual or methodological problem of the individual psychologist. They are also mnemonic devices which make it possible to summarize and convey a maximum of meaning with a minimum of words. Going beyond anything even hinted at in the paper, prescriptive theory might also help to make history a tool for investigation of the psychology of discovery, and also serve as a framework for studies using content analysis applied to historical documents.

Prescriptions are characterized by an oppositional character manifested in dominance and counterdominance, an implicit as well as an explicit nature, a philosophically based contentual character, a methodological character borrowed from the other sciences, a presence in other fields, an interlocking in schools of psychology (with some salient and others nonsalient), a clash of prescriptions at the national level and a participation of prescriptions at the national level, and a participation of prescriptions in the *Zeitgeist*. Since psychology seems to lack a unifying paradigm, it would seem that as a science it functions at the level of guidance by prescriptions.

NOTES

1. Others have expressed themselves about the lack of unity in psychology. If one were asked what is the most comprehensive treatment of psychology since Titchener's *Manual,* the answer must be the multivolumed *Psychology: A Study of a Science,* edited by Sigmund Koch (1959). Its general introduction makes considerable capital of the diversity of tongues with which psychologists speak and the preface comments that psychology proceeds along "several quite unsure directions" (p. v). To turn to but one other source, Chaplin and Krawiec (1960) close their recent book on systems and theories with the prophecy that the task of the future is "to integrate all points of view into one . . ."; to provide "a comprehensive theoretical structure with the integrating force of atomic theory . . ." (pp. 454-455).

2. A fortunate historical precedent for using prescriptions in this way is to be found in a quotation from Leibniz in his *New Essays Concerning Human Understanding* (1949). It may help to make clear what is meant. "The discussions between Nicole and others on the *argument from the great number* in a matter of faith may be consulted, in which sometimes one defers to it too much and another does not consider it enough. There are other similar *prejudgments* by which men would very easily exempt themselves from discussion. These are what Tertullian, in a special treatise, calls *Prescriptiones* . . . availing himself of a term which the ancient jurisconsults (whose language was not unknown to him) intended for many kinds of exceptions or foreign and predisposing allegations, but which now means merely the temporal prescription when it is intended to repel the demand of another because not made within the time fixed by law. Thus there was reason for making known the *legitimate prejudgments* both on the side of the Roman Church and on that of the Protestants" (Book IV, chap. 15, pp. 530-531).

3. Something akin to the prescriptive approach has been suggested in the past. In the early part of the last century Victor Cousin (1829), followed by J. D. Morell (1862), developed a synthetical system of the history of philosophy based upon a division into the four aspects of sensationalism, idealism, skepticism, and mysticism.
    In the '30s, Kurt Lewin (1935) was groping toward something similar in his discussion of the conflict between the Aristotelian and Galilean modes of thought. Lewin's shift of modes of thought from the Aristotelian to Galilean, although admitting of partial overlap, impresses me as too saltatory, too abrupt

in movement from qualitative appearance to quantitative reality, from search for phenotypes to search for genotypes, from surface to depth, from disjointed descriptions to nomothetic search for laws. They are, in my opinion, not so much a matter of qualitative leaps as they are gradual changes, with the older views still very much operative. Lewin's conceptualizing in relation to the historic facts seems similar in spirit to Piaget's brilliant strokes on the process of development. I suspect that if we were to take Lewin as seriously as did the American investigators who followed the leads of Piaget into painstaking detailed research, we would find that there was much blurring and overlap of these Lewinian shifts, as there seems to be at the Piagetian levels.

In applying the shift in modes of classification from the Aristotelian to Galilean syndrome, Brunswik (1956) placed psychology as showing the shift between Titchener in 1901 and Lewin in 1935. It is unfortunate that an arbitrary impression of finality emerges. Prescriptions, at any rate, are not conceived as emerging with such definitiveness; they appear gradually and tentatively, to disappear and then to reappear.

Brunswik (1955, 1956) also casually used the term "Thema" in somewhat the same broad sense that I use "prescription," but without working out its meaning or scope. He also used the same term to apply to the seeking of analogical similarity to the content of another science (1955) and even to psychological content as such (1956).

In his *Historical Introduction to Modern Psychology,* through the 1932 revision but not his 1949 revision, Murphy (1932), in summing up the decades of 1910 and 1920, utilized quantification as the integrating theme to unify psychology, but gave previous consideration to problem trends over the time in question, for example, from structural to functional, from part to whole, from qualitative to quantitative, and from experimental to genetic-statistical. It is important to reiterate that these were used as guiding themes only for a summary of two decades, and not for the earlier history of psychology. When Murphy faced the task of summarizing from the vantage point of the late 1940s, he abandoned this form of summarization.

Bruner and Allport (1940) analyzed the contents of psychological periodicals for the fifty-year period, 1888-1938, in terms of individual "author's problem, his presupposition procedure, explanatory concepts and outlook in psychological science" (p. 757). The material provided the basis for Allport's 1939 Presidential Address to the American Psychological Association. In his summarization, Allport (1940) indicated that his survey showed an agreement with an earlier one by Bills; he not only stated that psychology is "increasingly empirical, mechanistic, quantitative, nomothetic, analytic and operational," but also pleaded that psychology should be permitted to be "rational, teleological, qualitative, idiographic, synoptic, and even nonoperational" (p. 26). Thus, Allport and I show substantial agreement, since five out of six "presuppositions," as he calls them, are among those in my schema of prescriptions. The reason that one exception, operational-nonoperational presuppositions, is not included in my schema is that I consider it, as explained before, historically rooted in other older prescriptions.

Allport and Bruner's work cries out for follow-up, and I hope to have someone working on it in the near future. Allport did, however, use something akin to his schema in a comparison of American and European theories of personality published in 1957.

A more recent related publication is that of Henry Murray, who, in the course of an overview of historical trends in personality research, made a plea for "a comprehensive and fitting classification of elementary trends" (1961, pp. 15-16), which he then classified as regional, populational, theoretical, technique, data ordering, intentional (pure or applied), and basic philosophical assumptional trends. This last, the basic philosophical assumption, was not

in any way spelled out, so there is no way of knowing what he had in mind.
4. There is a precedent for considering the trends studies in terms of antithetical pairs. In his critical study, *Biological Principles,* J. H. Woodger (1929) considered the problems of biological knowledge to center on six antitheses: vitalism and mechanism, structure and function, organism and environment, preformation and epigenesis, teleology and causation, and mind and body. His emphasis was upon examining the current views circa 1929. Although he showed a lively appreciation of their historical roots, his task was not essentially historical.

W. T. Jones (1961) also has developed a means of evaluation of so-called "axes of bias" of order-disorder, static-dynamic, continuity-discreteness, inner-outer, sharp focus-soft focus, this world-other world, and spontaneity-process. Content high on the order axis shows a strong preference for system, clarity, and conceptual analysis, while that for disorder shows a strong preference for fluidity, muddle, and chaos. Illustrative applications to samples of poetry, painting, and documents in the social and physical sciences were made. Syndromes for the medieval, the Renaissance, the enlightenment, and the romantic periods were developed. The last, receiving the most attention, was characterized as showing soft-focus, inner-disorder, dynamic, continuity, and other-world biases. The results so far reported show it to be a promising technique.

Brunswik (1956) also speaks of the survival of dichotomizing doctrines, such as the four temperaments, as illustrative of a prescientific syndrome in psychology.
5. Of course, implicitness of historical trends is not a novel idea. Whitehead (1925) remarked that when one is attempting to examine the philosophy of a period, and by implication to examine a science as well, one should not chiefly direct attention to those particular positions adherents find it necessary to defend explicitly, but to the assumptions which remain *unstated.* These unverbalized presuppositions appear so obvious to their adherents that it may even be that no way to state them has occurred to them. In similar vein, Lovejoy (1936) has observed that implicit or incompletely explicit assumptions operate in the thinking of individuals and ages.
6. It should be noted that this looking to other sciences and finding evidences for prescriptions implies that paradigmatic sciences are not denied the presence of prescriptions. Exploration is, however, outside of the scope of this paper.

REFERENCES

Allport, G. W. The psychologist's frame of reference. *Psychological Bulletin,* 1940, *37,* 1-28.

Allport, G. W. European and American theories of personality. In H. P. David & H. von Bracken (Eds.), *Perspectives in personality theory.* New York: Basic Books, 1957, pp. 3-24.

Bruner, J. S. & Allport, G. W. Fifty years of change in American Psychology. *Psychological Bulletin,* 1940, *37,* 757-776.

Brunswik, E. The conceptual framework of psychology. In O. Neurath *et al.* (Eds.), *International encyclopedia of unified science.* Chicago: University of Chicago Press, 1955, pp. 655-760.

Brunswik, E. Historical and thematic relations of psychology to other sciences. *Scientific Monthly,* 1956, *83,* 151-161.

Chaplin, J. P. & Krawiec, T. S. *Systems and theories of psychology.* New York: Holt, Rinehart & Winston, 1960.

Cousin, V. *Coursde l'histoire de la philosophie.* 2 vols. Paris: Pichon & Didier, 1829.

Jones, W. T. *The romantic syndrome: Toward a new method in cultural anthropology and history of ideas.* The Hague: Nijhoff, 1961.

Koch, S. (Ed.), *Psychology: A study of a science.* Study 1. *Conceptual and systematic.* New York: McGraw-Hill, 1959.

Kuhn, T. S. *The structure of scientific revolutions.* Chicago: University of Chicago Press, 1962.

Kuhn, T. S. The function of dogma in scientific research. In A. C. Crombie (Ed.), *Scientific change.* New York: Basic Books, 1963, pp. 347-369.

Leibniz, G. W. *New essays concerning human understanding.* (Trans. by A. G. Langley) La Salle, Ill.: Open Court, 1949.

Lewin, K. The conflict between Aristotelian and Galilean modes of thought in contemporary psychology. In *A dynamic theory of personality.* New York: McGraw-Hill, 1935, pp. 1-42.

Lovejoy, A. O. *The great chain of being.* Cambridge: Harvard University Press, 1936.

Marx, M. H. & Hillix, W. A. *Systems and theories in psychology.* New York: McGraw-Hill, 1963.

Miller, G. A. (Ed.), *Mathematics and psychology.* New York: Wiley, 1964.

Morell, J. D. *An historical and critical view of the speculative philosophy in Europe in the nineteenth century.* New York: Carter, 1862.

Murphy, G. *An historical introduction to modern psychology.* (3rd. rev. ed.) New York: Harcourt, Brace, 1932.

Murray, H. A. Historical trends in personality research. In H. P. David & J. C. Brengelmann (Eds.), *Perspectives in personality research.* New York: Springer, 1961, pp. 3-39.

Watson, R. I. The historical background for national trends in psychology: United States. *Journal of the History of the Behavioral Sciences,* 1965, *1,* 130-138.

Whitehead, A. N. *Science and the modern world.* New York: Mentor, 1925.

Woodger, J. H. *Biological principles: A critical study.* New York: Harcourt, Brace, 1929.

POSTSCRIPT (1971)

Work on prescriptive theory has continued since this article first appeared in 1967. A paper, "A prescriptive analysis of Descartes' psychological views," derived from a longer manuscript on the history of psychology in the seventeenth and eighteenth centuries, serves as an illustration of how this point of view may be applied to an individual.[1]

Another article contrasts prescriptive theory with various other approaches to the dynamics of history.[2] It shows the interrelationship of the former with the Great Man and the *Zeitgeist* theories, and with the eclectic inductive contentual emphasis, both in its presentist and its nonpresentist form.

This paper also contains a brief discussion of the first dissertation in the UNH doctoral program in the history of psychology. It was carried out as a major aspect of its framework, specifically through use of content analysis categories. She plans publication in the near future.
by Barbara Ross and is entitled "Psychological thought within the context of the scientific revolution, 1665-1700." Dr. Ross used prescriptive theory

Kenneth Gibson of UNH proposes to study the frequency of acceptance, rejection, and irrelevance of the prescriptions, using the Presidential addresses of the American Psychological Association from 1892 to 1970 as the material for content analysis. Dominance and counterdominance, explicitness and implicitness, and the presence or absence of patterns will be studied.

A portion of an unpublished Master's essay at UNH by Joseph Mirabito involves the factor analytic study of ratings of prescriptive variables by a sample of members of Divisions 25 and 26 of APA. The nine factors that emerge each made psychological sense. For example, the first factor has positive loadings on methodological objectivism, quantitativism, nomotheticism, and inductivism, and a negative loading on methodological subjectivism. The methodological attitude that it expresses tells us something about the current scene in psychology in the United States. A note on his results will appear shortly.

NOTES

1. Watson, R. I. A prescriptive analysis of Descartes' psychological views. *Journal of the History of the Behavioral Sciences,* 1971, *7,* 223-248.
2. Watson, R. I. Prescriptions as operative in the history of psychology. *Journal of the History of the Behavioral Sciences,* 1971, *7,* 311-322.

Prolegomena to a Textbook
History of Psychology

JOHN J. SULLIVAN

1. *Introduction.* Determination of the nature of a textbook history is not high on any list of interesting theoretical problems challenging an historian of psychology. But anyone planning to spend a few years writing a textbook would be well advised at the outset to spend a few days thinking about the nature of the enterprise. We have learned from studies on mental sets the importance of specification of determining tendencies for the understanding and controlling of mental processes. If we view writing of a textbook history as a rational enterprise, as distinguished from an unreflective academic publishing project, the result may be judged wise or foolish, well or poorly done, coherent or disorganized, in terms of the goals of the specific textbook. Accordingly, here are specified a rationale and characteristics for a textbook history of psychology.

2. *Taxonomy.* Short reflection indicates that common elements found in histories of particular sciences are the following:

A. A theory, model, or set of proposals in a certain pattern which constitutes the organization of the subject matter of the science.
B. A sequence of events ordered in a temporal direction, the historical narrative.
C. A person with a particular set of cognitive dispositions, a particular intellectual style, certain problems to solve, and usually a sense of direction in which an adequate solution for the problems is to be sought.
D. A person's social or reference group, either a school or profession or national or cultural period.

Histories clearly differ in their emphases on one or another of these elements. A history of mathematics written for professional mathematicians

This is the first chapter of my *A Small Textbook on the History of Psychology* to be published by Prentice-Hall. The chapter is a prolegomenon to the book. Its aim is to give the student a set toward the rest of the book and to provide an overview of the schemes of categorization of the contents. Its function, in the argot of educational psychology, is to be an "advance organizer."

I have discussed the contents of this article with Mary Henle and William Woodward.

might conceivably be a history of different structural proposals for the special fields of mathematics. A popular writer on historical aspects of mathematics may well stress biographies of mathematicians, with little formal analysis of their contributions to mathematics. In the humanistic approaches to either scientists or the history of sciences, there is a tendency to stress the individual scientist and his existential conflicts, to take a biographical approach to the person. Analysis of his ideas is usually given explication in terms of coherence of his general perceptions of the world rather than the place of his ideas in the history of a special scientific discipline.

TABLE 1. MATRIX OF ELEMENTS OF HISTORIES OF SCIENCE

	A	*H*	*P*	*S*
A—Analysis of theory (Philosophy of science)	AA	AH	AP(H)*	AS(H)*
H—Historical narrative (Historiography)		HH	HP	HS
P—Descriptions of persons (Psychology)			PP	PS(H)*
S—Social groups (Sociology)				SS

In addition to these ten categories the system of combinations includes the following three-element histories:

AHP   AHS   APS(H)*   HPS

And one four-term construction:

AHPS

*(H) indicates that historical sequence is held constant. This type of study — the analysis of a theory, person, and group — would be about some historically important person — say, Diderot, his conception of science, his complex personality and style of thinking, and his relation to other Encyclopedists.

Table 1 indicates the possible combination of these elements of histories of science. This taxonomic scheme is based upon the combinatorial possibilities of any given number of elements. The general formula for the number of combinations of any set of n elements is 2^n-1. In this table of common elements in histories of science, the number is 2^4-1, or 15 combinations. If some type of history of science is not found in one of the combinations of this system, then it must be composed of elements other than those of this taxonomic system. No claim is made, of course, that all histories of science consist only of the above elements. The claim is that a systematic look at possible combinations brings order into a series of discussions on historiography. In the absence of such an ordering scheme, or another similar to it, literature on historiography has been a hodgepodge of unrelated issues. Such issues might be whether to write a history of ideas (the "what to worship" school) or of great men (the "whom to worship" school), whether to write an internal or an external history of science, whether scientific communities' acceptance of a particular paradigm depends more on the sociology of the community than it does on the prevalent philosophy of science, and so on.

3. *Component Fields.* In the classification system exhibited in Table 1, the set AA, HH, PP, and SS refers to basic disciplines that contribute to a history of science. It is also the set of disciplines in which the young historian of science ought to be well grounded. AA is the field of philosophy of science, viewed as an analysis of basic formal concepts used in scientific theories and research. It has roughly the relationship of Aristotle's First Philosophy to his books on physics and psychology, and is concerned with the justification (in Kant's terms, *quid juris* rather than *quid facti*) of induction, explanation, description, theory, concepts, scientific laws, causality, probability, etc. HH is the field of history. My own predilection is to view the term "history" as a property of, an aspect of, an intellectual discipline. History is always "of something" and is not properly an independent (Platonic) form. The special concern of this paper is with properties of a history of psychology.

PP refers to the field of psychology. Any historian ought to demonstrate some sophistication about contemporary psychology. It is particularly incumbent upon authors who will write histories of psychology to be sensitive to the psychological dimensions of men and groups. This does not mean, of course, that one must be committed to some form of psychohistory, but that one should give some indication of a general familiarity with the conceptual systems of contemporary psychology and an understanding of the state of the art of interpretation. Many historians ask of psychology that it provide more than the field can deliver in the way of psychological explanation. Explanatory principles of psychology are closely associated with the kind of data generated in the laboratory and clinic, and may be used to explain history only by extrapolations from original sources. And these extrapolations by historians frequently make psychologists cringe with embarrassment. Facile psychological generalizations about a particular historical period, in turn, make the professional historian less than happy. The history of the field of psychology is clearly a problem for the historian. Application of psychology to history is in the domain of the psychologist — once the historian has performed his labors and given us the most probable accounts of what actually happened.

SS refers to the field of sociology and the bordering discipline of social psychology. Problems of history are frequently cast in the form of interactions of individuals with a scientific community, a national culture, or a particular historical epoch. As in the case of psychology of the individual, sociology and social psychology cannot, in the present state of their development, provide the type of laws of social organization and change that historians need for explanation. Thus, historians are forced to give close descriptive accounts of the events they study, and either avoid or invent the sociological generalizations they need. If historians keep close to historical description, the narrative itself provides implied psychological and sociological explanations. The price the historian pays for this close contextual description-explanation is the same that an insightful novelist pays, the limited generality of his findings. In addition, what the historian chooses to describe, what he will consider relevant in a particular historical setting, is related to his conception of the psychology of the individual and the sociology of relevant social groups which are being studied.

4. *Two-Element Studies.* AH history may be called, following Bergmann,[1] "structural history." This type of study is based upon a distinction between structural, factual, and causal history. In writing structural history the historian analyzes theories and then places them in historical order. Such a history highlights formal similarities and differences of various theories. For instance, in Book IV of *Republic,* Plato presents a tripartite theory of mind that has properties similar to Freud's, which he introduced in *The Ego and the Id.* A structural historian makes an analysis of the theories of Plato and Freud and discusses similarities and differences of the two proposals. A factual historian, armed with this analysis, then has the problem of looking into the "history" of Freud's development of the theory, making sure to check the background of Freud in classical studies, texts he used in *Gymnasium* and in the university, the books in Freud's library, his letters between the writing of *Beyond the Pleasure Principle* (1920) and *The Ego and the Id* (1923), etc. From close examination of primary texts, letters, and other records of that time, a set of factual data is available for an estimation of whether there was any direct causal influence of Plato's conception on Freud. This type of history, establishing causal chains, is regarded by some as the essence of historical scholarship. Others, and I include myself in this group, think that it is usefully engaged in only up to a point. The point of diminishing returns undoubtedly depends upon the use of the historical narrative. For textbook histories, such diminishing returns occur early in historical studies. Samples of AH history are Bergmann [2, 3] and Sullivan.[4] Gillispie [5] says that he writes structural history, but obviously he does much more.

AP history would be a selection of an historically significant person and an analysis of his work. This is not history in any particular sense, but philosophical or cultural analysis. Perhaps an example of this type of work can be found in a section of "From Breuer to Freud" (Sullivan [6]), in which there is an analysis of the structure of early Freudian thought. The distinction to be made here between AP and HP is between philosophical analysis and literary historical description. Perhaps the distinction can be seen in R. B. Perry's [7] several works on William James and the recent more literary biography of Robert Jay Allen.[8] R. B. Perry tends to write AP history, whereas Allen writes HP history.

AS is a type of nonhistory presented at the Fourth Annual Meeting of the Cheiron Society [9] (Calgary, Canada, June 1972) by a group of philosophical psychologists from the Alberta Center for Advanced Study in Theoretical Psychology. The thrust of their presentation was to deny attribution of simple positivism to behaviorism by analyzing the range of theories in the behavioristic spectrum. In a paper, "Diversity of Behaviorism," by Kellogg Wilson,[10] the dimension of analysis was the cognitive content of the theories which ranged from a Skinner to Watson and Thorndike through a Spence-Hull and Tolman position to a Miller, Gallanter, and Pribram position (see Table 2). This type of analysis is not based upon an historical arrangement, but is, I believe, propaedeutic to the writing of the history of any set of doctrines, scientific or philosophical, which have a structure.

TABLE 2. THEORETICAL (STRUCTURAL) ANALYSIS (AS)

Low *Mentalism*				*High* *Mentalism*
I Radical behaviorism (Skinner)	II Connectionism (Watson, Thorndike, Guthrie)	III Behavior theory (Hull-Spence)	IV Purposive behaviorism (Tolman)	V Mentalistic behaviorism (Miller, Gallanter, Pribram)

HP history is simply the history of a person without analysis of his scientific doctrines. It is difficult to understand how a history of a scientific discipline can be written without referring in some way to the doctrines of the person that make him worthy of scientific or historical attention. However, this approach might be made on the basis that the person's work is generally understood to be important, and that it is of interest to inquire into the nature of his life. Someone might write a biography of Plato, Aristotle, Leibniz, Hume, Kant, or Darwin [11] that would be of interest to historians of science even if the details of his theory were not included. This sort of biography, which has been done on Newton [12] and Hume,[13] shades into the type of psychohistory Erikson [14] has given us of young Luther. In any event, such biographical approaches designed to humanize great thinkers require special skills and a type of research interest rarely exhibited by standard historians of science.

HS history refers to the history of a group of persons. This kind of work has been called, variously, "collective biography," "multiple career line analysis," or "prosopography." Classical examples appear in such studies of politics as Charles Beard's [15] explanation of the founding of the Constitution of the United States by an examination of the social and economic interests of the "founding fathers." Another classical example is Namier's [16] study of the members of British Parliament at the time of the accession of George III. Such a history could be an examination of a group of behaviorists belonging to any one particular group. Such studies of reactions, both of groups and of members of a group, to significant figures have been done with skill by David Krantz.[17] Burnham [18] has analyzed the history of the psychoanalytic and the behaviorist movements.

PS is the type of work, not necessarily historical, which relates a person to a social group, a social network. This kind of study does not appear as history except as in a case similar to AP history, in which the person happens clearly to be important historically. Study of a person's relations with his social group also contributes something important to an understanding of a period and to the diffusion of a particular doctrine. A classical example of this variety of study was presented at the 1971 Cheiron Society meeting by W. R. Whipple [19] — a study of the friendship network of William James that was so important in the diffusion of Darwinism.

5. *Three-Element Studies.* Two-element presentations tend to be either nonhistorical studies or historical studies done by nonhistorians with a special interest in a particular aspect of science. Historians generally tend to do broader studies, for one of the basic characteristics of historical sophistication is the multiple determination of historical events. Unlike the physical or social scientist who attempts to isolate his phenomena of interest in laboratory-type simplifications, historians attempt to interpret the phenomena of interest in terms of a rich historical context. To put it in another way in order to sharpen the contrast, the effort of the historian is to enrich contextual description, while the laboratory psychologist tends to deplete and to simplify the conditions associated with an event. The measure of an historian is the fullness of his description of relevant historical contexts; that of the experimental psychologist is the amount of control of the experimental context. One of the consequences of this distinction is that one would predict a natural affinity of the experimental psychologist for two-element structural histories (AH) and theoretical analysis of the AA type, and that the historian's presentation of complex contexts of events would be inconsistent with the intellectual style of the experimentalist.

A problem of the historian, like that of the philosopher, is, to use one of Horace Kallen's favorite images, that of orchestration of complex elements. It goes without being emphasized that skill in orchestration is quite different in its demands from simply writing a melody or being competent in playing an instrument.

Table 1 indicates that in our taxonomic system there are four three-element possibilities for history, one of which — APS(H) — is, strictly speaking, more of a cross section of an historical period than an historical sequence. An advantage of the AHP type of history is that, compared with the other kinds, it is easy to write and easy to understand. It is easy to write because the basic unit is the person who has a particular definable history and a particular scientific theory. When the basic unit is a group of people, as in AHS, there are problems in determining the limits of the group, the sampling of persons to study, the multiple career lines of individual members, and varieties of scientific theories held by members of a group. The sheer number of variables that do not admit of sharp limitation make the final conclusions inevitably tentative. This type of problem, however, is capable of resolution by modern factor analysis, but the kind of quantitative measures such procedures require are usually not generated by historical research.

As we become more sophisticated about social psychology and sociology, it becomes increasingly clear that individual behavior is under normative regulation and is strongly influenced by models and social reinforcements. Thus the notion of the "great man," alone in his study and generating great ideas, is a patent distortion of the psychological realities. Whatever position one takes toward B. F. Skinner's recent book, *Beyond Freedom and Dignity,* it has the undeniable merit of clearly indicating the mechanism by which we attribute properties to individuals in the absence of knowledge of the controlling variables. This book, however it may irritate historians on other grounds, should be welcome in that it stresses the controlling features of the contexts of behavior, a position which I understand is basic to an historical enterprise. A deficiency with three-element history is that either the social contexts are omitted in AHP or are stressed in AHS, but with the person left out. HPS amounts to historical sociology without emphasis on scientific analysis of a theory.

In AHS studies are found analyses of theories of groups of individuals, schools, or movements, presented historically. To illustrate some distinctive features of this kind of history, consider how the AS analysis of behaviorism by Kellogg Wilson, shown in Figure 1, appears in an AHS model. The AS dimension becomes the ordinate and the time dimension becomes the abscissa. Each scientist has his own career line on which his publications may be noted. See Figure 1.

FIGURE 1. STRUCTURAL HISTORY OF BEHAVIORISM (AH)

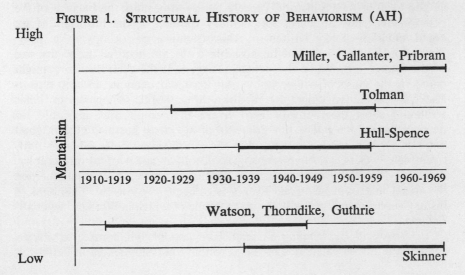

To sum up the characteristics of three-element histories: while they are more general than the two-element type, they still reflect a special interest. Special interest categories are related to the basic contributory disciplines of philosophy of science, historiography, psychology, or sociology.

6. *Four-Element Studies.* The convention for the taxonomic system here proposed is to call history proper only those works written with an AHPS format. A case has been made that we should distinguish between general and special histories, and that the special histories have the function of illuminating an aspect of an historical situation. The aspect chosen is related to such nonhistorical interests as historical sociology, historical psychology, an exercise in historiography, or criticism of past scientific theories. It might be objected by some historians, psychologists, or sociologists that to use the designation of history only for the four-element type of presentation is to expect too much of scholars. To be a psychologist, sociologist, historian, and philosopher of science is easily to require four lifetimes, so the argument might go. A counterargument is that in the sciences the old category systems of intellectual disciplines are changing rapidly and the problem of scientific research requires study of the inter-actions of a number of component systems. In the biological sciences today the competent researcher is expected to know physics, chemistry, and mathematics, as well as his normal specialty within the field of biology. As social sciences move out of the laboratory variety of study and into natural contexts, the researcher either joins a research team composed of various specialties or he acquires the specialties himself. Since history is the study of natural contexts of social action *par excellence,* it is expected that the historian will also have training in a number of fields as well as training that permits "orchestration" of the data from each of these fields into a coherent historical narrative.

The ideal of AHPS history is rarely achieved because the balance of the components tends to reflect the primary training of the historian. If we could envision books written in this tradition as occupying a four-dimensional space, it would be possible to locate histories near any one of the dimensions. When the person is stressed, the AHPS history might come in the guise of a biography. An excellent example of this type is Packe's [20] definitive biography of John Stuart Mill. Isaiah Berlin [21] has written a short biography of Karl Marx that emphasizes not only his personality and the intellectual contexts of his ideas, but also gives a good analysis of his work. Passmore's [22] is another example of this sort. Crombie's [23] classical *Augustine to Galileo* is a model of historiography; Peter Gay's [24] *The Enlightenment* is another example. Accentuation upon the social matrix of ideas and events is difficult to come by. This kind of history verges on cultural history, an example of which is Werner Jaeger's [25] *Paideia.*

7. *Historical Explanation.* It would be possible, of course, to discuss each of the fifteen categories of the taxonomy not only singly in detail but

also in relation to each other. Not all these relations are important for the historian, nor are they all relevant for the present discussion. Within the contexts of contemporary psychology, however, the relation between AH, structural history, and AHP, the history of persons in the development of scientific theories, is important. To persons trained in the experimental tradition as behaviorists, the history naturally preferred is the AH type. They tend to be suspicious of psychohistory even when it is accompanied by excellent historiography and competent theoretical analysis, which it rarely is. AH history, it will be recalled, is history of theories, with the scientist left out. As the logical empiricist movement fades, it appears that preference for an AH as opposed to an AHP history was ultimately based upon preference for a certain type of explanation. In the physical sciences the model was based upon explanation which was one of the subsumption of instances under a general law of classes of events. It involved the notion of logical entailment, such as is found in syllogistic logic — namely, that the premises of an argument imply the conclusions. In this explanatory machinery the scientist as a rational agent has no place. And if he has no place in such explanation, what history offers as explanation could be considered pseudoexplanation.

That there is only one paradigm of explanation is a reflection of a platonic emphasis of the unity of science movement. The criticism of Wittgenstein and his disciples has expanded the notion of explanation to encompass various different verbal games other than those in the physical sciences. Passmore,[26] a distinguished historian of contemporary philosophy, has given a classical statement of the issue and supporting examples for development of the concept of explanation that coincide with the practice of historians:

> My own view is that the peculiarities of history have been exaggerated. It no doubt looks peculiar when it is contrasted with mathematical physics, but it would be absurd to take mathematical physics as the typical example of inquiry; it could scarcely be more atypical. If we understand how explanation functions in everyday life, we shall have few difficulties with the procedures of the historian. . . . In everyday life there is a wide variety of circumstances under which we may offer, or be offered, what we should describe as "an explanation" of an occurrence. Consider the following:
>
> (1) "As I got into the streetcar, I noticed a large brown cylinder which was emitting a continuous clicking noise. The driver explained that I was to put my fare into it." In this instance I am confronted by an object which I do not know how to use. The explanation tells me how to use it, "what it is for."
>
> (2) "On the menu, there was something called 'scrod.' The waitress explained that this is young cod." As in case (1), I am being taught how to use something — a word. But the explanation now takes the form of a definition.

(3) "I asked him why I had to submit a report on a student at midterm. He explained that this is the common custom in American universities." My puzzlement in this case revolved about what I took to be an unusual procedure; the explanation consists in telling me that it is not unusual, that there is nothing to be puzzled about.

(4) "One of my students did not hand in his midterm paper. I asked him to explain." Here what I seek as an explanation is an excuse, a justification.

(5) "I found one passage in his essay very obscure. I asked him about it, and he explained what he was getting at." To explain is, in this case, to elucidate, to paraphrase, to make clear how something fits into a general context.

(6) "I asked him how he had gotten home, and he explained that he first caught a subway, then a streetcar, then a taxi." The explanation fills in detail. I already know that he got home; the explanation tells me by what stages he did so.

(7) "I thought Mary was winking at me, but they explained that she had a tic." In this case, to explain is to reclassify, or reinterpret.

(8) "I had always been told that all Americans were hearty hail-fellow well-met sort of people, but he explained that this is only true of the Mid-Western." "Explained to me" because I am puzzled about the discrepancy between what I had been told and what I have experienced; the explanation tells me that I have wrongly taken to be a universal characteristic of Americans what is, in fact, characteristic only of a special class of Americans.

(9) "I asked him why he wrote badly, and he explained that his school course laid very little stress on English composition." The explanation, in this case, refers to precedent conditions — this is a typical causal explanation.

The force of these "explanations" really turns on the fact that Passmore starts with a puzzlement that is resolved in one way or another. The role of the agent or individual who is puzzled in the scheme of things, as distinguished from his elimination in the explanations of theoretical physics, makes these explanations work. One of the important distinctions between science and history is that the scientist's role in resolving his puzzlements is part of his history and the history of the science, but not part of the explanatory corpus of the science itself.

8. *Textbook Histories.* Within the proposed taxonomic system, textbook history may be defined as the three-element type — either AHP, AHS, APS(H), or HPS. Clearly, textbook history is a specialized form and the goal may be focused on either persons, ideas, social groups, or the interaction of persons and social groups. Textbooks in the history of psychology, in my opinion, can be schematized as falling into three levels of abstraction: the lowest level stresses persons, the second level is about theories, and the highest level emphasizes methodological problems. This

is a dimension based upon a psychological interpretation of the problem of ease of communication. What seems cognitively simple for beginning students, the study of the ideas of persons, upon close examination proves to be quite difficult and complex. Methodology, which is apparently more abstract, is in structure more simple. Until students in the field have strong methodological training when they enter courses in the history of psychology, the best tactic seems to be to introduce the subject through discussions of "the great psychologists," and to hope that students will complete their studies with some sense of structural history. Historians of psychology are expected to acquire that methodological sophistication which distinguishes any specialist from psychologists who have only general knowledge of the field.

9. *A General Outline of the History of Psychology.* Although there is ambiguity in the concept of "history" and considerable variation in use of the term "psychology" in a broad historical view, we can take the various meanings of the phrase "history of psychology" and group them into three broad phases.

The first phase is best indicated in the classical Greek thought of Plato and Aristotle but, with minor modifications, is continuous in philosophy up to the philosophies of Hume, Kant, J. S. Mill, and Brentano. Theories of mind were an essential part of philosophical systems. Within these systems of philosophy, psychology functioned as a theory of mind which provided the substructure for theories of either epistemology or ethics, that is, problems of knowledge or conduct. For those psychologists today who wish for a psychology with broad social and philosophical relevance, this early philosophical psychology, and psychological philosophy, should be of great interest. The philosophical approach generally is to ask what mind must be like to account for problems of knowledge and the control of conduct. This approach is similar to procedures used generally in the humanistic disciplines. In these studies, where theories of mind are implied, the procedure is to construct a theory of mind based upon the evidence of humanistic literature. The mind of the Italian Renaissance painters was constructed from analysis of their paintings by Burkhardt.[27] The procedure is still in use by certain psychoanalytic writers, grafted on to standard psychoanalytic theory. Freud's studies of Leonardo da Vinci and Michelangelo are of this type.

The second phase of psychology was initiated in the latter half of the nineteenth century by a group of psychologically oriented philosophers. Wundt, Külpe, Brentano, and William James were empirical philosophers with a strong scientific orientation which took the form of psychological research. Philosophy to them was in many respects an empirical discipline, and the empirical part of philosophy was the study of mind. Their students, however, who were interested in theories of mind, became the first modern psychologists. But they were psychologists with strong systematic interests and definite philosophical commitments. These psychologists and their students founded the great systematic positions of Structuralism, Psychoanalysis, Gestalt theory, and Behaviorism. The technical working out of these psychological systems constituted the normal science of the second phase of the history of psychology. Modern psychology has been considered to have been founded with the revolt of Structuralism, Psychoanalysis, Behaviorism, and Gestalt theory from the classical psychology of the earlier period. Rather than being constructed on the basis of casual observations and common sense tailored to the constraints of philosophical systems or humanistic conceptions of man, theories of mind and behavior were constructed to explain laboratory and clinical data. However, the break from philosophy by psychologists was not sharp, for the systematic interests of the psychologists were patterned in the main on philosophical models.

In the third phase of psychology these great systematic positions have less prominence. In this period, roughly starting around 1950, the "heroic" systems of Freud, Köhler, and Hull seem to have been too quickly constructed on data too quickly gathered. Today less attention is paid to general systems of psychology and more to specific problems. The role of philosophy with regard to psychology has also changed. With the decline of broad systematic concerns in philosophy, which preceded by several decades the similar decline in psychology, the philosophers directed their attention to analysis of scientific concepts, clarification of the nature of scientific language, etc. Psychology has not outgrown philosophy; the relationship has simply changed. Philosophy of science is today of primary concern for theorists of psychology.

In broad overview, then, the various conceptions of psychology look like a chaotic conglomeration of "just one damn theory after another." If the theories are arranged in an historical order, a distinction can be made between them on the basis of different functions, different methods, and different data. With these criteria in mind, the three phases of psychology have been discriminated. A question arises as to whether it is possible, within each of these phases, to provide a system of ordering the various theories. An obvious requirement is that each ordering system within each phase of psychology elucidates important relations within each phase. Thus one ordering system would not suffice for the three different phases. Accordingly, three different systems of ordering are proposed.

10. *A Category System for the History of Theories of Mind: Twenty-three Ontologies.* With the growth of both physics and biology in the seventeenth century, the opinion became widespread that knowledge of the physical world was a construction, the basic data of which were the experiences of the scientist. Starting from experience as basic and the physical world as a construction led some philosophers to the conclusion that epistemology was the fundamental philosophical problem, that only minds exist, and that the properties attributed to the world depended upon the properties of mind. Growth of science and its magnificent

predictive successes led scientists to emphasize the existence of the world as independent of the mind of the scientist. The collision between a philosophy that was increasingly skeptical with regard to the claims of knowledge about the external world with the success of scientists in predicting physical events led to a radical reexamination of the problems of epistemology. Epistemology was then seen, by Realists such as Russell and by neo-Realists such as E.B. Holt and R. B. Perry, as having a role in ontological systems. Ontology replaced epistemology as the basic concern. It is from this standpoint that a set of categories for the characterization of theories of mind within philosophical systems is constructed.

For the purposes of the analysis of the history of mind, the following ontological elements are considered fundamental:

A. *Mental acts.* These acts are such events as thinking, judging, comparing, remembering, discriminating, etc.

B. *Mental phenomena.* The term "phenomena" refers to sense data, sensations, elementary reactions to external stimuli.

C. *Physical objects.* Under the influence of the elementarism of Newtonian physics, the ultimate constituents have been held to be either particles, mass-points, or, at one time, atoms. Whether physical objects are considered to be simples (particles) or composites is not crucial for the purposes of this category system.

D. *Relations.* Relations are between events, so in a sense they imply the existence of the events. The strong assertion of the function of relations, however, holds that the properties of events depend importantly upon the structures in which they appear. The weak doctrine of relations holds that the definition of the properties of an object does not entail its external relations.

These ontological elements are important in the development of theories of mind. If one holds that only minds exist, then the world may be constructed as an act of will or a reflection of the properties of mind. This position is not uncommon among mystics. If only minds and phenomena exist, then the external world is unknowable and is but a construction. If one starts with the existence of physical events and phenomena and minds, then the problem is how to arrive at intersubjective agreement on the structure of the world. The constraints put on subjectivity of the scientist to insure intersubjectivity, or public knowledge, result in the notion of objectivity. The relations of the world may be either constructed by a mental act, learned by experience of a mind that is essentially passive, or be presented because the world presents itself as structured (relationally). These alternatives, using the various ontological elements, have been traditional concerns of theorists of mind. Selection of one of these alternatives has historically influenced the various conceptions of psychology as they appeared in philosophical systems. We shall order these systems by these ontological elements. There are fifteen combinations possible with four elements.

The fifteen ontologies, however, do not constitute an exhaustive system. Plato and such religious thinkers as Plotinus and Aquinas do not fit into this system. Accordingly, a fifth ontological element would be the assertion of an ideal world, composed of either Platonic forms, mythological figures, theologically important personages, or souls. Positing of an ideal world occurs, after the stage of animism, primarily in those ontologies that have a mental act component. Belief in such a world was, during the time of the Scholastics, an act of reason; in the Protestant world after Kant, an act of faith. Eight of the fifteen ontologies have a mental act element. Thus, in addition to the original fifteen ontological combinations, these eight are repeated with the element of an ideal world, resulting in twenty-three ontologies.

Historically, only a very few of these ontologies have been held exactly by anyone. These positions are formulated as what would be called, in factor analytic studies, "marker variables." With these fixed ontological positions, each particular psychologist or philosopher may be studied carefully with the following questions in mind: Is mind conceived to be active or passive? Are phenomena the fundamental realities, or do they indicate events in the physical world? Are only the laws of the physical world and physical elements admitted into the psychology? Are relations a property of the physical world, an integration of phenomena by either sensory or central processes, or are they formed by a principle of learning?

In general, psychoanalytic theorists distinguish themselves from the rest of psychology by the assertion of a mind that acts, selects, chooses (in the Rorschach), defends itself, etc. Gestalt psychologists refer to relations in the natural world and/or as a result of nervous system integration. Behaviorists stress learning of relations and a mind that is passive. Existentialists emphasize the primacy of phenomena and add other elements, depending upon whether they are religious or atheistic in inclination.

11. *A Category System for the Classification of Psychological Systems.* In the second phase of psychology the "schools" were closely associated, as were schools of philosophy, with the personality and intellect of certain dominant figures. To discuss these schools is to discuss the formulations of particular men and their students. The category scheme that will be used is as follows:

    I. *Structuralism*
        W. Wundt
        E. B. Titchener
        J. P. Guilford
    II. *Gestalt Psychology*
        W–Gestalt (Wertheimer)
        K–Gestalt (Köhler)
        Gestalt predecessors: Goethe, Kant, Brown, Mach,
                    v. Ehrenfels

III. *Psychoanalysis*
The Foundations: Freud 1890-1905
Classical Psychoanalysis: Freud 1905-1920
Transition to Ego Psychology: Freud 1920-1939
Ego Psychology: Hartmann, A. Freud,
and E. Kris 1939-1960

IV. *Behaviorism*
Behaviorism$_A$—Watsonian. Experimental. Human and animal subjects. No mentalistic terms. Anti-introspection in methodology. Psychology defined as the science of behavior.
Behaviorism$_B$—Tolmanian. Experimental. Animal subjects. Mentalistic terms, "purpose" may be given if operationally defined. Mind both passive and given cognitive processes. Intervening variables.
Behaviorism$_C$—Hullian. Experimental. Human and animal subjects. Intervening variables. Formal theory. Quantitative relationships. Equations empirically derived. Afferent stimulus interaction leads to some relations, learning results in others.
Behaviorism$_D$—Skinnerian. Experimental. Human and animal subjects. Against intervening variables, formal theory.
Behaviorism$_E$—Estesian. Experimental. Human and animal subjects. Rational theory, equations rationally derived, checked empirically.
Behaviorism$_F$—Osgoodian. Human subjects. Experimental and psychometric study of meaning. Psycholinguistics. Mediational processes, Gestalt-like integrational processes on stimulus interaction, and response interaction.

12. *A Category System for the Study of Psychological Problems.* In the third phase of psychology the study of scientific problems ultimately resolves itself into determining either laws of succession of events or syndromatic laws which order concurrent events as, for instance, in factor analysis. The requirements of measurement are that some aspect of behavior of a subject under study is examined and related to some other aspect of either the environment or the individual. The format of the research is Behavior$_Y$ = f(X). With this format the various problems of psychology may be classified by grouping of the dependent and the independent variables in somewhat the following manner:

I. BASIC SCIENTIFIC FIELDS

Beh = f(physiological variables, variables correlated with hearing, vision, etc.)

Beh = f(perceptual variables)

Beh = f(learning variables, number, frequency, timing of reinforcement)

Beh = f(individual differences, intelligence, aptitudes, attitudes)

Beh = f(personality variables, ego strength, etc.)

Beh = f(social group variables)

As can be seen, the fields of psychology, according to this category system, vary from physiology to social psychology. If one goes further in the direction of physiological psychology, one comes to pure physiology; and when one goes further in the other direction from social psychology, one comes into sociology. Thus we see that this breakdown categorizes psychology from physiology to sociology. The system, however, does not include developmental studies.

With the schema presented above, the problem of thinking is conceived to be a complex process something like Kant proposed; it includes, as subprocesses, sensation, perception, learning, and the structure of intellect. A schema which is more general in terms of processes studied and which gives more emphasis to cognitive processes and value systems can be constructed as follows:

	A	*B*	*C*	*D*	*E*	*F*
A—physiological processes	AA	AB	AC	AD	AE	AF
B—behavioral processes, individual		BB	BC	BD	BE	BF
C—cognitive processes			CC	CD	CE	CF
D—social norms, values				DD	DE	DF
E—social behavior					EE	EF
F—physical settings						FF

Here are twenty-one basic relations, of which AA is pure physiology, one part of the physical system interacting with another. AB is the relation of a physiological variable interacting with a behavioral variable. BB is the interaction of two or more behavioral tendencies, for example, in a response hierarchy. CC is the interaction of cognitive processes — dissonance, consonance, etc. DD is study of value systems. EE is study of social behaviors of individuals. FF is study of physical geography, environment, etc., and their properties. EF is a study of the relations of physical environment to social behavior. With this category system one can locate most of the basic scientific works in the field of psychology. With six elements one can generate 63 combinations; only the first and second pairs are presented above. The auxiliary and metadisciplines are, of course, statistics, instrumentation, history, philosophy, biology, and sociology.

II. DEVELOPMENTAL FIELDS

Beh $= f(age)$; the general formulation
Beh $= f(8$ months to 12 years); child psychology
Beh $= f(12$ to 18 years); adolescent psychology
etc.

How the age span is divided varies according to whether one studies Freud's scheme of psychosexual development, Erikson's psychosocial development, Piaget's cognitive development, or simple physical growth measures. Study of development is not a basic field in the sense that learning and perception are. There are no new principles of learning or perception at the various developmental levels. Rather, different objects are responded to; different conditions are reinforcing.

III. APPLIED FIELDS

The general formulation here is that behavior is determined by situational variables. The fields are defined in terms of what situational variables are of interest.

Beh $= f$(school variables) — educational psychology
Beh $= f$(military variables) — military psychology
Beh $= f$(business and industrial situations) — industrial psychology

In these situations the basic laws of learning and perception are adjusted by the situational variables. Behavior is ultimately determined by the basic scientific laws, the developmental stage, and the situation in which the individual is placed.

13. *Conclusions.*

A. A well-formed psychology consists of (1) a set of basic scientific laws, (2) a set of developmental laws, and (3) a set of applications. The auxiliary disciplines are the bordering content fields of physiology and sociology and the instrumental disciplines of statistics, measurement, and computer sciences. History of psychology is the broad metadiscipline of both psychology and the auxiliary fields.

B. There are varieties of histories of sciences. A simple and rather obvious taxonomic system has been proposed here.

C. The elusive state of historical sophistication is defined differently in different types of history.

D. The historian's ideal of the description of what actually happened, and how it was seen in a particular historical period, is distinguished from textbook pedagogical goals.

E. Pedagogical considerations of long-term memory systems of the student result in a stress on a conceptual approach to the history of psychology.

NOTES

1. Bergmann, G. *Philosophy of Science*. Madison: University of Wisconsin Press, 1958.
2. Bergmann, G. The problems of relations in classical psychology. *The Philosophical Quarterly, 7,* 1952, 140-152.
3. Bergmann, G. *Realism*. Madison: University of Wisconsin Press, 1967.
4. Sullivan, J. J. From Breuer to Freud. *Psychoanalysis and Psychoanalytic Review, 1959, 46,* 2.
5. Gillispie, C. C. *The Edge of Objectivity*. Princeton: Princeton University Press, 1960, p. 524.
6. Sullivan, J. J. *Op. cit.,* 1959, *46,* 2.
7. Perry, R. B. *The Thought and Character of William James*. Cambridge: Harvard University Press, 1948.
8. Allen, G. W. *William James*. New York: Viking Press, 1967.
9. Symposium on Behaviorism, Fourth Annual Meeting of Cheiron Society, Calgary, Canada, June, 1972.
10. Wilson, K. Diversity of behaviorism. Unpublished paper read at Cheiron Society meeting, Calgary, Canada, June, 1972.
11. Gruber, H. Darwin's materialist philosophy and fear of persecution as factors in his early development. Unpublished paper read at Cheiron Society meeting, New York, May 1971.
12. Mossner, E. C. *The Life of David Hume.* Austin: University of Texas Press, 1954.
13. Manuel, F. E. *A Portrait of Isaac Newton*. Cambridge: Harvard University Press, 1968.
14. Erikson, E. *Young Man Luther*. New York: Norton, 1958.
15. Beard, C. A. *An Economic Interpretation of the Constitution of the United States*. New York: Macmillan, 1913.
16. Namier, L. B. *England in the Age of the American Revolution*. 2nd ed. London: Macmillan, 1961.
17. Krantz, D. Personal and impersonal channels of recruitment in the growth of psychological theory. Unpublished manuscript.
18. Burnham, J. C. *Psychoanalysis and American Medicine*. New York: International Universities Press, 1967.
19. Whipple, W. R. A new approach to the study of Darwin's influence on American psychology. Unpublished paper read at Cheiron Society meeting, New York, May 1971.
20. Packe, M. St. J. *The Life of John Stuart Mill*. New York: Macmillan, 1964.
21. Berlin, I. *Karl Marx*. New York: Oxford University Press, 1963.
22. Passmore, J. A. *A Hundred Years of Philosophy*. London: Duckworth, 1957.
23. Crombie, A. C. *Medieval and Early Modern Science*. Vols. I and II. Garden City: Doubleday & Co., 1959.
24. Gay, P. *The Enlightenment: An Interpretation*. New York: Random House, 1966.
25. Jaeger, W. *Paideia*. 3 vols. New York: Oxford University Press, 1944.
26. Passmore, J. A. Explanation in everyday life, in science, and in history. In G. H. Nadel (Ed.), *Studies in the Philosophy of History*. New York: Harper & Row, 1960.
27. Burkhardt, J. *The Civilization of the Renaissance in Italy*. Vol. I. New York: Harper & Brothers, 1958.
28. Danto, A. C. *Analytic Philosophy of History*. Cambridge: The University Press, 1968.

On Controversy and Its Resolution

MARY HENLE

We seem in psychology to be a little ashamed of our controversies. Or — what amounts to the same thing — we smile indulgently at the foibles of our elders. We attribute controversy to the Age of Schools, and we make it altogether clear that we are well past that age. The instinct controversy has recently been described as "one of the dirtiest of our controversial wash" (Krantz & Allen, 1967, p. 336). The Baldwin-Titchener controversy — some 40 pages of it — we say concerned nothing more than a tenth of a second in reaction time. What contemporary editor would have allotted 141 pages to the Wundt-Stumpf controversy on tonal distance? And who is interested in these disputes today? Psychology does not have a very good record in resolving its controversies; rather, we lose interest in them.

My theme will be that we need not be ashamed of our controversies or dismiss them as trivial. Controversy is not only useful, but probably unavoidable, since it arises out of essential properties of our cognitive functioning. Further, controversies have made positive contributions, and resolution — in one way or another — is sometimes possible.

Why are controversies in such bad repute? It seems that we dislike them because we see in them the intrusion of emotion in the rational structure of our science. We read, for example: "If science were a totally rational enterprise, controversy would, in all likelihood, not exist" (Krantz & Allen, 1967, p. 336). Again: "What is it that creates scientific controversy? Ego-involvement. Ego-bias" (Boring, 1954, p. 639). Also: "When two incompatible egoisms come together, they account for the wasted time of scientific warfare, for the dethronement of reason by rationalization" (Boring, 1955, p. 105). Elsewhere, Boring is still more explicit:

> Egoism and the need for prestige . . . tend to close the mind in controversy, a phenomenon which is illustrated in any thoroughgoing scientific quarrel. . . . Not distinct from egoism is the need for self-

A number of friends have read and criticized an earlier draft of this paper. I am grateful to Dr. Rudolf Arnheim for forcing me to clarify my thinking at crucial points and to Dr. John Sullivan and Dr. Theta Wolf for many helpful and interesting suggestions.

consistency. Every quarrel shows that too. When a man takes up a position, his pride prevents retraction. . . . Sometimes it is not respectable to be right if you have to change your mind out loud (1942, p. 612).

Let me begin my defense of controversies by pointing out that they have not, as a rule, been insignificant. The issue between Baldwin and Titchener was that of functionalism vs. structuralism. It was a controversy over the legitimate problems of psychology and the legitimate conditions of collecting psychological data. To speak of the controversy as if it were over a minor difference in reaction time is to rob it of its context and meaning. But when torn out of context, most scientific work sounds trivial. What does it matter, for example, if an eclipse arrives a little late? So do jets, and nobody minds very much. To the astronomer, of course, seeing the event in its scientific context, it would make a tremendous difference.[1]

But the main issue is undoubtedly that of the role of passion in controversy. Aside from the presence of personal attack, why do we see in controversy the operation of factors less than ideally rational? For the effects attributed to emotion, I will draw considerably on Boring, the psychologist who has been most interested in the analysis of controversy.[2]

1. It has usually been true in psychological controversy that neither side has changed its position. Boring comments: "Controversy is more than discussion. It involves emotion: and passion, while of itself irrelevant to scientific procedure, enters to prejudice reason and to fix the debaters more firmly in their opinions" (1929, p. 119). Again, he remarks: "Plainly there is a perseverative tendency in scientific thinking" (1929, p. 113). He quotes a remark of Max Planck: "New scientific truth does not triumph by convincing its opponents and making them see the light, but rather because its opponents eventually die" (1954, p. 640).

One of the most striking forms such a perseverative tendency takes is seen in the use of the ad hoc hypothesis to deal with contradictory evidence. As an example from the history of psychology, we may consider the famous constancy hypothesis. When many perceptual phenomena did not behave as they ought to have behaved from this point of view — the illusions, the constancies, contrast, perceived movement, and so on — nothing was easier than to add assumptions, untested and untestable, about the effects of unconscious inferences, errors of judgment, and the like. What could be better evidence for ego involvement in one's theoretical position than such frantic efforts to save it?

2. Controversy, it is said, blinds us to alternatives, so that we can see neither the point of our opponent nor the relevance of his arguments, or even of his data.

Thus, controversies in psychology have tended not to be settled by factual evidence. Krantz (1969) has shown this clearly in the case of the Baldwin-Titchener controversy, where there was little argument about what the facts were. As a matter of fact, both participants were pretty well aware of the facts before the controversy began (cf. Titchener's review article, 1895). As another example, the same seems to be true in the case of the long controversy over continuity in learning.

3. Another curious and apparently nonrational characteristic of controversies is that they may seem to die out, only to reappear in connection with a different problem. Thus the controversy over reaction times had died out by 1900 (Krantz, 1969, p. 12), but the structuralists and the functionalists had by no means lost interest in refuting each other's positions. Instead, they found new problems, new arenas, for their debates. It is easy to blame emotion for the refusal of certain debates to die out: passion would seem to motivate the search for new points of attack.

4. As Boring sees it, some personal need — enthusiasm, loyalty, egoism

gets the work done, but it may also blind you to the defects and short-comings of the work itself. . . . The truth of objectivity may be left for others to perceive, or even reserved for posterity (1954, p. 645).

5. Participants in controversy are frequently accused of still another apparently emotional indiscretion. In Boring's words:

Social attitudes also constrain thought. Here we have the influence of the schools, the need for men to stand together. The in-group magnify their agreements and rise to repel, or at least to depreciate, the out-group. . . . Wundt's students confirmed the tridimensional theory of feeling; others did not. Würzburg never found images for thought; Cornell did. Is feeling a sensation or not? Laboratory atmosphere largely determined what would be found in answer to that question . . . (1942, p. 612).

While other such effects can be gleaned from the literature, these should suffice. It can certainly not be denied that such phenomena may be observed in our psychological controversies. Must we conclude that — whatever the motivational advantages of emotion, of commitment, of intense interest, for scientific work — controversy does no more than reveal the scientist in his entirely human capacity for passion?

It will be suggested here that all these phenomena are characteristic of cognitive processes in general, and especially so when we are dealing with organizations of any complexity. The relevant facts are so well known that extended discussion is unnecessary.

1. What Boring calls a perseverative tendency in scientific thinking — what I would prefer to call perseverance — is necessary for all problem solving. In the case of problems of any complexity, most scientific problems certainly included, failure is assured if the thinker abandons his approach in the face of every obstacle. "Hold to your strategy, vary your tactics," advises Humphrey:

The strategy of thought, its general aims, must be carried through, in spite of all difficulties, with all the persistence one can summon. The tactics must be altered to suit the particular difficulties that arise during the process of solution (1948, p. 62).

Wertheimer, describing his talks with Einstein about the thinking that culminated in the theory of relativity, quotes his subject as saying: "During all those years there was a feeling of direction, of going straight toward something concrete" (1959, p. 228, note 7). Examples are familiar: Newton, it is reported, came to discover the law of gravitation by always thinking about it. Gauss worked for four years to prove a theorem (Humphrey, 1948, p. 129). Poincaré offers numerous instances of his prolonged efforts to solve particular problems (1952).[3]

Perseverance in a wrong direction, of course, leads to foolish processes or to error. Einstellung is a well-known phenomenon in certain kinds of problem solving. Similarly, in the case of systems of thought, perseverance in a nonessential direction may be unproductive: the most familiar example in American psychology is Titchener's structuralism, which Heidbreder describes as a "gallant and enlightening failure" (1933, p. 151).[4]

But coherent thinking requires persistence in a given direction. Such persistence leads, at times, to failure, but it is essential for cognitive achievement.

2. The fact that it is often impossible to see the relevance of an opponent's arguments, or even of his data, may be derived from one of the most basic phenomena of all cognitive processes: a given item appears different in different contexts. First demonstrated in the case of perception, where an item may not even retain its identity in a new configuration, as Ternus has shown, the statement may be exemplified everywhere in thinking and in understanding. At the most commonplace level, a word has different meanings in different sentences. At a somewhat more complex level, the meaning of a statement will depend upon the author to whom it is attributed, and thus upon the context of ideas in which it is set (Asch, 1948). Wertheimer has given compelling instances in which "a thing may be true in the piecemeal sense, and false, indeed a lie, as a part in its whole" (1934, p. 137).

For purely cognitive reasons, then, it is scarcely surprising that a fact in the context of Titchener's system would have different significance from the same fact in the context of Baldwin's thinking. That the facts of the case did not change the mind of either participant in this controversy is testimony, not to the emotional character of controversy, but to the powerful role of context in endowing facts with meaning.

Once more it must be added that the effects of context may, on occasion, lead to error. Functional fixedness, as one example, is an expression for the fact that an object that could be used to solve a particular problem —

that could be relevant in a particular context — is not seen as relevant because of its known relevance to some other context.

Because of the power of context in determining the meaning of items, contexts themselves are usually difficult to change. New items, immediately interpreted in the light of a body of ideas, lose much of their potential ability to threaten those ideas. When the organization in question has the complexity of a theoretical system, reorganization is, of course, exceedingly difficult. In commenting on Einstein's achievement in reorganizing physical thinking, Wertheimer remarks:

> In appraising these transformations we must not forget that they took place in view of a gigantic given system. Every step had to be taken against a very strong gestalt — the traditional structure of physics, which fitted an enormous number of facts, apparently so flawless, so clear that any local change was bound to meet with the resistance of the whole strong and well-articulated structure. This was probably the reason why it took so long a time — seven years — until the crucial advance was made (1959, p. 232).

Given the difficulty of achieving reorganizations of complex systems, one can understand the tendency to use ad hoc hypotheses to patch up a system rather than attempt to achieve a new theoretical framework. Nor is this necessarily irrational where the apparently contradictory facts are neither central nor overwhelming in number. The necessity for perseverance in thinking has been pointed out above.[5]

But to return to the main point: facts do — and ordinarily must — find their meaning in context. If we failed to interpret facts, we could not explain them or even think about them. We would be in the position of Thurber's man who "doesn't know anything except facts," and we would obviously not be solving scientific problems.

3. It was pointed out that controversies often seem to die out, only to reappear in a new connection. In other words, the controversy has been transposed. Transposition first became known in perception, and it has wide relevance to thinking processes as well. Organized bodies of knowledge, which may be challenged at a number of points, are, of course, particularly conducive to such transposition.

4. That we are often unable to see the defects of our own work as clearly as we see those in the work of an opponent is most likely largely a matter of the difficulty of achieving reorganizations of already organized material.

5. The influences attributed to schools seem to be even more simply explainable. That different findings are obtained in different laboratories is a matter of the conditions set up, the tasks presented, the instructions to subjects and to experimenters, and the like. One special case will be considered below.

I have been suggesting that we do not need to look to emotional factors to account for the phenomena of controversy, but that we are dealing with basic characteristics of cognitive processes. The same factors — the role of context and the rest — that enable us to have any coherent view of the world or any theoretical framework are the ones that make it difficult for us to resolve our controversies. Is this to say that passion does not enter into controversy? By no means. Wundt did insult Stumpf (Boring, 1929), and Titchener's term "polite invective" might at times be applied to both participants in the Baldwin-Titchener exchange.[6] Certainly, passion and commitment figure in controversies; but, apart from name-calling, they doubtless function by way of processes of the kind described here.

This is another chapter that cannot be treated here; but I would like to indicate a direction by quoting a passage from John Stuart Mill.[7] Here intellectual and "moral" sources of erroneous opinions are discussed; the latter, for Mill, consist of indifference to the attainment of truth and of bias:

> But the moral causes of opinions, though with most persons the most powerful of all, are but remote causes: they do not act directly, but by means of the intellectual causes; to which they bear the same relation that the circumstances called, in the theory of medicine, *predisposing* causes, bear to *exciting* causes. Indifference to truth cannot, in and by itself, produce erroneous belief; it operates by preventing the mind from collecting the proper evidences, or from applying to them the test of a legitimate and rigid induction; by which omission it is exposed unprotected to the influence of any species of apparent evidence which offers itself spontaneously, or which is elicited by that smaller quantity of trouble which the mind may be willing to take. As little is Bias a direct source of wrong conclusions. We cannot believe a proposition only by wishing, or only by dreading, to believe it. The most violent inclination to find a set of propositions true, will not enable the weakest of mankind to believe them without a vestige of intellectual grounds — without any, even apparent, evidence. It acts indirectly, by placing the intellectual grounds of belief in an incomplete or distorted shape before his eyes. It makes him shrink from the irksome labour of a rigorous induction, when he has a misgiving that its results may be disagreeable; and in such examination as he does institute, it makes him exert that which *is* in a certain measure voluntary, his attention, unfairly, giving a larger share of it to the evidence which seems favourable to the desired conclusion, a smaller to that which seems unfavourable. It operates, too, by making him look out eagerly for reasons, or apparent reasons, to support opinions which are conformable, or resist those which are repugnant, to his interests or feelings. . . . But though the opinions of the generality of mankind, when not dependent on mere habit and inculcation, have their root much more in the inclinations than in the

intellect, it is a necessary condition to the triumph of the moral bias that it should first pervert the understanding. Every erroneous inference, though originating in moral causes, involves the intellectual operation of admitting insufficient evidence as sufficient; and whoever was on his guard against all kinds of inconclusive evidence which can be mistaken for conclusive, would be in no danger of being led into error even by the strongest bias. . . . If the sophistry of the intellect could be rendered impossible, that of the feelings, having no instrument to work with, would be powerless (1881, pp. 513-515).

To return parenthetically to the role of passion in scientific work, Boring points to its motivating effects: "Out of egoism are derived the drive and enthusiasm that lead men to undertake research, to keep at it, to publish the results, to keep promoting the knowledge and use of these results" (1954, p. 640). With T. S. Kuhn (1962), I prefer to view normal science as puzzle solving, with the demands of the problem itself and the curiosity of the scientist supplying the motivating forces. This is not to minimize the role of passion in scientific work. But passion for what? For the work, I am suggesting, not merely the passion of egoism.

If one considers controversy to be irrational to a high degree, this has certain consequences for its resolution. Thus Boring recommends that we cultivate both judiciousness and effective prejudices (1929, p. 121) — judiciousness with a view to reducing fruitless controversy, and effective prejudices with a view to getting the work done. He holds out the hope that, if we do not outlive our outmoded views, at least science will (1954, p. 641). And Krantz considers that "to accomplish . . . confluence of views, some form of persuasion must occur" (1967, p. 337).

If one holds controversy to be a consequence of normal modes of cognitive functioning, the problem of its resolution changes. But since, as I have mentioned, psychology has not been notably successful in resolving its controversies, let us first look briefly at some effects of controversy even in the absence of resolution.

My references will largely be to recent controversies. It should be noted that these are not controversies in the grand style of the nineteenth century. We do not find a critique, a reply, a rejoinder, an *AntiKritik*, a *Schlusswort,* and still another *Schlusswort*. Rather, we are fortunate to find a critique and a rejoinder. But the changes, I suspect, are changes in editorial policy, not in the dynamics of controversy.

1. Controversy leads to research undertaken in the hope of settling the issue. We have seen that controversies tend not to be settled by factual evidence. "But facts are facts," as William James put it (1890, I, p. 193), "and if we only get enough of them they are sure to combine. New ground will from year to year be broken, and theoretic results will grow."

2. Since controversy arises where existing research leaves questions of interpretation, it may lead to an improvement of techniques and of research designs.

Köhler makes this effect of controversy explicit in a reference to Postman's criticism of his work on the nature of associations:

The experiments, I will candidly say, are perhaps not yet entirely conclusive. But I am grateful to Postman; his arguments tell me exactly what further tests must now be done in order to reach a clear decision. At times, work in psychology does become a lively affair (1969, p. 132).

Another controversy which seems to have led to improved research design and procedures is the one over learning and awareness; still another example is the long controversy over subliminal perception.

3. Controversy may lead to a clarification of issues. This may take the form of a clarification of the implicit assumptions of one's opponents. For example, Krantz and Allen point out that "McDougall forced a clarification of the underlying assumptions of radical behaviorism" (1967, p. 336). Many similar examples could be given.

Köhler once remarked that it is the responsibility of each scientific generation to make explicit the implicit assumptions of its forebears. Controversy enables us to do this within a generation — at least for uncommitted outsiders, if any exist.

4. Some positive effects of controversies, quite independent of their resolution, have been indicated. It must now be added that the criticism which is essential to controversy may lead to changes that are not necessarily advances:

a) A hardening of position. Titchener in 1898 saw functionalism as having a great future; of course, by this he meant that its future was assured to the extent to which it could be taken over by his own experimental psychology (1898, p. 465). In later years his position hardened — in part, no doubt, as a result of his continuing debate with the functionalists. (This is, however, not an unmixed effect of controversy. In part his position hardened because, as he systematically set forth his ideas about science, it became clear that functionalism in no way fit.) At any rate, in *Systematic Psychology* he wrote: "Functional psychology . . . is a parasite, and the parasite of an organism doomed to extinction" (1929, p. 254). The image no longer suggests a great future, indeed no future at all.

b) A restricting of position. In a minor controversy in which I was once involved, the opponents first described what they called "pure phenomenological psychology" as concerned with nonconceptualized experience; under criticism, they seemed to add a condition not previously discernible: "ppp" deals with experience that is conceptualizable but not conceptualized (Brody and Oppenheim, 1967, p. 332). That this is a restriction, not simply a clarification, is seen from the circumstance that it would exclude mystical experience which, before the criticism, was the most plausible material on which they could draw for their conception of "ppp."

c) A position may become more extreme under criticism. Krantz and Allen have indicated that this was one effect of attacks on early behaviorism by McDougall and others (1967, p. 336). Similarly, most of us have seen ourselves pushed under attack into extreme positions we didn't really hold.

Still, controversies are sometimes resolved. How?

1. Resolution may be the result of mutual decision that new methods should be used to settle issues. The decision may not be explicit at the time; and it may be made by those who inherit a controversy rather than by those who initiated it.

A number of early scientific controversies disappeared when scientists agreed to decide them by empirical evidence rather than by authority. In the controversy on the comets of 1618, for example, one of the arguments brought against Galileo was a biblical story. He took the trouble to answer the argument, but this, of course, did not resolve the issue; it could be settled only later by the methods of empirical science. Again, Harvey had to contend mainly with the authority of the Galenists. Here is one of his replies:

> . . . Who will not see that the precepts he has received from his teachers are false; or who thinks it unseemly to give up accredited opinions; or who regards it as in some sort criminal to call in question doctrines that have descended through a long succession of ages, and carry the authority of the ancients — to all of these I reply: that the facts cognizable by the senses wait upon no opinions, and that the works of nature bow to no antiquity; for indeed there is nothing either more ancient or of higher authority than nature (1649).

This controversy, too, disappeared when the higher authority of nature was generally recognized.

Likewise in modern times, controversies may drop out with the introduction of new methodology. Krantz and Allen (1967) have shown that the instinct controversy in psychology disappeared for this reason: an experimental methodology was being introduced for problems of social psychology. (Revival of interest in instinct in contemporary ethology had to await acceptable methodology for problems in this area.)

2. Occasionally a controversy can be resolved by showing that the alternatives as formulated are too narrow. Thus Köhler has shown that both nativists and empiricists have seen their problem too narrowly. Both have neglected all those factors which the organism shares with the rest of nature — thus, factors independent of the heredity of the individual or the particular species, and likewise independent of the individual experience of any member of the species. Thus a perceptual phenomenon that is unlearned need not depend upon the existence of inherited mechanisms.

The dichotomy as formulated, in short, leaves out a very large part of the story:

It is three factors by which events in organisms . . . are generally determined. First, the invariant principles and forces of general dynamics, secondly, anatomical constraints which evolution has established, and thirdly, learning. . . . Why so much talk about inheritance, and so much about learning — but hardly ever a word about invariant dynamics? It is this invariant dynamics, however constrained by histological devices, which keeps organisms and their nervous systems going (Köhler, 1969, pp. 89-90).

Here is a case, I think, in which it does not matter whether nativists continue to oppose empiricists. The controversy has been superseded: once it is seen that three factors are involved, not two, the controversy loses its meaning. If we do not realize that this controversy has been bypassed, so much the worse for us. The next generation will find it out.

3. In still other ways, a controversy may be shown to be a pseudo-controversy. Arnheim has suggested, for example, that the controversy over imageless thought arose because the Würzburg psychologists did not know what to look for in examining their consciousness for images. The experienced content did not correspond to their notion of an image (Arnheim, 1969, p. 102). They thought of images as replicas of objects, ignoring the essential abstractness of images.

If Arnheim is right, the imageless thought controversy disappears. It then becomes a pseudocontroversy arising because the two sides were talking about different things, but using the same name for them.[8]

4. A controversy may be resolved by formulating a more inclusive theory which will in some sense incorporate the competing positions. For example, Mary Calkins (1906) attempted to resolve the conflict between structuralism and functionalism by finding for both a place within a broader context: her own self-psychology. But in order to do this, she had first to ask: What is essential about each approach — that is, specifically what is the problem of reconciliation?

As to structuralism, the essential thing, she thought, is not its atomistic unit, whose inadequacies the functionalists had already pointed out. If this were the essential thing, there would be no point to the reconciliation. Rather, it is the method of structuralism which is to be retained: the analysis into irreducible elements and the classification of experiences. Within the new context, the structural task is the analysis of consciousness regarded as experience of a self (1906, p. 70).

What about functionalism? Again Calkins went to what she regarded as essential — here, too, a type of psychological analysis. This she viewed as embodying two conceptions:

. . . first, and fundamentally, the conception of consciousness in terms of the relations to environment which it involves; second, the conception of consciousness in terms of the significance or value of these relations (1906, p. 72).

The first of these conceptions may be made to coincide with self-psychology; the second may be subsumed under it. In short, "functional psychology, rightly conceived, is a form of self-psychology" (1906, p. 75).

Today we are not much interested in this solution by Calkins, but the reason does not lie in any inadequacy of the solution. Rather, we no longer experience the conflict: we are no longer interested in structural problems in the Titchenerian sense; and, on the other hand, functionalism never became a developed system of psychology, but has persisted as a flavor, an interest of contemporary psychological theories. As a matter of fact, Calkins herself lost interest in this solution as she came more and more to "question the significance and the adequacy, and deprecate the abstractness" of structural psychology (cf. 1930, p. 40).

It should be noted that Calkins took *two* steps, not one, to resolve the controversy. First she decided *what* was to be reconciled; then she placed the apparently conflicting material within a larger framework. There have been many recent attempts to resolve controversy; one reason for their failure has been the omission of the first step. And, more serious, we have tended to try to resolve the controversy while staying within a framework not sufficiently broad to encompass what is of value in each point of view.[9]

Anatol Rapoport (1967) has suggested a similar method as a means of escape from paradox. (He is concerned only with step 2; but since he is dealing with clear-cut logical problems, this makes no difficulty.) Apparently insoluble problems, he shows, can sometimes be solved by broadening the logical framework in which they are presented.

This procedure, it seems to me, applies not only to the resolution of theoretical conflict and to escape from certain kinds of paradox, but much more generally to the resolution of conflict. We may restate this method of solution in more formal and more general terms. Given conflicting demands $|a|$ and $|b|$, resolution is possible only when a configuration is found — say, abc — which includes both. Solution is possible in the larger context because the components alter their character within the configuration. $|a|$ is not the same item as the a in abc, and may thus not be in conflict with the b of abc. Furthermore, our focus is no longer on $|a|$ but on the configuration.

Once more, particular items look different when seen within a broader context: the conflicting claims look different, and the conflict may therefore sometimes be resolved. The same influence of context which has been seen to make the resolution of controversy difficult can be used for just that purpose. Perpetuation of controversy, as well as its resolution, may be seen as Gestalt problems.

In summary, most of the methods of resolution of controversy listed above may be seen to be means of superseding the controversy rather than resolving it. To free a science of a pseudocontroversy is a positive achievement. True resolution has been discussed in terms of setting conflicting positions within a broader framework; but this method has rarely been used in psychology. Indeed, if it is envisaged, as Calkins did, as a means of reconciling general theories, it seems today to be premature. Meantime, rather than look away from controversy, we may recall its productive consequences:

> Heated argument is to be avoided. But to set opposing points of view into plastic relief is our obligation.

Goethe's maxim (Curtius, 1964, p. 122) seems to be good advice to contemporary psychology.

NOTES

1. Since this point will become relevant in a more specific connection below, further discussion is postponed.
2. Reference will also be made to a discussion of the instinct controversy by Krantz and Allen (1967) and one of the Baldwin-Titchener controversy by Krantz (1969).
3. Persevering in efforts to solve a problem is not, of course, necessarily a matter of continuing in the same line of thinking. But it must be remembered that the perceived problem itself contains directions for its solution.
4. Enlightening, of course, for future generations of psychologists who were saved from Titchener's errors by his very thoroughness in working out his approach.
5. Polanyi points to evidence by D. C. Miller that appeared to contradict the theory of relativity, and he comments: "Little attention was paid to the experiments, the evidence being set aside in the hope that it would one day turn out to be wrong" (1958, p. 13).
6. I am unable, however, to confirm Krantz's finding (1969) that some 40 percent of Titchener's final article (1896) in this exchange was devoted to "implicit or explicit attack upon the professional or personal character" of his opponent. Only if no distinction is made between criticism—which is the function and the value of a polemical article—and invective, can I approximate this figure. To blur this distinction seems to me to be a serious error.
7. These problems need, of course, to be dealt with much more specifically. For one such attempt, cf. Henle, 1955.
8. Cf. Titchener (1896, p. 237): "I almost wonder whether Professor Baldwin and myself are not using the term 'reaction experiment' in two totally different senses."
9. Some eclectic failures to resolve controversies have been analyzed from a different point of view by Henle (1957, 1965). The method here under discussion is not eclectic in the sense used in those papers. There, eclectics in psychology were shown to attempt to resolve differences by ignoring them. Calkins' resolution is offered in full awareness of the differences in the points of view to be subsumed under a more comprehensive theory.

REFERENCES

Arnheim, R. *Visual thinking.* Berkeley and Los Angeles: University of California Press, 1969.

Asch, S. E. The doctrine of suggestion, prestige and imitation in social psychology. *Psychological Review,* 1948, *55,* 250-276.

Boring, E. G. The psychology of controversy. *Psychological Review,* 1929, *36,* 97-121.

Boring, E. G. *Sensation and perception in the history of experimental psychology.* New York: Appleton-Century, 1942.

Boring, E. G. Psychological factors in the scientific process. *American Scientist,* 1954, *42,* 639-645.

Boring, E. G. Dual role of the *Zeitgeist* in scientific creativity. *Scientific Monthly,* 1955, *80,* 101-106.

Brody, N. and Oppenheim, P. Methodological differences between behaviorism and phenomenology in psychology. *Psychological Review,* 1967, *74,* 330-334.

Calkins, M. W. A reconciliation between structural and functional psychology. *Psychological Review,* 1906 *13,* 61-81.

Calkins, M. W. Autobiography. In C. Murchison (Ed.), *A history of psychology in autobiography.* Vol. 1. Worcester, Mass.: Clark University Press, 1930, pp. 31-62.

Curtius, L. *Goethe: Wisdom and experience.* Trans. by H. J. Weigand. New York: Ungar, 1964

Harvey, W. *A second disquisition to John Riolan.* Trans. by R. Willis. In R. M. Hutchins (Ed.), *Great Books of the Western World.* Chicago, London, and Toronto: Encyclopedia Britannica, 1952, Vol. 28.

Heidbreder, E. *Seven psychologies.* New York: Century, 1933.

Henle, M. Some effects of motivational processes on cognition. *Psychological Review,* 1955, *62,* 423-432.

Henle, M. Some problems of eclecticism. *Psychological Review,* 1957, *64,* 296-305.

Henle, M. On Gestalt psychology. In B. B. Wolman (Ed.), *Scientific psychology.* New York: Basic Books, 1965, pp. 276-292

Humphrey, G. *Directed thinking.* New York: Dodd, Mead, 1948.

James, W. *The principles of psychology.* New York: Holt, 1890.

Köhler, W. *The task of Gestalt psychology.* Princeton: Princeton University Press, 1969.

Krantz, D. L. The Baldwin-Titchener controversy. In D. L. Krantz (Ed.), *Schools of psychology.* New York: Appleton-Century-Crofts, 1969, pp. 1-19.

Krantz, D. L. and Allen, D. The rise and fall of McDougall's instinct doctrine. *Journal of the History of the Behavioral Sciences,* 1967, *3,* 326-338.

Kuhn, T. S. *The structure of scientific revolutions.* Chicago: University of Chicago Press, 1962.

Mill, J. S. *A system of logic* (8th ed.). New York: Harper, 1881.

Poincaré, H. *Science and method.* Trans. by F. Maitland. New York: Dover, 1952.

Polanyi, M. *Personal knowledge.* Chicago: University of Chicago Press, 1958.

Rapoport, A. Escape from paradox. *Scientific American,* 1967, *217,* No. 1, 50-56.

Titchener, E. B. Simple reactions. *Mind,* 1895, *4(N. S.),* 74-81.

Titchener, E. B. The "type-theory" of the simple reaction. *Mind,* 1896, *5 (N.S.),* 236-241.

Titchener, E. B. The postulates of a structural psychology. *Philosophical Review,* 1898, *7,* 449-465.

Titchener, E. B. *Systematic psychology: Prolegomena.* New York: Macmillan, 1929.

Wertheimer, M. On truth. *Social Research,* 1934, *1,* 135-146.

Wertheimer, M. *Productive thinking* (enlarged ed.). New York: Harper, 1959.

PSYCHOLOGICAL
MOVEMENTS

Gestalt Theory:
Early History and Reminiscences

FRITZ HEIDER

The early history of Gestalt psychology is rather involved, and for the purposes of this paper I will concentrate on one strand of its development, namely, the one which is most commonly mentioned in texts and which is also the one with which I am most familiar. It begins with Ehrenfels, goes on to the Graz school with Meinong and Benussi, and then leads to Berlin with Wertheimer, Köhler, and Koffka. And in tracing this history I will deal principally with the relation of Ehrenfels to the Graz school and the relation of Graz to Berlin, neglecting some of the other figures like Bühler, G. E. Müller, Katz, and Rubin, who made important contributions to the development of Gestalt psychology.

Ehrenfels, the author of the paper on Gestalt qualities (6), lived from 1859 to 1932. He was born in Vienna, and in 1885 got his Ph.D. in Graz with the philosopher Alexius Meinong. I may mention here that I, too, got my degree with Meinong in Graz, though it was 35 years later, in 1920. Ehrenfels was one of Meinong's first students and I may have been the last to write a dissertation with him.

Ehrenfels must have been an interesting person, enthusiastic and emotional. He had musical and poetic talents. The composer Anton Bruckner tutored him in counterpoint. He was a passionate Wagnerian and even wrote texts for operas himself. He was a friend of Freud (10, p. 46) and wrote articles on sexual morals in which he advocated legalized polygamy (4).

His famous paper appeared in 1890, the year of James' *Principles of Psychology*. It was not an experimental paper, but it contained some observations and reflections about form perception which were stimulated by remarks of Ernst Mach. It was in this paper that Ehrenfels pointed out that the experience of a melody does not simply consist of the sequence of experiences of single tones, as it should according to the then-prevalent atomistic theory of sensation elements. He insisted that there is another feature present besides the sensations — a feature that cannot be derived from them and which he called the Gestalt quality.

Ehrenfels was partly an innovator, partly a conservative. He was an innovator in showing that the sensation theory could not take care of the

63

Gestalt phenomena, and he was a conservative in that he essentially accepted the old theory of sensation and only added a new part.

It is to be noted that in pointing out the existence of this aspect of experience he was not satisfied with using phenomenological observation, but went beyond that and, following Mach, resorted to a kind of functional proof based on the fact of transposability. When one plays the same melody in different keys, the tone sensations change while the Gestalt quality stays the same. According to the theory of sensations, you could not have equality of the wholes with inequality of the parts. This argument of transposability rests on simple judgments of equality and inequality. The fact that he did not limit himself to the description of a number of examples of Gestalt experiences, but also used this more explicit proof, is probably the reason why the Berlin Gestalt theorists singled out Ehrenfels as a significant forerunner of their own theories.

As the second step in the development of Gestalt notions, historians often mention the Graz school with Meinong and Benussi. The city of Graz is the capital of Styria in the southeastern corner of Austria, with the boundaries of Hungary and Yugoslavia only 20 or 30 miles away. In its center is a big park spreading over a rocky hill where an old fortress once stood. Retired people come from all over Austria because of the mild climate, and spend their time sitting in the park, feeding the brightly colored little birds and the squirrels that eat from their hands. One looks down on a broad river and across at the surrounding hills that seem to be made for leisurely hikes.

Meinong was professor of philosophy and psychology in Graz. He was six years older than Ehrenfels and lived from 1853 to 1920. Meinong was a close friend of Ehrenfels, though he was very different from what I imagine Ehrenfels to have been. When I knew him he was in his sixties, a rather short man with a full beard. He was practically blind, yet a very efficient person, sober and well-organized, and the lectures seemed to come out of his mouth ready to be published. After getting used to Meinong's talks, everybody else seemed sloppy, messy, and diffuse. During his lectures he stood behind the desk; he seemed to speak without emotion, the only interruption in the even flow of words being an odd kind of snort when he was at a loss what to say next. We students practiced that snort at home till we could do it almost as well as he.

Meinong was a student of Brentano, as was Husserl, who became the ancestor of existentialism. However, Brentano did not think highly of either of them, and in their later years, at least, they were not on good terms with each other. Husserl had once published a remark which Meinong interpreted as an accusation of plagiarism, and from that time on Meinong completely ignored Husserl and never mentioned his name in his lectures or his writing, though the two had much in common. At present Husserl's reputation overshadows that of Meinong, but in the early 1900s it was the other way around. Many of the most prominent English philosophers of that time were influenced by Meinong — for instance, Bertrand Russell and G. E. Moore. And the poet T. S. Eliot wrote a paper on Meinong when he was at Harvard (8).

When I wrote my thesis, there was, in addition to Meinong, another professor of philosophy in Graz who had to pass on it. I did not consciously plan this, but it so happened that the first part of the thesis was in terms of Meinong's theories, which at that time I had really mastered, while the second part was closer to natural science, the field of the other philosopher. Meinong was pleased with the thesis and said the first part was especially excellent, while the other man said that he liked the second part very much but he didn't care for the first. So I passed.

I confess that during my study with Meinong I was often irritated with Meinong's scholastic way of thinking; a recent writer has described it as having the faults of elementarism and of a piecemeal progress (8, p. ix). It is only in the last years that I have realized how much I actually learned from him.

Meinong's great invention or discovery was really a new discipline which he called "object theory" (8). By "object" he meant anything our thinking or experiencing is about or to which it refers. He maintained that one can study and classify these objects and their features and that they have some kind of independent being, regardless of whether they are part of the existing nature or whether anybody actually thinks about them or not. In this way Meinong treats all the possible parts of the world of our experience, the past and the future, the objects of our guesses, hopes or fears, even the absurd and impossible. Meinong's description of this world of objects shows a certain similarity to Lewin's description of the life space, but the similarity does not go very far. It is significant that Meinong talks about objects, while Lewin talks about space. I will say no more about Meinong's object theory except to add that it is a remarkable production by a mental giant and that I would not be surprised if sometime in the future a psychologist would find it useful in a study of cognition as a kind of mathematics of concepts.

Here we are really only interested in Meinong's contribution to the development of the Gestalt idea (8, pp. 22 ff.). Disregarding some of the subtlety of his concepts, I can state it briefly as follows. Ehrenfels had tried to show that there are two kinds of elements: sensations and Gestalt qualities. Meinong, in his passion for clearly articulated theories, developed the idea of his friend and former student and said that there is a two-step process. The first step leads from stimuli to the sensations, and the second from sensations to Gestalt. The first step is mainly determined by external factors — that is, by the stimuli — while the second goes on by virtue of an internal factor, an act of the subject, which he called the act of production. This is the theory of *Gestalt production* of the Graz school. Ehrenfels seems to have accepted this idea for the most part, in spite of the statement in his paper that the Gestalt qualities require no special activity and that they can appear simultaneously with the sensations. The meaning of Meinong's theory will best be seen when we look at the experiments of Benussi that are based on it.

Benussi (16), who lived from 1878 to 1927, was also a student of Meinong, and taught at the University of Graz. He was an elegant-looking, lean person with a finely chiseled and melancholy face and a dry skeptical smile. He went around in a black laboratory smock and when he took a walk he put on a black hat with a wide brim and puffed on a long black cigar. One year there was a student who was often seen walking with him, much shorter, but in exactly the same black outfit. Benussi mostly worked in a darkened room where he had a cot, along with his apparatus, and he often spent the night as well as the day there. He did not give many courses, perhaps because his health was not good. I remember one course in which he used his students as subjects for a whole semester in an experiment on guessing the number of dots in a long series of patterns, and he did this without giving us any idea of the purpose of the experiment. I finally rebelled and told him humbly that I would like to learn psychology from him. He was very friendly, gave me a key to the laboratory, and said that all the apparatus was at my disposal but that he did not have much time.

Benussi was an Italian from Trieste, which at that time belonged to Austria, and he had an Italian accent. His father had strong Italian and anti-Austrian political sentiments, and the young Benussi must have shared them and all the time felt himself an outsider in Graz. At the end of World War I he became an Italian citizen and left Graz, finally becoming professor at Padua, where I visited him in 1926. I had the feeling then that he was rather depressed and homesick for Graz. He had made a respected place for himself in Austrian and German psychology, and probably never received the same recognition as an Italian psychologist. He died in 1927, not yet fifty years old, a marginal man who stood between two cultures.

Benussi was the first to make experiments in the field of Gestalt perception, beginning in 1902; and when Wertheimer's famous paper appeared in 1912, he had already published a long series of studies. He was mainly interested in getting experimental evidence for the existence of Meinong's second step, the internal factor of the act of Gestalt production. This led him to the study of Gestalt ambiguity, those cases in which the perceived figure varies although there is no change in the stimuli, that is, no change in the external factor. He reasoned that this variation must be the effect of the act of production. Thus he investigated the influence of the subject's way of grouping dot patterns, of fatigue, of practice or learning, and of individual differences, that is, of just those factors which the so-called "new look" school emphasized a few years ago (1).

We see that Benussi, especially at the beginning, was primarily concerned with a problem of classification: Do sensations and Gestalten belong to two different classes or to the same class? But in trying to get an answer to this question experimentally, he became involved in the study of connections between conditions and effects.

During the years from 1902 to about 1912, Benussi must have felt that he was in the position of a pioneer battling with the old-fashioned view that perception begins and ends with the study of sensation elements. But in the years immediately preceding World War I, his experiments were suddenly and unexpectedly attacked from another side, the new Berlin group. And he found himself forced out of the role of the progressive rebel into that of a defender of an established view.

To see how this came about, let us consider the Berlin Gestalt psychologists. Necessarily, my treatment of them will be sketchy and incomplete. I will not try to present them as persons since so many of you have known them.

Wertheimer's 1912 paper (22) on apparent movement is usually described as the first experimental paper on Gestalt theory, and in the light of later developments this makes good sense. Actually, the term "Gestalt theory" does not, as far as I can see, occur in the paper. Wertheimer talks about a number of theories of apparent movement that had appeared in the literature, among them also the theory of Gestalt quality, and he quotes Ehrenfels and the Graz school. However, as we shall see, he presents this theory principally for the purpose of showing where it differs from his own.

Careful observations by himself and by his subjects Köhler and Koffka played an important part in this investigation, and I would like to digress here briefly and talk about the relation of the Berlin group to their teacher Carl Stumpf. Boring says that Stumpf brought phenomenology into psychology (2, p. 369) and that it was his influence that brought about the "experimental phenomenology" which was so important for the development of Gestalt psychology. In support of that statement I will quote from a typed account of the celebration of Stumpf's seventieth birthday in April 1918. There was an address by Wertheimer in which he first said how much they missed Köhler, who had gone to Teneriffe to work with chimpanzees and had been interned there for the duration of the war, as well as Koffka and Lewin, who were also absent because of the war. Then he compared Stumpf's method with that of other psychologists. There are some, he said, who approach nature as an enemy; they set up traps and try to defeat her, or they are like sportsmen who want to show off their own skill and strength. He then addressed Stumpf, "How different are you!" And in describing Stumpf's method he used an illustration: "With one African tribe there exists the following custom: When they want to show a guest that they trust him, a mother puts a baby into his arms and says, 'Hold the child'. That is how you hold the facts in your hands, and what you have taught us, reverence for reality." One can understand these words in different ways, but it is quite likely that Wertheimer was talking here about the free, unbiased description of experience, the kind of phenomenological description which we meet in his paper.

In studying apparent movement, Wertheimer presented his subjects with many variations of the basic setup, with two alternating exposures a and b at a distance from each other, asking them to describe what they saw. He investigated the influence of different kinds of stimulus patterns on the perceptual experience and discussed the relation of the results to a number of different theories. Not classification of perceptual constituents, but the study of condition-effect connections, is in the center of his study. According to the production theory, the experience of the subjects should have contained two separate entities, a and b, as the foundation on which the experience of movement of one single object is then based. However, there were many descriptions which did not at all fit this schema. Sometimes two entities were seen, but only one seemed to move while the other remained still; or each moved part of the way toward the other without ever making contact; or the two never appeared as separate entities, etc., etc. Other theories were refuted by similar arguments. At the end of the paper Wertheimer sketched his own theory of some kind of whole process which occurs as the direct effect of the stimulus pattern. He seems to address Benussi when he says that it is one-sided to stress Gestalt ambiguity; there are also compelling Gestalt stimuli which can be seen in only one way, and research will have to study them as well (22, p. 252).

In the course of subsequent years, these suggestions were gradually worked out in greater detail. It seems that the first more thorough presentation of the new theory occurs in a paper by Koffka, though it is now generally understood that the theory came mainly from Wertheimer. Koffka's paper appeared in 1915 and is entitled "A debate with Benussi."

Meinong's theory and Benussi's experiments thus served as a foil to set off the new theory. Koffka explicitly rejected the two-step process and, with it, the concept of the sensations as basic elements in perception. I do not want to trace all the arguments Koffka brought against Benussi in this paper (1915), but I would like to call your attention to a very significant passage in his *Principles of Gestalt Psychology,* which appeared twenty years later. In it he stated the main objection of the Berliners to the Graz theory. He said that the remedy which the Graz school proposed for the difficulties of the sensation theory was not acceptable because it was vitalistic and introduced a profound dualism into psychology (12, pp. 559 f.).

Here we touch upon one of the central themes of the Berlin Gestalt theorists, the attempt to create a monistic world view, "to integrate nature, life and mind," as Koffka said (12, p. 684), to treat the realm of science and the realm of meaning and value in the same terms (15). They abhorred vitalism because it implied the presence of a mysterious metaphysical agency that reaches into the world of nature from outside and is somehow made responsible for the order of the world as we perceive it. The two steps of the production theory belong to two different realms of discourse, and this dualism conflicted with the fundamental monism of the Berliners.

With Ehrenfels, the two-step Gestalt idea attained cosmic proportions.

In 1916 he published a book titled *Kosmogonie,* which means the development of the ordered universe (7). This can hardly be called a scientific book. It contains a mixture of mythical visions and science, and propounds a dualism with two principles opposed to each other: one, a tendency toward unification, order, law, and Gestalt; the other a principle of chaotic variety and disorder which stimulates the unifying principle to react with ever new forms. A creative Gestalt principle confronts the formless chaos and imposes some order on it. Ehrenfels hoped that the book contained "the essential constituents of a new religion," and his Gestalt-forming principle was identified with God. One of the main themes of the book was the anti-Darwinian thesis that Gestalt processes and organismic order can never arise from the chaos of chance events. Thus, out of Meinong's theory of production Ehrenfels made a myth of the development of the universe. As the act of production imposes order on the chaos of sensations, so the godlike Gestalt principle forms order out of the resisting world chaos.

Twenty years later Koffka said at the end of his book, *Principles of Gestalt Psychology* (12, p. 683), that the word "Gestalt" carried ". . . in its connotation the chaos-kosmos alternative; to say that a process, or the product of a process is a Gestalt means that it cannot be explained by mere chaos, the mere blind combination of essentially unconnected causes." This could also have been said by Ehrenfels. But the difference between their views appears when we ask for the true reason for the emergence of the Gestalt. For Ehrenfels, it is a mystical and vitalistic principle. For the Gestalt psychologists, it is dynamical self-distribution and self-regulation within the limits that the boundary conditions (e.g., stimuli) prescribe.

Returning to Benussi, I want to add a few words about his personal relations with the Berlin group; they were cordial and friendly despite the theoretical disputes. He once visited a German congress at which he met the three Berlin psychologists, and apparently they had a very good time together. He talked in a rather wistful way about these youngsters who were newcomers in the field of Gestalt psychology but had very interesting ideas. He must have been pleased and flattered that they treated his work respectfully and that Koffka wrote a long paper on his experiments. When I went to Berlin in 1921, Benussi sent me letters of introduction and told me to be sure to look up Wertheimer who, he said, was a remarkable man.

In turn the Berlin group had a high regard for Benussi. Of all the people with whom they had theoretical disputes, he is probably the one for whom they had the greatest respect. This is expressed, for instance, in the obituary of Benussi that appeared in the *Psychologische Forschung,* the journal of the Berlin group. It said that with him, psychology had lost one of the most prolific experimenters, and it called him a man of genius who always attacked basic problems with untiring energy (18). Already in 1913 Köhler had written that Benussi had accomplished much that was important in his experiments, in spite of the fact that he was handicapped by Meinong's theory (13, p. 70). Benussi quoted this passage in his next paper and added that without this theory he would never have been able to plan the experiments, and that he would go on using it (1, pp. 397-98). It is possible, however, that the attacks of the Berlin group made Benussi less sure of the production theory in spite of this demonstration of loyalty. In his later papers he used Meinong's terms less frequently, and in reading them one sometimes has the feeling that there is an unexpressed doubt in the background: "Are these young rebels right after all?" Thus he was also a marginal man in his work, standing between Graz and Berlin, as he stood between Austria and Italy.

I want to add that the issues discussed in these controversies are not yet completely dead. In 1967 Ulric Neisser published an interesting book on cognitive psychology, in which he says that the roots of his approach are at least as old as the act psychology of the nineteenth century. His "central assertion is that seeing, hearing, and remembering are all acts of construction" (17, p. 10). We recognize dim shades of the act of production of the Graz school in these words. Neisser even talks about two stages in these processes. However, there is a great difference between what Neisser means and Meinong's two stages.

The debate between Benussi and the Berliners occurred mainly before or at the beginning of World War I. Benussi had left Graz at the end of the war and Meinong died in 1920. His death meant the end of the Graz school, and in 1921 I found myself increasingly restless in Graz. An opportunity came to go to Berlin and I gladly took it, though I cannot claim to have foreseen how exciting the twenties would be for a psychologist in Berlin. I did not yet know much about the Gestalt psychologists and I went more or less by chance; but having arrived, I realized how lucky I had been. I audited courses by Wertheimer and Köhler, as well as the seminars of Lewin with whom I soon had long discussions. I went every day to the psychological institute in the palace which the Kaiser had had to leave at the end of the war just three years before. The institute was in a corner of the palace where the minor Prussian princesses were said to have lived. It was an intricate warren of rooms of all sizes. Every so often Koffka came for a visit from Giessen, and then Wertheimer and Köhler raced with him from one room to another and he was shown all the new apparatus and phenomena. Everything was fresh and growing and of great importance. One had the feeling that something remarkable was happening there, something that would influence the history of psychology for a long time to come. The big courses by Wertheimer and Köhler were popular and fashionable with the young Berlin intelligentsia. Their books and papers were eagerly read and vehemently discussed as soon as they appeared.

When I arrived, everybody told me that I must read Köhler's book on the physical Gestalten right away (14). It had been published just a year before, in 1920. Later, another high point was the publication in 1923 of Wertheimer's paper on unit forming factors (23). In connection with this paper, I would like to discuss some questions that may be of interest to historians.

We saw that in general the aim of Wertheimer was to find coordinations between stimulus configurations and experienced wholes. This was Wertheimer's goal in the paper on apparent movement, and it was also the cardinal point in his essay on unit-forming factors. He asked the question: What features of the stimulus pattern make for the impression that certain parts of the visual field form units?

Though this question seems to be obvious now, it was less so then, and it is perhaps an example of the *Zeitgeist* that Wertheimer asked it just at that time. Arguments stemming not from psychological research, but from the field of the history of art, raise some interesting questions. Wertheimer published his paper in 1923, but he said in it that he had already developed its main points in the years 1911 to 1914. It was exactly during the same years that Picasso, one year younger than Wertheimer, developed his style of breaking up the visual appearance of objects, as was shown to perfection a few years later in pictures like the "Three Musicians," which he painted in 1921. If one looks at these pictures after having read Wertheimer's paper, one realizes immediately that Picasso's new technique consisted partly in destroying the natural units of familiar objects by opposing one unit forming factor to another. One specific part of the picture may make a good unit with a table according to one factor, but according to another factor it belongs to the wall. True enough, unit-forming factors were used in older pictures, but more often they were used to help in a redundant way to segregate one object unit from others, e.g., a person from the landscape. One has the feeling that Picasso's introduction of these strange visual contradictions implies a more conscious use of these factors.

It is highly unlikely that the two men knew about each other, yet in a sense the perceptual phenomena with which they were dealing were the same. In the *Autobiography of Alice B. Toklas* (19) we read that when Gertrude Stein and Picasso walked down a boulevard in Paris during World War I, they came across camouflaged cannon. Picasso was spellbound and said: "It is we who have created that" (Stein, 1933, p. 110). The Gestalt psychologists, on their side, were of course conscious of the fact that camouflage makes use of unit-forming factors, and there was a rumor that Wertheimer or Koffka helped in improving it.

However, this tenuous contact by way of camouflage does not mean that there was an influence in either direction as far as Wertheimer and Picasso were concerned. We have to assume two independent developments reaching a culmination at the same time. It seems hardly possible that this occurred purely by chance, and one is tempted to speak of the influence of the *Zeitgeist*.

Boring mentions the dual role of this elusive factor. On the one hand, it is facilitating and we see several people getting the same new idea at about the same time. On the other hand, it may prevent new thoughts from being accepted if they emerge when the times are not yet ripe for them (2, p. 89). The history of the discovery of the unit-forming factors also serves as a good example of this second role.

I have here a brief quotation from a book in German in which the author talks about the conditions on which the perception of a spatial whole depends, and he says there are mainly four: first, the closed Gestalt (he even uses the word *Gestalt*); second, a color which is different from that of the background; third, the employment of the eye within the contour (he means the differentiation of the figure within the contour); and fourth, what he says is most important, the motion of the whole in front of the ground. This paragraph obviously implies an awareness of the figure-ground distinction and of some of the unit-forming factors with which Wertheimer has made us familiar under the names (in translation) of *closure, similarity,* and *common fate.* But it comes from Herbart's book on *Psychology as a Science,* first published in 1825 (9, p. 99). This would seem to be one of the cases where we can assume that something important was overlooked because it appeared before the *Zeitgeist* was ready for that sort of thing. In the same book (p. 101) we also find intimations of transposability in Herbart's discussion of the reproduction of Gestalten. He mentions the fact that we can read writing with equal certainty, whether it is in black on white or in white on black. And, like Ehrenfels, he points out that this cannot be explained on the basis of reproduction of sensations. What Ehrenfels calls the Gestalt quality, Herbart calls "a dark or dim spatial picture which is reproduced equally by the forms regardless of the specific color," and he says that these pictures are made of a stuff that is much more common than all sensations, that we continually elaborate it, mix and transpose it, and that we falsify everything with it. Perhaps somebody will eventually find that Mach was familiar with these pages and then the chain would be complete.

However, this seems to be a case in which the *Zeitgeist* showed its power by preventing the public from realizing the importance of a published idea. It took Wertheimer to teach us to understand Herbart's remarks on perception, just as it took Freud to give meaning to what Herbart said about repression and other phenomena. There are probably still many insightful passages in Herbart and in other writers of his stature, and the spirit of the times will eventually catch up with these passages.

REFERENCES

1. Benussi, V. Gesetze der inadäquaten Gestaltauffassung. *Arch. ges. Psychol.*, 1914, *32*, 396-419.
2. Boring, E. G. *A history of experimental psychology.* 2nd ed. New York: Appleton-Century-Crofts, 1950.
3. Boring, E. G. *History, psychology, and science*: Selected papers. R. I. Watson & D. T. Campbell (Eds.) New York: Wiley, 1963.
4. Brod, M. Christian v. Ehrenfels zum Gedenken. *Kantstudien*, 1932, *37*, 313-314.
5. Brunswik, E. Prinzipienfragen der Gestalttheorie. In E. Brunswik et al., *Beiträge zur Problemgeschichte der Psychologie.* Jena: Fischer, 1929, pp. 78-149.
6. Ehrenfels, C. v. Ueber Gestaltquälitaten. *Vtljsch. wiss. Philos.*, 1890, *14*, 249-292.
7. Ehrenfels, C. *Kosmogonie.* Jena: Diederichs, 1916.
8. Findlay, J. N. *Meinong's theory of objects and values.* 2nd ed. Oxford: Clarendon Press, 1963.
9. Herbart, J. F. *Psychologie als Wissenschaft.* II. Teil. In J. F. Herbart, *Säemtliche Werke,* Vol. VI. Langensalza: Beyer, 1892.
10. Jones, E. *The life and work of Sigmund Freud.* Vol. 2. New York: Basic Books, 1955.
11. Koffka, K. Zur Grundlegung der Wahrnehmungspsychologie: Eine Auseinandersetzung mit V. Benussi. *Zsch. Psychol.*, 1915, *73*, 11-90.
12. Koffka, K. *Principles of gestalt psychology.* New York: Harcourt, Brace & Co., 1935.
13. Köhler, W. Ueber unbemerkte Empfindungen und Urteilstäuschungen. *Zsch. Psychol.*, 1913, *66*, 51-80.
14. Köhler, W. *Dit physischen Gestalten in Ruhe und im stationären Zustand.* Braunschweig: Vieweg, 1920.
15. Köhler, W. *The place of value in a world of facts.* New York: Liveright, 1938.
16. Musatti, C. Benussi, Vittorio. In *Dizionario Biografico delgi Italiani.* Roma: Instituto della Enciclopedia Italiana, 1966. Vol. 8, pp. 657-659.
17. Neisser, U. *Cognitive psychology.* New York: Appleton-Century-Crofts, 1967.
18. Psychologische Forschung. V. Benussi (obituary). *Psycholog. Forschung,* 1928, *11*, 1.
19. Stein, G. *The autobiography of Alice B Toklas.* New York: Harcourt, Brace & Co., 1933.
20. Weinhandl, F. *Die Gestaltanalyse.* Erfurt: Kurt Stenger, 1927.
21. Weinhandl, F. Christian von Ehrenfels, sein philosophisches Werk. In F. Weinhandl (Ed.), *Gestalthaftes Sehen.* Darmstadt: Wissenschaftliche Buchgesellschaft, 1967, pp. 1-10.
22. Wertheimer, M. Experimentelle Studien über das Sehen von Bewegung. *Zeitschrift für Psychologie,* 1912, *61*, 161-265.
23. Wertheimer, M. Untersuchungen zur Lehre von der Gestalt. II. *Psychologische Forschung,* 1923, *4*, 301-350.

Why Did Their Precursors Fail
and the Gestalt Psychologists Succeed?

Harry Helson

Those who experienced the first two and a half decades of the Gestalt movement and followed its various developments will remember the excitement and enthusiasm it engendered. More than any other movement in experimental psychology, it appeared like a bright meteor lighting up the otherwise dim sky of perceptual theory. In a paper prepared for delivery before the APA, Köhler (1967) referred to the excitement and enthusiasm among the early Gestalt group, and this spirit was certainly communicated to many of us before we met and heard him and Wertheimer, Koffka, and Lewin in person. Yet it was not an altogether easy point of view for non-Germans to understand, because it was deeply rooted in German tradition or, rather, traditions.

There was the tradition of adopting an explicit point of view — usually that of the Ordinary Professor or *Geheimrat* — the tradition of working in the framework of specific hypotheses whose proof or disproof was more important than particular facts or statistical significance. And there was the tradition of batting ideas around along with the discussions of experimental results.

Contrast German interest in theory with Titchener's response to Dallenbach when the latter asked him what color theory he believed in and Titchener replied: "Why, I believe in none of them. Facts are all important. Carry your theories lightly" (Dallenbach, 1953). The Gestalt psychologists were concerned with concepts, ideas, and assumptions underlying the interpretation of data, and this in itself marked a new departure in experimental psychology.

They did not carry their theory lightly, nor did they regard the theories of others lightly. They showed us that we must take fundamental assumptions as seriously as we do experimentally established facts or highly sophisticated statistical treatments. Theories do make a difference, and here I am reminded of an illustration given by Whitehead in this connection: Just as slight turns in the tracks in a railroad yard determine whether one goes north, east, south, or west, so even small differences in theory may have important consequences on where one finally comes out in scientific work.

The title of this talk has imposed a rather difficult task on me, even though I chose it. For some have denied that Gestalt psychology was successful, and others have found much of value in its precursors. Indeed, Köhler (1959), in his presidential address to the APA, felt that Gestalt psychologists had exerted little influence on American psychologists working either in perception or learning theory. Perhaps he was too pessimistic in this conclusion, but we must grant right at the beginning that terms like "success" and "failure" are relative, never absolutes. Of course, Gestalt was not a complete success, nor were its precursors or rivals complete failures. Without Mach, Husserl, and von Ehrenfels, it is doubtful if there would have been Gestalt as we know it. At least to that extent their precursors were extraordinarily successful, and if it had not been for the dualistic views of the Meinong-Benussi school, we would not see and appreciate the importance of the monistic views of Wertheimer and Köhler.

We come close here to the influence of the *Zeitgeist,* the general climate of opinion, as Boring (1950, 1955) defined and emphasized it in many publications on the subject of "great men and scientific progress." As he pointed out, the *Zeitgeist* has both good and bad effects, but most great advances are made by combating it even though it may provide the matrix out of which creativity and discovery emerge to advance knowledge.

Going further, Boring denies that there are huge leaps in scientific knowledge because all ideas can be traced to previous concepts; but here I think he underestimated the importance of even slight differences in emphasis or nuance, in effects of context, in the predominance of a concept within a thinker's outlook. Yes, James and von Ehrenfels did speak of whole qualities, but with Wertheimer the concept of wholeness was central in his thinking, not just one among many other ideas. The importance of wholeness is not as apparent in any of Wertheimer's predecessors or contemporaries, who invoked a variety of other concepts to account for the formation and properties of wholes.

There are many reasons for what I have called the success of the Gestalt movement as contrasted with its precursors and contemporaries, but I will concentrate on what appear to me to be the most important ones.

First and foremost, it was a radical movement. I once referred to the Benussi group as the left-wing Gestalters with their assumption of higher level processes to account for whole qualities, and Koffka said: "No, we are the radicals in rejecting such processes," and he was, of course, right.

Gestalt was a radical departure from established ways of looking at and interpreting things psychological. Just as in the politico-economic-social world only radical movements force great leaps forward (sometimes backward), so in science, the more a point of view forces radically new interpretations of extant data, the greater is its impact. Somewhere Koestler has said: "He who does not shock his contemporaries is no true teacher of posterity." The Gestalt attack on analytical introspection, its rejection of attention, unconscious processes, past experience, and association as explanations of perceptual and ideational processes, its program of proceeding *von oben nach unten* rather than *von unten nach oben* as in the older approaches, all forced reconsideration not only of the methods and theories current up to 1912, but also of the data chosen for experimental manipulation. Wholes, forms, large perceptual units, and groupings took the place of static descriptions of reduced experiences. Contrast the Titchener-Dimmick treatment of phi-movement with the studies of Wertheimer and of Koffka and his co-workers, who not only described but formulated the necessary and sufficient conditions of several types of apparent movement: alpha, beta, gamma, and delta movement as well as the case in which no movement is perceived from really moving objects (cf. stroboscopic effects).

Their position was buttressed with beautiful new experiments and demonstrations, without which they would have been merely another group of armchair theorists.

The revolutionary position of the Gestalt psychologists was in some ways more extreme than that of John B. Watson and the early behaviorists. While these workers dispensed with experiential or conscious data, they did not deny the validity of the analytical method of the Wundt-Müller-Titchener school. This approach Wertheimer rejected *in toto*. Wertheimer and his colleagues cut away from mentalistic concepts as surely as did Watson — but in a positive way, by concentrating on whole properties immediately given without the intervention of psychic acts or contents. Criticism of a point of view does not vanquish it unless it presents something better. In this respect Gestalttheorie, not behaviorism, vanquished introspection by broadening the concept of immediately given, palpable data.

Still another precursor of Gestalt, the imageless thought movement, failed in its primary mission because it offered nothing fundamentally or theoretically new in dealing with thinking. They still resorted to cross-sectional analysis when they invoked the "imageless thought" as an added element to explain the purposiveness and logicality of thought processes. Contrast this approach with the Gestalt view that a train of thought is a temporal process, like a melody in having beginning, transitional, and end phases; and contrast the Gestalt concept of insight with trial and error to explain sudden solutions in both animals and men.

While Koffka (1935) seemed to resort to older views in his use of the trace and Wertheimer seemed to revert to associationistic principles in his use of such factors as similarity and nearness in explaining formation of groups, it must be remembered that these concepts were meant to apply to whole, organized units, and were not meant to be used in the old analytical sense of cementing elements to form complexes.

A second reason for the success of the Gestalt movement was its experimental, factual, and concrete approach. To be sure, Benussi was an active experimentalist, and others also dealt with factual data; but the great theorizers, Husserl, Meinong, and von Ehrenfels, were primarily philosophers rather than psychologists in our modern sense. These men dealt almost wholly in concepts, while the Gestalt psychologists drew from experiments performed under carefully controlled laboratory conditions.

Two main directions, before Wertheimer, can be discerned in attempts to account for the form qualities of Mach and von Ehrenfels: (a) reduction of the form quality to parts and relations, with corresponding bifurcation of perception into sensory and nonsensory psychological processes; (b) retreat into philosophical and logical abstractions far removed from experimental validation. A good example of both these tendencies is found in Lipps' reduction of form quality to relations among elements. Thus Lipps (1899) distinguished between accidental relations *(Beziehungen)* and necessary relations *(Verhältnisse)*. He asserted, "The house is red" involves an accidental relation between house and its color, while "Triangles have three angles" involves a necessary relation. But Lipps confuses logic and psychology here because the perception of the house as red under the given conditions of observation is psychologically as necessary as the perception that a triangle has three angles. Logically the relations are different, but psychologically the two expressions are on a par as phenomenologically given data. Similarly, Meinong and Husserl developed the logical and philosophical considerations rather than the psychological realities inherent in the problem of the form quality. It remained for Wertheimer to formulate a position with respect to these complex phenomena that was truly psychological and capable of experimental investigation.

With the reemergence of attention theories, it is well to remind ourselves of the objections raised by the Gestalt psychologists against this concept as a general explanation. Thus, in the attention theory of G. E. Müller, it is assumed that rapid shifts of *attention* from one element to another are responsible for formation of wholes or complexes. The complex theory of Müller does require extremely complicated gyrations of attention to perceive even a three-letter word. In addition to the three acts necessary to perceive the individual letters, a fourth is required to unite them into a unitary whole. As Köhler (1925) pointed out, this theory needlessly complicates the explanation of complex perceptions, and for perception of a long word it becomes fantastic. That this account of Müller's (1923) attention theory is not overdrawn can be checked by reading his statement of it in his book *Komplextheorie und Gestalttheorie*.

The factors determining the formation of Gestalten were taken out of the psyche and put into stimulus and/or physiological configurations. Thus, whatever makes four dots appear as a square is due to their structure, not to higher psychic activities in the individual. By objectifying Gestalten, the threefold division of object, content, and act was no longer necessary or desirable. In place of added psychic elements and acts, the Gestalt psychologists postulated the reality of whole properties, both in stimulus and in physiological configurations. As early as 1912, Wertheimer asserted that if phi-phenomenon cannot be distinguished from "real" movement, then the physiological processes underlying the two must be the same, and one must adopt a holistic view of brain processes as well as of perceptual phenomena. Similarly, animal learning was envisaged in objective terms, for the concept of insight was operationally defined in terms of sudden drops in learning curves, direct paths to goals (or as direct as prevailing conditions allow), and part activities viewed in relation to attainment of ends (food or other incentives).

The trend taken by behavior theorists since Watson reveals a strange reversal. Behaviorism that started with a rejection of mind, consciousness, and all other subjective concepts returned to a host of new ones in later formulations that attempted to deal with problems of animal learning. Today, needs, drives, frustrations, anticipations, appetitive states, fear, pain, curiosity, pleasant and unpleasant emotions, incentives, and many other subjective concepts that Hall (1967) referred to as "motivational antecedents" now permeate otherwise behavioristic approaches to behavior, with just as much disagreement over these concepts as was the case in earlier debates regarding the products of introspective analysis.

Paradoxically enough, while emphasizing the reality of forms, structures, and what Meinong called objects of higher order, the Gestalt psychologists rejected dualistic theories involving subjective acts, contents, and non-sensory processes, whether invoked to account for perceptual, learning, or other data. Their essentially suppositionless theory (except for the postulate of organization or wholeness) was, indeed, a radical departure from both preceding and succeeding attempts to deal with the new facts uncovered by Mach, von Ehrenfels, Meinong, and others. This radical stance extended to their treatment of memory, learning, and other temporally extended phenomena and paid off in new experiments, new observations, and new fields of inquiry and application (e.g., Arnheim's 1954 approach to the visual arts).

A third reason that in my view contributed to the great leap forward in Gestalttheorie was its emphasis on physiological thinking. While employing phenomenological methods, they went beyond them by seeking explanations in neural processes. In his 1912 paper, Wertheimer proposed the short-circuit theory of the phi-phenomenon, and this was followed by other physiological theories and experiments, for example, Köhler's (1920) book devoted to physical and physiological Gestalten, his later theory of electrotonus to explain figural aftereffects (Köhler & Wallach, 1944), and physiological experiments carried out by Köhler and his co-workers (referenced in Köhler, 1957). Here the Gestalters anticipated the tremendous surge in physiological psychology we are witnessing today. Granted that their physiologizing was subject to the most telling criticism (cf. Lashley, Chow & Semmes, 1951), the fact that they looked for and postulated physiological correlates of Gestalt phenomena shows their approach was in tune, if not with the times, at least with future trends. In this they were aided by the fact that the concept of Gestalt lent itself to physiological models, something that was not true of the concepts of their precursors and contemporaries: *Akt, Gestaltqualität,* objects of higher order, etc., conceived as psychic or the products of mental processes or contents, did not inspire physiological work or thinking. Although their specific physiological models have not been generally accepted, the field approach to physical and physiological processes is destined, I believe, for a long life. In one of his later papers, Köhler (1957) referred to the fact that interest in the use of microelectrode techniques had led to a neglect of molar phenomena in the brain. Köhler's position that brain physiology could fruitfully take a more holistic approach is supported by a statement of a field-theoretical physicist who maintains that the inertia of a particle vanishes if there is no other matter in the universe (Sachs, 1969). If the inertia of a particle depends on all other matter, as Sachs claims, how much more must local regions of the brain depend upon their interactions with neighboring and more remote regions! Important facts and questions will not be downed, and I agree with Köhler that some problems will yield only to more molar probings. But this is for the future. It is mainly the legacies that future workers find fruitful that determine a theory's place in the history of science.

A fourth aspect of Gestalttheorie that was of great importance was the fact that it was mainly a descriptive rather than a constructive or constitutive type of theory. Progress in science is accelerated by transitions from constitutive to descriptive theories.

Gestalt as such is not what Einstein called a "constructive theory"; that is, it makes no assumptions concerning hypothetical constituents (Klein, 1967). Rather, Gestalt, like thermodynamics, as described by Einstein (Klein, 1967), "is a theory of principle which starts from empirically observed general properties of phenomena . . . and deduces from them results of such a kind that they apply to every case which presents itself" (p. 510). That is why the laws of thermodynamics, in Einstein's view, will not soon be overthrown. Properties of symmetry, Prägnanz, accentuation, closure, leveling, etc., are considered to be inherent in wholes, with no assumptions as to how they got there or from what constituents they might derive. In this sense Gestalt is descriptive, ahistorical, and agenetic. But Gestalttheorie had its constructive aspects, too, in Wertheimer's short-circuit theory of phi-phenomenon and in Köhler's theory of electrotonus for figural aftereffects, and these have proved to be its weakest aspects. Its descriptive contributions are as valid today as when they were first formulated over half a century ago.

The fifth and almost final reason for the success of Gestalttheorie is one that some may contest with me or, at least, with my way of putting it. It is, however, the most important of all and, therefore, should perhaps have been first on my list to gain the advantage of primacy. It is the fact of *simplicity*. No complex theory will survive if a simpler theory will do its work.

Said Einstein on simplicity:

A theory is the more impressive the greater the simplicity of its premises is, the more different kinds of things it relates and the more extended its area of applicability (quoted by Klein, 1967, p. 509).

More recently, Tukey (1969) has also stressed the importance of simplicity in scientific theorizing.

The simplification achieved by Wertheimer can only be appreciated by those who read the writers dealing with essentially the same problems: Mach, von Ehrenfels, Cornelius, Meinong, Benussi, Höfler, Husserl, Schumann, Witasek, and others (cf. Helson, 1925, 1926). For example, Mach ascribed the difference between a square perceived as resting on a side and one resting on one of its corners to "mechanical and intellectual operations," not to a difference in perceived Gestalt (in spite of the sameness of geometric form). Relational theories operating with "elements" were supposedly simpler than the Gestalt concept, but they actually prove to be more complex; for if it is assumed that perception of a figure is a matter of seeing the parts in relation to each other, then in seeing a square it would be necessary to perceive four lines and four right angles, but this is a much more complicated and different process than seeing the square (Helson, 1925).

While the Gestalt movement was concerned mainly with perceptual processes, it also contributed to the simplification of thinking about learning and animal behavior. Transposition of a brightness discrimination was attributed by Köhler to reactions to "structure functions" rather than reactions to parts in relation. The animals, said Köhler, perceived a brightness gradient and, if trained to choose the "up" side of the pair of stimuli in one situation, would continue to do so in a new situation even though it meant rejecting the specific stimulus previously chosen and rewarded. The degree of simplification and objectivation achieved in the Gestalt interpretation can best be appreciated by considering alternative theories offered at the time for Köhler's results:

> Jaensch following Schumann explained the structure-function reaction by means of "transitional sensations." The theory of transitional sensations was based upon the hypothesis that over and above the primary sensory processes are other experiences which accrue to the primary. By means of these transitional states the animal compares the stimuli and can discriminate between them. . . . Koffka, defending Köhler's theory, denied that transitional sensations can explain the transfer from one situation to another, since no addition of elements can account for sameness of structure. Once the configurational similarity is admitted, elements become superfluous. Furthermore, the transitional sensations are not observed; only the primary "sensations" are in consciousness at the moment the judgment is made. *"Wir sehen im Farben-Paar ein Zueinander, eine Struktur, dazu brauchen wir kein Uebergangs-Erlebnis, wohl aber setzt das Uebergangs-Erlebnis die Existenz einer Struktur voraus"* (quoted in Helson, 1925, p. 352).

The whole point of theory is a reduction, simplification, or unification of the welter of data. Now this does not mean that theories are necessarily simple, but they do *simplify thinking* about the facts they deal with.

Modern atomic theories are infinitely more complex than those of the ancients, but they are less complex than the sum total of the phenomena they explain. Anyone not steeped in small particle work soon becomes lost in the welter of electrons, protons, muons, positrons, nucleons, mesons, pi-mesons, etc. An adequate theory of the modern small particles of physics would help enormously in seeing the relations among these entities, at least by laymen. Theories, even difficult and complex ones, are preferable to the welter of data accumulated by purely empirical approaches.

The Gestalters achieved in one fell swoop an enormous simplification of behavioral theory and thereby rendered most of their predecessors' thinking obsolete. Those who have pointed out the dangers of oversimple theories, while stressing one valid point, have missed another, perhaps more important one, namely, the role of theory in the economy of thinking. The simpler the theory, the greater is the saving in thinking about scientific data.

Finally, we must take into account the personalities of the chief actors in the Gestalt drama. Köhler, Koffka, and Wertheimer were a close-knit group, and they formed an ingroup with those who studied and worked with them. We cannot underestimate the power of numbers in forming a school or movement. A power law with exponent greater than 1 seems to apply here.

Boring has listed a number of traits that individuals must possess in order for their ideas to predominate in their time. My list is somewhat different, but it has much in common with his. Such individuals must, of course, be creative, but they must be more. What Boring called aggressive, I would prefer to call courageous. It takes courage to challenge stereotypical thinking and to take the consequences of a radical position. It also takes integrity and dedication — one does not develop theories easily even when ideas come in flashes. Like the mathematician who must often work hard to prove a correct hunch, so the theorist must think through a welter of approaches and data to reach the nub of the question. By their frontal attacks on associationism, reductionism, attention, unconscious processes, and practically every other concept current in their time, the Gestalt psychologists did not endear themselves to most of their colleagues. However, the brilliance of their work and their quiet urbane manner in personal contacts were saving graces.

There are many more facets of their work and personalities that contributed to their success, but I will not attempt to cover them all. Those of us who had the privilege of knowing Wertheimer, Koffka, and Köhler, realize how many and varied were the traits and talents that were brought to bear on the development of Gestalttheorie. Truly, they formed a Gestalt of intellect, feeling, and appreciation. We shall not soon see their collective like again.

REFERENCES

With a few exceptions, only more recent publications are listed as the older, historical literature is fully documented in Helson (1925, 1926).

Arnheim, R. *Art and visual perception.* Berkeley: University of California Press, 1954.

Boring, E. G. Great men and scientific progress. *Proceedings of the American Philosophical Society,* 1950, *94,* 339-351.

Boring, E. G. Dual role of the *Zeitgeist* in scientific creativity. *Scientific Monthly,* 1955, *80,* 101-106.

Dallenbach, K. M. The place of theory in science. *Psychological Review,* 1953, *60,* 33-39.

Hall, J. Motivation and affectivity. In H. Helson & W. Bevan (Eds.), *Contemporary approaches to psychology.* Princeton: Van Nostrand, 1967.

Helson, H. The psychology of Gestalt. *American Journal of Psychology,* 1925, *36,* 342-370, 494-526.

Helson, H. The psychology of Gestalt. *American Journal of Psychology,* 1926, *37,* 25-62, 189-223.

Klein, M. J. Thermodynamics in Einstein's thought. *Science,* 1967, *157,* 509-516.

Koffka, K. *Principles of Gestalt psychology.* New York: Harcourt, Brace 1935.

Köhler, W. *Die physischen Gestalten in Ruhe und im stationären Zustand.* Erlangen: Verlag der philosophischen Akademie, 1920.

Köhler, W. Komplextheorie und Gestalttheorie. *Psychologische Forschung,* 1925, *6,* 358-416.

Köhler, W. Psychologie und Naturwissenschaft. *Proceedings of the 15th International Congress of Psychology,* Brussels, 1957, 37-50.

Köhler, W. Gestalt psychology today. *American Psychologist,* 1959, *14,* 727-734.

Köhler, W. Gestalt psychology. *Psychologische Forschung,* 1967, *31,* xviii-xxx.

Köhler, W. & Wallach, H. Figural after-effects: An investigation of visual processes. *Proceedings of the American Philosophical Society,* 1944, *88,* 269-357.

Lashley, K. S., Chow, K. L., & Semmes, J. An examination of the electrical field theory of cerebral integration. *Psychological Review,* 1951, *58,* 123-146.

Lipps, T. Zu den Gestaltqualitäten. *Zeitschrift für Psychologie,* 1899, *22,* 383ff.

Müller, G. E. *Komplextheorie und Gestalttheorie.* Göttingen: Vanderhoek & Ruprecht, 1923.

Sachs, M. Space, time and elementary interactions in relativity. *Physics Today,* 1969, *22,* 51-60.

Tukey, J. W. Analyzing data: Sanctification or detective work? *American Psychologist,* 1969, *24,* 83-91.

Wertheimer, M. Experimentelle Studien über das Sehen von Bewegung. *Zeitschrift für Psychologie,* 1912, *61,* 161-265.

E. B. Titchener
and His Lost System

RAND B. EVANS

When E. B. Titchener died in 1927, the work completed toward his long projected series of books on systematic psychology consisted of only three chapters, and those dealt with general and introductory considerations. The important chapter on method, which was to be the final chapter of the first volume, the *Prolegomena,* was never written and no trace of notes on the other volumes has been found.[1]

There were hints in those last years that a change was in the wind at Cornell [2] and that the new books would unfold a system very different from that published in 1910.[3] We shall never know exactly what Titchener's thinking was on systematic matters at the end, but there is sufficient evidence to give an idea of the direction of that thought.

It may seem surprising to suggest a major change in systematic thinking on Titchener's part during that last decade. Those last years of Titchener's life have often been represented as unproductive.[4] Even Boring commented that he thought Titchener had "gone to seed."[5] Perusal of the number of pages of Titchener's printed work during that period might give support to such a contention, but it is somewhat dangerous to judge Titchener or his tactics in present-day terms. To understand Titchener, it is necessary to understand the attitudes and privileges of the nineteenth-century German *Gelehrter* and of Wundt in particular, for it is in that image that Titchener patterned his professional life. Titchener's personal publications, some 50 notes and articles during that last decade, represent only a minor aspect of his thinking and activity.

It is tempting to use a military analogy to represent Titchener and his relation to his school. Titchener served much as a commander-in-chief and tactician. It was he who held the total battle-plan against "the enemy," and it was he who set the direction and timing of attack. The Cornell faculty served as field generals in charge of implementing directives, sending reports to headquarters, and seeing to the training and activities of the graduate students who were, of course, the troops. With doctoral theses and minor studies as their weapons, these troops would assault one adversary, perhaps Würzburg, and then another, perhaps Act psychology. Titchener's notes and articles were used to tie the theaters of conflict together, to demonstrate the significance of a given battle, and to present the manifesto for a new assault.

If one looks at Titchener and his school in this way, the production of those last ten years comprises some 110 papers.[6] The notes of graduate students, as well as correspondence between Titchener and his students, show rather clearly how much of the writings of students was Titchener's own expression.[7]

What about the system, then? The system commonly represented as structuralism, or Titchenerism, is that of Titchener's *A Textbook of Psychology,* published in 1910, although Titchener specifically objected to professional criticism of his system based on a general textbook because "a text-book . . . is written for the student and not for the professional psychologist. . . ."[8] At any rate, the description of psychology found in the *Textbook* stuck, and not that in the many articles written for professional consumption. Unfortunately, most authors seem to have assumed that Titchener's systematic thought solidified in 1910 and that the system remained the same over the next seventeen years. Scientific systems, if they are at all viable, are in a constant state of flux, although the changes may be barely observable to the casual observer. Titchener's system presents no exception.

A study of the total output of Titchener's school shows not a sudden change, but a gradual development of thought over a number of years.[9] As a reference-point, we might do well to begin with that system of 1910. Titchener described psychology then as the study of experience in terms of the experiencing individual. "We are concerned in psychology with the whole world of human experience; but we are concerned with it solely under its dependent aspect, as conditioned by a nervous system. . . ."[10] It was, in short, an elementistic system with the problems of analysis, synthesis, and explanation in terms of the nervous system. Titchener was dealing with the facts of experience, not the values or meanings commonly attached to those facts. Values and meanings were in the domain of common-sense man and technology, not for scientific psychology. He was devoted to understanding the IS of experience, not the IS FOR, and he held fast to the faith that experience could be stripped of meaning and left as bare facts, sheer existences.

The elementary processes of the system were three: sensations, images, and affections.

> Sensations are, of course, the characteristic elements of perceptions. . . . Images are, in just the same way, the characteristic elements of ideas. . . . Lastly, affections are the characteristic elements of emotions.[11]

The perception, the idea, and the emotion were the "given" of experience. They were reduced to their characteristic elements by means of analysis, just as the chemist breaks down complex substances into further unanalyzable substances.[12] Titchener carried out this analysis by an elaborate system of introspection, far more elaborate than that of Wundt.[13] These elements, these products of analysis, were not static, however, but were considered processes capable of being observed in various aspects or attributes.[14]

"A mental element," according to Titchener, "can be identified only by the enumeration of its attributes." [15] Attributes of sensation were listed as quality, intensity, duration, and clearness (extent was included, but not for every sensation). Image carried the same attributes as sensation, although Perky's thesis had already cast doubt as to the existence of image as something separate from sensation. Image had been virtually relegated to a subclass of sensation in 1910, or at least, along with sensation, to subclasses of some more basic elements.[16] Edwards' thesis would resolve the matter, leaving the system with two elements, sensation and affection.[17] Affection was accompanied by the attributes of quality, intensity, and duration, but neither clearness nor extent.

Titchener accepted Külpe's doctrine of inseparability and independent variability of attributes, but only to a point. Inseparability he held to be generally true:

> The attributes of any sensation are always given when the sensation itself is given, and the annihilation of any attribute carries with it the annihilation, the disappearance, of the sensation itself. . . . A sensation that has no quality, no intensity, no duration, etc., is not a sensation; it is nothing.[18]

As to the matter of independent variability, however, Titchener had his reservations:

> We are told . . . that the attributes of sensation are independently variable; quality may be changed while intensity remains constant, intensity changed while quality remains constant, and so on throughout the list. Is this statement true? Relatively, yes: true for certain cases and under certain conditions. . . . Absolutely true, however, the statement is not. In certain cases and beyond certain limits the variation of one attribute implies the concomitant variation of another. . . . What I wish to emphasize is the fact that there are bound attributes as well as free, and that the test of independent variability, useful enough for a preliminary survey, must be applied with caution when we demand accuracy of detail.[19]

These sensory processes, with their concomitant attributes, were synthesized at the next level to simple perceptions (those with a single attributive basis) and complex perceptions (those with the multi-attributive basis). The structure then progressed by further integrations to more and more complex mental states.

This is only a crude representation of some aspects of Titchener's system, but perhaps it will suffice to show something of the development that would take place over the following seventeen years. Two trends will be considered in particular: the structure of the system (at least first-level structure) and the methodology of observation.

The first apparent shift away from the systematic stance of the *Textbook* concerned the elemental structure of the system. In 1913 Carl Rahn, in his doctoral thesis under J. R. Angell, attacked the logic behind the concepts of sensation as process and attributes in Titchener's system.[20] The criticism touched on several points, but the most important had to do with the relation of elements to attributes:

> What is the method by which these attributes of the element are determined? Titchener tells us that the element is not further analysable by introspection. On the other hand we are told that the element presents different aspects or sides, called attributes, that can be separately attended to. Thus attended to they are discriminated, and what is this other than further analysis? Is it other in kind than that which yielded the elements? And are the precipitants of this further analysis of another sort? [21]

Rahn attacked Titchener's views on sensation and attribute in a roundabout way, first identifying Titchener's views with those put forward by E. B. Talbot in an article printed in the 1890s and then turning Calkins' criticism of Talbot on Titchener. Calkins had said:

> Either the sensation has attributes, but then it is complex, no element and has lost its excuse for psychological being; or the sensation is an irreducible and unanalysable element, but then its simplicity is absolute, not to be trifled with, and not to be explained away by reference to any second process of analysis into elements, which yet are not elements, but only "attributes," "aspects" or something equally vague and meaningless.[22]

Titchener responded to Rahn's use of this criticism and others in his "Sensation and System." [23] As well constructed as was Rahn's criticism, Titchener was still able to get around it with the Wundtian device of burying the opposition in a multitude of references to past publications. In escaping Rahn's criticism, however, Titchener seemed to shift ground, or at least several men in the Cornell laboratory and elsewhere thought so, although Titchener never admitted a shift. He seemed to shift sensation from an observable entity to a classificatory term.[24]

> Sensation is a classificatory term. . . . We get our systematic notion of it . . . as the outcome of abstractive analyses performed under various psychological determinations; in other words — while the common-sense notion, colored very likely by biology or physiology, is always with us — we build up the notion of sensation, in a strict procedure, from observations of its empirical aspects or attributes. . . . In point of fact . . . all experimental investigations of sensation deal with attributes: with qualities, intensities, durations, what not. Even the sensation of Wundt's system, which is constituted solely of quality and intensity, is to be observed under its two attributes in separate experiments. But be that as it may, I should certainly maintain in my own case that a sensation, taken in this way as a psychological object of the first order, must ordinarily, by the number and heterogeneity of its

attributes, exceed what is called the "range of attention. . . ." All observation of psychological objects of the first order is, I conceive, observation of attributes.[25]

Just when Titchener made the transition in his own mind from the directly observable "sensation" to the classificatory concept of sensation is not clear. It was certainly possible in the days of the *Outline,* and there is no definite statement to the contrary in the *Textbook.*[26] One may only speculate here; but more than likely, Rahn caught Titchener in an insufficiently explicit description of position. Titchener may not have even realized he had made the transition until Rahn's criticism. Whatever the cause, Titchener would use sensation as an observational term less frequently after 1915.[27]

Mental elements were dropped from Titchener's course in Systematic Psychology as early as 1918, and the system started out from "the ultimate 'dimensions' of psychological subject-matter: quality, intensity, protensity, extensity and attensity." [28] Four years later, in 1923, Titchener announced to an inquiring Boring that he was ready to shelve the concept of elements "for something still more fluid and still more pregnant" — attributive dimensions.[29] Even earlier in a letter to Ruckmick, Titchener made the change in his systematic thought clear.

What I am concerned with in my own thinking is the number and nature of the dimensions of the psychological world, just precisely as the physicist is concerned with mass and time and space as the dimensions of his physical world.[30]

Dimensions in the form of qualitative or intensive series had been in the system from the days of the *Outline,* but F. L. Dimmick's work on the black-grey-white series seems to have revived interest in the matter.[31] Dimmick's little note is important because it seems to have led Titchener to reorganize his thinking about the color pyramid and to begin questioning intensity as an independent attribute, although, as has been shown, Titchener had not held to independent variability as a rule for attributes for some years. The idea of quality and intensity as interactive dimensions seems to have gained ground somewhat later.[32] Relating this to the black-grey-white series, grey becomes not the midpoint of an intensive series running from black to white, but an end-point on many qualitative-intensive dimensions. The final result was a recasting of the color pyramid.[33]

This work on the pyramid sparked similar work in models of the other modalities:

Our first step in grappling with this dimension is, of course, to secure the intramodal arrangements, such as we already have in the color pyramid, the taste and smell figures, and possibly in my own touch pyramid.[34]

This concern with series led to a search for a general theory of quality. The matter of quality was important to Titchener, as he seems to have seen in it a major distinction between the world of the physicist and that of the psychologist.[35]

> I have sometimes dallied with the idea that quality too must have a generalized psychological theory, identical in principle for all the modalities. I think we have at some time in the past discussed the possibility of bringing all the modal qualities together; at any rate I have long thought that even if all the psychological qualities do not form a continuum, they may form a sort of hinged or interconnected total — so that to put it crudely, the color pyramid somewhere hooks on to the smell prism, and that to the taste pyramid, and so forth.[36]

If Titchener was serious in his statement that he was dealing with psychological dimensions *"just precisely"* as is the physicist with mass, time, and space in the physical world, this sort of interrelated dimensional arrangement would be just the sort of thing he would seek. By Titchener's own definition, the physicist uses interrelated dimensional explanations, defining one dimension in terms of the other.[37]

One sticky problem with all this talk of dimensions of experience, rather than elements and attributes, is what happens to affection. If sensation is invalid as an observable entity, then what of affection? If affection is nothing more than dimensional experience, how do those dimensions fit into the rest of the system? There seems to have been thought given at one time to making affection a sensory attribute.[38] The problem was solved with J. P. Nafe's doctoral thesis. His results were simple and surprising:

> The affective qualities, pleasantness and unpleasantness, turn out, under direct observation, to be modes of pressure: *Pleasantness is a bright pressure, and unpleasantness is a dull pressure.*[39]

This removed any question of affection as a separate element, just as Perky and Edwards had done with image. What was created, then, was another qualitative or, at most, a protensive dimension. The bright and dull pressures of simple feelings became, then,

> . . . qualities within the continuum of pressure qualities (what we call the touch pyramid), this continuum contains all the pressures there are, whether sensory or anything else; and no quality is intrinsically sensory.[40]

Sensation and affect had vanished, removing any need for the discrimination between sensory and affective dimensions, although the term was used now and again in a purely systematic way. In 1926, Titchener would chastise a graduate student:

> You must give up thinking in terms of sensations and affections. That

was all right ten years ago; but now, as I have told you, it is wholly out of date. . . . You must learn to think in terms of dimensions rather than in terms of systematic constructs like sensation.[41]

So the first level of Titchener's old system reduced to the five dimensions of quality, intensity, protensity, extensity, and attensity, with quality taking precedence over the others. In this form, protensity and extensity became somewhat more primitive than in the system of the *Textbook,* protensity changing from time to a "pre-temporal welling-forth," and extensity from space to a "pre-spatial spread," as in Katz's film color.[42] Even intensity as a separate dimension from quality was being questioned.[43] By 1927 research was under way on simple combinations of attributive dimensions, with particular emphasis on Katz's modes of appearance of colors, and on extensions of the dimensions previously known as affect.[44] Titchener's untimely death and the quick disintegration of his school never allowed systematic organization of this later work.

This development of systematic thinking was not the only change going on in that last decade. Sometime in the early 1920s, or perhaps even earlier, Titchener began to question the rigid system of introspection that had been the hallmark of his work since the turn of the century. He seems to have come to the belief that there were at least two possible ways to proceed in the study of qualitative dimensions. In a long letter on the topic in 1926, Titchener wrote:

One may work by way of unequivocally determined observation; that is, one may set one's observers to observe under a specific rubric, such as pitch (which one borrows from music), or brightness (which one borrows from visual analogy); having got one's rubric, one naturally takes advantage of the standardized procedures, so that the results take the form of judgments of comparison, which can be mathematically treated. Under either of the rubrics mentioned, one gets pretty results — results that seem to indicate that the rubrics themselves are psychologically identical. One gets no assurance, however, that one is dealing with straight quality.

One may also use a generally determined observation, in which one directs the observers to observe quality simply and the judgments of comparison are given in terms of like and unlike. Here the guiding thread for the experimenter must be the qualitative series. I suppose Henning worked on odours in this sort of way. If one can't have recourse to qualitative series one must try some other methodological trick as Nafe did in his study of the affective qualities. The former method, with specification, is logically posterior to the other, but in practice is a good deal simpler. It has the advantage that one may employ observers who are only moderately trained. The second or general method is magnificent if one can take time to live with the experience for a term of years, and if during this period one can strip oneself of all biases and prepossessions. . . .[45]

This "magnificient" method of generally determined observation with its requirements of great familiarity with the experience and absence of systematic constriction seems to have been the method adopted as an alternative to the rigid introspective method in the later years of Titchener's systematic and experimental work. Some evidence of this trend is shown in the theses of Bixby, Kreezer, and Hazzard.[46] In practice, the time interval for familiarity with the experience was somewhat less than years, but the freeing of observers from systematic bias seems to have been seriously attempted. The systematic bias of greatest importance to the matter at hand was, of course, the presupposition of discontinuous elements and attributes as well as the accompanying special vocabulary.

The phrase "to strip oneself of all biases and prepossessions" is an important one in understanding Titchener's thinking at this time. It is very near Titchener's definition of the method of phenomenology:

> Phenomenology demands that you dispense with theory, that you face the world impartially and describe as faithfully as you can.[47]

It may seem a contradiction of terms to refer to "Titchener's phenomenology," but in terms of method, this seems to have been the way Titchener was moving. Students used the term at the time in their correspondence, and Titchener used it himself, as we shall see.[48] This is not to say that the more traditional approach of controlled introspection was abandoned, just that a less constricted approach was allowed into the Cornell laboratory. As early as 1912, Titchener had discriminated between the phenomenological and descriptive approaches:

> I would warn the reader against confusing descriptive psychology with a "phenomenological" account of mind. . . . I mean by a phenomenological account of mind, an account which purports to take mental phenomena at their face value, which records them as they are "given" in everyday experience; the account furnished by a naive, commonsense, nonscientific observer, who has not yet adopted the special attitude of the psychologist, but who from his neutral standpoint aims to be as full and as accurate as the psychologist himself.[49]

Titchener was not particularly confident that such an analysis was possible, at least not in 1912. But even though his terms were generally negative at that time, he did not completely reject some role for phenomenology.

> A roughly phenomenological account, a description of consciousness as it shows itself to common sense, may be useful or even necessary as the starting point of a truly psychological description. . . . The psychologist may also have recourse to phenomenology after the event, after he has completed his own first analysis, as an additional check upon the singly motivated and more technical description. Or again, the elaborate phenomenology that issues from a foregone epistemology may be of service as indicating possible lacunae in psychological description.[50]

This sounds encouraging, but Titchener in 1912 hastened to add that "phenomenology . . . is not psychology." [51] The phenomenology Titchener was referring to was that of Husserl, however, and he specifically differentiated between Husserl's phenomenology and that of Stumpf and Brentano.[52] But even here Titchener was emphatic: ". . . no form of phenomenology—phenomenology of mind, *Gegenstandstheorie,* science of selves—can be truly scientific, for the reason that the implied attitude to experience is multiply motivated and fluctuating, while the minimum requirement of science is a fixed and constant point of view." [53] Titchener, so far as the record shows, would always reject Husserl's phenomenology as being the study of the "extracted and essential meanings and the application of applied logic." [54] However, somewhere along the line — just where and when is hard to say — Titchener saw the need for a form of the phenomenological method, perhaps to correct for the "lacunae" of the strict Titchenerian introspective terminology.

It should be clearly understood that Titchener was not advocating the content of Husserl's phenomenology, nor the Akt of Brentano, nor the Funktion of Stumpf. It was phenomenology as method he was introducing to the Cornell laboratory — "meticulous, minute description, i.e., description in the most pregnant sense."[55] It was this type of observation that was urged on experimenters and observers in Titchener's letters between 1925 and 1927:

> As regards the plan of experiment, you have to remember what you are after is not a determination of conditions but a straight phenomenology. What you then want to get is a straight descriptive account of what the observers see; the reports will at first, in all probability, be rough . . . but as the observations are repeated you ought to get a full and detailed account of the phenomena.[56]

It would seem that somewhere along the line, descriptive psychology and phenomenological method became compatible:

> If you take a perfectly casual phenomenological attitude, you see what they tell you to see; but if you vary your attitude a hair's breadth in the direction of critical observation, you get all sorts of other things under your eyes.[57]
>
> A very simple visual vocabulary will see you through if you will only keep it mobile, and use it freely in face of the phenomena without letting yourself be biased by preconception.[58]

The last thesis actually edited by Titchener for publication was F. L. Bixby's "A Phenomenological Study of Luster" and the method employed was phenomenological. Kreezer's thesis, though completed under H. P. Weld, was carried out in large part during Titchener's lifetime, and it bears the definite mark of Titchener's phenomenological method.[59]

It is important to note that phenomenology was the method employed, but that there was no basic change in the object of study — existential contents, that is, the facts of experience separated from the values and meanings of experience. The word "existential" seems to have been the source of concern in some quarters when it was published, but Titchener merely introduced it in his lectures and in *Prolegomena* to stand in opposition to the term "intentional" used in the discussion of Act psychology.[60] Titchener gave no evidence of swinging toward intentionalism, neither toward Brentano nor Gestalt.[61] The organization of the system had changed and a new attitude had been added to the observational repertoire — that of meticulous, unbiased observation — but the basic study of the contents of experience remained the same.

These developments only scrape the surface of Titchener's final system. We shall never know the implications of all these changes for the overall system Titchener was preparing. Even the chapter on Method for the *Prolegomena* would have been enough to give a better understanding of what the system would have become. We shall never know where he might have gone with a life-span like that of Wundt. His faith in the study of the contents of experience remained firm and probably would have continued so. Some writers have suggested a shift toward behaviorism or physicalism, but no evidence of such changes of a compelling sort has been presented, and there is a goodly bit of evidence to the contrary.[62] In his last major psychological paper that remains extant, a talk given before the Experimentalists at Princeton in 1925, Titchener gave his view of psychology's progress and future as follows:

We have, I think without question, passed from infancy to childhood. Our independence of physiology is a guarantee of that: we no longer feel any necessity of consulting physiology when we lay out our investigations; we do not necessarily borrow physiological apparatus and procedures; it does not occur to us to imitate physiology in the presentation of results; in a word, we are out of our physiological leading-strings. It is pleasant and reassuring, certainly, if while an inquiry is in course or after it has been brought to completion we can make a cross-correlation with physiology; but we feel ourselves, none the less, to be independent; we do not lean upon physiology. That sign, then, seems unequivocal; and there is another, which a bold spirit might interpret to the effect that we are approaching adolescence —I mean the radical change that has been wrought over the whole field of the science since it turned to phenomenology. We can trace the impulse to this change directly to Hering; and if Hering has had to wait a long time before coming to his own, that is partly because he was himself otherwise entangled in a rather crude form of empirical psychology.[63] Phenomenology is not yet, is not of itself, experimental psychology; but it provides today a safe and sure mode of approach to the analysis of our psychological subject matter; and our recourse to it, our realization of its promise may perhaps be taken as a sign of adolescence. If, then, Godfrey Thompson is right, and the intellect is most alert and most capable at the age of sixteen, we may congratulate ourselves that experimental psychology is nearing that critical point, and we may expect far better things from it in the near future than have been accomplished in the past.[64]

So the system of 1925-1927 was very different from that of 1910, both in organization and method, although it is possible to see the later Titchener by careful analysis of the earlier. Existential experience had become completely sensory or, perhaps more accurately, dimensional. A new approach had been added to the acceptable methods of experimental psychology— that of phenomenological observation.[65]

We come, then, full circle back to the *Prolegomena*. To what kind of systematic work was it to be the prolegomena? Would it have been a great catalogue of the facts of psychology, like Wundt's *Grundzüge?* Some of his students thought so, and Titchener seems to have intended a work on those lines in his earlier years.[66] At some time in the post-*Textbook* period, however, Titchener's position changed, as had Wundt's before him.[67] Just when this happened and why, there is not yet enough evidence to say. In 1924 Titchener wrote:

> I think I must have told you, when you were here, that I thought it was impossible in our generation to write a system of psychology. That position I still adhere to. I have, however, never denied that we are now in a position to write at psychology systematically; and this is all that I myself have in mind to do. A system of psychology, full rounded out and complete, could hardly nowadays be more than philosophical — at any rate that is my judgment still. But I think we have a large enough body of data to be able to present the subject in a systematic schema so that future generations may see that we had not been altogether dependent upon philosophy for our conceptual scaffolding.[68]

Why these important developments, which were well known by members of the Cornell department and by several important researchers outside of Cornell, should have become lost in the post-Titchener systematization and ignored in books on psychological systems is an important question. The answer is complex, having to do with changes in psychology in the late 1920s, with Titchener's relations with his own department and ex-students in other departments, and with the thinking and development of Titchener himself. All that, however, is another story.

NOTES

1. Published posthumously as *Systematic Psychology: Prolegomena*, Macmillan: New York, 1929, under the editorship of H. P. Weld.
2. W. B. Pillsbury, The psychology of Edward Bradford Titchener. *Philos. Rev.*, 37, 1928, 105.

3. E. B. Titchener, *A Textbook of Psychology*, Macmillan: New York, 1910.
4. Julian Jaynes, Edwin Garrigues Boring: 1886-1968, *J. Hist. Behav. Sci.*, *5*, 1969, 102.
5. E. G. Boring. Letter to R. M. Ogden, Aug. 18, 1928, Cornell University Archives.
6. W. S. Foster, A bibliography of the published writings of Edward Bradford Titchener 1889-1917, in *Studies in Psychology: Titchener Commemorative Volume*, Louis N. Wilson: Worcester, Mass., 1917, 323-337; Karl M. Dallenbach, Bibliography of the writings of Edward Bradford Titchener, *Amer. J. Psychol.*, *40*, 1928, 121-125.
7. Notes of conversations with E. B. Titchener by Cora Friedline, Archives of the History of American Psychology, University of Akron, Akron, Ohio.
8. Titchener, Sensation and system, *Amer. J. Psychol.*, *26*, 1915, 258. Titchener would have preferred criticisms be leveled on the basis of his *The Psychology of Feeling and Attention*, Macmillan: New York, 1908; *Lectures on the Experimental Psychology of the Thought Processes*, Macmillan: New York, 1909; as well as articles such as Prolegomena to a study of introspection, *Amer. J. Psychol.*, *23*, 1912, 427-448; The schema of introspection, *Amer. J. Psychol.*, *23*, 1912, 485-508; and Description vs. statement of meaning, *Amer. J. Psychol.*, *23*, 1912, 165-182. This material as well as the *Textbook* will be covered by the phrase "system of 1910."
9. Some of this ground has been covered before by E. G. Boring in his article, Titchener and the existential, *Amer. J. Psychol.*, *50*, 1937, 470-483, and is repeated here for the sake of continuity.
10. Titchener, *Textbook*, 25.
11. *Ibid.*, 48.
12. *Ibid.*, 37 f.
13. At least one of Titchener's early students was repelled by this elaboration of Wundt's introspective method. M. F. Washburn, Some recollections, in Carl Murchison (Ed.), *History of Psychology in Autobiography*, Vol. 2, 1930, 343.
14. Titchener, *Textbook*, 50.
15. Titchener, *Lectures on the Experimental Psychology of the Thought Processes*, 214.
16. Titchener, *Textbook*, 52-55, 198 f.; C. W. Perky, An experimental study of imagination, *Amer. J. Psychol.*, *21*, 1910, 422-452.
17. A. S. Edwards, An experimental study of sensory suggestion, *Amer. J. Psychol.*, *26*, 1915, 99-129.
18. Titchener, *The Psychology of Feeling and Attention*, 8 f.
19. *Ibid.*, 9ff.
20. Carl Rahn, The relation of sensation to other categories in contemporary psychology: A study in the psychology of thinking; *Psychol. Rev. Monog. 67*, 1913. See, particularly, 19-25, 39-41.
21. *Ibid.*, 22.
22. *Ibid.*, 23 f.; E. B. Talbot's article was The doctrine of conscious elements, *Phil. Rev.*, *4*, 1895, 154. Calkins' retort is found in her Attributes of sensation, *Psychol. Rev.*, *6*, 1899, 506. M. F. Washburn attempted to mediate between these views in her Some examples of the use of psychological analysis in system making, *Phil. Rev.*, *11*, 1902, 445. Titchener was well aware of Calkins' position since he included the reference to her article as well as Talbot's and Washburn's in his *Textbook*, 57, and in the notes to his *Feeling and Attention*, 325. One can only speculate as to why Titchener waited for Rahn's use of these criticisms to respond. Perhaps Titchener thought the Washburn distinction between Calkins' and Titchener's elements was sufficient reply, although Washburn tells us that Titchener objected to the paper when she delivered it at one of his seminars. M. F. Washburn, *op. cit.*, Some recollections, 344.

23. Titchener, Sensation and system, 258-267.
24. W. S. Hunter, James Rowland Angell: 1869-1949, *Amer. J. Psychol.*, *62*, 1949, 445; E. G. Boring, Titchener and the existential, *Amer. J. Psychol.*, *50*, 1937, 472 f.
25. Titchener, Sensation and system, 259.
26. Titchener, *An Outline of Psychology*, Macmillan: New York, 1899, 2nd edition, *37 f.* Titchener once wrote to Boring, "For Wundt, of course, a sensation was observable precisely *as* its two attributes, because two fall within the 'range of attention.' So he could call a simultaneous observation of quality-intensity the observation of 'a sensation,' though what he and his men observed (and said so) was just the intensity-quality. . . . For me, whose systematic sensation has been steadily growing more complex, a complete observation of a sensation (as sum of attributes), has long been impossible; the range of (observational) attention forbids. My memory is that in the old *Outline* I made 4 attributes simultaneously observable (6 units being at that time the 'range of attention') as a sensation. The object in observation of sensation has always been attributive, by definition and by practice. So long as the attributes were two (or under 6 . . .), one could still talk of observation of sensation. As attributes increased, one could not, and so one naturally spoke more and more discriminatively of observation of attributes" (Letter, E. B. Titchener to E. G. Boring, Sept. 24, 1923, Cornell University Archives).
27. Titchener, Lectures on elementary psychology, Cornell University, 1916-1925. Notes by Karl M. Dallenbach, in the author's collection.
28. Titchener, The term "attensity," *Amer. J. Psychol.*, *35*, 1924, 156; Titchener, Lectures on systematic psychology, 1918-1919, Notes by L. B. Hoisington, copy in the author's collection .
29. Titchener, Letter to E. G. Boring, Oct. 10, 1923, Cornell University Archives and Harvard University Archives.
30. Titchener, Letter to Christian Ruckmick, Oct. 26, 1922, Cornell University Archives.
31. F. L. Dimmick, A note on the series of black, grey, and white, *Amer. J. Psychol.*, *31*, 1920, 301 f. One source has it that it was Titchener who wrote the note under Dimmick's name. There is little doubt that the reorganization was due to Titchener and Dimmick's conversations, although the idea seems to have been the product of the atmosphere of the whole Cornell laboratory (K. M. Dallenbach, Letter to E. G. Boring, Oct. 3, 1951, Cornell University Archives).
32. Titchener, Visual intensity, *Amer. J. Psychol.*, *34*, 1923, 310 f.
33. *Ibid.*, 310.
34. Titchener, Letter to Christian Ruckmick, Oct. 26, 1922, Cornell University Archives; see also Titchener's Models for the demonstration of sensory qualities in Notes from the psychological laboratory of Cornell University, *Amer. J. Psychol.*, *31*, 1920, 212 f.
35. *Ibid.*, Letter to Ruckmick, Oct. 26, 1922.
36. Titchener, Letter to E. G. Boring, Nov. 19, 1924, Cornell University Archives. Also quoted in Boring's Titchener and the existential, *Amer. J. Psychol.*, *50*, 1937, 478.
37. Titchener, *Systematic Psychology: Prolegomena*, Macmillan: New York, 1929, 141.
38. Titchener, Letter to Junichiro Horiguchi, Dec. 9, 1925, Cornell University Archives.
39. J. P. Nafe, An experimental study of the affective qualities, *Amer. J. Psychol.*, *35*, 1924, 508.
40. Titchener, Letter to Horiguchi.
41. *Ibid.*
42. Titchener, The term "attensity," 156.

43. *Ibid.* See also Letter from E. B. Titchener to E. G. Boring, Nov. 19, 1924, Cornell University Archives; also quoted in Boring's Titchener and the existential, 478.

44. Dallenbach, Bibliography of the writings of Edward Bradford Titchener, 125; E. Frances Wells, An experimental study of affective experience, Thesis, Cornell University, 1928.

45. Titchener, Letter to E. G. Boring, Nov. 11, 1924, Cornell University Archives. Also quoted in Boring, Titchener and the existential, 477.

46. F. L. Bixby, A phenomenological study of luster, *J. Gen. Psychol., 1,* 1928, 136-174. This was the last thesis edited by Titchener for publication. George Kreezer, Luminous appearances, *J. Gen. Psychol., 4,* 1930, 247-281; F. W. Hazzard, A descriptive account of odors, *J. Exper. Psychol., 13,* 1930, 297-331. This work was completed under the direction of L. B. Hoisington, Titchener's right-hand man. It was well under way before Titchener's death.

47. Titchener, Lectures on perception, Cornell University, Lecture 17, July 27, 1920. Notes by K. M. Dallenbach, in the author's collection.

48. F. L. Bixby, Personal communication, 1969.

49. Titchener, The scheme of introspection, *Amer. J. Psychol., 23,* 1912, 489 f.

50. *Ibid.,* 490.

51. *Ibid.,* 490.

52. *Ibid.,* 490.

53. *Ibid.,* 490.

54. Titchener, Lectures on perception, Cornell University, Lecture 4, Summer, 1920. Notes by K. M. Dallenbach, in the author's collection. After studying Husserl's writings for a year, Titchener's evaluation is said to have been, "There is nothing in him" (E. G. Boring, Review of Titchener's *Systematic Psychology: Prolegomena, Psych. Bull., 27,* 1930, 127).

55. Titchener, Lectures on perception, Cornell University, Lecture 4.

56. Titchener, Letter to Max Meenes, March 10, 1925, Cornell University Archives.

57. Titchener, Letter to E. G. Boring, Feb. 8, 1926, Cornell University Archives.

58. Titchener, Letter to J. P. Guilford, Jan. 4. 1926. Cornell University Archives. Guilford was an observer in Bixby's study at the time.

59. The exact dates when Kreezer's experiment was carried out are not given, but the times at which the various observers left Cornell indicate the experimental work must have been completed before Titchener's death. George Kreezer, Luminous appearances, *J. Gen. Psychol., 4,* 1930, 247-281.

60. Titchener, Lectures on elementary psychology, Cornell University, Lecture 2, Oct. 7, 1919. Notes by K. M. Dallenbach, in the author's collection. See also Titchener's *Systematic Psychology: Prolegomena,* 256.

61. Had Titchener experienced a softening of heart regarding Act psychology, he would surely have considered a revision of his criticisms in the *Prolegomena.* Letters to C. S. Meyers (Feb. 19, 1925) and to C. A. Ruckmick (Oct. 1, 1925) show clearly that there was no intention of the slightest change in the *Prolegomena* manuscript. As to Titchener's view of Gestalt psychology, we find him referring to it as a fad and adding: "There is really no remedy for all these eccentric movements except time and the general logic involved in the progress of the science all round" (Letter to G. Tschelpanow, Oct. 25, 1924). One finds, however, in reviewing Titchener's letters, a decidedly softer tone toward Gestalt psychology after Koffka's stay at Cornell than before. In 1925 he would say to Otto Klemm: "I heartily agree that the Gestalt investigations will bring in a good psychological harvest, my one fundamental criticism is that the Gestalt psychology is not identical with psychology as science" (Letter to Otto Klemm, Oct. 27, 1925). In 1926 he wrote to President Lowell of Harvard: "[Köhler] and the other configurationists have done much good work, and some brilliant work, the results of which can be taken up fairly easily into the main body of

experimental psychology. It is clear, however, that the school must enlarge its space; it is impossible to rear a complete science on the foundation of a single concept" (Letter to A. L. Lowell, April 19, 1926). All letters from Cornell University Archives.

62. Boring, Titchener, meaning and behaviorism, in *Schools of Psychology: A Symposium*, David Krantz (Ed.), Appleton-Century-Crofts: New York, 1969; Boring, Titchener on meaning, *Psychol. Rev.*, *45*, 1938, 94. Titchener's attitude toward Behaviorism in the late years is clearly shown in his letters. "Behaviorism has spread over the country in a great wave, more or less as Freudianism did a few years ago. The actual experimental work that the behaviorists turn out is good enough; but the general logic of their position is ridiculously crude. . . . I don't think that the movement will continue very long" (Letter to G. Tschelpanow, Oct. 25, 1924). "The more freely the behaviorists write, the more obviously do they expose themselves to criticism" (Letter to C. Ladd-Franklin, Oct. 5, 1923). Both letters from Cornell University Archives.

63. Here is another jab at Act psychology. Empirical psychology and the Act psychologies of the Brentano stripe were used as equivalents in much of Titchener's writing. Titchener, Brentano and Wundt: Empirical and experimental psychology, *Amer. J. Psychol.*, *32*, 1921, 108-120; Empirical and experimental psychology, *J. Gen. Psychol.*, *1*, 1927, 176 f.

64. Titchener, Experimental psychology: A retrospect, *Amer. J. Psychol.*, *36*, 1925, 322 f.

65. It should be clearly understood that Titchener was not saying that phenomenological observation had replaced the traditional introspective method. Titchener seems always to have discriminated between the phenomenological and psychological attitude. The effect of these attitudes was one task given to George M. Scheck for his doctoral thesis in 1924. Titchener, Letter to L. B. Hoisington, Mar. 11, 1924. Cornell University Archives.

66. W. B. Pillsbury, The psychology of Edward Bradford Titchener, *Phil. Rev.*, *37*, 1928, 104 f.; Boring, Review of Titchener's *Systematic Psychology: Prolegomena, Psychol. Bull.*, *27*, 1930, 121 f.

67. Titchener, Wilhelm Wundt, *Amer. J. Psychol.*, *32*, 1921, 173.

68. Titchener, Letter to G. Tschelpanow, Oct. 25, 1924. Cornell University Archives.

Introduction to John B. Watson's Comparative Psychology

RICHARD J. HERRNSTEIN

To find out what behaviorism was, consult this book; for without a doubt John B. Watson defined it, shaped it, promoted it, and coined its terminology. To find out what it is now is a harder task, perhaps even a futile one. Today psychologists cannot even agree that the field is still alive; the earliest obituaries started appearing in the 1920s and have not stopped yet. Nor can they agree if the field was ever verdant, or barren from the beginning, as it was according to the traditionalists who were called to arms by Watson's attacks in this book.

Let us hold aside for a few pages the pristine clarity of Watson's behaviorism, and consider the contemporary scene, of which any view is bound to be idiosyncratic. The view to be depicted, it should be noted, is a favorable one, arising in a conviction that the behavioristic revolution in psychology is but one aspect of the evolution of scientific psychology out of philosophical speculation.

After Watson, behaviorism trifurcated, yielding three important and distinct roads, disregarding the numerous false starts and minor pathways that a thorough portrayal would require. The main roads are known by the names of the men who took the first steps down them. There is Edward Chace Tolman (1886-1959), the Berkeley professor whose systematic work, *Purposive Behavior in Animals and Men,* was published in 1932. There is Clark L. Hull (1884-1952), the Yale professor whose first systematic work, *Principles of Behavior,* was published in 1943, but only after a series of theoretical articles during the 1930s had adumbrated the larger work, and who is therefore in effect Tolman's contemporary. And there is B. F. Skinner (1904-   ), the still active Harvard professor whose first book, *The Behavior of Organisms,* was published in 1938, but whose influence has grown only in the last decade or so. It is surprising how much of a story is told by the titles of these three books to one who is already familiar with the story. All three display the word "behavior," and do so meaningfully, for each man was reacting against an

This essay is the introduction to J. B. Watson's *Behavior: An Introduction to Comparative Psychology,* originally published in 1914 and reissued in 1967 by Holt, Rinehart & Winston.

older view of psychology as the study of mind. "Behavior" is the word that identifies them with Watson's revolution, but each man was trying to modify behaviorism, as succinctly revealed in the other words of the titles.

All three of the new behaviorisms were disputing the central feature of Watson's scheme, the characterization of behavior itself. For Watson, behavior was movement, actual physical movement of the body, the activity of muscles and glands — whether on a large scale, as in locomotion, or so small as to be hidden from casual observation, as in the case of the hypothesized movements of the larynx in Watson's theory of thought. For none of his followers was Watson's simple definition of behavior acceptable. For all of them, behavior was a more abstract entity, more closely allied to what a layman might call an "act," rather than to what he might call a "movement." In the vocabulary of psychology, the new behaviorists were "molar" in their approach to behavior instead of "molecular," as Watson was.

It was E. C. Tolman who applied the words "molar" and "molecular" in this sense, even though he was using a terminology he had found in the writings of C. D. Broad. In Broad's book *The Mind and Its Place in Nature* (1925), there was a contrast between molar behaviorism and molecular behaviorism, with the former referring to the idea that every psychological process can be identified with a bit of behavior and the latter referring to the idea that every psychological process has a physiological basis. Although this was a significant issue in itself, Tolman's usage preempted Broad's, at least in the American psychological literature. Tolman was concerned with a different problem, one that had already been the source of some discussion even before Watson might have stimulated it. For example, in 1915 — published too soon after the present book to have been a reaction to it — E. B. Holt discussed in *The Freudian Wish* the profound contrast between a creature moved by isolated reflexes and one moved by reflexes acting in some sort of mutual coordination or integration. The first kind of creature, of whose existence Holt was skeptical, is a mechanical system triggered into action from moment to moment by the stimuli impinging on it. The second kind of creature, by virtue of the integration of its reflexes, is behaving with respect to some stable aspect of its environment, notwithstanding the momentary variations in stimuli. Consider, said Holt, the example of the bee foraging for nectar. Viewed as the first kind of creature, a description of its activity would consist of a recital of minute movements touched off by the momentary pattern of visual, olfactory, and tactual stimulation. Viewed as the second kind, the description would also reveal that these movements are coordinated to equip the bee to forage for nectar. The fact of its foraging— probably the most reliable fact of all — would never emerge in the first account, which is an inadequacy great enough to invalidate it as psychological description, said Holt. Behavior, innate or learned, argued Holt, is organized so as to be linked to its objective context rather than to be elicited by whatever representation of the context happens to be adventitiously portrayed in the momentary stimuli.

Holt was arguing against neither the reality of reflexes nor the adequacy of a scientific account of behavior; he was fully in favor of both. Rather, he was arguing for a description of behavior in terms of the objects in the creature's environment around which behavior was so self-evidently organized. In other words, purposiveness was a property of behavior that Holt was unwilling to forego in his account. The other anticipators of molar behaviorism, like the psychologist William McDougall or the philosopher Ralph Barton Perry, similarly believed that a proper description of behavior must encompass the terminal events for a sequence of acts, as well as the initiating ones — the goals, that is, in addition to the stimuli.

Watson's behaviorism, when it came along, left out these goals. He was opposed to the idea of purpose because a purpose cannot be a cause of behavior in the sense that a stimulus is; and, with his deterministic faith, he was persuaded that a stimulus would eventually be found for every bit of behavior. Moreover, purpose is not directly observable; it arises only in introspection, of which, more than anything else, Watson wanted to rid psychology. And so his behaviorism was molecular, restricted to isolated movements triggered by momentary stimulation — that is, the very approach that Holt, along with others, had condemned. The new behaviorists did not, however, follow Watson's line. Each tried to create an objective, deterministic psychology, as scientific as Watson's was supposed to be, but molar, dealing with the fact that behavior had objective reference, that it was goal-directed. The three new behaviorisms can, then, be seen as three distinct attempts to reconcile empirical science with purpose.

It may seem strange that behaviorism was confronted with the problem of purpose. After all, had not some eminent prebehaviorists — William James, for example — focused their attention on purpose as the key to the mind? The answer, of course, is yes, but the prebehaviorists were content to deal with purpose introspectively, and if there is one thing uniting all species of behaviorists, it has been a distrust of introspection. Purpose, then, became behaviorism's special problem.

Tolman's behaviorism was a frontal assault on the problem of purpose, as evidenced by the title of his systematic book, *Purposive Behavior*. . . . He tried to find an objective criterion of purposiveness to replace the subjectivity of the earlier psychologists and settled on "docility," in the sense of teachability. Thus, a rat learning to thread its way through a maze — for many years Tolman's favorite experimental situation — gains its reward progressively more efficiently, which Tolman took as the proof of purpose and cognition in the rat. His revision of behaviorism did more than restore the importance of purpose. The criterion of purpose as docility, given the importance of purpose in his definition of behavior, made Tolman's behaviorism, unlike Watson's, little more than the study of learning itself. Of course, what was really involved was a matter of emphasis rather than of total exclusion or inclusion. Tolman's book, as well as Watson's, discussed both learning and instinct, but there was a clear shift in primary concern.

The coalescence of behaviorism and learning theory that distinguishes Watson from Tolman also distinguishes Watson from both Hull and Skinner, each of whom, by similar but distinct chains of argument, re- defined behavior so as to make crucial the capacity to learn. For Hull, as for Tolman, behavior is molar rather than molecular. The essence of molarity is again the goal-directedness of global acts, although Hull did not make his criterion of molarity as explicit as Tolman had. Hull was committed to a more mechanistic view of psychology than was Tolman, and so strove for a formula that would at once capture the adaptiveness of behavior as well as the simple reflexive analysis that Watson had favored. Hull's solution, again betrayed by the title of the systematic work, *Principles of Behavior,* was a quasi-axiomatic structure of first principles, patterned after Newtonian mechanics, from which theorems presumably followed with geometrical precision to predict what animals actually do. Among these first principles was the concept of reinforcement, the technical term for the idea that organisms tend to repeat rewarded acts, which was supposed to account for adaptiveness and purpose by the selective effects of past success on subsequent behavior. Whereas Tolman wanted to make purpose scientifically respectable by identifying it with the capacity to learn, Hull wanted to explain it away altogether. His stratagem was to propose a theory of learning that made no reference to purpose, but did not suffer the implausibility of denying adaptiveness. In fact, the index of Hull's book contains no references either to purpose or cognition. The frontal assault on the problem of purpose was distinctively Tolman's; Hull (and Skinner, as will be shown later) preferred a more indirect approach. But from a far-removed vantage point, one can see that Hull, like Tolman, was creating a behaviorism of adaptive behavior. And in so doing, Hull, like Tolman, became a learning theorist.

Skinner, too, sought to deal with behavior at the adaptive level and also formulated a learning theory that distinguishes his variety of behavior- ism. And once again the distinctive feature of the approach is captured in the title of his systematic book, *The Behavior of Organisms,* for Skinner wanted a rigorous commitment to the study of behavior itself, not inferred entities like purpose (Tolman) or first principles from which behavior could be deduced (Hull). Skinner's behaviorism has therefore been properly called a "descriptive" behaviorism, one presumably stating all its laws and predictions in terms of behavior itself. But for all of its stark empiricism, Skinner defined behavior not as Watson did, in terms of actual movements, but in terms of the effects of movement on the environment. Skinnerian research typically uses animals working in confined chambers and getting food or water for their labors. For example, a rat may be rewarded by a small pellet of food for depressing a lever protruding into a chamber. For Skinner, all the different ways of pressing the lever are grouped together into a single class of behavior, a single response-class identified by the property of operating the lever and without regard to anatomical configuration. In Skinner's analysis, the behavior is "lever-pressing," a characterization that the true Watsonian could have forgiven only on the grounds of expedience; each of the many ways a rat can press a lever is a different response in the Watsonian scheme of things. Like Hull, Skinner leaves the "purpose" out of his system in any explicit form, but it is there nevertheless, since each class of behavior is defined by its consequences.

The excuse for this excursion into modern behaviorism is simply that there seems to be no better way to judge the impact of Watson on psychology than to consult the judgment of time itself, as made known in the contributions of his intellectual heirs, of whom Tolman, Hull, and Skinner are both primary and representative. The judgment of time is clear, or at least as clear as it can become in just fifty years. Watson's behaviorism has been judged to have been too intimately linked to an analysis of behavior in terms of muscle twitches and gland secretions. It failed to solve the uniquely psychological problem of purpose. It failed to take into account the transcendent importance of learning in the dynamics of behavior, and also to recognize the difficulties in creating a satisfactory theory of learning. But if all this seems like a harsh judgment, it is not really. For Watson's goal was as much to see psychology become a natural science — predictive, experimental, and useful — as it was to advance the substantive particulars of his theory of behavior. And in that, his heirs support him entirely, and have made their modifications in the hopes of furthering the very same goal.

Watson's behaviorism was a reaction against the psychology of the time, primarily against the introspective German structuralists searching for the contents of the mind, but also against those American psychologists who, although themselves opposed to structuralism, had not fully abandoned the introspective method. His alternative to introspection was the direct observation of behavior, in the laboratory and in natural situations, with the goal of finding the connections between behavior and its underlying physiology. At the time this book was written, Watson was clearly in the Darwinian tradition, trusting in the continuity of species to provide clues in animal behavior for an understanding of behavior in general. Watson's psychology was reflexological; behavior was to be analyzed into the quasi-mechanical connections between stimuli and responses. In some instances, he could point to relatively well-isolated simple reflexes, in the higher organisms as well as in the lower. In other instances, when discussing instinct, he argued that reflexes may become concatenated in long sequences to produce complex adjustments. And, finally, when discussing habit — which was the current term for the study of learning — Watson further argued that these, too, are but networks of concatenated reflexes, differing from instinct only in the genesis of the pattern and order of the individual movements and not in the movements themselves.

A large part of the book is an attempt to substantiate the reflexological approach to behavior, and thereby to all of psychology. The flavor of Watson's dialectical method is best obtained from a concrete instance, for example, the treatment of learning (pp. 256-259). Watson recognized that the capacity to learn poses several problems for a reflexological theory. There is the problem that learning is often, indeed usually, an adaptive change in behavior. An animal gains skills not for their own sake, but for the benefits they bring: food, shelter, and so on. In fact, the course of learning is little else than a growing facility in gaining these benefits. For the reflexologist, who may not ascribe the growing facility to a conscious mental process, the adaptiveness of learning is a challenge, if not a refutation. Watson's answer was Darwinian. He pointed out that because of its long evolutionary history, the animal is likely to have adaptive reflexes, disposing it to approach the things it needs and to shun the things that might damage it. The creatures that were remiss about approaching food or potential mates were at so serious a disadvantage in the race for survival that their descendants are not around to testify to the essentially mechanistic control of behavior. What we see around us instead, said Watson, are the descendants of the animals with the right reflexes, misleading us to see adaptiveness as the cause, instead of the effect, of the psychological mechanism.

But inherited reflexes, whether adaptive or not, do not explain how behavior changes at all, which is an even more fundamental property of learning, and a reflexological theory seems to imply that new behavior cannot be produced during the lifetime of any given creature. Watson made this implication explicit by saying that the only changes in behavior are in the pattern of movements, never in the movements themselves.

Suppose, said Watson, a rat is confronted with a box which it is motivated to open. (Watson did not specify the motive, but since the example is hypothetical, we may assume that the rat is after food.) We observe the rat and find that most of its movements are irrelevant to the task at hand; but a few, such as approaching the box, digging away at the sawdust that obscures the latch, and so on, are essential. Eventually, in this hit-or-miss way, the rat gets the box open and is fed. On subsequent occasions, the rat's behavior becomes progressively more focused on getting the box open, until at last the rat approaches the job in full command of the necessary skills. To all appearances, granted Watson, it is as if the rat had acquired new behavior, not readily attributable to inherited reflexes, for the required skills depend on wholly arbitrary features of the situation. Watson's answer here was statistical. Suppose, he said, that we put ten slips of paper, numbered 1 to 10, in a container and draw them out randomly one at a time until a certain numeral, let us say 5, is drawn. Then we return all the slips drawn, after tallying them, and repeat the game. It can be shown, said Watson, that the number 5 would, in the limit, turn up twice as often as any other number, let us say 9, that one might compare it with. It is, in principle, equally likely that 9 would come before 5 or afterward, but since drawing is terminated at 5, half of the occurrences of 9, on the average, are prevented. This, said Watson, is similar to what is happening with the rat's movements. The sequence of movements is reflexive and random, but the "drawings" are artificially terminated at the occurrence of the critical movements, and, therefore, the critical movements will occur more often than any others.

At this point, Watson affirmed that the sheer practice of a movement increases its frequency. Given the law of practice, it follows that the animal's behavior will evolve toward the minimal configuration of effective and necessary movements, with the superfluous ones tending to vanish. By chance, it is possible that some superfluous ones will also get practiced and therefore strengthened; but that, said Watson, is why the world is not populated by virtuosos, and not a problem with his theory.

As a theory of learning, Watson's was far from original. The idea of learning by practice is undoubtedly ancient and had already been incorporated into experimental psychology by Hermann Ebbinghaus, the German psychologist who invented the nonsense syllable and the procedures for studying rote memorization. And Watson also discussed the importance of "recency," another favorite of the rote-memorization psychologists, which held simply that, all other things being equal, a more recent response is more likely to be repeated than a less recent one. But there was very little in Watson, taken item by item, that was original. The novelty of the approach was its comprehensiveness. Neither Ebbinghaus, nor any of his followers, was willing or disposed to use the principle of frequency as an argument against the importance of adaptiveness, as Watson was. Nor had it been used before as part of an argument for a reflexological approach to all of psychology.

Watson's example of the rat and the box would have served well as the paradigm for a different sort of learning theory. In 1898, a young American psychologist named Edward L. Thorndike published a monograph describing the learning of chickens and cats in an apparatus similar to Watson's hypothetical device, but destined to make Thorndike famous as the inventor of the "puzzle box." The animal was placed inside the box, from which it could escape and be fed by tripping a latch mechanism. Thorndike collected curves of the time taken to escape on successive trials, which, as would be expected, revealed a fairly orderly decrease to a minimum value. These were "learning curves," among the earliest in the literature of psychology and therefore of historical importance in their own right. From these data and from other observations of the animals, Thorndike formulated his laws of learning, of which the most important was the law of "effect." An animal, this law says, repeats actions that have gained it satisfaction and avoids actions that have cost it discomfort; in other words, an animal is influenced by the "effects" of its actions. Here is not the proper place to discuss the history of this hedonistic principle, except to note that in Thorndike's time it was already a widely held, if loosely stated, theory of learning among psychologists in the Darwinian tradition. It was a theory that neatly guaranteed the adaptiveness of behavior, a requirement that Darwinians were naturally sensitive to, given their concern with adaptiveness on the broader scale of evolution. Thorndike, too, was a Darwinian, and so his adherence to a hedonistic account is compatible with his general convictions. Curiously, Watson was also a Darwinian, as numerous passages in this book demonstrate, and yet he chose a non-hedonistic theory as his own.

Thorndike has not been remembered as a behaviorist, although his contribution resembles Watson's, with its insistence on objective data, on experimental rather than anecdotal or introspective observation, on the suitability of animal subjects in the psychological laboratory, on the usefulness of science instead of its more abstract justifications, on an interest in action at the expense of a concern with cognition. In many ways, as a matter of fact, the modern behaviorists owe more to or, at least, are more like Thorndike than like Watson. Like them, Thorndike was caught up most directly in the question of the learning process, and was content to deal with behavior at the level of act rather than of movement. His law of effect has continued to be a vital issue in psychology.

Why, then, do we call Watson a behaviorist, and not Thorndike? The answer is partly chronological. Watson coined the vocabulary of behaviorism, and he did so after Thorndike had already reached a level of eminence that virtually prohibited him from changing his affiliations. But part of the answer is also substantive, dealing with learning theory itself. Watson felt that the law of effect, along with all the other versions of the hedonistic principle, is untenable because it seems to speak of the animal's state of mind. For Watson, and thus for the early behaviorists, the state of pleasure or otherwise in the mind of a chicken is unknown and unknowable, and hence could not possibly enter into a behavioristic account. Judging from what has happened since, Watson was wrong about what could be incorporated into behaviorism and what could not, for most of the modern versions still retain the law of effect in some form or other.

The contrast between Thorndike and Watson need not be mere speculation, for Thorndike wrote one of the few reviews of this book. In general, the review is favorable. Thorndike commended Watson for his devotion to experimentation, for his contribution to animal psychology, for his distrust of introspection, for his detailed and scholarly accounts of particular pieces of experimental apparatus and instructions as to their use, for his criterion of prediction as the measure of scientific truth, and for almost everything else we have come to think of as behaviorism. But he disagreed with a theory of learning based exclusively on frequency and recency, and took pains to refute in Watson's own terms the statistical argument outlined earlier. For, as Thorndike pointed out, the theory works only if the various responses constituting the animal's behavior are equi-probable, as the example with numbered slips of paper tacitly assumes. If, on the other hand, the correct response happens to be very much less probable than some other response, the practice will selectively strengthen the other response. Thorndike thought something more was needed to focus on the correct response, presumably his own law of effect.

It is not only in Thorndike's work that one encounters significant similarities to Watsonian behaviorism. Watson was writing in a period of rapid change in psychology, and many of the landmarks that are sometimes credited to Watson were, in fact, only signs of the times. The Watsonian predilection for neurological theorizing was too widespread to be documented here, but a few examples are William James's *Principles of Psychology* (1890), W. B. Pillsbury's *Essentials of Psychology* (1911), and Knight Dunlap's *An Outline of Psychobiology* (1914). The interest in animal psychology was, of course, an offshoot of Darwinian theory, already formulated in such books as G. J. Romanes' *Animal Intelligence* (1882), C. Lloyd Morgan's *Introduction to Comparative Psychology* (1894), and H. S. Jennings' *Behavior of the Lower Organisms* (1906). The idea that nineteenth-century psychology had been neglecting the study of behavior was stated in many places, many of them seemingly unlikely, such as William James's *Talks to Teachers* (1898) and William McDougall's *Physiological Psychology* (1905). By 1914, there were already self-conscious schools of psychology with systematic positions not very different from Watson's. There were the Russian reflexologists, of whom Pavlov was the outstanding figure, and about whom there will be more later. There were also the German biologists, typified by Jacques Loeb, who subscribed to a mechanistic account of behavior in terms of tropisms and other forced movements.

It should not be surprising, then, that Watson's book was not ushered into the intellectual community to the blare of trumpets. Thorndike thought it was a good book, useful in the classroom for bringing together the growing body of fact and method in the field of animal psychology. And Harvey Carr, Watson's successor at the University of Chicago six years before, also wrote a favorable review emphasizing the value of the book as a text, but criticizing Watson's tendency to become overly polemical and his failure to recognize the importance of the learning process in the description of behavior. The experts were, of course, right in one sense. Watson's behaviorism was not all that new. The traditional introspective psychology against which he was railing was already mortally weakened, particularly in the hostile environment of American pragmatism. But the experts were wrong in another sense, for in this reaction against the old psychology, Watson was to be the most potent catalyst. Young students, coming into psychology innocently unaware of the ferment therein, gravitated to Watson's brand of objective psychology and, in so doing, made an important figure of him.

Because this book was so much a part of what was happening in psychology, it was not immediately seen as the beginning of a revolution. But within a very few years, there were behaviorists, self-conscious about their membership in a new school. Watson's writings took on the quality of a new orthodoxy, which is not to suggest that obedience was required, for the behaviorists fell into factional dispute virtually immediately. Nor is it to suggest that Watson's views became static, for in his later books his theory changed, mainly in highlighting its more radical aspects and in diminishing its dependence on the experimental findings of behavioral research, the very feature that both Thorndike and Carr had praised. As Watson's ideas became more clearly distinguishable from the historical stream from which they emerged, they became less defensible.

Most of the radical ideas were already in this book, but often not fully elaborated. There is the attack on the idea of images. Watson wrote, "There are no centrally initiated processes" (p. 18). What seems to go on in the mind, said Watson, is either not going on at all in any scientifically demonstrable way, or else is going on as small-scale behavior, too small to be grossly detected, but potentially measurable by a sufficiently sensitive instrument applied to the right muscles. There is Watson's distinction between man and beast (Chapter X), which reduces to the existence of language in the one and not in the other. There is the identification of language with habit, differing in no fundamental way from any other kind of habit. There is the relegation of thought to small-scale habits, many of them language habits, and thus to be detected at some future time as movements of the larynx. There is the identification of emotion with stimuli arising in the erogenous zones of the body. What is missing from this book and what later became one of the most potent, and therefore most outrageous, aspects of Watson's behaviorism is the almost unrestrained environmentalism, and the concomitant claim that by proper training virtually anyone can do anything. Within ten years, when he wrote *Behaviorism* (1924), Watson had come to recognize the importance of learning so well that he felt justified in saying:

> Give me a dozen healthy infants, well-formed, and my own specified world to bring them up in and I'll guarantee to take any one at random and train him to become any type of specialist I might select— doctor, lawyer, artist, merchant-chief and, yes, even beggar-man and thief, regardless of his talents, penchants, tendencies, abilities, vocations, and race of his ancestors. I am going beyond my facts and I admit it, but so have the advocates of the contrary and they have been doing it for many thousands of years.

Behaviorism was reviewed in the book review section of Sunday's *New York Times,* a distinction reserved for few books by experimental psychologists and for which Watson's book qualified by virtue of its radical thesis and, of course, its author's eminence. The reviewer, Evans Clark, said, "These lectures show that he has hardly yet made a beginning [in his program to create a science of behavior] — some experiment[s] on infants, some investigation of the relation of the muscles and glands to conduct, and a few other scattered tests — but that he should have done even that marks a new epoch in the intellectual history of man." The concern for instinct that marks the book reprinted here had so far faded that Watson had begun to doubt if there were any human instincts at all. And if Watson was only doubting, some other behaviorists, such as the Chinese psychologist Z. Y. Kuo and the American sociologist L. L. Bernard, felt they had grounds for the positive denial of all instincts.

Watson's involvement with learning was not like that of Tolman, Hull, or Skinner. For these modern behaviorists, the importance of learning emerged from an attempt to redefine behavior itself in a psychologically valid way; but for Watson, the definition of behavior seems to have come easily, and he seems to have had no inclination to question it. Behavior was reflexive first and always. Instead, the change seems to have come about when he recognized the importance of the work on conditioned reflexes by I. P. Pavlov, the Nobel Prize-winning Russian physiologist. It was a recognition that must have come after the present book was written, judging from the critical tone and the brevity with which he disposes of Pavlov in the chapter on apparatus and methods (pp. 65 ff.).

Starting in the first years after the turn of the century, Pavlov began publishing brief reports of his studies of salivary conditioning, studies that soon began to attract interest in the Western world. What became clear only later was that Pavlov was part of a movement in Russia toward objective psychology, similar to the one that Watson promoted in America, but considerably ahead of it chronologically and technically. In 1863, I. M. Sechenov, a leading figure in physiological circles in Russia, published a monograph entitled *Reflexes of the Brain*. Unlike most of Sechenov's publications, which concerned conventional neurophysiology and neuroanatomy, this one was a wholly speculative treatise on the idea, first, that all behavior is composed of reflexes and, second, that all of psychology can be reduced to the study of behavior. Sechenov argued that only complexity distinguishes these "reflexes of the brain" from the spinal reflexes that physiologists usually study, and hence there is no basic distinction between the mental life of an organism and its simple bodily functions. He argued further that the ancient distinction between voluntary and involuntary behavior vanishes in the light of reflex integration and reflex inhibition — already well-established physiological phenomena in the 1860s—so that all activity, mental or otherwise, is equally involuntary.

Sechenov's radical thesis attracted attention among Russian intellectuals. He had adoring disciples and bitter opponents. He was seen as the pioneer for a positive and useful science, and as an unholy heretic who threatened the best values in life. He won eminence among a circle of young and fervent scientists, but he got into trouble with the authorities over his monograph, which for a time was banned. A few years later, he resigned his professorship at the Medico-Surgical Academy in St. Petersburg, and then later returned to his alma mater, Moscow University. These personal notes about Watson's Russian predecessor may seem pertinent later, when the details of Watson's personal and professional life are briefly noted.

Among the young men stimulated by the daring of Sechenov's mechanistic view of psychology was Ivan Petrovitch Pavlov, as he said in 1923 in the preface to *Lectures on Conditioned Reflexes*. By 1923, Pavlov had achieved great scientific eminence in two fields, enough in either one to earn him a place in the history of the biological sciences. In 1904, he had been awarded the Nobel Prize for his experiments on the reflexes of the alimentary canal, but his Nobel Prize lecture, entitled "The First Sure Steps Along the Path of a New Investigation," outlined research in a new field, that of conditioned reflexes.

The experimental methods that assured his eminence in the study of digestive reflexes proved to be the source of his diversion to the study of behavior. Instead of the usual acute experimentation of the physiological laboratory, in which the experimental animal is sacrificed for the sake of a few brief observations, Pavlov invented chronic methods, restoring the animal as nearly as possible postoperatively to normal function, while still allowing observations to be made of the parts of the digestive system. In particular, Pavlov measured the secretions from the glands of the gastrointestinal system by diverting the appropriate duct away from its usual pathway and having it empty into a vial on the outside of the animal. Years of his life were spent devising ways to keep his subjects, usually dogs, as healthy and comfortable as possible under the circumstances, not only for humane reasons, but also because the delicate adjustments of the gastrointestinal system were so easily thrown awry by the smallest disturbance.

Although his caution was rewarded by a rich harvest of discovery about the operation of the digestive system, it also led to his encounter with "psychic secretion," his term for glandular activity produced mentally rather than physiologically. Pavlov found that the gastrointestinal glands are primarily reflexive, which is to say that they are triggered into appropriate action by various definite and specifiable stimuli arising from particular substances in the canal itself. All of this was in accord with the physiological knowledge of the time, and with the Darwinian argument for adaptive reflexes. However, because his experiments were chronic and because dogs learned the daily routine, the glands were often thrown into action by remote stimuli, such as the approach of the experimenter or the sight of a particular substance. These secretions could hardly have been inherited reflexes, for such details of a laboratory's operation could have no representation in the hereditary endowment of the animal.

For a time, Pavlov was content to distinguish between the physiological secretions, produced by natural agents, and the psychic secretions, produced by expectations of the dog based upon its experience in the laboratory, and he disregarded the latter except in his efforts to minimize them. But at some point, the kernel sown by having read Sechenov as a young man developed into an eagerness to study these "higher" reflexes— reflexes of the brain, as Sechenov called them. Pavlov said more than once in his writings that the point at which he decided to investigate the psychic secretions was precisely the point at which he decided to call them psychic secretions no longer. The significant insight was that these "unnatural" secretions are, in fact, just as physiological, just as orderly, just as amenable to scientific scrutiny, and, finally, just as natural as are the reflexes whose study had won him the Nobel Prize. They differed only in being acquired instead of inherited, and in revealing the operation of the nervous system at a higher level than the inherited digestive reflexes. The inherited reflexes are designed, in the biological scheme of things, to enable the animal to manage its internal environment, whereas the acquired reflexes enable the animal to cope with its surroundings. Pavlov devised a terminology for his new insights. The acquired reflexes were called "conditioned reflexes"; the inherited ones, "unconditioned reflexes," as a means of capturing the distinction between reflexes that are contingent upon other circumstances and reflexes that are not. From about 1902 until his death in 1936, Pavlov worked exclusively and productively on the properties of conditioned reflexes, creating a new field of inquiry that has ultimately become international, after several decades during which it was largely Russian.

Curiously, this story of Pavlov, Sechenov, and the discovery of a way of investigating the process of learning by objective methods could be virtually retold by substituting V. M. Bekhterev for Pavlov, for Bekhterev was another young Russian physiologist who transformed Sechenov's speculations into a program of research. Bekhterev's terminology was different from that of Pavlov. He spoke of association reflexes instead of conditioned reflexes. He studied motor responses, such as leg flexion, instead of the secretion of the salivary gland. And in certain technical ways, the type of learning he examined differs from Pavlovian conditioning. But the two men share an objective approach to traditionally subjective psychological issues, and share also in having been ahead of Watson in method, if not in conception. Pavlov, writing in 1923, acknowledged the contribution of Bekhterev and Watson, among others, to the growth of objective psychology, but granted priority to only one man as regards experimental work, and that was Thorndike.

Pavlov, ordinarily the epitome of the cautious scientist, content to let his data do most of the speaking for him, could not restrain his enthusiasm for the vista that opened up when he contemplated a science of behavior based on conditioned reflexes. In 1923 he wrote:

> About myself I shall add the following. At the beginning of our work and for a long time afterwards we felt the compulsion of habit in explaining our subject by psychological [i.e., subjective] interpretations. Every time the objective investigation met an obstacle, or when it was halted by the complexity of the problem, there arose quite naturally misgivings as to the correctness of our new method. Gradually with the progress of our research these doubts appeared more rarely, and now I am deeply and irrevocably convinced that along this path will be found the final triumph of the human mind over its uttermost and supreme problem — the knowledge of the mechanism

and laws of human nature. Only thus may come a full, true and permanent happiness. Let the mind rise from victory to victory over surrounding nature, let it command for its service prodigious energy to flow from one part of the universe to the other, let it annihilate space for the transference of its thoughts — yet the same human creature, led by dark powers to wars and revolutions and their horrors, produces for itself incalculable material losses and inexpressible pain and reverts to bestial conditions. Only science, exact science about human nature itself, and the most sincere approach to it by the aid of the omnipotent scientific method will deliver man from his present gloom, and will purge him from his contemporary shame in the sphere of interhuman relations.

If the potentialities of this approach to behavior could raise a man of Pavlov's sobriety to such heights of excitement, could it long leave Watson unmoved, as he was in 1914 when he wrote the present book? Clearly, the answer is no, for in his later works the importance of conditioned reflexes gradually dominated all of the other features of Watson's behaviorism. The process had already begun by 1915, when Watson's presidential address to the American Psychological Association ("The Place of the Conditioned Reflex in Psychology") argued that introspective accounts are properly replaced by conditioned responses in a behavioristic psychology. Not only was Pavlovian conditioning a practical, objective, and deterministic framework in which to cast as much of psychology as one's imagination encompassed, but it was built upon the reflex itself, Watson's first love in psychological analysis. The marriage was a natural, and there were no impediments to it. It is not surprising that in the everyday psychology of popular literature, and in too many psychology texts as well, Watson's behaviorism is equated with Pavlovian theory.

Watson's conversion to the conditioned reflex went hand in hand with a change in the scope of his behaviorism. Instead of a mere faction within an academic discipline, it became a program for social control and improvement. During the 1920s, Watson's books became more and more concerned with practical questions in human affairs and more and more devoid of scholarly contact with the rest of psychology. The books themselves were usually compilations either of articles that had appeared in various popular magazines or of popular lecture series. Here is a sampling of some of the titles that appeared over his name: "The Behaviorist Looks at Instincts" (*Harper's,* 1927); "Feed Me on Facts" (*Saturday Review of Literature,* 1928); "The Weakness of Women" (*The Nation,* 1928); "Can We Make Our Children Behave?" (*Forum,* 1929); "It's Your Own Fault" (*Collier's,* 1928); "The Heart or the Intellect?" (*Harper's,* 1928); "Are Parents Necessary?" (*New York Times,* 1930). The articles are interesting, forceful, and assertive, but they are also propagandistic, sometimes simplistic, and occasionally unscholarly. They seem to betray a mischievous pleasure in shocking their audience — the educated, conventional

American middle class — by questioning cherished beliefs regarding child-rearing, marriage, religion, and so on. Watson was attacking certain aspects of morality in the name of behaviorism, and the main weapon for his assault was Pavlovian conditioning. This may explain why even today Watson, behaviorism, and Pavlov are held in contempt by many non-psychologists who are, of course, unable to see how much this later stage in his career was the result of his personal experience and how little it had to do with the scientific movement of which he had been a part.

The rebellious streak in Watson's character is frankly revealed in an autobiographical sketch he wrote for Carl Murchison's *History of Psychology in Autobiography* (Vol. III, 1936). John Broadus Watson was born near Greenville, South Carolina, in 1878, the son of a prosperous farmer, and was educated in district schools in the countryside and in the public school of the town of Greenville. Of himself as a pupil he said, "I was lazy, somewhat insubordinate, and, so far as I know, I never made above a passing grade." His childhood interests seem to have tended toward the violent, having been arrested on two occasions for sheer hell-raising. Yet even as a young boy, he had an aptitude and fondness for the chores around a farm, including carpentry. In his later life, the manual skills showed up as an interest in the technical aspects of psychological research, an interest that is unmistakable in the book here reprinted.

At the age of sixteen he entered Furman University, a Baptist school in Greenville, where he stayed for five years to earn an A.M. Although he appears to have found college neither interesting nor worthwhile, he decided after graduation to seek further study, choosing the then new University of Chicago, apparently because one of his teachers at Furman had studied there and because he had heard of John Dewey, who was then teaching the gospel of pragmatism at Chicago. Watson went to Chicago to study philosophy, but was diverted into psychology, perhaps influenced by Dewey's strong interest in psychological matters at that time. There were exceptional men at Chicago, in and around the periphery of psychology. Watson acknowledged a profound debt of gratitude to James R. Angell, who was then in psychology and who later became president of Yale, for his "erudition, quickness of thought, and facility with words." Angell was in those years the leader of American functional psychology, a school that insisted upon a concern with the dynamic aspects of an organism's adjustments to its environment, as well as with the static properties of consciousness. It is easy to see Watson's behaviorism as a radical extension of Angell's functionalism. Watson studied also under H. H. Donaldson, the eminent neurologist, and Jacques Loeb, the transported German biologist, who by this time had his own version of objective psychology, based, in a metaphoric way, on the botanical concept of tropisms. Watson was apparently tempted to write his dissertation under Loeb, but was advised against it by Angell and Donaldson because, according to Watson, Loeb was not considered a "very 'safe' man for a green Ph.D. candidate," presumably because of the heterodoxy of his views. Instead, Watson took his degree under Angell and Donaldson, working on the behavior of the white rat in relation to the growth of medullation in its central nervous system.

Philosophy, his original interest, seems to have gotten away from him. Watson said he studied it and took a good many courses, but gained so little understanding from them that he gradually lost his interest. He studied with G. H. Mead and Dewey, important names of the times, but it made little impression. About Dewey, Watson said, "I never knew what he was talking about then, and, unfortunately for me, I still don't know." But the break with philosophy was not a rancorous one; Watson's fondness for Mead was still evident in 1936 in his autobiography.

Watson flourished at Chicago. When he earned his doctorate in 1903, both Donaldson and Angell offered him positions, the one in neurology and the other in psychology. Watson chose psychology, staying on first as Assistant and then as Instructor until he was offered a job at Johns Hopkins University in 1907. The offer from Hopkins came from James Mark Baldwin, another of the leaders of American functionalism, and was originally for an Associate Professorship, but while Watson hesitated in his reluctance to leave Chicago, it was raised to a full Professorship. Watson could not refuse this, and so moved into a major university with a major position in 1908 at the age of 29. At Hopkins, Watson was fortunate to encounter yet another group of outstanding men. In addition to Baldwin, there was Knight Dunlap, a psychologist who was himself already tending toward behaviorism; H. S. Jennings, a zoologist who had written one of the earliest major books on comparative psychology and who had a keen sense of the demands of objectivism on psychology; A. O. Lovejoy, the prominent neorealist philosopher; and, after a few years, the brilliant K. S. Lashley, a biologist who came to Watson from Jennings' laboratory and who went on to become the most outstanding physiological psychologist America has yet produced.

The book reprinted here was the product of this period in Watson's life, easily the best with regard to scholarly and scientific activity. Watson was active in his laboratory, working on sensory processes in animals, and in professional psychology at large. He was elected president of the American Psychological Association in 1915, just one year after this book was published. The book was itself an expansion upon a series of lectures that Watson had given at Columbia University in 1913. Its first chapter is almost identical to an article entitled "Psychology as the Behaviorist Views It," published in 1913 in the *Psychological Review* and usually taken as the founding manifesto of Watsonian behaviorism.

The disruption of this productive existence was augured by Watson's experience in World War I. He tried to enlist as a line officer, but was found unfit because of poor eyesight. Instead, he was called to aid in the problems of personnel selection for the army. Being an officer was a nightmare for Watson. His stubborn independence guaranteed that he would clash with the military hierarchy in general and with a few officers in particular. About one of them, he said in his autobiography, "His egotism and self-seeking soon made every one in the personnel section of aviation understand why it is that some officers fail to return from expeditions even when not engaged by enemy troops." About officers in general, he said (excepting West Point and Naval Academy graduates), "Never have I seen such incompetence, such extravagance, such a group of overbearing, inferior men."

After the Armistice, Watson returned as promptly as possible to Hopkins, eager to resume his scientific life. He started work on the conditioning of infants, and began to assemble the material for *Psychology from the Standpoint of a Behaviorist,* which was published in 1919, and which is a far more doctrinaire argument for behaviorism than the present one. But he had barely settled back into his old routine when he was asked to resign his professorship. The incident is still too obscured by unsubstantiated rumor to be fully recounted, but it was undoubtedly related to his divorce, after sixteen years of marriage, from Mary Ickes, a sister of the Harold Ickes who was to become Roosevelt's Secretary of the Interior, and his almost immediate remarriage to Rosalie Raynor, who was Watson's student as well as his collaborator in a famous experiment on the Pavlovian conditioning of a fear reaction in a child. Today, the scandal of Watson's resignation and the furor it provoked in the Baltimore newspapers seem very much out of proportion to the incident itself. Mores have changed greatly in forty-five years; nevertheless one might wonder if Watson was not in some measure paying for the novelty of his psychological theories and the radical tone in which he was disposed to pitch them.

Unlike his Russian predecessor Sechenov, Watson was not temperamentally disposed to wait for the storm to abate and then return to the sort of academic position his eminence and abilities fully justified. Instead, he chose to turn his back on the intellectual community that had so abruptly turned against him. He went to work for the J. Walter Thompson Co., the advertising firm, and rapidly brought his great talents to bear on the world of commerce. Four years after his resignation from Hopkins in 1920, Watson became a vice-president of the company. In 1936, he moved to another firm, William Esty and Co., also as vice-president, where he remained until his retirement in 1946. Life as a businessman seems to have satisfied him, for he wrote with enthusiasm of the challenges of his new life. But he retained an understandable hostility toward the academic community, one which often appeared in his later writings as a conviction that universities fail to equip students with the knowledge and skills that they will eventually need.

For about a dozen years after his resignation from Hopkins, Watson continued to develop the behavioristic credo in lectures, popular articles, and books. In addition to *Psychology from the Standpoint of a Behaviorist,* which came out shortly before the scandal broke, he wrote *Behaviorism* (1924), *Psychological Care of Infant and Child* (1928), and *The Ways of Behaviorism* (1928). As the years passed, the discipline of scholarship became progressively less evident in his writings, while the skills of persuasion, perhaps sharpened by his job, became progressively more so. Then, in the middle 1930s, Watson finally reached the end of his psychological career, too occupied, as he said, with "business, my family and my farm." In 1958, at the age of eighty, Watson died, an event not unnoticed in academic circles, for the conservative *American Journal of Psychology* published an obituary with a photograph, a distinction reserved for only the very important members of the profession.

And very important he had been, notwithstanding the flaws that may be found in his contribution to psychology. The reflex, Watson's analytic unit, has not become the basis of scientific psychology or even of modern behaviorism. Pavlovian conditioning is generally regarded as but one kind of learning among several, and probably not even the most important in complex human behavior. Radical environmentalism has given way to a more plausible synthesis of nature and nurture. Even introspection has persisted as a method in psychology, albeit with far less status than before Watson's attack. The higher mental processes, like language and thought, are viewed by virtually no one as mere habits localized in the peripheral musculature. The list of Watson's mistakes could be multiplied, but to do so is to distort what actually happened, for Watson's importance was more sociological than substantive. It was not his theories that changed psychology, except insofar as they were the medium by which he argued for psychology to be a natural science, more closely allied to biology than to philosophy, empirical instead of polemical. His insistence on the importance of experimentation was far more significant than the fact that his own experiments yielded little of permanent value. And his optimistic enthusiasm for a predictive science of behavior was to have far more impact than the fact that his enthusiasm was often unfounded. Of course, Watson was but part of the growth of objective psychology, in clear continuity with his precursors, but circumstances and his talents singled him out for special influence. In America at least, Watson is the link between the dawning objectivism of nineteenth-century psychology and the almost unquestioned empiricism around us today.

Schools and Systems:
The Mutual Isolation of Operant
and Non-Operant Psychology
as a Case Study

DAVID L. KRANTZ

The present research studies a contemporary example of a "school" whose adherents could be directly questioned. The choice of operant conditioning as a case study was suggested by the perception of some non-operant researchers that there is a closed group of committed, if not overly committed, individuals who maintain and explore the idea system initially developed by B. F. Skinner. A total of 35 open-ended taped interviews were performed, with the majority of the individuals being more senior, high-status individuals in operant conditioning (60 percent of the respondents held editorial positions on one or both of the two operant journals).

Since an earlier study on "schools" (8) strongly suggested that the nature of relationship and communication between competing approaches is an important characteristic in defining and understanding the nature of "schools," the following presentation will focus upon this aspect. Following an assessment of the character of the interrelationships, an examination will be made of the external interactions between operant and non-operant psychology and the internal development within the movement.

MUTUAL ISOLATION: CITATION DATA

To index the relationship between operant and non-operant psychology, the mean percentage of self-citations per article in the *Journal of the Experimental Analysis of Behavior* (JEAB) — the oldest operant journal — summed across articles per year, was computed.[1] The obtained

This article, which has been abridged by the editors, appeared in its original form in the *Journal of the History of the Behavioral Sciences*, 1972, *8*, 86-102.

curve, shown with the self-citation of the *Journal of Verbal Learning and Verbal Behavior* (JVLVB), partially to control for JEAB being a relatively new journal, and with the self-citation of the *Journal of Experimental Psychology* (JEP), one of JEAB's and JVLVB's source journals and the highest self-citing journal in psychology (15), is shown in Figure 1. Clearly the slope of JEAB's self-citation curve is greater than that of JVLVB, both contrasting with the slightly decreasing rate of JEP's self-citation.[2] It would not be overinterpreting these data to say that JEAB, by increasingly citing itself, is isolating itself from other approaches.

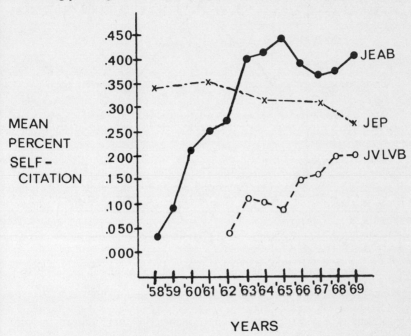

Figure 1.   Mean percent of self-citation of JEAB, JVLVB, JEP, across years.

Reciprocally, JEAB's findings are being isolated by other approaches in psychology. In two recent learning texts, Deese and Hulse (1) and Hall (2), JEAB citations constitute .012 and .006 of all citations.   In contrast, JVLVB articles are cited .026 and .018 in these two books. Although text citations mirror to some extent the accepted "paradigm" of a field (9), they often lag behind the changes occurring in a field. A more current index is the degree to which JEAB's major source journal, *Journal of Comparative and Physiological Psychology* (JCPP), cites JEAB.[3] As shown in Figure 2, JEAB's publications are not being incorporated into its source journal, JCPP, to the same extent as JVLVB's publications are in its source journal, JEP.[4] In summary, the citation data indicate that there is a mutual isolation of operant research, by JEAB, in

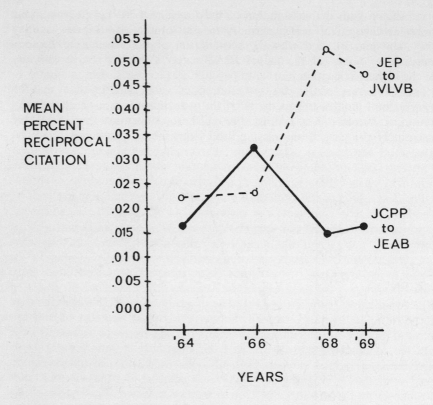

Figure 2. Mean percent of reciprocal citation of JCPP to JEAB, and JEP to JVLVB, across years.

its high self-citation, and by other approaches in their failure to cite operant findings.

EXTERNAL RELATIONS

The Columbia Program

Following World War II, a program utilizing Skinner's *The Behavior of Organisms* (11) as its source was developed by Keller and Schoenfeld at Columbia University. This program provided a setting for the recruitment and training of future operant conditioners.

At the core of the Columbia program was the Introductory Psychology course, where all of the diverse topics in psychology were treated from the perspective of Skinner's behavioristic approach. With supportive laboratory experience, this approach was in marked contrast to traditional introductory courses that contained a potpourri of topics, each embodying dissimilar theoretical approaches. A casual comparison of the course's text, *Principles of Psychology* (7) by Keller and Schoenfeld, with such introductory books of the period as Munn or Boring strongly indicates the difference in approach.

The Columbia course was so successful that enrollments exceeded departmental facilities. Students from the natural sciences and engineering were now attracted, as contrasted to the largely humanistically oriented students of the past. Soon most of the Columbia College undergraduate curriculum was revised in line with an operant conditioning approach. A relatively small graduate program in operant conditioning then evolved, with many of its students coming directly from the undergraduate program.

The description of the Columbia program (6) soon came under attack by Wendt (13). His comments can be viewed as symptomatic of a growing response to the operant movement: "The requirement by a department of adherence to any system of thought in its courses, be it Wundtian structuralism, neo-Thomistic humanism, or Skinnerism, eventually results in an inbred department and its isolation from the rest of science and from other disciplines." He then went on to describe the developmental stages of an academic cult from a small number of enthusiasts in the basic course, to the hiring of similarly minded faculty, the lack of support of and the eventual dropping out of dissenters, leading to the eventual isolation of the cult. He concluded: "I recognize that the Columbia system is enthusiastically received by the students. But all cults have that advantage which rests on the fact, well-known to students of propaganda, that simplification introduced into confusion has high acceptance value. The worth of an educational policy must rather be evaluated by its long-run contributions to the pursuit of truth. . . . Systems have their function when eagerly developed by individuals, but their administrative imposition on a college can be only harmful in the end."

Skinner, in an unpublished memorandum written at that time (12), wondered what Wendt meant by a "cult." There was little description, Skinner continued, of the system embodied in the Columbia course, just an analysis of enthusiasts, dissenters, and inbreeding.

Skinner stated that the systematic position embodied in the course was not unique to him or to operant conditioning. Rather, he viewed the nature of the Columbia course as an undergraduate curriculum based upon logical analysis of the field of behavior rather than upon historical accidents or external reasons for emphasizing particular areas. Although such an approach involved omission and simplification, it remained a promising experiment in undergraduate teaching.

A comparison between Wendt's and Skinner's views indicates that they were not completely confronting each other. What concerned Wendt (14) was the prospect of increasing numbers of individuals becoming deeply committed to a systematic position, with restriction of systematic options and isolation of the approach within psychology. Skinner's response, in contrast, focused upon the idea system itself, stressing its relationship and value to psychology independent of the social means of development and perpetuation.

The fact that Wendt found criticism necessary is interpreted by respondents working at that time as follows: "It means we were having an effect. People don't bother to criticize things that aren't influential." Nor was Wendt alone in his criticism. What contributed to this conflict was the often militant posture of some operant conditioners in the late '40s and early '50s. As one respondent summarized the situation, "We were getting the tough guys [referring to the natural science-oriented students]. As they began to be good, they began to question their teachers. There was a sense of power. There is a little bit of arrogance. We could do things they couldn't do." Again, "you'd be really telling a guy that spent ten years of his life on a problem like latent learning, 'you wasted your time'. How do you expect him to respond? The essential fact about an aversive stimulus is that it reinforces any performance that removes it. And there is nothing more aversive than a threat of withdrawal of reinforcement when it concerns your bread and butter and your status." As one respondent characterized the early '50s: "It took guts to be an operant conditioner then. Everyone was belligerent."

Whether there was a "cult" of operant conditioners is largely a semantic question, but clearly a cluster of individuals existed at Columbia, and subsequently at Harvard, who perceived interrelationship in terms of a strong commitment to the operant orientation. Contributing to the feeling of a "group" were strong friendship relationships, frequently based on the sharing of a new and potent approach to psychology. As one respondent characterized Columbia of that period, "It was an exciting place. You could go into the laboratory and produce an observable behavioral change. People were excited and shared what they were finding." In part, the sense of a "group" was also fed by the outside criticism. "We never had any acceptance, so we banded together."

The Founding of JEAB

Whereas the discussions surrounding the Columbia program highlight the social separation between operant and non-operant conditioners, the following description of the founding of JEAB underlines the intellectual differences that were a primary basis for the social factionalism.

The impetus for founding this journal was the difficulty experienced by many operant conditioners in publishing their research in available psychological outlets. Most operant conditioners, in submitting their papers to JEP and JCPP, found a nonreceptive editorial policy. Although non-operant researchers also had difficulty in publishing during this same period, particularly in JCPP, the operant conditioners perceived their problems as being greater. The difficulties centered around the operant conditioner's employment of single subjects measured across time. Since both JEP and JCPP, the highest status outlets for animal research, were not accepting their articles, operant conditioners published their material in less visible sources, particularly in the *American Journal of Psychology* and *Science,* along with such lower-status outlets as the *Proceedings of the New York Academy of Sciences* and *Psychological Record.*

From the perspective of the operant conditioner the journals' evaluations were unfair and totally irrelevant to their stated concerns. Particularly, as one respondent pointed out, operant conditioning methodology is quite close to that of psychophysics; in this area the use of such designs was quite acceptable to the journals, particularly JEP. Rejection of the operant conditioner's animal studies, using a similar psychophysical design, was based, in part, on the modal nature of animal research where large-sample, between-groups designs were the norm, rather than upon what the operant conditioner considered reasonable "scientific" grounds. A unique archival source with editorial standards appropriate to the literature of operant conditioning was felt necessary.

The accounts of the founding of JEAB are conflicting on the question of whether a new journal was justifiable in terms of the amount of available operant conditioning literature extant at that time. It is generally agreed that the population of operant conditioners active in research in 1957 was approximately two dozen. Since the founding of JEAB, the movement has undergone marked growth. Testimony to this growth is the continued flourishing of JEAB. Moving from a state of concern as to whether the first year's issues would appear and from financing largely by the contributors, JEAB now has a constant flow of manuscripts and a large number of subscribers. Where the number of active researchers was approximately two dozen when JEAB was founded, by 1967 there were 342 unique authors with 125 (36.6 percent) contributing two or more articles to JEAB.

The most striking growth index of the movement is the increase in membership in Division 25 of the APA. Where the greatest percentage gain in members was 37 percent between 1966 and 1968 for all other APA divisions, Division 25 increased by 110 percent, with a rank of 16th out of 29 divisions. With the appearance of a recent handbook of operant research (5), the continuing flow of introductory and reading texts from an operant point of view, the exponential sale of *Walden II,* teaching machines, and the omnipresent Skinner box in most psychology departments, there is little question that operant conditioning is a vital movement within and outside psychology.

As the operant movement has grown, there have been gradual differentiations, with more specific research interests developing a sizeable number of practitioners, particularly in such areas as applied behavioral analysis and, in part, behavioral pharmacology. The following analysis of three internal changes — the founding of a second journal; the discussions surrounding a proposed third journal; and the perceptions of insiders and outsiders of the movement — raises the question as to whether these events represent not only expected internal differentiations but splinterings within the movement as well.

INTERNAL RELATIONS

The Founding of JABA

In 1967 a second operant journal, the *Journal of Applied Behavioral Analysis* (JABA), was organized. The founding of this journal constitutes, in contrast to JEAB, less of a break from established norms in psychology. Rather, it represents a development that was internal to the operant conditioning movement and, in addition, an assimilation of a partially separate set of developments.

Although the impetus for the founding of JABA arose partially from within JEAB, the individuals concerned with the domain of problems covered by JABA derive only in part out of the experimental JEAB tradition. A larger segment of the practitioners in this area developed from a partially separate tradition originating with Bijou and Baer. Neither Bijou nor Baer was originally trained in an operant orientation, but they came to use operant techniques in an applied setting while colleagues at the University of Washington. They and their students have developed a tradition that is intellectually similar to that of the experimental tradition.

The applied behavioral analysts have had few of the publication problems that faced the JEAB founders. One available outlet for their research has been JEAB; however, the frequency of applied papers has been relatively low. The general absence of applied literature in JEAB cannot be interpreted as a form of ingroup hostility to another part of the ingroup; rather, JEAB has made it very clear, in its editorial policy, that articles must meet certain criteria of control. One particularly vexing control problem for the applied behavioral analyst is the necessity to take the subject through a number of changes in conditions. Although such reversals are quite easy to perform on pigeons or rats, they are often difficult with children, psychotics, retardates, etc., the populations that interest the applied behavioral analyst. Thus some applied articles were rejected by JEAB for editorially defined reasons; however, some respondents questioned the narrowness of JEAB's concept of control.

It is important now to consider the relationships between JEAB and JABA. As the JABA people perceive it, their research provides a needed dimension to operant research; JABA provides the "acid test" for JEAB's findings. As indicated by the discussion surrounding the choice of title for the new journal, the concern of the applied behavioral analyst is not simply to show one more instance of how an experimental law operates;

rather, its direction is to test the power of these laws in different settings. As one respondent pointed out, many insignificant variables can produce seemingly potent effects because of the lack of competition among variables in highly controlled, limited settings. When such variables are placed in the "noisy" environment of real life, they may be of limited importance. Many of the behaviors investigated in laboratory settings do not represent "significant" responses of the organism to its environment for they are not part of his response repertoire in "real life" settings. It is the shared expectation of the applied behavioral analysts that the potency of experimental laboratory findings will be demonstrated again in such "noisy" settings.[5]

The JEAB respondent's perception of the applied behavioral analyst, at the time of JABA's founding, was multifaceted. The greatest percentage of JEAB respondents indicated that they were not sufficiently aware of the work of the applied behavioral analyst to make any judgment. A smaller percentage indicated a concern about the competence level of applied behavioral analysts, suggesting that they are less well trained, less able to control not because of the demands of the experimental situation, but rather as a function of insufficient methodological sophistication.

In addition, questions were raised about the applied behavioral field, centering around attempts to extend behavioral principles and laws to societal levels. From the perspective of both applied and experimental operant conditioner, such extensions are possible but have been inadequately represented by a small core of "zealots" who are concerned with the remaking of the world where the concept of control ceases to be a problem of science but becomes one of values and ethics. Generally respondents felt that such concerns by the intellectual community are irrelevant to their research activities since they fail to recognize the pure science ideal, embodied both in the experimental and applied traditions, which contains no implication concerning values and ethics.

A Third Journal (?)[6]

Where some JABA authors were critical of JEAB's concept of control, the individuals involved in the founding of a third operant journal question many of the editorial policies of both JEAB and JABA. These individuals seek both intellectual and financial separation from the already established operant journals.

The impetus behind the discussions of a third journal was the feeling that JEAB's and, to a lesser extent, JABA's editorial policy did not mirror the ongoing intellectual changes within the operant movement; rather, the editorial policies reflect an inbred conservative element in the field. It was felt that there is a broader spectrum of findings and issues in operant conditioning which are not being adequately represented in the two extant journals. As one individual commented, "JEAB is treating us like JCPP treated them."

The third journal is perceived by its founders as providing services not provided by JEAB and JABA, particularly a broader editorial policy allowing for dialogue between researchers through published commentary and reviews of findings. The journal's founders view themselves as representing a broad cross section of the field rather than as a "fringe" or "splinter" element within the movement. (A number of the individuals willing to serve on the new journal's editorial board have held similar positions on JEAB and JABA.) In short, from the perspective of the founders, the new journal is not directed at splintering the movement but at broadening its present boundaries.

Insiders' and Outsiders' Perception

The choice of operant conditioning as a case of a "school" was suggested by such outsider perceptions as follows:

> . . . Sometimes I am concerned by the fact that disciples of operant conditioning have formed a tight little club known as Division 25· (Experimental Analysis of Behavior). Here and in their *Journal of the Experimental Analysis of Behavior* they talk and write to each other, guaranteeing positive reinforcement on a rich, fixed or variable, interval schedule (3).
>
> Not since J. B. Watson's time has any band of behaviorists seemed so assertive in its likes and dislikes and so convinced that its techniques and experimental approach will not only change psychology but in the process reshape the world (4).

Whereas some outsiders see "school"-like activity, it was the overwhelming consensus of the respondents that this characterization was meaningless and failed to recognize the nature of ongoing activity. They pointed to the large differences in research interests, strategy, and even assumptions that distinguished many members of this so-called "school." Another aspect of this problem is suggested in the following remark: "Many individuals, myself included, use operant methods without subscribing to the religion."

The issue raised by this statement concerns the bases and criteria for perceived scientific affiliation and identity. For those younger psychologists (i.e., trained after the founding of JEAB) in the interview sample, professional identification was seldom as an operant conditioner. They perceived their work in terms of the topic of research rather than affiliation with a strategy of study. This perception was shared, as well, by the pre-1958 operant individuals, but they possessed, in addition, the awareness of participation in an historical set of events which are the shared properties of many operant conditioners and, in part, serve to define the identity of the group. Among these shared events are: the experience of outgroup hostility, the journals' rejection of their papers, the founding of JEAB, and education at

Columbia and Harvard. The relevant history for younger operant conditioners occurs within a period where the approach had its own journal and a sufficiently large number of active individuals in many subareas to sustain not only within-operant communication but communication within an operant specialty.

With success, the movement's cohesiveness has decreased with its internal differentiations and the increased blurring of its boundaries. When the group was small and the movement young, the sharing in the effectiveness of the approach and in a common history provided the source of identity. Now the approach has lost some of its newness, it has been proven successful to the point that a growing literature has evolved, technological innovations have been made in laboratory and environmental settings, and, at least on the instrumentation level, it has been incorporated in a number of areas within and outside psychology. But it is still the case that the research of many operant conditioners, however they identify themselves, remains distinct and unincorporated within psychology.

The question still remains as to whether there is a "school" of operant conditioners. The answer is a very qualified "yes" in the sense that there is a group of individuals who subscribe in varying degrees to the assumptions and strategies of a psychology initially proposed by Skinner. The character of the "school" has changed over time. Yet to call these individuals members or disciples of a "school" is to engage in stereotypic perception and to reify their activities on dimensions which are mysterious to the operant conditioner and often undelineated by the outsider.

For the operant conditioner, his daily activity consists in researching highly specialized research topics where there is only an implicit holding of underlying systematic assumptions. It is likely that when a state of attack occurs upon the assumptive base of these research activities, that "school"-like character of operant conditioning will be shown. Given the existing mutual isolation between operant and non-operant psychology, as embedded in the overall trend within psychology toward increasing, often nonoverlapping specializations, "school"-like confrontation seems decreasingly probable. The "Age of Schools" may still be with us — it is just that the conditions do not allow for their expression.

DISCUSSION

Broad issues can seldom be directly attacked in science. Each scientist examines one aspect of the broad issue in the expectation that the cumulative search of all researchers will solve the general problem. However, these smaller explorations often redefine themselves into problems of a general nature and develop an autonomous life.

How, then, can science reverse the trend of differentiation and achieve a cumulative, integrated, critically evaluated body of knowledge? Polanyi (10) suggests the mechanism of "mutual control."

> It consists . . . of the simple fact that scientists keep watch over each other. Each scientist is both subject to criticism by all others and encouraged by their appreciation of him. This is how *scientific opinion* is formed, which enforces scientific standards and regulates the distribution of professional opportunities. It is clear that only fellow scientists working in closely related fields are competent to exercise direct authority over each other; but their personal fields will form *chains of overlapping neighborhoods* extending over the entire range of science.

The present case study indicates that such mutual control breaks down if the scientists perceive that the control is inappropriate. In the case of the founding of JEAB, and the possible founding of a third operant journal, the existent editorial constraints were perceived as irrelevant and restrictive. By establishing a journal with standards specific to their concerns, the approach creates its own internal controls while at the same time providing potential immunization from external constraints.

What lies at the root of the mutual isolation of operant and non-operant psychology is differing belief systems on the nature of psychology, on the basis of which divergent views on such problems as method, modes of explanation, significance of problem areas, are derived. Whereas such differences in belief during the "Age of School-Systems" were related to different areas of study (for example, behaviorism and learning, Gestalt psychology and perception), the present divergences in belief exist in the same domain, namely, learning. When the same domain was studied during the era of schools and systems, direct confrontation often occurred in the form of controversy (8). It may well be a hallmark of the emergence of psychology from the era of "little science" to "big science" that, rather than confrontation, the contemporary strategy of conflict resolution is disregard.

In the case of the mutual isolation of operant conditioning and general psychology, there are differences in belief that differentiate operant conditioning from other approaches in psychology; to what extent these differences involve incommensurability between the conflicting systems is at this point unclear. However, given the perceived polarity between some operant conditioners and practitioners in other approaches in psychology, there appears to be little desire on the part of either side to shift, assimilate, and integrate the different faiths and the empirical generalizations generated from them.

Unless such attempts at integration occur, each segment will develop its own set of empirical priorities and its own list of criteria for acceptable research and scientific significance. Such a prognosis can only lead to increasing the already existing isolation, unless it turns out that one of the faiths — the faith of the operant conditioner or the faith of another approach to psychological knowledge — gains consensus, at least for some period of time.

NOTES

1. Given the difference in the number of JEAB and JVLVB articles available for potential citation during the journals' publication histories, a conditional probability index of citations could have been employed for Figures 1 and 2. However, the determination of an appropriate available pool of citable papers necessary for such a weighting involved so many arbitrary decisions and assumptions that the present more direct measure appeared the least biased.
2. Comparison of the JEAB and JVLVB self-citation slopes, for comparable publication histories (JEAB, 1958-1965; JVLVB, 1962-1969) yielded a $t = 4.68$, $df = 7$, $p < .01$.
3. A 2 x 4 analysis of variance indicates a significant difference in the incorporation rate of JVLVB vs. JEAB citation by their respective source journals. This effect is interactive with years, with the major divergences appearing in 1968 ($t = 5.70$, $df = 597$, $p < .01$) and 1969 ($t = 2.92$, $df = 527$, $p < .01$).
4. Respondents expect that the new journal, *Learning and Motivation,* will replace JCPP as the primary source for JEAB, with high reciprocity of citation between them. Editorial changes in JCPP have led some authors interested in JEAB findings now to publish in this new journal.
5. The foregoing discussion implies that JABA research will be more dependent on JEAB than vice versa. It has been suggested that applied settings will not solely test the generality of findings from laboratory environments but may feedback new variables and dimensions to the laboratory for study. Since JABA has, at the time of this writing (September 1970), only a two-year publication history, it is premature to determine any trends in reciprocal citation between JEAB and JABA.
6. At the time of this writing (September 1970) the journal's founders had organized a steering committee for evaluating the feasibility of such a journal.

REFERENCES

1. Deese, J. & Hulse, S. *The psychology of learning.* 3rd edition. New York: McGraw-Hill, 1967.
2. Hall, J. *The psychology of learning.* Philadelphia: J. B. Lippincott & Co., 1966.
3. Harlow, H. William James and instinct theory. In R. MacLeod (Ed.), *William James: Unfinished business.* Washington, D. C.: American Psychological Association, 1969.
4. Hearst, E. The behavior of Skinnerians. *Contemporary Psychology,* 1967, *12,* 402-404.
5. Honig, W. (Ed.), *Operant behavior: Areas of research and application.* New York: Appleton-Century-Crofts, 1966.
6. Keller, F. & Schoenfeld, W. N. The psychology curriculum at Columbia College. *American Psychologist,* 1949, *4,* 165-172.
7. Keller, F. & Schoenfeld, W. N. *Principles of psychology.* New York: Appleton-Century, 1950.
8. Krantz, D. L. The Baldwin-Titchener controversy. In D. Krantz (Ed.), *Schools of psychology.* New York: Appleton-Century-Crofts, 1969.

9. Kuhn, T. *The structure of scientific revolutions.* Chicago: University of Chicago Press, 1962.
10. Polanyi, M. *The tacit dimension.* Garden City, New York: Doubleday & Co., 1966.
11. Skinner, B. F. *The behavior of organisms.* New York: Appleton-Century, 1938.
12. Skinner, B. F. Private communication, 1970.
13. Wendt, R. The development of a psychological cult. *American Psychologist,* 1949, *4,* 426.
14. Wendt, R. Personal communication, 1970.
15. Xhinghesse, L. V. & Osgood, C. E. Bibliographical citation characteristics of the psychological journal network in 1950 and 1960. *American Psychologist,* 1967, *22,* 778-791.

BACKGROUND
STUDIES

Five Classic Doctrines
of Man

ROBERT B. MACLEOD

The alternative doctrines of man may be classified and subclassified in many ways. For the sake of simplicity we shall identify them as they emerged in the early history of psychology. We shall call these the *classic doctrines of man*. As the Greeks and early Christians wrestled with the problem of understanding man's place in the universe, they propounded, at varying times, five significantly different ways in which man can be understood. Each of these has survived the test of history. Each has absorbed the content furnished by fresh thought and new discovery, but each still stands as a challenge to curiosity.

The early Greeks were seeking for a simple way in which nature and life could be understood. Some writers have referred to this early period as the hylozoistic period, a period during which they sought a *hule* (fundamental substance), which could be united with a *zoe* (principle of life). The hylozoists were pioneer scientists. They looked outward upon the world and tried to find a reasonable explanation for it. Yet they realized, perhaps dimly, that they, the theorists, had something to do with the nature of the theories they were building. The early Greeks gave us theories of nature; but implicit in their theories was the thought that man, the theorist, might be an integral part of the process of theory building. Greek curiosity naturally and inevitably became focused upon man.

Historians sometimes call this second period the anthropological period, the period during which scientific inquiry gradually became directed toward the study of man, and philosophers began to appreciate the role of the human factor in the direction of philosophic thought. This is probably an oversimplification, since Greek philosophers at all times included man in their attempts to explain nature. Nevertheless, about the beginning of the fifth century B.C., there emerged a group of teachers, known as the Sophists (wise men), who courageously challenged the traditions of their elders and kept insisting that philosophic inquiry, i.e., scientific inquiry, should begin with the study of man. How can one develop a theory of the world, they asked, without first scrutinizing the processes whereby one perceives and

This is an abridged version of a chapter in a forthcoming book, *Persistent Problems of Psychology*.

131

thinks? It was the Sophists who for the first time made human experience and behavior a legitimate subject for scientific inquiry.

PROTAGORAS AND THE RELATIVISTIC DOCTRINE OF MAN

The greatest of the Sophists was undoubtedly Protagoras (480-411 B.C.). "Man is the measure of all things." This is the quotation for which Protagoras is famous. To paraphrase, "Everything that we know is in part a function of the knowing agent." The data of direct experience may be accepted as such; what is not given in direct experience must always be questioned. Protagoras kept insisting, on the one hand, that the scientist should never depart from the available data, and, on the other hand, that he should scrutinize the available data and squeeze them for what they are worth. The implication is that knowledge may extend beyond immediate experience, but that, in the last analysis, the intents and the limitations of the thinker will determine the nature of the product.

The Protagorean doctrine dramatizes a distinction that runs through Greek philosophy — indeed, through all philosophy — namely, the distinction between appearance and reality. Appearances *(phenomena,* in the correct sense of the term) are the familiar things, events, and relationships of everyday perception. That appearances are deceptive is a truism. The stick in the water appears bent; the tiny cavity in the tooth feels large to the tongue; the mirage in the desert, the hallucinations of the insane, the faces in the clouds — all are appearances that are clearly at variance with reality. If our direct experience is limited to appearances, how can we discover what is real? Sometimes we think we have adequate tests. We can withdraw the stick from the water and see that it is "really" straight; we can look at the tooth-cavity in a mirror and see that it is "really" small. When we do so, however, we are merely substituting one percept for another; the second percept, however more satisfying it may be, is no less an appearance than is the first. Even when we demonstrate a high degree of coherence among our percepts, we have no assurance that we are perceiving what is really there. At best, said Protagoras, we can have an opinion; even if we have true knowledge, we can never know that it is true.

The challenge of Protagoras is even more disturbing when we leave the realm of simple perception and begin to construct theories. Just as what I perceive is a function of my powers of perception, so what I think is a function of my thought processes. The world of the worm is limited to what the worm can perceive and comprehend; the world of man is structured by the capacities and motives of man. The perceiver and thinker can never transcend his own perceiving and thinking processes.

Protagoras presents us with a relativistic philosophy, with man as the inescapable determiner of all relations. Philosophers have responded to relativism with two types of answer. One answer, skepticism, is defeatist. The skeptic simply concedes that he does not know anything; his brother, the agnostic asserts not merely that he does not know anything, but that he cannot know anything. Both can easily be tripped. We can ask the question: Is the statement "I do not know anything" a true statement? The agnostic must answer "yes," in which case he has affirmed a truth and denied his position. If the skeptic answers with "I do not know whether or not I know anything," he is then asked the further question, "Is it true that you do not know?" And so *ad infinitum*. But there have been no really skeptical philosophers. The more common response of philosophers has been to try to find within the data of experience a justification for the transcending of experience. The very phenomena (appearances) themselves, they say, require us to believe in the existence of a reality that is nonphenomenal and about which we can make true statements. And these statements, they add, are not dictated by man's perceiving and thinking processes; they represent, rather, the accommodation of man's perception and thought to what is independent of man's perceiving and thinking.

The direct consequences of relativism for psychological theory may be recognized in three types of emphasis that have recurred from time to time in the history of our subject. We shall term these (1) phenomenalism, (2) projection theory, and (3) introjection theory. Each is a logically definable position which, in actual fact, is seldom defended without reservation or compromise.

The *phenomenalist* would accept at face value the Protagorean thesis that the individual cannot transcend the world of appearances, but would argue that appearances (phenomena) are worth studying in their own right. For him, psychology can be nothing more than the observation, description, and classification of phenomena. Since we can have no independent knowledge of an external world, of a deity, or of any other postulated reality, it is fruitless to try to correlate phenomena with the constructs of the other sciences. In fact, the consistent phenomenalist would have to argue that, since the pointer readings of the physicist or astronomer, the observations of the biologist, and the conceptualizations of the historian are all, in the last analysis, human experiences, therefore these sciences can represent nothing more than the ordering of arbitrary selections of phenomena. From this point of view, each of the other sciences must be regarded as a subdivision of psychology. While such a thesis has occasionally been advanced, it has never won many followers.

The *projection theorist* takes as his starting point the motivated individual, and proceeds to demonstrate the relativity of all other psychological phenomena to the inescapable fact of motivation. We believe what we wish to believe, we accept as legitimate goals of conduct only those that are consonant with our basic needs, we perceive even the size and color of objects in accordance with their "value" to us. The world, as man apprehends it, is merely an outward projection of man's inner needs, desires, aspirations, and anxieties. God, the projectionist would assert, was made in the image of man, not man in the image of God.

One of the best examples of projection is the ink blot test, developed and standardized by the Swiss psychiatrist, Rorschach. Rorschach found that what you see seems to depend on the kind of person you are. It is as though you project into the ink blot the essential characteristics of yourself. In a similar way, a picture — the Thematic Apperception Test — will yield from different people widely different stories, each person "projecting" into the picture a meaning that reveals his own inner propensities and conflicts. There seems to be ample evidence to support the judgment that the way things appear to us depends in important ways on the way in which we ourselves are organized.

Projection theory is thus a relativism of the world to the individual. Its basic datum is the motivated individual, and it sees the world as a projection — a throwing out — of the individual's characteristics. Psychology, from this point of view, is an expansion of the theory of motivation.

Introjection theory is the opposite of projection theory. It is a relativism of the individual to the world. Its most common expression is in the theory of cultural relativity, a doctrine which has recently received considerable support from anthropological researches. The introjection theorist sees the individual as a creature of his culture. It is a fact of common observation that people of approximately the same biological constitution, but born and reared in different cultures, develop in accordance with the pattern of their culture.

The introjection theory is thus a learning-oriented theory. Man is to be conceived, not as a dynamo of energy, dictating and shaping his world, but as a lump of putty, conforming to pressures that come from without. The individual becomes an individual as he is battered into shape by forces over which he has no control.

DEMOCRITUS AND THE MATERIALISTIC DOCTRINE OF MAN

Perhaps the easiest, and certainly the most popular, escape from relativism is by way of materialism. The materialist argues that basic reality is of the nature of matter, and that the phenomena regarded as mental are merely other forms of material substance. The materialist philosophy had its followers among the Greeks, and in one form or another it has been accepted as a working philosophy by possibly a majority of modern scientists.

Our Greek example of the systematic materialist is Democritus (ca. 460-ca. 370 B.C.). Only fragments of his writings have come down to us, but these are impressive. The evidence indicates that many centuries before the emergence of modern atomic physics, Democritus had conceived of the universe as composed of an infinite number of small, indivisible, indestructible units ("atom" means "uncuttable"), differing only in size, shape, weight, and motion. The popular belief before Democritus was in four fundamental but essentially different types of substance — earth, air, fire, and water — the mixture of which in varying proportions could account for all the phenomena of nature. But Democritus, with his passion for simplicity, could not rest content with a pluralism of elements. There must, he believed, be one primary substance to which everything can be reduced. This substance might take different forms and behave in different ways, but there must be an underlying unity to nature. The explanation of nature must ultimately be in terms of what we now call physics. In the last analysis, there can be no laws other than the laws of physical science.

This is the essence of the materialist position. But how does the materialist account for the phenomena of mind? For Democritus, the answer lay in the atoms. Atoms are indivisible and indestructible, but they differ in size, shape, and motion. Some atoms are smaller, smoother, and livelier than others. These are the "soul" atoms. When a person thinks, the "soul" atoms are agitated; when he wills, the motion is transmitted outward; when he perceives, atoms from the outside world pass through the sense organs and set up similar motions in the "soul" atoms. Thus the apparent difference between the mental and the physical is overcome. Mind and matter are essentially the same, mind being merely a subtler form of matter.

Democritus was first and foremost a physicist, but he seems to have developed a fairly complete psychology within the limits of his atomic theory, even assigning different psychological functions to different parts of the body — thought to the brain, anger to the heart, appetite to the liver — and he found the secret of the good life in gentle motions of the soul-atoms. Our interest, however, is less in his specific conclusions than in the broad doctrine of man he presents. For Democritus, man is a part of physical nature, to be explained in terms of physical laws. His psychology is the prototype of a psychology that has been popular for more than two hundred years.

The materialistic doctrine of man in ancient Greece did not long survive Democritus. An alternative doctrine propounded by Plato found readier followers, and the grand synthesis of Aristotle, reinterpreted by the Christian Church, was to dominate the thinking of the Western world for many centuries. The materialist faith in physical science was never completely lost, but in an intellectual world ruled by the theologians a frank materialism came to be regarded as a heresy of the worst sort. With the emergence of the new science of the sixteenth century, a materialistic account of physical nature began to appear possible, but it was not until the eighteenth and nineteenth centuries that any serious efforts were made to reestablish it as a doctrine of man.

Modern materialism in psychology began with the Newtonian revolution in physics; it gained strength as Darwin began to close the gap between man and animal and must now be regarded as the doctrine of man most generally accepted by scientists. True, the conception of matter is being drastically revised by modern physicists, but the prevailing materialist view is that, however we conceive of matter, there is nothing in the structure or functioning of man that cannot eventually be restated in terms of physical law.

PLATO AND THE IDEALISTIC DOCTRINE OF MAN

Simple, massive, and convincing as was the materialism of Democritus, it was a radically different alternative to the relativistic doctrine of man that appealed most strongly to the Greeks. Not the physical but the mental, not matter but reason, promised to furnish the laws in terms of which man and his relation to the universe could be understood. The system became known as Idealism, a system that encompassed not merely psychology but also all the other basic philosophic disciplines, and that was destined to guide a great tradition that has continued to the present. Greek idealism asserted that the Idea, the rationally derived concept, is the fundamental element of reality, that the material world is only a partial expression, even a degradation, of the world of ideas. Man, from the point of view of the idealist, is a partial embodiment of ideal realities that transcend the world of matter.

The great spokesman for Greek Idealism is Plato (427-347 B.C.), but the thinking of Plato can never be divorced from that of his teacher, Socrates (ca. 470-399 B.C.). Socrates might be listed as one of the Sophists, i.e., a member of the new profession of teachers who contributed so richly to the intellectual life of Athens during the fifth century B.C. He thought of himself as a "spiritual midwife," whose privilege it was to assist his pupils in the birth of their ideas. Sometimes the birth was painful, and sometimes the product was a monstrosity, but Socrates had faith in the process of reasoning. Through the dialogues of Plato we gain the impression of Socrates as a diabolically ingenious debater, humble before the truth, but never before an opponent. It is clear that Socrates challenged both the relativistic and materialistic doctrines of man. He believed that reason was not only a capacity of man, but a force that could penetrate appearances and reveal reality in its true form There is no moral problem, he insisted, that cannot be solved by clear thinking. In the last analysis, virtue and knowledge are one. Like Protagoras, he believed that the first duty of the scientist is to understand himself; unlike Protagoras, however, he believed that self-knowledge contains within itself the means whereby the world of appearances can be transcended. One of the most interesting of Plato's Dialogues is the *Protagoras,* in which Socrates is presented as the opponent of relativism. How much is Socrates and how much is Plato, we cannot say; but at least we have here Plato's answer to the relativistic challenge.

For the idealist, the inescapable fact about man is that he can think and that, by clear thinking, he can discern the reality behind appearances. Thinking, then, not mere observation, is the true instrument of science; and the finest example of science is obviously mathematics. In mathematics we may have to compromise with appearances when we use algebraic symbols and geometric designs, but the sensory content of these is irrelevant. It matters little whether we use x or y, alpha or beta, to represent a quantity, whether we convey the notion of triangularity by red or green, thick or thin lines. The idea of quantity or of triangularity is what is essential, and the more skilled we become, the less we depend on sensory supports. Any triangle we may draw is imperfect, but this does not hinder us from grasping the essence of triangularity. In mathematics we come closest to commerce with pure ideas.

Science, from the idealist's point of view, is thus a discovery. The ideas are there to begin with as the essential structure of reality. The philosopher (scientist) is the one who can apprehend the ideas most clearly. The ideas of causality, of opposition, of beauty, and of goodness are not products of the scientist's thinking; they are part of the reality that is gradually becoming known to him. His knowledge can never be complete, for reality contains more ideas than the human mind can ever grasp, but he has in the inner consistency of his own thinking an indication as to whether or not he is on the right track. Truth is there for us, and it is up to us to learn how to recognize it.

Plato's doctrine of man is built on the assumption that man is a rational being who, through reason, can come to a knowledge of reality, but whose reason is often disorganized by irrational forces. From Plato we have inherited the famous doctrine of "the faculties," a doctrine that has had a long and honorable history and is now generally rejected; but it has had such a universal appeal that it cannot be lightly discarded. The Platonic doctrine was altered somewhat by the Christians, and it is still with us. When in our judgments of ourselves and others we distinguish between "rational" and "irrational," between "higher" and "lower," we are speaking the language of Plato.

Plato's doctrine of man comes out most clearly in the *Republic*. No idealist can divorce his psychology from his ethics, esthetics, epistemology, and metaphysics. In the *Republic* it is the problem of social ethics that absorbs Plato, and in trying to solve it, he presents his psychology. What, he asks, is the nature of justice? Justice is a social concept that demands a theory of society. Through the wit and wisdom of Socrates, Plato examines and deflates all the standard theories of social justice: justice as the interest of the stronger, justice as a social compromise, and so forth. He concludes that the principles that underlie the just state must reflect the principles in accordance with which the individual attains the Good Life. What are these principles? In the good state there are three classes of people: the workers, who cannot be entrusted with many decisions, and whose virtues are industry and sobriety; the soldiers (auxiliaries), who must defend the state and whose virtue is courage; and the philosopher-kings (guardians), who make the decisions and whose virtue is wisdom. Thus in the ideal state there are those who think, those who enforce the decisions of the thinkers, and those who do the work. It is a good state when all elements are in harmony with one another, with the wise men taking the lead.[1]

The state is, however, really a reflection of the nature of the individual. Corresponding to the three classes of society, there are in the human soul three fundamental divisions of powers: appetite, spirit, and reason. If the Good Life is to be achieved, reason, supported by spirit, must maintain control over appetite. In Plato we have the finest statement of the Greek ideal of the Life of Reason as the highest goal of man.

Let us take a closer look at each of the three parts of the soul, as Plato describes them.

1. The appetitive part is man's lower nature, and Plato characteristically locates the appetites in the lower portions of the body. In modern terminology, the appetites might be labeled as instincts, primary drives, or basic needs. In the Freudian system they are assigned to the Id. The appetites cannot be disregarded, for they are essential to living; but they are irrational, and they must be kept under control.

2. The spirited part is a little more difficult to identify, but Plato seems to have had in mind the power in man that gives him courage. He located it in the heart, and in his social analogue he likened it to the soldier class. In Plato's thinking, man's spirit was linked with his reason as part of his higher nature. It accounts for ambition, tenacity of purpose, defiance of danger. Like a spirited stallion, it can carry one to victory; but, also like the stallion, it can run wild and create havoc unless it has a skillful rider.

3. The rational faculty is man's supreme endowment. Through reason man can attain truth, recognize beauty, and achieve the Good Life. Reason enables man to penetrate the world of appearances and grasp the real world of Ideas. Like Democritus, Plato located reason in the head (possibly, it is suggested, because the head is the most nearly spherical portion of the body, and the sphere is the mathematically perfect figure), but its location in the body is unimportant. Reason is the highest faculty of an immaterial and immortal soul. When the soul takes up residence in the body, it is inevitably hampered, and sometimes degraded, by the association; but it can, through reason, progress toward emancipation. When man achieves the Life of Reason, he has conquered his appetites and is living in the World of Ideas.

There are few contemporary psychologists who could identify themselves as idealists, and still fewer who would call themselves Platonists. Idealism is not popular today. Nevertheless there is much in modern psychology which, possibly unrecognized, is reminiscent of Plato's doctrine of man. Plato's conception of the human soul as an immaterial entity that pre-exists, takes temporary residence in a body, and then — when the body dies — flits to another body in another world, has been incorporated into many theological systems, but in recent times it has seldom found favor with scientists.

The truly crucial points might be listed as follows:

1. Man is to be understood as in essence nonmaterial. He deals with the material world, but he is not a part of it. Thus the reductive procedure of the materialist is rejected.

2. Man possesses certain unique faculties that differentiate him from all nonliving things, and possibly from the animals. The highest of these is reason. He is thus a rational being.

3. Since the capacity for reasoning is what permits man to grasp the ideas which constitute the essence of reality, the understanding of man himself must be based on the logical analysis of his experience. An idealistic psychology is likely to be a rigorously deductive system, using the test of logical consistency rather than that of correspondence with observation.

Much of Plato's rationalism was absorbed into the later Aristotelian and Christian psychologies. Something akin to a pure Platonism might be recognized in the recurrent attempts to explain the nature of man in terms of formal logical and mathematical models. Such an effort was made in the early nineteenth century by Herbart. More recent examples might be drawn from the factor analysis movement. When, for instance, the psychologist uses statistical tools to identify the "pure" factors in intelligence or personality, he does not pretend that these factors are data of direct observation or that they will ever be directly observed; they are deduced from observation and tested by logic and mathematics. Yet, as the psychologist progressively refines his analysis, he believes that he is approaching a series of statements that are true. The factors are not entities in a material world; they are more like Plato's ideas, essential relationships to which the material world conforms.

ARISTOTLE AND THE TELEOLOGICAL DOCTRINE OF MAN

Aristotle's philosophy is regarded by some scholars as a major alternative to that of Plato, and by others as essentially an extension and systematization of Plato's thought. The issue need not concern us here. In the Aristotelian treatment of man, however, we find a central principle which, although present in Plato, is developed with such clarity as to warrant its being labeled an Aristotelian doctrine. This is the teleological principle, in terms of which the understanding of man is to be sought in the implicit purpose which gradually reveals itself in his development. The battle over the status of purpose in scientific explanation always goes back to Aristotle.

Not only did Aristotle (384-322 B.C.) explore and write about the problems of all the traditional philosophic disciplines; he also systematized and enriched the store of knowledge in all the sciences of nature. For the psychologist the basic source is *De Anima,* but Aristotle's psychological theories crop up in many other works as well, notably the *Logic,* the *Ethics,* the *Poetics,* the *Rhetoric,* and even in his work on biology.

Before examining the Aristotelian doctrine of man, we must examine briefly his general approach and a few of his basic concepts. Aristotle has sometimes been classed as a Realist, but the meaning of this term has been so confused in its history that it adds little to our understanding. He could with equal correctness be classed as an Idealist, for his philosophy resembles that of Plato more than it does that of many of the modern Realists. Aristotle agreed with Plato in rejecting a simple materialism and in insisting that a final explanation must be in terms of nonmaterial principles. He disagreed with Plato's belief in Ideas as independent existences; for him the Ideas are the forms of material substance, except in the case of God, who is Pure Form. Thus the Ideas cannot, except through a process of abstraction, be separated from matter, any more than matter can be conceived, except through abstraction, as an independent existent. The task of the philosopher-scientist is, through the study of formed matter in all its concrete instances, to derive the principles of form (the Ideas). Thus one of the crucial differences between the two lies in the role they accorded to the observation of particular instances. For Plato, the particular thing or event can conveniently *illustrate* a principle that unfettered reason can grasp directly without observation; observation of the particular is, as it were, a pedagogical device, an aid to communication. For Aristotle, *the principles reveal themselves through the observation of particulars,* although the principles cannot be formulated except through the operation of reason.

The Aristotelian method in science is that of observation, classification, and then deduction of implications. The revival of Aristotle's method of induction had much to do with the emergence of the new science in the sixteenth century.

If we are to understand the Aristotelian doctrine of man, however, we must be clear about the conceptual framework within which he observed, classified, and interpreted the phenomena of nature. It is immaterial whether we regard this as a set of preconceptions or as a set of conclusions. To oversimplify, here are some of the main concepts we must keep in mind:

1. *Matter and form.* Any object exists as a concrete reality in space and time. It is composed of something (matter), but it exists only as something particular (a stone, a tree, a human body); i.e., it is formed matter. Through a process of abstraction one can conceive of formless matter or matterless form, but these are simply conceptions. The reality we know is matter that has form; but form cannot be reduced to terms of matter.

2. *Potential and actual.* Potential means "what is possible"; actual means "what is." A block of marble is potentially a great number of

different statues, but it is not potentially a human being. A human being is potentially a criminal or a saint, but he is not potentially an elephant. In each case the actual form of matter has placed certain restrictions on the number and kind of forms that might be actualized from it. The hypothetical formless matter is potentially anything, since it contains all possible forms. Thus any actual thing contains various potentialities, but the range of these is a function of actual form.

3. *Inherent properties.* Formed matter has certain properties, but some of these are essential and others are accidental. A piece of iron, when dropped, will fall to the ground rather than float in the air, because iron is inherently heavy. Heavy objects fall; light objects, like balloons, rise. The same piece of iron might be heated or cooled, but its particular temperature is an accident of circumstance. Iron is heavy, but it is not essentially hot or cold. So far as temperature is concerned, the only inescapable fact about iron is that it is capable of variations. This capacity is inherent in iron, but the particular temperature is an accident. Thus we may distinguish between properties that are inherent and properties that are accidental. If we wish to know the true nature of the object, we must identify the properties that are really inherent.

4. *Causality.* The answer to the question "why?" naturally begins with "because." When you release the stone, why does it fall? Because you dropped it? Because it is heavy? Or because of something else? Whatever follows the word "because" reveals your theory of causality.

For Aristotle there are four types of cause, all of which participate in every event: the material, the efficient, the formal, and the final. Let us consider the familiar billiard ball example. Ball A, struck by the cue, strikes Ball B, and then Ball B moves at the appropriate angle with the appropriate velocity. What causes the movement of Ball B? The efficient cause is clearly the force transmitted from A to B. But we must also consider the material cause. If A were a balloon, it would not cause the same movement in B. Then there is a formal cause; the flatness of the table and the roundness of the balls are also important. "On a cloth untrue with a twisted cue and elliptical billiard balls," the result would be quite different. Lastly, there is the intent of the billiard player. If he is a skillful player, he has taken advantage of all the other conditions to produce the desired result. The purpose expressed through the event is the final cause. ("Final" here means "end," not in the sense of "coming to a stop," but in the sense of "goal to be attained.")

Material, formal, and efficient causes are all consonant with a materialist explanation. The materialist explains events in terms of antecedent and concomitant conditions. What Aristotle added was the final cause, the teleological principle without which, he believed, no object or event in nature could be fully explained.

5. *The teleological principle.* Teleology means the doctrine of ends or purposes. To be a teleologist is to insist that we cannot understand a thing or an event without reference to the purpose behind it or inherent in it.

There are two kinds of teleology: a transcendent and an immanent (indwelling) teleology. The transcendent teleologist believes in a purpose behind events, possibly in a God who has planned in advance all that is to come. Nearly all the traditional religions have been centered on a transcendent teleology. The immanent teleologist believes that there is an inherent purposiveness within the processes of nature. Nature as a whole, and every process within nature, is directed toward a goal.

Aristotle shared with the enlightened Greeks of his day a belief in a Supreme Being who embodied the *Summum Bonum* (the Highest Good), who was the First Cause and the Final Cause of all existence. In this sense he was a transcendent teleologist. For us, however, it is Aristotle's immanent teleology that is interesting. He believed that the purposes of the Supreme Being are built into nature. Every natural object or process has its *entelechy* (inherent purpose) in accordance with which it behaves. It is appropriate that light objects should rise and heavy objects fall; that cats should behave like cats and dogs like dogs; that man, if he is to be fully human, should exercise his capacity for reasoning.

Aristotle's teleology thus brings into a single focus his distinctions between matter and form, potential and actual, essential and accidental properties, and final causes as contrasted with the other types of cause. Any object is to be regarded as having its own inner nature which is gradually actualized as it comes into being, the discovery of which is the basis of our true understanding of it.

Within this framework Aristotle gives us a consistent interpretation of man. It is true that man is a part of physical nature, i.e., is composed of matter; but the essence of man, the soul, belongs in the category of form. It is something that is gradually actualized during the course of his development. Soul is not to be regarded, after the fashion of Plato, as something essentially independent of the body; it is, rather, the formal principle in accordance with which the body operates. Aristotle is accordingly much less convinced than was Plato of the immortality of the soul. He concedes that the rational principle is indestructible, but whether it can survive as a concrete entity is less clear.

In the first chapter of *De Anima,* Aristotle defines the problem of psychology as that of ascertaining "the nature and essence of soul and its attributes." The essence of soul, we have seen, is that it is a formal principle, the form of organization of the body. But what are its attributes? The attributes of soul can be ascertained only through systematic observation. In his speculation about "essences," Aristotle was carrying on the rational tradition of Plato, a tradition that was to dominate psychological thought for many centuries. In his search for "attributes," he was launching the empirical movement in psychology. Rational psychology is concerned with the origin, the nature, and the destiny of the soul. Empirical psychology is concerned with the observation, classification, and interpretation of the manifestations of soul in human experience and behavior. For Aristotle, both kinds of psychology were legitimate; but the empirical movement in psychology was not revived until long after the rebirth of science in the sixteenth century. Aristotle's empirical findings were frozen into a rational pattern, and his spirit of empirical inquiry was lost.

The inherent purpose of any object is to behave in accordance with its own inner nature. Just as a ship that is too long and narrow to maintain stability is not a proper ship, and a horse that has lost one of its limbs is not a proper horse, so a man whose conduct is not guided by reason is not behaving as a proper man. The task of the scientist is to gain an understanding of the inner nature of things, to observe particular structures and processes, and to show how they play a part in fulfilling general purposes.

What, then, are the essential structures and purposes of man? Aristotle's analysis is too rich and detailed to be presented here. Essentially, man is an animal, but he is a *rational* animal. As an animal he possesses the structures necessary for growth, reproduction, perception, and locomotion. His animal nature provides him with appetites which, as Plato had pointed out, must be kept under control; with senses which enable him to respond to the world about him; with mobility which permits him to escape danger and pursue his goals. As a rational being he behaves within the context of his animal nature, but he is able to transcend it. Reason, however, cannot operate by itself; it must make use of what is furnished by the lower faculties. The laws of pure reason are to be found in the discipline of Logic, but reasoning as it actually takes place is clouded by perception, memory, and imagination. Hence Aristotle's interest in the lower faculties.

Aristotle's study of the processes of cognition gave us a theory, possibly wrong but beautifully simple, which has appealed to psychologists ever since. The basis is the doctrine of the senses. There are five senses, the gateways of the mind: vision, audition, taste, smell, and touch, which give us the five basic qualities out of which all experience is constructed. There is, besides, a *sensus communis,* a second-order common sense that integrates the data of the individual senses into percepts; and there are the capacities of memory and imagination which permit us to retain and recombine the data of the several senses and preserve them as ideas. There are, furthermore, the principles of association — similarity, contrast, and contiguity in space and time — which account for the fact that one idea can suggest another. Thus, even before reason enters in, we find that mental life, like physical nature, is behaving in accordance with law. Sensations, percepts, and ideas are phenomena of nature that can be studied as such and can form the basis of a science. This is perhaps Aristotle's greatest contribution to the scientific study of man.

The rational principle, however, was for Aristotle something to be derived not from observation but from logical deduction, and the laws of thinking are, accordingly, the laws of logic. Knowledge has as its content the data of the senses, organized and interpreted by reason. The central faculty of reason is thus the only faculty of the soul that can apprehend pure form, i.e., can abstract form from its material setting, and can consequently know truth. In his treatment of reason, Aristotle follows in the footsteps of his teacher Plato. Even today psychologists still find it difficult to disentangle the empirical psychology of thinking from the formal categories of logic.

Aristotle's distinction between peripheral sensory processes and central intellective processes has played an important role in the history of cognitive theory. The assumption is that certain elementary data (givens) are provided by the senses and that these are then reworked by the mind. The persistent question is: How much of knowledge comes from the senses, and how much from the mind?

THE RELIGIOUS DOCTRINE OF MAN

It is with some hesitation that one speaks of *the* religious doctrine of man. The religions of the world have been so varied in their beliefs and practices that one sometimes despairs of finding any common characteristics. Nevertheless each religion has contained an implicit doctrine of man, and one is tempted to believe that all religions, from the most "primitive" to the most "emancipated," have enough in common to distinguish their doctrine of man from the nonreligious doctrines. Religion will here be identified as an attitude which involves: (1) a belief in an order of reality that transcends the material, which may or may not be personified as a deity; (2) a feeling of reverence (self abasement, or possibly only fear) with respect to the transcendent order; and (3) the acceptance of certain obligations upon personal conduct, which may be merely constraints. Religions have differed in their relative emphasis on these three components — some stressing theology, others ritual, and still others ethics — but all three are present to some extent in every religion. From the religious point of view, man must be considered as something apart from the natural order of things; or else, nature must be reinterpreted in terms other than those of conventional science.

Both Plato and Aristotle might, according to these criteria, be considered as exponents of a religious doctrine, and some of the teachings of both were absorbed into Christian theology. Their doctrines, however, were essentially rationalistic. Although God, as in Aristotle, might be identified as Pure Reason, neither Plato nor Aristotle believed that the understanding of man required the assumption of supernatural laws. The best examples of the religious doctrine of man are to be found in the religions of the Middle East and the Far East. For our present purpose, the Hebraic-Christian tradition will have to suffice.

The religion of the West is rooted in the Hebraic tradition. The Hebrew conception is of man as a free spirit. Whereas the Greek philosophers paid little more than lip service to their religion, and Greek rationalism is consequently at bottom an alternative to, rather than an interpretation of, the current religious doctrines, the thinking of the Hebrew prophets was centered on the implications for conduct of an unchallenged religious faith. There was no room in the Hebrew tradition for the kind of free speculation that secured for Athens its unique place in intellectual history, for to think freely would be a denial of faith. The Hebrews consequently gave us no great philosophic systems. Nevertheless, the Hebrew faith in God, when combined with the Greek faith in reason, was destined to give us an elaborate philosophy that included a clear and consistent doctrine of man.

The Christian doctrine of man was first formulated by Paul (d. ca. 67 A.D.). Paul's heritage and education included the culture of both the Hebrews and the Greeks. Paul's religion is a religion *about* Jesus, not to be confused with the religion *of* Jesus. Jesus belongs in the tradition of the Hebrew prophets who believed that they had a mission from God to save their people. For him, deliverance (salvation) was the result of an inner act of self-dedication to the will of God. "He that loseth his life, will save it."

The Christian doctrine of man must be understood in the context of Christian theology. For the early Christians the ultimate reality is God, the creator of the universe, the shaper of man's destiny. God is a spirit, transcending space and time, omniscient, omnipresent, and omnipotent. Man is also a spirit, i.e., he contains within him a spark of the divine, but he is a spirit enclosed within a mortal body. Only as he conquers the weaknesses of the flesh is he able to achieve full communion with God and attain his true end, which, in the words of the Shorter Catechism, is "to glorify God and enjoy him forever." The Christians accepted literally the Hebrew legend of man's fall from a state of grace into a state of sin, and interpreted the history both of the individual and of the race as the upward striving of man toward the reestablishment of unity (atonement) with God. To this the Christians added the conception of the Christ as the intermediary between God and man, through whose sacrifice man's salvation is rendered possible.

The early Christian doctrine obviously has much in common with that of Plato; but there is an important difference. Both Plato and Paul regard the life of man as a battle between the forces of his higher and lower nature, and for the Christians this battle became a grim life-and-death affair dramatized as a struggle for the soul of man between God and the Devil. Both the Greeks and the Christians are agreed that man's lower nature is revealed in his impulses and appetites. Both the Greeks and the Christians believed that if man is to achieve the Good Life he must conquer his lower nature. Characteristically, however, for the Greeks (Socrates), wisdom must be preceded by a conviction of ignorance; for the Christians (Paul), salvation must be preceded by a conviction of sin.

It is in the interpretation of man's higher nature, however, that we find the most important difference. For the Greeks the Good Life is the life governed by Reason. Socrates argued that knowledge and virtue are one, that moral problems can be solved only by clear thinking. Plato recognized the "spirited element" in man, but held that it should support but not control man's reason. In Aristotle's system the capacity for reasoning is unique to man. In the Christian doctrine of man, Plato's "spirited element" is broadened in its conception to include the Hebrew notion of Spirit, and it is promoted to a position above that of Reason. Reason alone cannot secure salvation; it must be Reason governed by Faith. Faith is the nonrational orientation of the whole individual toward the true and the good, i.e., toward God. *Credo ut intelligam.* One cannot fully understand unless one first believes.

The Christian doctrine of man is thus an extension, but also an inversion, of the Platonic doctrine. Man is an immaterial and immortal entity, dependent not on his own rational powers but on his God for all that he is to achieve. The secret of the Good Life is not merely clear thinking but right willing. The individual who has accepted the will of God will know what is true and will be guided to what is right. This is a transcendent teleology. There is a natural order, but above and beyond it there is a supernatural order which gives direction to the natural. Man can have absolute knowledge of what is true and what is good only when this has been revealed by the supernatural being.

The fifteen centuries since Paul bear witness to the persistent and passionate effort on the part of Christian theologians to clarify their thinking about the nature of man and his relation to God. Paul, as we have seen, was a child of both the Hebrews and the Greeks. As the architect of Christian doctrine he drew on both traditions. But there were certain inconsistencies that he never succeeded in resolving. Most of these were theological, which we cannot consider here. So far as the doctrine of man is concerned, however, there were two great unsolved problems: (1) the problem of human freedom, and (2) the relation between faith and reason, i.e., the problem of revelation. Neither has ever been finally answered, but two of the noblest attempts are to be found in the writings of Augustine and Thomas Aquinas, the former a Platonist, the latter an Aristotelian.

Augustine (354-430) was for a thousand years one of the dominant influences in Western thought and did more than any other to fuse the Idealism of Plato with the religious fervor of Paul into a consistent Christian theology. In the writings of Augustine, notably the *Confessions* and the *City of God,* we have perhaps the best expression of the religious doctrine of man. The only reality is spiritual. The Idea of Good (in Plato's sense) is the Supreme Spirit, or God. God created the universe in accordance with a plan, and in doing so endowed man with the potentiality of knowing with certainty that which is true. The process is that of observing one's own experience. God has implanted in us ideas of the eternal, which, if we are disciplined by faith, we can recognize. Mere observation of nature (science) gives a knowledge of temporal things, but knowledge of the eternal can result only from "divine illumination."

Since God is the sole creator, and man but a partial expression of God's will, it follows that man can *learn* from the study of nature but can *know with certainty* only through divine revelation. Science is thus disparaged as interesting but inconsequential, useful for the conduct of practical affairs, but irrelevant to the solution of man's deepest problem, which is to attain salvation.

Augustine accepted Plato's solution of the mind-body relationship. The cognitive problem disappeared once the principle of divine revelation was accepted. The esthetic experience became a by-product of the relation of man to God; contemplation of the divine fills one with the ecstasy of love. It was the problem of Will that resisted solution, and that has plagued all theologians before and since. If God created the universe, and is thereby responsible for all that is, how can man be considered responsible for his actions? Augustine, spurred by his study of the Greek rationalists, wrestled with the problem and also failed. In his earlier years he apparently favored a doctrine of freedom. As he became more and more embroiled in the controversies of the church and in the refutation of heresies, he seems to have moved in the direction of determinism. At any rate, with Augustine the problem comes into clear focus. Either man is free to make choices or, pushing the Christian theology to its full implication, man's fate is completely predestined. The controversy was to rage for many centuries, both in the Roman Catholic and later in the Protestant churches, and in modern science the problem emerges again as the alternative between determinism and indeterminacy.

Quite apart from his significance for religion and theology, Augustine is to be recognized as one of the great expositors of what was to become a fundamental method of psychology: the meticulous observation of one's own consciousness. Truth can be realized only through the discovery, in one's own consciousness, of what God planted there. The introspective method exemplified by Augustine's *Confessions* is far from the "dispassionate" inspection of experience advocated by the modern phenomenologists, for Augustine in his introspection was passionately searching for God. Whatever the motive, however, we find in Augustine's scrutiny of his own experience an approach which was later to become explicit in the writings of Descartes, Husserl, and even Sartre.

Augustine gave us a Christianized version of Plato. He had read some of Aristotle's works, but he was not challenged by Aristotle's interest in nature. For him the revelation of God through human experience was completely convincing and satisfying. Thomas Aquinas (1225-1274) is generally regarded as the greatest of the Christian interpreters of Aristotle. Reformulated by the modern Neo-Thomists to take into account the subsequent centuries of scientific discovery, the Thomistic system may now be accepted as the basic philosophy of orthodox Roman Catholicism.

What is of greatest importance to us as psychologists is the relation between Faith and Reason. The Greeks had exalted Reason as the secret of the Good Life. The Early Christians made Reason subservient to

Faith. For the Mediaeval Christians the problem of reconciling the two was the great challenge. In the system of Thomas Aquinas we have a defense of Faith *through* Reason, a rational doctrine of man that incorporates a belief in God, in the immortality of the human soul, and in the freedom of man to choose between right and wrong. Whether or not we accept such a doctrine, we must respect its clarity and consistency.

The Thomistic psychology is rationalistic in the Greek sense, but at the same time fundamentally religious. It provides an orderly account of the capacities and tendencies inherent in man, and it leaves room for an empirical science that describes, classifies and, in a limited sense, explains the relation between mind and body, the basis of cognition, and the basis of conduct; but it holds stubbornly to the belief that in his essence man is not a member of the natural order and must be understood ultimately in terms not of natural but of spiritual law.

RECAPITULATION

We have completed our review of five classic doctrines of man that have come down to us from the early speculations of the philosophers. None can be considered a fully scientific doctrine in the modern sense of the term "science," in that they lacked the discipline that we now consider essential to the scientific method. They did represent, however, sincere attempts to solve the persistent problems that arise when one wonders about the nature and the attributes of man.

To recapitulate, we have:

1. *A relativistic doctrine,* which, denying any absolutes, regards man as an accident of circumstance, possessing no intrinsic properties, capable of limitless variation.

2. *A materialistic doctrine,* which regards man as a part of physical nature, to be explained ultimately in terms of physical law.

3. *An idealistic doctrine,* which sees in man the temporary actualization of an ideal rational order.

4. *A teleological doctrine,* which finds in man an inherent nature, intelligible only in terms of an immanent purpose which reveals itself in his behavior.

5. *A religious doctrine,* which regards man as primarily a spiritual being, not exclusively a part of the natural order, not to be understood solely in terms of natural law.

These doctrines are not mutually exclusive. We might simplify by opposing the religious to the nonreligious, the materialistic to the non-materialistic, the relativistic to the absolutistic. On the other hand, we might cluster together the idealistic, the teleological, and the religious doctrines, as they were in fact clustered in the system of Thomas Acquinas. What is important, however, is not the particular list of doctrines, nor the men who have been used as their illustrations, but the historical fact that man, in his quest for an understanding of himself, has at different times seen the problem in different ways, considered different data as relevant, used different methods, and accepted different constructs as explanatory. As we pursue the story of man's thinking about man, we see, in the perspective of history, that the implicit assumptions of the psychologist are fully as important as are his explicit assertions.

NOTES

1. One cannot resist the famous quotation from Jowett's translation of the *Republic* (Book V, 473): "Until philosophers are kings, or the kings and princes of this world have the spirit and power of philosophy, and political greatness and wisdom meet in one, and those commoner natures who pursue either to the exclusion of the other are compelled to stand aside, cities will never have rest from their evils,—no, nor the human race, as I believe—and then only will this our state have a possibility of life and behold the light of day."

Gestation of the Instinct Concept

SOLOMON DIAMOND

Early in the twentieth century, before anti-instinctivism had become a way of life, and almost an instinct, with American psychologists, George Bohn was prominent in the radical left of European psychobiologists. It is to him that we owe the guiding line for most of this discussion: *"Qu'est-ce que l'instinct? Un mot. — What is instinct? A word"* (11, p. 313). As an expression of the disdain with which the instinct concept has so often been dismissed, these words have been quoted innumerable times.

The thought was not original with Bohn. It was almost a commonplace in the eighteenth century, when many writers looked upon instinct as a reality than a stick that does not have two ends" (29, v. 2, p. 193). survival of medieval disputations. Guer, for example, wrote in 1749 that instinct is "a chimera . . . a word void of meaning, which has no more And Rouillé D'Orfeuil (in a book called *L'Alembic Morale,* that is, an apparatus for distilling ideas) said that "men have imagined the word instinct, which they pretend exists in animals like a spring inside a watch" (54, p. 352).

These examples remind us that the anti-instinct movement did not originate in the twentieth century. It was especially vigorous in the eighteenth, but it was already explicit in the sixteenth. Periodically new adherents reassert it with the enthusiasm of innovators, so one might suppose that by this time they would be beating a horse which, if not dead, at least had all the instinct knocked out of it. But the instinct concept has never given up the ghost, and today the experimental work of the ethologists has made it more vigorous than ever.

Instinct is indeed only a word. But one may make the same charge against any of the conceptual constructs which are stock and trade of psychologists, such as *emotion, intelligence,* and *reflex.* It may nevertheless be enlightening to trace the history of the word, to learn why, more than any other word in our professional vocabulary, it is regarded as an expression of that semantic absurdity which (to play hob only slightly with Hobbes' epigram (32)), is the privilege above all of those who profess psychology.

This is not a problem on which I launched deliberately. I found myself rather, willy-nilly, often more nilling than willing, attacking bits of this intriguing problem, much as one returns compulsively to a giant jigsaw puzzle. One cannot sweep it back into the box half-done, and one cannot recover use of the table on which it is spread without completing it. Although I have not brought this particular jigsaw puzzle to completion, an interesting picture has begun to emerge.

Let us look first at *instinct*'s parentage and relations, so that we may avoid any tendency to regard it (as Guer explicitly did) as an illegitimate "foundling." *Instinctus* is a participial form of the Latin word *instinguo*— to prick, and hence to excite or urge. The Sanskrit root, *tig,* meaning sharp, also gave rise to a cognate Greek word, *stixo,* meaning to prick or puncture, but this word had no noteworthy psychological career. English descendants of *instinguo* include *distinguished* (which means marked for recognition with a sharp tool), *instigation* (which can sometimes be used to translate *instinctus),* and that most indispensable tool of all psychologists, *stimulus* (which is a contraction of an older form, *stig-mulus,* originally a prod for mules and slaves, and now applied with the same bland indifference to rats and students).

We look now at how this word was used by classical authors and by the early Christian Fathers.[1] Because instinct is not a verb in English, I will occasionally resort to a barbarous neologism, *instincted.* Tacitus used this word in his account of how the soldiers of a Roman army were instincted by their officers to join a rebellion against the emperor (58:1, 70). The range of the word was extended by Cicero: finding no Latin equivalent for the Greek *enthusiasm,* he used *instinctus* to describe the origin of oracular utterances which were inspirational rather than based on a reasoned analysis of events (14:1, 18). He used it also to refer to the heavenly inspiration of poets (15:1, 26). Lucretius declares himself to be similarly instincted by his longing for the approbation of the muses (42:1, 925). Instinct was ready-made, therefore, as a word which the Christian Fathers could use to discuss heavenly inspiration, but the distinctive genius of the new religion showed itself in applying it also to instigation by the devil. Tertullian used *instinctus* to describe the origin of our irrational souls, as coming not from God, but being instincted by the devil (60:16, 1). He used it also, in his earthy way, to say that the physical act of sex must be instincted by the soul (60:27, 5). Lactantius used it to deplore the divisive instigations of demons (40:4, 30). About this time the arch of Constantine was erected, and the inscription on the arch praised the emperor as *instinctus divinitatis,* divinely inspired (16, p. 183). Augustine used *instinctus* to state the libidinal source of adultery (6:4), and also to explain how evil spirits sometimes inspire correct forecasts by astrologers, in order to mislead men into trusting them (7:2, 17).

We learn from these examples that no aura of sacredness attaches to the word *instinct.* It is a motivational term, which can be applied as readily to urgings of a sinful nature as to those of divine origin. It usually points to an external source of motivation. There is no hint of any entity, instinct.

Another point of interest is that in classical times this word is not applied to animal behavior (although it may be used to allude to the fact that our animal natures instigate some of our actions). Almost a thousand years will pass before *instinct* is used to describe animal behavior. It is therefore natural to ask whether the concept of instinct may be present without this verbal label. In this connection, three authors especially demand our attention: Seneca, Galen, and Nemesius.

Letter No. 121 of Seneca's *Moral Epistles* (57) appears in the Loeb Classical Library under the title "On instinct in animals." However, if *instinct* is a mere word, Seneca is guiltless of using it. The letter states that animals have an inborn knowledge of their own bodily capacities, as well as a natural love of self which directs them to acts of self-preservation. Seneca dismisses as untenable the hypothesis that they are forced to act as they do simply to avoid pain consequent on any other course of action. Instead, he believes that they have "by nature" some kinds of knowledge which men gain only from experience, and this permits them to perform skilled acts without practice. The focus of his account is epistemological.

Galen (26: v. 2, pp. 700-702) saw proof of natural wisdom in an experiment with a newborn kid. He took the animal from its mother's womb and brought it into a room in which there was an array of dishes containing milk, wine, oil, vinegar, and water. The kid wisely chose the milk. Galen (25, p. 70) also makes other observations on the unlearned behavior of young animals: the young calf butts before its horns have appeared; the young shoat tries to use tusks it does not yet possess; birds try to fly before they are capable of doing so; the newly hatched snake crawls, without instruction, into the rocks. He concludes that "in every case the body is adapted to the character and faculties of the soul." Animals owe their skills to nature, not to reason. When he describes the process of human birth, he comments also on the sucking behavior of infants (25, p. 673). I quote from the fine translation by Margaret Tallmadge May, to which I shall however take one exception:

> Then is it right to praise Nature for all these things, or has the greatest wonder of them all — the instruction of the animal being born in the actions of all the parts — not yet been told? For not only did she prepare a mouth, esophagus, and stomach as instruments of nutrition; she also produced an animal that understands right from the beginning how these are to be used. . . .

I have stopped in the middle of a sentence, to emphasize that the focus is still on understanding. The sentence continues: "and she instilled into it a certain instinctive faculty of wisdom by which each animal arrives at the nutriment suitable for it." But take note that the word translated "instinctive" literally means "natural." The Greek language has no special word for instinct, and we must still wonder if they have the concept without such a special word.

Nemesius wrote in Greek, about two centuries after Galen. He is a man trained in medicine, who late in life took office in the church. He says that God has given animals a certain natural cleverness; also, that the uniformity of behavior in individuals of a like kind proves that their cunning is due to nature and not to reason. These statements use the word *physis*. It is the same word used by Galen in the passage just quoted, or when he writes of natural faculties; and it is also in the title of Nemesius's treatise, *Peri Physis Anthropon* — *On the Nature of Man*. In these passages, the medieval and Renaissance translators of Nemesius into Latin (47) write *natura*, and his early English translator (48) writes *nature*, where a recent English translation (59) writes *instinct*.

I conclude that for each of these ancient authors, the problem as they saw it was only to discover a source of knowledge, other than experience, to explain the cunning of animal behavior. They pointed to nature as that source. But it is no more correct to translate this as *instinct* than it would be to translate it as *heredity*. The ancient world did not possess a differentiated instinct concept.

This primary concern with cognitive problems continued to dominate the thought of the Arab philosophers. They accepted Aristotle's statement that man has a faculty of reason not shared by animals; but, like Aristotle, they were concerned chiefly with the faculties that animals and men have in common. Al-Farabi, in the ninth century, said that one such faculty [*wa'am*] [2] was a kind of practical judgment which is capable of recognizing, prior to experience, that a certain object may be either harmful or beneficial (66). By this faculty, he said, a sheep recognizes that the wolf is potentially harmful to it, but that another sheep is a safe companion. Christian scholars learned of this faculty chiefly through the writings of Avicenna (8), and to them it became known as *vis aestimativa*, the estimative faculty (cf. Goichon, 27A, arts. 610:28 and 785-790). Usually they would ignore the fact that for Avicenna and the other Arab philosophers this was a faculty shared by both men and animals, and, crediting it to animals only, they would say that it did for them what *cogitativa*, the power of thought, did for men.

This theory is important to us because it is associated with instinct in the work of Thomas Aquinas. But in itself it is not an instinct theory. The sheep behaves as it does, although it is not capable of making a rational judgment based on generalizations from sensory data, because it can nevertheless make a valid assessment by utilizing information not obtained through the senses. In many situations, men were thought to do the same.

Instinct was not used in relation to animal behavior until late in the thirteenth century, around the year 1270. At that time it appears in the work of Albertus Magnus and Thomas Aquinas. (Latham (41) also records it as present in the work of Robert Kilwardby, but I have not been able to find this. It would in any case probably be derivative from Aquinas.)

In Albert the Great, I have searched for *instinct* only in his great work *On Animals;* there it occurs twice. Once he says that the speech of pygmies, whom he regards as animals rather than as men, results from an instinct of nature rather than from the use of reason (1:1,3). Elsewhere (1:21, 16) he says that no animal is susceptible of being taught except through an instinct of nature *(nisi cum instinctu naturae)*. But then he tells how the various senses (particularly vision and hearing) and the various inner faculties (including imagination, memory, and the estimative faculty) participate in learning by different animals. He shows that their capacity for instruction depends on the degree to which they share these faculties. Only man is capable of rational or intellectual learning, or, as we say now, of purely cognitive learning, *à la* Tolman or Piaget. The learning of animals is always directed by their appetites, by pleasures and pains, fitting the Hullian model. This is the meaning of the statement that they cannot learn "except through an instinct of nature." No conflict is seen between instinct and learning. He uses the phrase "natural instinct" to describe one of the conditions of animal learning, not to describe the wonders of unlearned adaptive behaviors. So Albert does not have an instinct concept.

Notice that at the same time that the word *instinct* has entered a new context, it has also acquired a traveling companion. From this time forward, we shall have to distinguish between the simple word *instinct* and the new phrase, *natural instinct*.

We come now to Thomas Aquinas, whose psychology is rich in motivational theory. We must consider three of his works: the Disputation, *De Anima,* in which the phrase *natural instinct* appears once; the *Commentary on Aristotle's De Anima,* in which the word *instinct* does not appear, although it is used repeatedly by translators; and finally the *Summa Theologica,* in which *instinct* occurs so frequently as to justify the statement in an Italian etymological dictionary that the word was given general currency *(diffuso)* by Thomas.

First, the Disputation (2). In the passage which concerns us, Thomas defines five conditions of complete sensory knowledge. They include initial reception by the sense organ, discrimination of this sensory effect from others, its conservation in memory, recognition of the implication *(intentio),* and the power of recall. Here is Thomas' statement of the fourth condition; in giving it I use the word *impulse* where Thomas wrote *instinctus.* I will justify this later. Thomas writes:

> It is necessary [to perceive] some implications which the senses do not apprehend, such as harmfulness and usefulness and others of this sort. Men attain such knowledge by means of inquiry and comparison, but other animals by a certain natural impulse, as the sheep naturally flees the wolf as something harmful. From this we see that in other animals this is arranged by the faculty of estimation; but in man by the cogitative faculty, which draws conclusions from the particular implications. Therefore it is called the particular reason, and passive intellect" (2, v. 2, p. 330).

That is, the sheep, unlike a man, is responding to an impulse which is natural, meaning corporeal, human thought being incorporeal. Thomas, like Albert, insists on the exclusive determination of animal behavior by corporeal or natural influences, and he is not talking about any mysterious new entity called *instinct*. He is really not so much interested in explaining or even describing animal behavior as in maintaining the distinction between rational men and irrational beasts, despite certain similarities in their external actions.

In the *Commentary* on *De Anima* (3), two passages interest us. One is the discussion of that same estimative faculty. The *Commentary* exists in English translation (24), but there you will find the estimative faculty only in footnotes, for in the text it has been translated into *instinct*. Where, for example, a literal translation would be that "in irrational animals the apprehension of intentions is done by the natural estimation," the translation reads: "But the lower animals' awareness of individualized notions is called natural instinct" (24, art. 397).

Elsewhere in the Commentary, Thomas talks about the wonderful sagacity of the ants and the bees. He says that their actions are not directed by constructive use of imagination, but by natural *inclinatio*. The translation tells us that "ants and bees behave so cleverly, not because they are aware of definite images distinct from exterior sensations, but by a natural instinct" (24, art. 644). One wonders, why not *inclination?*

We come now to the *Summa Theologica,* Thomas's great final work, which should contain the justification for these substitutions. In it, the word *instinctus* occurs more than 100 times (21). It is used most often in reference to *divine instinct, inward instinct,* and the like (e.g., 2-II, q. 97.2). When the source of instinct is the Holy Ghost, the translation prepared by the Dominican fathers, which makes a point of the fact that it is "literal," usually renders it as *prompting* or as *inspiration* (e.g., III, q. 29.1). When the source is demonic, they usually write *instigation* (e.g., I, q. 114.3). All of these uses refer to the motivation of human behavior by various spiritual, noncorporeal agents, under exceptional rather than ordinary circumstances. There are 25 instances in which the word appears in the phrase *natural instinct*. Some of these also relate to human behavior. For example, the law of nature, which is the basis of moral feeling, is said to be instilled by natural instinct (e.g., I, q. 113.1 and 2-II, q. 93.1). It is expressed in primitive burial practices, or in a primitive disposition to prayer. An important aspect of this natural moral law is that it was operative in mankind before they had received any revelation of religious truths; that is, it is *not* prompted by any external spiritual agent. Nor is there anything extraordinary about its occurrence. It is a routine natural event, which has its basis in bodily processes.

Now, if the proper "literal" translation for *instinctus* is sometimes *inspiration,* sometimes *instigation,* sometimes *prompting,* what synonym will serve best for this use? It seems to me that spontaneous moral feelings and the law of nature are expressions of natural *impulses*. Promptings, instigations, and inspirations are all initiated by external agents. But the *instinctus naturale,* or *ex natura,* is an impulse initiated by the body. That is the meaning of *natural instinct.*

If we set aside those few but important instances in which this phrase, however we translate it, applies to human behavior, we are left with about 20 cases in which it applies to the behavior of irrational animals. Here are a few of these, exactly as they appear in the translation by the Dominican fathers (5), except that I have substituted *impulse* for *instinct* wherever the word appears.

For the sheep, seeing the wolf, judges it a thing to be shunned, not from reason, but from natural impulse (I, q. 83.1).

But irrational animals have not the command of the appetitive movement; for this is in them through natural impulse (1-II, q. 15.2).

Animals by means of their members do something from natural impulse; not through knowing the relations of their members to these operations (1-II, q. 16.2).

The senses do not apprehend the future: but from apprehending the present, an animal is moved by a natural impulse to hope for a future good, or to fear a future evil (1-II, q. 41.1).

Certainly no absurdities result from this change, and it serves to emphasize Thomas' important contribution, which is that he has broken away from the exclusively cognitive concern of his predecessors, to emphasize the motivational aspects of these actions. However, he still assigns them to the estimative faculty. He does not regard them as at all analogous to the divinely instinctive thoughts of a prophet. Spiritual instinct is transmitted from soul to soul, spirit to spirit; but natural impulse, from matter to matter. What we must hold in mind is this very simple fact: *natural* impulse is not *super*natural. In the future, other men will assert that each humble ant is providentially directed by the Master of the universe. For them, instinct will become what we now call a hypothetical construct, "like a spring inside a watch." But as presented by Thomas, the process is an expression of God's natural creation; it is a *machina ex deo,* rather than a *deus ex machina.*

Despite my preference for *impulse* as a translation of *instinctus* in most contexts, in what follows I go back to writing *instinct* whenever the corresponding word appears in other languages, so that the reference will always be clear.

The next figure in our story is Dante, who introduced instinct, but not natural instinct, into vernacular literature. Writing in Latin, in an early but posthumous work, he followed Thomas by stating that lower animals are guided by *instinct of nature* (*nature instinctu ducantur*) (20A: I, 2(5)). But in the *Paradiso,* when Dante is transfixed by the awesome spectacle of the universe, Beatrice tells him that divine *istinto* directs all things on the great sea of Being: it directs the flame to rise toward the moon, and the stone to fall toward the earth (20: Canto 1, 112-114).

For the next 250 years, whenever we find *instinct* mentioned in regard to animal behavior, it will invariably be as *natural instinct,* which has none of the noble and sublime connotations associated with the simple word *instinct.* This rule is very strikingly illustrated by the very first occurrence of the word in English. This is in John Lydgate's early fifteenth-century story of the Trojan wars, where Hector declares that even animals, "beasts of reason rude and blinde," desire vengeance through "instynt of kinde" (43, II: 2215-2216). I supposed at first that Lydgate must have found *instinct* in his source, a thirteenth-century Latin account by Guido delle Colonne (17). He did not. The corresponding passage in Guido only mentions irrational animals. But what, precisely, does "instynt of kinde" mean? In Middle English *kinde* means *nature,* so that *instinct of kinde* is the literal equivalent of *natural instinct,* and conforms to the rule.

There was very little development in the use of natural instinct. Gregor Reisch's *Margarita Philosophica* (52) is an encyclopedia that was widely read throughout the sixteenth century. The account of the estimative faculty states that it perceives intentions that are not directly sensed, and it does this either by natural instinct (as in the case of a sheep which has not previously experienced the wolf's deception), or as a result of experience (as in the case of an ass which avoids a ditch after having once fallen into it), or finally by reason (as when we judge that cherries are sweet because they are red). The next chapter deals with fantasy, the faculty which composes new pictures from previously received sensations. In men this faculty is embellished by reason, which leads to different effects in different individuals because of their different experiences; but in beasts it is governed by natural instinct, and that is why all swallows build their nests, and all spiders weave their webs, with the same skill. This differs somewhat from Thomas Aquinas. Thomas said such behavior must be due to natural inclination (*operantur naturali inclinatione,* which his translators generally render as *natural instinct*) because they cannot really "fantasy" anything apart from immediate sense impressions (3, art. 644; cf. 24, art. 644). The *Margarita Philosophica* grants them fantasy, but says it is unvarying.

This theme recurs in other discussions of natural instinct, or, better said, it is introduced into discussions of human behavior in order to highlight its volitional nature. There is no independent discussion of natural instinct as such, nor any effort to explain its operation. Scaliger's refutation of Cardano's *Subtleties of Nature* provides one example. Cardano dealt with the emotions as related to volition. Rejecting this idea, Scaliger (55) affirms that only men can will, while the actions of animals (who do have emotions like those of men) can only be said to be instigated. They are, he says, *instincted* by nature.

Another example is provided by Figliucci's *Filosofia Morale,* which is written in the vernacular. Figliucci speaks rarely of animals, and he conducts his dialogue about human virtue on an intellectual plane which gives little opportunity for instinct. At one point, however, the student asks why animals do not differ in their pleasures, as men do, and he receives the answer that it is because the behavior of animals is forced by *istinto naturale,* while that of men is varied by will (23, p. 487b).

We do not always find instinct where we expect it, and I think it important to mention some of these negative instances, to establish the fact that instinct is far from being a universally employed device even when it seems most apropos.

I read Spanish far less fluently than I would like, but still immeasurably more readily than I read Latin. So I prefer to read Vives in the authoritative Spanish translation by Lorenzo Riber, and only check back to the Latin as need may arise. In modern Castillian dress, the "great Valenciano" tells us that the sheep fears the wolf because of a "secreto instinto y estimulo natural" (64, v. 2, p. 1171), but the original speaks of a "secret natural stimulus" (63, p. 71). In Spanish we read about "el instinto de conservacion" (p. 1235), but in the Latin it is an appetite, that is, something corporeal. Even the conventional references to natural instinct are absent. Vives cannot be unfamiliar with the idea, but he feels no need to use it, although his twentieth-century translator does.

The *De Anima* of Melancthon (45), a book with strong physiological emphasis, is also free of any reference to instinct.

I had expected to find *instinct* in Conrad Gesner's great natural history, but I was disappointed. Gesner's monumental work runs to many thousands of folio pages, but then, the pictures help. But he is a systematic writer, and there is little reason to expect *instinct* anywhere if it does not appear in his account of the sheep's fear of the wolf, or the hen's fear of the hawk. The ants and bees do not come within the scope of his natural history. But in the dedicatory epistle to the initial volume he piously states that "the skills of the smaller animals . . . are no less to be wondered at because they do not issue from their own reason and will, but from the wonder-working of God, who by nature arranges that they shall perform alone many things that men can do only after a long life of practice" (27, f. a2). That is all. He too must be familiar with the doctrine of natural instinct, for no man is more widely read or has a more tenacious memory, but he finds no occasion to mention it. Perhaps Gesner and Vives would have agreed that *instinct* is only a word.

Meanwhile, the anti-instinct movement has found a beginning. Jerome Rorarius (53) wrote a slender book in defense of animal reason, which however waited 120 years for a publisher, until the Cartesian controversy had established a market for it. Bishop Rorarius is a candidate for election as the patron of anti-instinct theorists, for 200 years before Condillac he explicitly rejects natural instinct as an explanation for animal behavior. There is just one weakness to his claim. After reading his repeated rejections of natural instinct as the explanation for animal skills and animal sagacity, it is startling to be told that elephants share the universal human acceptance of the rite of purification by water, something known to the most savage men, and thus evidently "imparted to our minds by some natural instinct" (p. 105). So we must seek another candidate.

In 1575, in the *Examen de Ingenios* (33), translated as *The Examination of Men's Wits* (34), the Spaniard Huarte ridicules attempts to explain animal behavior on the basis of "vain instincts of nature." Here are his words, as they were presented to the English public in 1594, in Richard Carew's translation:

> Vulgar Philosophers, seeing the marvelous works which brute beasts perform, affirme it holds no cause of marvell, because they do it by natural instinct, in as much as nature sheweth and teacheth each in his kind what he is to do. And in this they say very well, for we have alreadie alleaged and prooved, that nature is nothing else than this temperature of the foure first qualities, and that this is the schoole-maister who teacheth the soules in what sort they are to worke: but they terme instinct of nature a certain masse of things, which rise from the noddock [base of the skull?] upward, neither could they ever expound or give us to understand, what it is. . . .
>
> All this [he has meanwhile been talking about individual differences among dogs and horses] cannot be reduced to those vaine instincts of nature which the Philosophers faine. For if you aske for what cause one dog hath more instinct than another, both comming of one kind, and whelpes of one sire, I cannot coniecture what they may answer, save to flie back to their old leaning post, saying, That God hath taught the one better than the other, and given him a more naturall instinct (34, pp. 33, 37).

And finally, with reference to human infants:

> The child so soone as it is borne, knowes to sucke, and fashion his lips to draw foorth the milke. . . . Well I know they will answer, That God hath given them this naturall instinct as to the brute beasts, wherein they say not ill, if the naturall instinct be the selfe same with the temperature (p. 40).

This vigorous anti-instinct statement should not be taken to imply that Huarte will rely on experiential determinants of behavior. True to his own time, Huarte believes that an ignorant servant girl can suddenly converse with her physician in correct Latin if her "temperament" is brought to the proper pitch by the fever of her illness.

Huarte represents a kind of watershed in our story. It is difficult to learn who were the "vulgar philosophers" whom he treats with such disdain, and to what extent they found their way into printed books more ephemeral than his, but it is certain that from this time forward the word *instinct* appears with increasing frequency, and Huarte himself is partly responsible for the change. His book had at least 70 editions before the end of the seventeenth century, in Spanish, Italian, English, French, Dutch and Latin (34, intro.). One measure of its importance is the fact that half a century after its appearance a French physician, Guibelet (30) wrote a much longer book in earnest refutation. But before coming to that, let us look at what has been happening to *instinct* in vernacular French and English.

Instinct does not appear in French until the sixteenth century, later than in English. It is used then chiefly in the sense of *instigation,* and almost solely in relation to voluntary human actions; however, the surgeon Ambroise Paré is reported as writing that in women, abortions are instincted by natural causes (35). Its use in the modern sense begins with Montaigne (65), although the word does not occur where we might most expect it, in the lengthy and famous discussion of animal behavior in the "Apologie de Raimond de Sebonde" (46, Bk. 2, 12). Montaigne had translated Sebonde's *Natural Theology,* and in this translation we read that animal actions are "poussées, par violence ou necessité de nature" (56, v. 9, p. 130). In the "apology," Montaigne asks why we should call forced in animals the same behavior which we regard as freely willed in ourselves. But elsewhere Montaigne says that the instinct of cruelty is a human frailty (46, Bk. 2, 11), and when discussing parental love he conjectures that this, if anything, might be a "truly natural law, that is, an instinct" imprinted in men and beasts alike (46, Bk. 2, 8). When Charron, who has been called Montaigne's secretary, restates his views regarding animal behavior at the opening of the seventeenth century, he shows the influence of Huarte by specifically rejecting the natural instinct hypothesis (23, Bk. 1, 8(7)).

In England too, Lydgate aside, application of instinct to animals comes late. In 1513 Thomas More wrote of "a secret instinct of nature in men's hearts" which alerts them to great events about to occur (28, v. 2, p. 777). The Oxford English Dictionary gives several other examples of the word's use prior to Shakespeare. One of these relates to a "natural instinct of friendship" in trees, as part of a moral discourse on marriage (62); none relates to animals. *Instinct* does not appear in concordances of the works of the sixteenth-century poets Thomas Wyatt (31), Thomas Kyd (18), or Edmund Spenser (49). It was used once by Marlowe, who died in 1593 (19).

You will recall that Huarte appeared in English translation in 1594. This is the year after Marlowe's death, and Shakespeare, 30 years of age, is already the author of *Venus and Adonis,* the *Rape of Lucrece,* and ten early plays (44), in which the word *instinct* does not appear (10). Then came the explosion. In the first part of *Henry IV,* in a long comic scene probably written in 1596, Shakespeare indulges in what is almost an orgy of instinct. Prince Hal and a companion had made a mock attack in the darkness on Falstaff and three henchmen, and put them to flight. As the facts are disclosed, Falstaff tries to excuse himself as having been "a coward on instinct," because "the lion will not hurt the true prince." Throughout the scene, Prince Hal pokes fun at him repeatedly for this instinct of cowardice. Shakespeare has solitary references to instinct in half a dozen later plays. In two of these there is further reference to animal behavior. Coriolanus, when he steels himself to resist the impulse to behave mercifully toward the populace of defeated Rome, says, "I'll never be such a gosling to obey instinct." (In the end, of course, he gives in to his mother's plea, which shows that the gosling imprint was not to be denied.)

And in *The Tempest* we are told that "the very rats instinctively had quit" a ship not seaworthy. These references to the instinctive guidance of animal actions without reference to natural instinct are possibly the first departures from a convention which had been unbroken for more than three centuries, and they are clear evidence of a changed point of view. There had, however, been some premonitions of this relaxation. First, in that book by Scaliger, although the text spoke of animals being "instincted by nature," the entry in the index reads "instinct in beasts" *(instinctus in brutis)*. Possibly the index compiler, like a modern headline writer, twisted the language to fit the entry into the narrow column of the index. (Not an influence on Shakespeare, however, for Farmer (22) very effectively disposed of Bishop Warburton's assertion that Scaliger's book was "well known to Shakespeare.") Second, in the passages I cited from Huarte, in which *instinct* occurred seven times, the qualifying *natural* was once omitted. But it is Shakespeare who is the first to drop nature altogether from this context. It is a hint that even animal instinct may soon be given a supernatural quality.

From Shakespeare one turns instinctively to Francis Bacon (9). The *Essays,* published in 1597, include such phrases as "secret inclination toward love of others," "disposition towards goodness," and "natural fear" which children have of darkness. These are contexts in which *instinct* might appear, but does not. In 1605, in *The Advancement of Learning,* he makes a conventional use of instinct in stating that the "light of nature" (in one of its two meanings) "is imprinted upon the spirit of man by an inward instinct, according to the law of conscience" (v. 6, p. 395). In the posthumous *Sylva Sylvarum,* his references are to *natural instinct:* there he speaks of the need to study "the secret instincts of nature," and wonders about secret passages of sympathy between persons of near blood and "the like passage and instincts of nature between great friends and enemies" (v. 5, arts. 986, 987).

Thus, at the beginning of the seventeenth century, *instinct* was beginning to show a vigor and popularity which it never had before, and before the middle of the century it was a topic of lively interest. The sharp line of separation between men and animals was being blurred, and therefore it is not surprising that as discussion moved out of the old Latin strait-jacket into free vernacular forms, confusion should begin to appear between the inspirational instinct of humans (in which animals never shared) and the natural instinct of animals (in which humans always had some portion). In consequence, instinct advances from a platitude to a subject of controversy, as some men toss all instinct into a single basket, and others attempt to toss it all out as one tub of bathwater. In closing, I want to mention briefly three obscure men who engaged in this controversy, and who are noteworthy to us because they explained instinct at length, which is something that had never been considered necessary before.

Guibelet is first, in 1627. Two chapters in his refutation of Huarte (30) are devoted to the defense of instinct. Guibelet is deceptively sensible when he rebukes Huarte for trying to explain too much with his one answer to all questions: temperament. But then we read that temperament and the four elements are inadequate because they do not help us to understand those influences which come from the heavens, and which account for the occult properties in plants and minerals, and for instincts in animals. If infants nurse with their lips instead of their ears, it is because "this is a choice which comes only from the soul, which gives this instinct to the lips of the infant, just as God and nature gave it to the soul" (p. 153).

Pierre Chanet, in 1644, directed a similar refutation against Charron, whose influence was spreading in new editions long after his death. Chanet (12) is scandalized by the thought of crediting animals with reason, and insists that instinct must explain their behavior. For him, instinct is a divine direction given to things both animate and inanimate, which directs them in ways that cannot be explained by their natural faculties. His very definition excludes the possibility of natural instinct. It is instinct which directs the planets in their course, for how else can a planet, after hurtling in one direction, turn about and rush just as fast in the other? And if only natural forces governed the growth of plants, they would all be perfectly round instead of sprouting leaves of different shapes. The complex bodily organization of fleas, or the instinctive fear which rats have of cats, cannot be due to heredity, since these creatures are often born without parents, from piles of dirt or from the filth in ships. Since all such phenomena are not explicable by natural faculties, they must be effects of instinct.

Guibelet and Chanet express a point of view which is strongly at variance with that of Thomas Aquinas, since for them animal instinct is not natural but supernatural. They represent a development that must be regarded as scientifically retrogressive. After the long gestation of the instinct concept, the service which they render in defending it is closer to being an act of abortion than to assisting at its birth. But we have a hero waiting in the wings. Chanet's great service was to provoke La Chambre to response, and then to engage in controversy with him. Although the focus of their controversy was on animal reasoning, instinct also had a prominent part in it, and some of La Chambre's views on instinct anticipate modern developments in important respects.

Not that La Chambre is free from absurdities. He is no Gassendi and no Descartes, and he builds hypothetical structures with the abandon of a three-year-old building towers of blocks. But he has a keen eye for behavior in man and animals, and a receptive mind for every new fact that is announced. I shall limit myself to a bare listing of three features of his theory:

1. The basis of instinctive behavior is innate imprinting of ideas in the brain, which function in the same manner as ideas which have been acquired by experience and stored in memory (39). This means that instinct has a physical basis in brain structure.

2. So-called sympathies and antipathies among animals, when they are not based on associative learning, are to be explained by special sensitivities to stimulating characteristics such as odors, and not by occult heavenly influences; they appear mysterious to us only because we cannot sense these qualities (38). (The same sort of explanation had been put forth earlier by Digby (21A) as an anti-instinct theory.)

3. Behaviors such as laughing and weeping are not to be understood as merely expressive, but constitute innate patterns of social signaling, which evoke suitable response in other individuals (36, 37).

I think these bare statements are sufficient proof that with La Chambre the instinct concept has at last emerged as something more than a word. It will be in the toddler stage until Reimarus (51), its childhood will not end before Darwin, and I would not dare to declare now whether it has yet emerged from adolescence into maturity; but in the seventeenth century, not earlier, its long gestation is ended. It is then no longer merely a parasitic adjunct to the theory of man's superiority over other animals, but it begins to point in new directions toward explanations of some of the facts of human and animal behavior.

NOTES

1. Most of the following instances are mentioned in Lewis' and Short's *Latin Dictionary,* but see the *Thesaurus Linguae Latinae* (61) for an extended list.
2. A student, Mr. George Bishara, informs me that in contemporary Arabic this word can mean *delusion,* that one of its meanings in the Koran is *mirage,* and that it can be defined in general as "a perception without basis in reality." As the faculty of estimation, it refers to correct perceptions without basis in reason.

REFERENCES

1. Albertus Magnus. De animalibus. Ed. by H. Stadler. *Beiträge zur Geschichte der Philosophie und Theologie des Mittelalters,* 15-16, 1921.
2. Aquinas, Thomas. De anima. In *Quaestiones disputatae.* Ed. by P. Bazzi *et al.* (8th ed.) Rome, 1949. 2 vols. Vol. 2, pp. 279-362.
3. Aquinas, Thomas. In *Aristotelis librum de anima commentarium.* Ed. by A. M. Pirotta. (4th ed.) Rome, 1959.
4. Aquinas, Thomas. *Summa theologica.* Ed. by P. Caramello. Taurini, 1952-1956. 5 vols. in 3.
5. Aquinas, Thomas. *The Summa theologica of Saint Thomas Aquinas literally translated by the Fathers of the Dominican province.* London, 1912-1921.
6. Augustine. De bono conjugale. In *Opera omnia,* VI. (*Patrologia latinae, XL.*) Ed. by J.-P. Migne. Paris, 1887. Cols. 373-396.
7. Augustine. De genesi ad litteram. In *Opera omnia,* III (1). (*Patrologia latinae,* XXXIV.) Ed. By J. -P. Migne. Paris, 1887. Cols. 245-486.
8. Avicenna. *Psychologie d'Ibn Sina, d'après son oeuvre As-Sifa.* Arabic text with French transl. by J. Bakos. Prague, 1956. 2 vols.
9. Bacon, F. *Works.* Ed. by J. Spedding, R. E. Ellis, & D. D. Heath. Boston: 1861-1864. 15 vols.

10. Bartlett, J. *A complete concordance of . . . Shakespeare.* London, 1953. 2 vols.
11. Bohn, G. *La naissance de l'intelligence.* [1909] Paris, 1929.
12. Chanet, P. *De l'instinct et de la connoissance des animaux.* La Rochelle, 1646.
13. Charron, P. *De la sagesse, suivant la vraye copie de Bourdeaux.* Paris, 1657. (Orig. ed. Bourdeaux, 1601.)
14. Cicero. De divinatione. In *De senectute, de amicitia de divinatoine.* With transl. by W. A. Falconer. Cambridge, Mass.: Harvard University Press, 1923.
15. Cicero. *Tusculan disputations.* With transl. by J. E. King. Cambridge, Mass.: Harvard University Press, 1927.
16. Cochrane, C. N. *Christianity and classical culture.* New York, 1944.
17. Columnis, Guido de. *Historia destructionis Troiae.* Ed. by N. E. Griffin. Cambridge, Mass.: Medieval Academy of America, 1936.
18. Crawford, C. *A concordance to the works of Thomas Kyd.* Louvain, 1906-1910.
19. Crawford, C. *The Marlowe concordance.* Fourth Part. Louvain, 1928.
20. Dante Alighieri. *La divina comedia, III. Paradiso.* Ed. by N. Sapegno. Firenze, 1957.
20A. Dante Alighieri. *De vulgari eloquentia.* Ed. by A. Marigo. (3rd ed.) Firenze, 1957.
21. Deferrari, R. J. and Barry M. L. *A complete index of the Summa theologica of Saint Thomas Aquinas.* Baltimore, 1956.
21A. Digby, K. *Two treatises. In the one of which, the nature of bodies; in the other, the nature of mans soule; is looked into.* Paris, 1644.
22. Farmer, R. An essay on the learning of Shakespeare. In *The plays of William Shakespeare.* London, 1793. 15 vols. Vol. 2, pp. 1-83.
23. Figliucci, F. *Della filosofia morale.* Vinegia, 1552.
24. Foster, K. and Humphries, S. *Aristotle's De anima in the version of William of Moerbeke and the Commentary of St. Thomas Aquinas.* New Haven: Yale University Press, 1965.
25. Galen. *On the usefulness of the parts of the body.* Transl. by Margaret T. May. Ithaca, N. Y.: Cornell University Press, 1968. 2 vols.
26. Galien. *Oeuvres anatomiques, physiologiques, et médicales.* Transl. by Ch. Daremberg. Paris, 1854. 2 vols.
27. Gesner, C. *Historia animalium. I. De quadrupedibus viviparis.* Frankfurt, 1602. (Orig. ed. Zurich, 1551.)
27A. Goichon, A-M. *Lexique de la langue philosophique d'Ibn Sina.* Paris, 1938.
28. Grafton, R. *Chronicle at large and meere historye of the affayres of England.* London, 1568.
29. Guer, J. A. *Histoire critique de l'âme des bêtes.* Amsterdam, 1749. 2 vols.
30. Guibelet, J. *Examen de l'examen des esprits.* Paris, 1631.
31. Hangen, E. C. *A concordance to the complete poetical works of Sir Thomas Wyatt.* Chicago, 1941.
32. Hobbes, T. *Leviathan, or the matter, forme, & power of a commonwealth ecclesiasticall and civill.* London, 1651.
33. Huarte, J. *Examen de ingenios para las sciencias.* Leyden, 1652. (Orig. ed. Baeza, 1575.)
34. Huarte, J. *The examination of men's wits.* Transl. by R. Carew. [London, 1594.] Facsimile reprint, with historical introduction by C. Rogers. Gainesville, Fla.: Scholars' Facsimiles & Reprints, 1959.
35. Huguet, E. *Dictionnaire de la langue française du seizième siècle.* Paris, 1946.
36. La Chambre, Cureau de. *Caractères des passions* [I]. Paris, 1648. (Orig. ed. 1640.)
37. La Chambre, Cureau de. *Caractères des passions, V. Des larmes,* etc. Amsterdam, 1663. (Orig. ed. Paris, 1662.)
38. La Chambre, Cureau de. *Discours de l'amitié et de la haine qui se trouvent entre les animaux.* Paris, 1667.

39. La Chambre, Cureau de. *Quelle est la connoissance des bestes, et jusq'ou elle peut aller.* In *Caractères des passions, I-II.* Amsterdam, 1658. Pp. 543-599. (Appeared 1645 as a supplement to *Caractères des passions, II,* but often missing from surviving copies.)
40. Lactantius. *Firmiani Lactantii opera.* Ed. by O. F. Fritzsche. Leipzig, 1842-1844. 2 vols.
41. Latham, R. R. *Revised medieval word-list from British and Irish sources.* London, 1965.
42. Lucretius. *De rerum natura.* Ed. By W. E. Leonard & S. B. Smith. Madison, Wis.: University of Wisconsin Press, 1942.
43. Lydgate, J. *Troy book.* Ed. by H. Bergen. Early English Text Society, Nos. 97, 103, 106. London, 1906-19.
44. Magnus, L. *Dictionary of European literature.* London, 1927.
45. Melancthon, P. *Liber de anima, recognita ab autore.* Witenberg, 1584. (Orig. ed. 1552.)
46. Montaigne, M. de. *Essais.* Ed. by P. Coste. Geneva, 1727. 5 vols.
47. Nemesius. *De natura hominis, graece et latine.* Halle, 1802. (This reprint of the Plantin ed. of 1585 has been reprinted in facsimile, 1967.)
48. Nemesius. *The nature of man.* Englished by G. Wither. London, 1636.
49. Osgood, C. G. *A concordance to the poems of Edmund Spenser.* Washington, D. C., 1915.
50. Rand, E. K. & Wilkins, E. H. *Dantis Alighierii operum latinorum concordantiae.* London, 1912.
51. Reimarus, H. S. *Allgemeine Betrachtungen über die Triebe der Thiere, hauptsächlich über ihre Kunsttriebe.* (4th ed.) Hamburg, 1798. (Orig. ed. 1760.)
52. Reisch, G. *Margarita philosophica, cum additionibus novi.* Baislea, 1517. (Orig. ed. Heidelberg, 1496.)
53. Rorarius, H. *Quod animalia bruta ratione utantur melius homine.* Amsterdam, 1666. (Orig. ed. 1654.)
54. [Rouillé D'Orfeuil, A.] *L'Alembic moral, ou analyse raisonnée de tout ce qui se rapporte à l'homme.* Maroc, 1773.
55. Scaliger, J. C. *Exotericarum exercitationum lib. xv de subtilitate ad Hier. Cardanum.* Frankfurt, 1576. (Orig. ed. Paris, 1557.)
56. Sebonde, R. La théologie naturelle de Raymond Sebon. In Michel de Montaigne, *Oeuvres complètes.* Vols. 9 and 10. Paris, 1932, 1935.
57. Seneca. Letter No. 121. In *Ad Lucilium epistulae morales.* With transl. by R. M. Gummere. Vol. III. Cambridge, Mass.: Harvard University Press, 1925. Pp. 396-411.
58. Tacitus. *The histories.* With transl. by C. A. Moore. Vol. V. Cambridge, Mass.: Harvard University Press, 1925.
59. Telfer, W. *Cyril of Jerusalem and Nemesius of Emysa.* London, 1955.
60. Tertullian. *De anima.* Ed. by J. H. Waszink. Amsterdam, 1947.
61. *Thesaurus Linguae Latinae.* Leipzig, 1900-. Vol. 7, cols. 1982-1985.
62. Tilney, E. *A brief and pleasant discourse of duties in marriage, called The flower of friendshippe.* 1568.
63. Vives, J. L. *De anima et vita.* [*Basile,* 1538.] Facsimile reprint, Torino, 1963.
64. Vives, J. L. Tratado del alma. In *Obras compledas.* Transl. by L. Riber. Madrid, 1947. Vol. 2, pp. 1147-1319.
65. Wartburg, W. *Französisches etymologisches Wörterbuch.* Vol. 4. Basel, 1952.
66. Wolfson, H. A. The internal senses in Latin, Arabic, and Hebrew philosophic texts. *Harvard Theological Review,* 1935, *28,* 69-133.

The Problem of Animate Motion
in the Seventeenth Century

JULIAN JAYNES

Motion is now so much the domain of physics that it is difficult for us to appreciate that this was not always so. Before the seventeenth century, motion was a far more awesome mystery. Shared by all objects, stars, ships, animals, and men — and, since Copernicus, the very earth itself — it seemed to hide the answer to everything. The Aristotelian writings had made motion or activity the distinctive property of living things, an idea that occurs naturally to children and primitive peoples of all centuries. Because they moved, the stars were thought by no less a scientist than Kepler to be animated. Motion perplexed Gilbert, who became convinced that magnets had souls because of their ability to move and be moved. And Campanella in his Neapolitan prison, when he understood what Copernicus was saying, that the earth really moved, exclaimed, "Mundum esse animal, totum sentiens!" [1] In a world so sentient and alive, motion is everywhere. And one of the major intellectual developments of the seventeenth century gathered itself to this theme. I shall try to show in this essay that when this idea of animate motion is clarified, one result is the sorting out of the sciences by their subject matter as we know them today.

The background of this concern with motion is complex. In the Aristotelian heritage, motion was of three kinds: change in quantity, change in quality, and change in spatial locality. While the sixteenth century was beginning to use the word only in its third sense as we do today, the mysterious aura of its other two meanings hung about it like ghosts into the next century.

There was a practical background as well. The sixteenth century, with its political upheavals and religious wars, had seen the beginning of engineering as a political, military, and mercantile necessity. The tricks of the trade were called machines, from the Latin *machina,* meaning a trick or device, ways of making physical objects animate to do work that otherwise men or beasts would have to do. There had, of course, been a long history of such tricks. In the earliest times, machines had been mostly for enjoyment, such as the "automata," originally some kind of dancing dolls moved externally by an elaborate hidden mechanism of strings, weights, and rollers. Such automata are used to illustrate the principles of animate motion in both the Aristotelian writings on the subject, particularly

166

701B of *De Motu Animalium,* and then in Galen who was copying him. Machines later came to be used for practical purposes and, instead of making dolls dance, were made to lift weights or pump water. Particularly in the Roman period, mechanical devices of all sorts were brought to bear on many practical problems. And a usually neglected part of the Renaissance was the reawakening of that Roman fascination with the possibilities of mechanical engineering. Its first text appeared at the end of the sixteenth century in Jacques Besson's *Théâtre des Instruments* (Paris, 1594). And Galileo himself, at about the same time, spoke of the kind of problems that were arising in the shipbuilding yards at Venice, or in handling artillery, or in the pumping of water in mines, problems which Leonardo da Vinci had brushed with his vision a century earlier.

This tremendous increase in the number of different devices to obtain motion induced a curiosity about the ingenuity of God or nature, which could make animals or stars move. One of the great turning points in science was when man-made machines became the hypotheses or models of natural phenomena. As early as the fourteenth century, when clocks worked by wheels were still new, it was suggested that the stars were actually a piece of clockwork. While the Greeks had made the analogy that the automaton was like animal movement, some scientists in the seventeenth century, as we shall see — e.g., Descartes — were to insist that the two were identical. Motion, therefore, haunted by ancient meanings that made it seem more than it was, and pushed into central focus by the practical necessity of harnessing it to man's use, was a central problem of the century in a unique way.

The story begins when Fabricius ab Aquapendente (1537-1619) and Galileo (1564-1642) were rivals for the intellectual attention of Venice a few miles from Padua.[2] In 1610 Galileo emulated the older man Vesalian in fame-getting ways by holding his own public demonstration, not of anatomical dissections, but of his new thirty-power telescope with which he was soon to discover the moons of Jupiter, the rings of Saturn, and the cause of the shine of the Milky Way. But even at this time, Galileo was retreating from this data-collecting into reasoning about motion. The ensuing arguments between Galileans and Aristotelians created an atmosphere of discussion about motion under the overhanging pillared galleries of Padua that involved the whole university. And the aging Fabricius, just before he was poisoned,[3] was swept up into this youthful intellectual *mêlée,* writing his last work on animate motion in 1618, *De Motu Locali Animalium.*

This work should be compared to its similarly titled inspirations, the two brief Aristotelian treatises on the same subject.[4] The latter are exciting patchwork, remarkable for discovering the problems rather than for solving anything. Coming from them to Fabricius' work is like emerging from a teeming, disorderly, and exciting town into a neat meadow, a more coherent panorama of observations. Because species of the same class often exhibit different modes of motion or combinations of them, he organized his material according to the type of motion: creeping, flying, swimming, walking in bipeds, and, finally, walking in quadrupeds and multipeds. These modes of locomotion are correlated with the nature of a particular ground, whether the habitat is level or hilly, wet, sandy, or grassy. Moreover, the variability of a particular terrain or habitat finds itself mirrored in the variability of the locomotions of the particular animals living there. Not having the advantage of Galileo's *Della Scienza Mecanica,* which did not appear until 1634, Fabricius' mechanics of these motions only began what Borelli was to complete at the end of the century. But the work also contains much that is new: the first real description of the peristaltic movement, an attempt to derive all locomotions from two archetypes, walking with diagonal limbs in unison and leaping with opposite limbs in unison — an idea begun in the Aristotelian works,[5] and a fascinating section relating wing structure in birds and insects to their flight behavior. Whereas the Aristotelian writings everywhere assume that everything in nature has a function, Fabricius turns this into a principle of economy, that there is nothing extra in behavior. And instead of the Aristotelian principle that nature does what is best, Fabricius states that nature perpetuates what is best.[6] This change of verb is a giant step between ancient and modern biology. But in spite of these huge ideas that squeeze in among the detail of Fabricius' observation, the work as a whole is a failure and merely reopens the problem.

William Harvey (1578-1647) was Fabricius' best student, and most of his work can be considered an extension of Fabricius'. Recently, a new manuscript of Harvey's has been discovered.[7] Somewhere around 1627, while putting the final touches on his work on the motion of the blood, he began a notebook for his own work on the problem of animate motion, with Aristotle as "my General" and Fabricius as "my Guide." But either because of the ravages of the English civil war, or more probably because of Harvey's despair with the problem, only the notes have survived. They are a fascinating failure, altered and crossed out as Harvey's restless and unsatisfied thought frustrated and teased itself further and further into the unresponsive mysteries of behavior. He tried to refine Fabricius' classification of animal movement in terms of the means of propulsion, the kinds of movements involved, whether sequent, simultaneous or alternating, or the particular organs used. He pushes Fabricius' ecological determinism into generalizations that merely return us to Aristotelian loose ends which, for example, classify human gaits as to whether they resembled "a duck, a crane, a crow, Jew of Malta, ambling Turk,[8] servile trot, etc." The physiology is essentially Galenic in its resort to animal spirits, but breaks off into exasperated splurges of metaphor. The brain in particular is compared to a choirmaster, who performs behavior with an exquisite sense of rhythm and harmony. When the brain was removed — and here he cut off the head of a chicken and watched its behavior to prove it — behavior is disorderly, for muscles are like separate living creatures that have to be directed in harmony by the choirmaster of the brain. And from this metaphor, too, comes his emphasis on rhythm in muscular coordination, how each muscular system has a subrhythm of tension and relaxation just as the beat of the heart has its systole and diastole. Such rhythms range from the very short period of the heart to such seasonal rhythms as when "frogs and swallows hide in winter and give forth no movements," showing that he had read the erroneous statement of Olaus Magnus in 1555 on the hibernation of swallows as an explanation of their seasonal appearance in Britain. The emphasis on rhythms is a huge thought, but with Cromwell battering the king's armies outside his windows (Harvey was a loyalist), it was scarcely a propitious time for a naturalistic investigation.

In fact, his very emphasis on order and harmony reflects the civil commotion all about him. Political struggles of his day become a model of learning. The muscles of the organism are compared to a commonwealth of persons [9] that must be governed by a set of laws, where no citizen is useless and where, once order is established, there is no more need of a separate monarch to preside over each several task. Cromwell had Charles I beheaded just at this time. Harvey meant that, in learning, we are conscious of each part of a total action, but that once the action is learned, "one thing follows another in its accustomed order," and no monarch of conscious control is necessary. Harvey's interest in learning was something new to science, though the subject had become fashionable in educational discussions at Padua when Harvey was there around 1600. He is an elementarist on one page, saying that learning proceeds from parts to wholes, from particular movements that "connect up and are commanded as one whole." [10] While on another, he astonishes us with a Gestalt pronouncement that "nature thinks of the works to be performed and not of the movement of the muscles." [11] But the book as a whole is a failure, and the deletions and lacunae in the manuscript demonstrate that these were Harvey's feelings as well.

The notebook ends with lists of metaphors that might generate some kind of truth. The choirmaster model is reiterated. Or the heart is compared to a general or king, the brain to a judge or sergeant-major, the nerves to leaders or magistrates, and the muscles to soldiers — all, be it noted, enclosed within the animal without relating to its environment. A new metaphor through which to "see" behavior was indeed needed before any further progress could be made. But it was not to be found in Harvey's beautiful and grand similes to music or architecture or government, so complimentary to the reader, but in something much less inspiring, an hydraulic statue, and by someone far more insensitive: René Descartes.

In 1614, Descartes,[12] a maternally deprived eighteen-year-old student, suffered the first of several breakdowns and hid himself away in Saint Germain for two years. The only recreation available at that then rural village near Paris was a visit to the royal gardens. They had recently been designed for the new Queen by her fountaineers, the Francini brothers, and consisted of a cascade of six enormous terraces cut into the steep bank of the Seine. Each terrace ended in a row of dark subterranean grottoes connected by stone vaulted corridors, and in these high gloomy echoing chambers, flickering with torch light on their sculptured ceilings and walls and often filled with eerie music from a hydraulic mechanical organ or mechanical singing birds, were the Francinis' masterpieces: complicated hydraulic statues that moved, danced, or even spoke.[13] Descartes had been a student at the King's Jesuit school at La Flèche and so, I presume, would have been allowed in. I am suggesting that these glistening, fizzing statues in their eerie torch-lit world became the surrogate friends of a brilliant intellect unable to cope with people. Descartes tells us himself [14] how he made them move without knowing it; how, on entering, he trod on hidden plates that, for example, when he approached a bathing Diana, caused her to hide her bronze allurements in bronze rose bushes, and when he tried to follow her, caused a stern Neptune to clank and hiss forward to intercept him, creaking his dripping trident puritanically over the delighted philosopher's head.

These images, perhaps aiding his recuperation with their paradigms of behavioral control, perhaps stayed at the very depth of Descartes' thinking. He seems to view the entire physical world as though it were modeled on the Francinis' work. It was nothing but a vast machine. Just as in the Queen's gardens, there was no spontaneity at any point. He loathed animism. He loved the statues. Later he named his only child, an illegitimate daughter, Francine, perhaps after their creator. All moved by fixed principles of extension and motion. He was even contemptuous of action at a distance, for this was nothing but animism, and of course found Kepler unreasonable when the latter took the world for a ·single animal, a leviathan that roared in caverns and breathed in ocean tides. Except for human consciousness, there is only matter, dead matter, measurable and orderly matter, matter that acts on other matter by pushing or pulling matter next to it. And all goes on with the regularity, precision, and inevitability of a smoothly running machine made of nothing but matter.

Sometime between the period of his breakdown and 1633, he wrote his *L'Homme,* and then, in the winter of 1645-46, *Passions de l'âme.* Both may have been haunted by these early experiences in his late teens. Particularly in the former, he asks: What is the difference between the hydraulic statues and the people from whom he has fled, or between the bronze animals in the Orpheus grotto and real animals?

As for animals, the answer seemed self-evident. There was no difference whatever. Animals were mere water statues, not conscious, not really living — machines without will or purpose or any feeling whatever. He dissected them alive (anesthetics were far off in the nineteenth century), amused at their cries and yelps since these were nothing but the hydraulic hisses and vibrations of machines. Everything was the same. The hollow nerves and cavities of the brain were the Francinis' pipes, full of animal liquids. He called them spirits, and in some places referred to them as a subtle air, but it is more correct to think he meant the cerebro-spinal fluids that were filtered from the blood of the cerebral arteries. The muscles and tendons are merely like the "various engines and springs" which moved the statues. The nerve pipe fed into the muscle, and when the fluid came down, it billowed the muscle out like a balloon, and so made the limb move.

Now the important thing about this conception is not its hydraulic neurophysiology (though the hydraulic model is to return again and again in modern psychology) but the treadle side of the business Unlike Harvey's metaphors, the model of the statue demands that animate behavior be thought of in an environment that triggers these limb movements. The objects affecting the sense organs themselves were the treadles which the visitors stepped on, thus making the statues work. Descartes seems to have two ideas of how this came about. In some passages, he has what I will call with more correctness than taste the flush-toilet model. He thought he had found in his dissections that there was a thread running through the center of a nerve. So he considered that the sense organs contracted when stimulated, pulling this thread which ran through the nervepipe all the way up to the brain, which there pulled out a little valve allowing the animal fluids to gush back down and billow out the muscle.[15] But this couldn't explain very much, certainly not the variations in the intensity of muscular movement. So in other passages he speaks of the transmission of sensation to the brain being hydraulic as well, perhaps as a wave of pressure rising to the brain and there — and this is extremely important — reflecting back,[16] just as the water pressures were reflected in the joints of the Francinis' pipes, a reflection of the fluids that returned them down other pipes to billow out appropriate muscles. This is the beginning of the idea of the reflex.[17] The Francini brothers from Florence had built more than they knew; they had created the essential image behind modern psychology.

But Descartes' rapier-like attack on animism in animals stopped short of himself and his own species. He couldn't quite say that he himself and other non-bronze men are merely machines — as La Mettrie was to say later. In fact, the big feature of his philosophical method in his *Discours* was its new starting point in self-consciousness. And for Descartes to conceive of one of these bronze spurting statues to introspect, perhaps to suddenly spout bronzily at him *"Cogito, ergo sum,"* was a rather disconcerting thought. Never bothering to appreciate the problem he had initiated by beginning with a mechanical model as his premise, he backed out of it by calling his self-consciousness a thing, in the same sense that the statue was a thing. There were two such things, mind and body. Instead of harmonizing the discrepancy of viewpoint by analyzing in a skeptical fashion his own thought processes as he should, he simply asserted the discrepancy was in nature rather than in his own thinking. Without a quiver of the plume in his hat, he reified his own consciousness into a substance, perhaps even like the mists that hung glistening in the air over the beautiful hydraulic automatons in their irresponsible grottoes, an airy substance uncontrolled by the pipes, springs, and water pressure; in fact, the soul — the soul that has its own laws, is not dependent on the brain, and has innate structuring and innate ideas prior to experience; the soul that is the misty origin of volition and unbounded place of thought, that at least could be imagined at death to rise, either steamy with sin or misty with innocence, to a heaven situated somewhere above the engaging motions of Saint-Germain.

But even this mind, in Descartes' compulsively mechanical and materialistic thinking, had to be joined to the body, though there was no rational necessity to do so. Recent Paduan anatomists had mentioned the pineal gland, whose function is just becoming known today.[18] Since it is in the center of the head, and is single rather than double, as most other parts of bilaterally symmetrical animals, here was the great tiny bridge between the two worlds where the whole mystery of creation was concentrated, where thought meets extension and mastered it, and where extension moves toward thought and is perceived. The soul or mind squeezed the pineal gland this way and that, nudging the animal fluids in the human brain into the pores or valves,

> and according as they enter or even only as they tend to enter more or less into this or that nerve, they have the power of changing the form of the muscle into which the nerve is inserted, and by this means making the limbs move.[19]

Animals, according to Descartes, had no pineal gland (even though it had been first discovered in animals!), and thus no bridge to the other realm, no thoughts. If they had any thoughts, they would say so and tell us about them. Their silence condemns them into mere automation.

It was all so clear and simple that anyone could remember it and everyone did. Thought so novel, so attractive in its bold, clear images amidst the remaining murk of scholasticism, and so flattering to the human species (everything immortal this side of the pineal gland) could not but lift up the attention of a century already impatient with ancient philosophy and longing for a new one. Like magic, a prevaricating magic I might add, it swept all the old insolubles and scholastic confusions out of sight and effort, and into the mists of consciousness, leaving the visible world merely a catching clockwork like the flickering grottoes hissing with hydraulic life at Saint-Germain.

It is important to appreciate the enormity of the reaction to Descartes so that we realize the importance even of his mistakes. Brilliant and arrogant, he was just that bit beside the point on most of the psychological problems he tackled as to stir calm reflection into heated discussion. As to the problem of animate motion, the reaction to Descartes is in three phases: (1) the refutation of the localization of soul action in the pineal gland; (2) the refutation of his theory of nerve-muscle action and, with it, the long history of the doctrine of animal spirits; and (3) the continuation of his emphasis on animal motion being caused by stimuli.

Archaic for its own day, the errors of Descartes' physiology were pointed out one by one as they appeared. The year following the publication of *Traité de l'Homme*, N. Steno (1638-1686), the young Danish theologian and physiologist, found himself "obliged to point out . . . the vast difference between Descartes' imaginary machine, and the real machine of the human body"; [20] he showed that the pineal gland existed in animals as well as in man (as had been known before), and in no case had the rich nerve supply which the Cartesian theory demanded. The drivewheel of Descartes' animal machine had been the brain, with its ventricles full of valves; but as had long been known, the brain was unnecessary to many animal movements. Redi noticed the movements of decapitated snakes. So did Boyle, who also went searching for the seat of the soul in snakes by removing one internal organ after another until his specimens even . . .

> two or three days after the skin, the heart, and the entrails are separated from it are seen to move in a twining or wriggling manner, may appear to be manifestly sensible of punctures, being put into a fresh and vivid motion when it lay still before, upon the being pricked especially on the spine or marrow, with a pin or needle.[21]

And the chance finding that a decapitated tortoise moved three days afterward provoked an anonymous writer for the recently begun *Philosophical Transactions of the Royal Society* to exclaim that this was a "sore blow" to the Cartesians, "so the Disciples thereof are here endeavoring to heal the wound."

But if the Cartesian soul was not in these locations, perhaps it might be in the blood. Blood transfusions, following the technique of blood infusion developed by the architect Sir Christopher Wren, were begun by Richard Lower. Lower replaced the blood of a sheep with the blood of a calf, after which the sheep bounded away and reacted to a dog in typical sheep-like fashion, proving that habits and instincts are not situated in the blood.[22] Descartes' idea that the soul had a particular location or isthmus in the body and Steno's immediate disproof had thus begun a quandary that was both futile and regressive, and would last well into the next century.

The second aspect of Descartes' physiology to be refuted was his concept of muscle action and, with it, a part of the long tradition of animal spirits. The importance of this refutation must be understood against the larger background of the rivalry between the two great medical theories of the seventeenth century, the Physiatric and the Chemiatric. The former, stressing physical therapies, surgery, and anatomy, was the chief trend of the century, and became even more prominent after the exciting success of Galileo's mechanics, Harvey's theory of circulation, and the many mechanical inventions of the time. But the older Chemiatric School, with its chemical and alchemical therapies and theories, was nevertheless still flourishing in the haunted heritage of that wondered, wandering cabalistic drunk, Paracelsus, particularly in Germany and Holland, where he had established it. Early in the seventeenth century, a new offshoot of the Chemiatrics appeared, calling themselves Rosicrucians, still a going concern today. From this time to our own, the Rosicrucians have kept alive the older mystiques about motion, referring to vital forces that pass through one body to another. Like Paracelsus, they wallowed in undulant metaphors, using them as explanations, as in the analogy of animate motion with magnetism that later grows into Mesmer's "animal magnetism" and thence into hypnosis.

In general, the Chemiatrics saw the thickening of muscle tissue in contraction as a swelling of the animal spirits similar to the swelling up of a liquid during fermentation. Van Helmont (1557-1644), their most respectable member, did so, although he buried the causative part of the problem of animate motion in spiritual occult agencies called "blasses," interacting with the body through the pylorus, which were little else than the *archei* of Paracelsus revived for a more critical age. The influence of this idea of muscle action went quite beyond the Chemiatric school itself. John Mayow (1645-1679), for example, perhaps because of Lower's experiment, thought the air rather than the blood was impregnated with a "certain, universal salt, of a nitro-saline nature, that is to say, with a vital, fiery and in the highest degree fermentative spirit" [23] whose particles are breathed in and become the animal spirits that account for animate motion. This idea, like Rosicrucian doctrine, has also lasted into our own time, its most recent manifestation being the orgone theory of Wilhelm Reich.[24]

Descartes had simply taken over this idea of muscle action and crystallized the problem beautifully and wrongly with the simplicity of his vision. The animal spirits that had begun as a confused doctrine over a thousand years before in Alexandrian physiology had indeed come to this. If this could be disproved, if it could be shown that the muscle was not swelled up by liquid or airy animal spirits, the Chemiatrics had lost their most promising solution to the problem of animate motion and therefore much of their hold on seventeenth-century thought. And this is precisely what happened.

The famous experiment of Jan Swammerdam (1637-1680) was one of the most important of the century. What a brilliant simplicity it was! Dissecting out the gastronemius muscle of a frog with its attached nerve, he immersed it in water, pinched the nerve, and showed that there was no displacement of the water as the muscle contracted.[25] Nothing could therefore have been added to the muscle. Even the very demonstration of such an artificial irritation of the nerve-muscle preparation ruled out all notions of animal spirits being flushed down from the ventricles of the brain, as Descartes had arrogantly insisted. The experiment was definitive. The Chemiatric theory of animate motion was never a serious scientific trend again.

The more agreeable side of Descartes' influence on the problem of animal motion is not in physiology. It is in the idea that animate motion is to be understood by correlating it with physical stimuli which occasion it. Even Descartes' critics could not escape the power and fascination of seeing behavior in this new way. Swammerdam in particular, a thorough physiatric, carefully related the behavior he observed to stimuli. He noted the contraction of the pupil of the eye when irritated by a "particle of light," the peristalsis of the intestines in proportion to their contents, and how trains of images, just like trains of muscular contractions, can follow each other "urged by one cause of motion to another."

And this emphasis is repeated by Francis Glisson (1597-1677) in England, who, I venture, could not escape knowing Swammerdam's widely discussed work. Referring to the Chemiatric theories in his posthumous *De Ventriculo,* Glisson explained how "this explosion and inflation of spirits has now for some time past been silent, convicted by the following experiment." [26] And then he went on to perform the same sort of experiment as Swammerdam to show that muscles did not increase in bulk during contraction. His experiment with somewhat less elegance used the intact human arm submerged under water. He also stressed certain aspects of Swammerdam's terminology that brought into general biology that unfortunate concept of "irritability."

In a different way, the stimulus-response paradigm is continued in the sometimes fantastic work of Thomas Willis (1621-1666), a celebrated physician at Oxford.[27] His work is an astonishing combination of worth and worthlessness, so that even contemporaries dubbed him "a lucky dissector" who "too soon fell in love with his first thoughts." And those first thoughts were indeed his inspiration from Descartes. Willis was little better than Descartes on the nerves, conceiving them not as tubes, but as "cords lightly strung," the animal fluids slithering down the outside of them into the muscles. His conception of the brain was even more baroque than Descartes', complete with ventricles like halls of mirrors and windows, with actual images projected on the white wall of the *corpus callosum* by the *corpora striata*. Images undulate about the brain, pushed hither and thither by hydraulics more fantastical than Descartes', and were stored in the folds of the cortex. The brain even produced its own light that shone out through the eyes in ancient Platonic fashion, so that he could believe an elderly gentleman who once quaveringly told him that "after an extra good bout of wine he could see to read print clearly on a very dark night."

But Willis' importance resides not in his fantasies, as Descartes' does, but in his two emphases. First, he carries through all his work the Cartesian idea of behavior as a reply or response to stimuli. He even used the metaphor of an echo, and differs from Descartes in making the periphery, as well as the brain, the seat of what Marshall Hall in 1833 called the reflex.[28] Second is his emphasis on the hierarchy in the nervous system. The cerebrum presides over voluntary motion and is higher than the cerebellum presiding over involuntary motion. Each has its own memory.

This is the first and proper solution to a problem that perplexed many of the writers I have dealt with. Van Helmont had ascribed voluntary and involuntary motion to two occult "blasses." Descartes had hidden the problem of voluntary motion in the depths of his nonphysiological human soul, all other behavior being automatic. And Swammerdam, appalled at this mixture of science and metaphysics, had gone too far the other way in refusing to admit the distinction. Willis put the matter in the right direction, which led to considerable experimental work in the next century on the effects of destroying parts of the nervous system. The important result was to solve the problem of animate motion by classifying it according to the parts of the nervous system necessary to it.

What was happening was now becoming clear. The problem of animate motion, when separated from physics, has two solutions: correlating it with stimuli or with parts of the nervous system.

But there is another solution. And it is the morose and quarrelsome Giovanni Borelli (1608-1679), a troubled and swaggering thinker, who is the very summing up of this seventeenth-century obsession with the problem of motion.[29] In one of his early works, he had spoken of the attraction between bodies that we have come to call gravity, explaining the movements of the moons of Jupiter as a resultant between such an attraction and inertia — and this twenty years before Newton. But he lacked the calculus that Leibniz and Newton were inventing even at that very time, and the definitive statement had to wait for Newton's great *Principia* in 1687. And after a stormy life studying astronomy, fever, kidney function with Bellini, and geometry, and scrapping with the Accademia del Cimento, the scientific society to which he belonged (they met in semisecrecy and were supposed to publish anonymously, which was too much for his ego), Borelli retired to a monastery and spent his last years finishing the work for which he expected fame (and received posthumously), his *De Motu Animalium*. It was published in two parts, in the two successive years after his death, and is concerned with the problem that had persisted since the century had begun.

The first part solves much of the problem Fabricius and the Aristotelian writings had opened. Following Galileo's mechanics and Steno's ideas on the structure of muscle, with diagrams and equations meant "to ornament and enrich" his subject, Borelli showed the bones to be true levers — the length of the limb, the distance to the muscle, or differences in the center of articulation all influence the force necessary to make the movement. When he examined the flight of birds and the swimming of fish, he first looked for the center of gravity, even as Aristotelian writings had done, but with the new Galilean emphasis. One of his sections is entitled "The Quantity of Air Acted Upon by the Wing of a Bird in Flight Is in Shape a Solid Sector Swept out by a Radius Equal to the Span of the Wing." He demonstrated that "the power of the muscles that beat the wings is ten thousand times greater than the weight of the bird." And from this he deduced that the story of Icarus is impossible since our pectoral muscles could never reach this ratio. It is to be noted that he is never concerned with the initiation of animate motion, only its mechanics.

In the second part, Borelli went on to apply mechanics to internal motions. He calculated the forces necessary for Harveian circulation, the heartbeat, and respiration, and attempted to apply mechanics to liver and kidney functions with less successful results, biochemistry being unknown. This is, of course, the exciting beginning of physiological biophysics. And thus the seventeenth-century's fascination with motion produced major discoveries in physiology as well as in physics and psychology.

My underlying purpose in this essay has been to suggest that much of modern science has structured itself out of these seventeenth-century divisions of the problem of motion. During the Renaissance many thinkers kept and nourished a mystique about motion that confused it with both life and change. Partly because this mystique was so intellectually haunting, and partly because motion by machines was becoming more and more important in the European economies, it became the central intellectual concern as the century begins. Even before Galileo disengaged the physical problems of mechanics from this mystical confusion, Fabricius separated out the biological problems of animal motion. He failed to find a solution, but succeeded in correlating animal motion with environment in a remarkably prescient way. Harvey also struggled with the problem, but made no advance in it whatever. What was needed was a new metaphor or paradigm for animal motion, one that would differentiate it from the motion of physics. And this, as I have shown, was supplied by Descartes' analogy of organisms with hydraulic sculpture. How ironic that this materialistic idea, by considering animate motion as a response to stimuli, distinguished it forever from the motion of inanimate objects! Even by 1680 it was somewhat trite to point out, as did Perrault, that, for example, the flowing of a river which "seems to seek the valley," [30] indicating choice and desire, is in reality a wholly different kind of thing than the sense-caused movements of animals.

Three solutions followed. First, the paradigm that animate motion is a response to stimuli led directly to the notion of "irritability" and of the reflex, and thence to the stimulus-response psychology of more recent times. Secondly, the explanation of animate motion was felt to be in the nervous system, just as a machine is explained by its parts. This led immediately to the study of the localization of function. Willis' idea of the independence and separate functions of parts of the brain was pursued by Boyle, Perrault, Bohn, Chirac, Du Vernez, Preston, and others, and led to the development of neurology in the next centuries. Thirdly, another kind of explanation was found in the descriptive mechanics of the organism treated as a physical system. After Borelli, there was so little more to say of a fundamental sort that the subject, except for a brief flurry of interest in the late nineteenth century in Marey and others, did not receive further attention until modern biophysics.

The seventeenth century, then, sorted out the mystical and confused problem of motion into our several modern sciences. Perhaps the most important lesson from all this is to realize the tremendous generative power of metaphor and analogy in the beginnings of science. This is particularly evident with respect to the two kinds of motion. Physics in the seventeenth century is anthropomorphic about matter, applying animate terms like attraction, force (originally muscular strength), inertia (originally referring to an idle and unemployable person), and acceleration (to hasten one's steps) to get started. The reverse occurred with Descartes when he applied the inanimate statue analogy to animal motion.

Newton's *Principia* in 1687, coming after this history, is of course the major answer to the seventeenth-century concern with the problem of motion. Newton's laws of motion make it all the more clear that physical behavior is a quite distinct thing from animate behavior. Hardly any physicist would ever again think of the world as living because it moved, as Kepler and Campanella had done, and even as Newton was tempted to do at one time. Animate behavior is different. Its explanation resides no longer in the explanation of motion, but only in the correlation of that motion with a nervous system and the stimuli around it. This is a huge and important step.

NOTES

1. Thomas Campanella, *De Sensu Rerum,* Bk. 1, Ch. 9.
2. One student wrote home in 1549 that Padua was "an infinite resorte of all nations where all kynds of vertue maie there be learned" Clare Howard, *English Travelers of the Renaissance* (New York, 1913 p. 53).
3. Cf. *Biographie Universelle.*
4. The *Peri Zoon Kineseos and the Peri Zoon Poreias* of the Aristotelian works. I refrain from ascribing them to Aristotle since they are obviously multi-authored and are collections of scraps from various sources from the fourth to second centuries B. C.
5. *Peri Zoon Poreias,* 705A.
6. A relevant passage remarkably prescient of nineteenth-century biology is the following (my translation): "In truth, nature fulfills her aim by so bestowing behavioral movements and functions among animals that they preserve themselves through them; this consists in a preservation of the ablest in obtaining food, in continuing the species, and in avoiding injury" (*De Motu Locali Animalium secundum totum,* Padua, 1618, p. 8).
7. William Harvey, *De Motu Locali Animalium* (1627), ed. and trans. by G. Whitteridge (Cambridge, 1959).
8. Perhaps indicating something about the flamboyance of acting style of the time, since these are obviously references to two characters from Marlowe's plays.
9. An analogy made also in the Aristotelian *Peri Zoon Kineseos,* 730A30.
10. Harvey, p. 122.
11. *Ibid.,* p. 123.
12. I am here advancing a theory about Descartes. I have not been able to find more pertinent evidence than I have here cited, and I realize I am being more inferential than scholarly. Descartes nowhere (that I know of) refers to the

Francini statues by name or actual place, or as to when in his life they so probably impressed him.

13. For further descriptions of these grottoes, see Paul Gruyer, *Saint Germain* (Paris, 1922) and Georges Houdard, *Les Chateaux Royaux de Saint Germain-en-Laye* (Saint Germain, 1911-12). John Evelyn, the diarist, visited them in 1644 and described them as already beginning to decay.

14. Descartes, *L'homme,* ed. by Cousin (Paris, 1824), IV, p. 348.

15. *Ibid.*

16. Article 38 of *Passions de l'âme.* The only passage where any reflex-like word appears in Descartes is in this sense in Article 36, where he speaks of "les esprits réfléchis de l'image ainsi formée sur la glande. . . ."

17. The two important works on this history of the reflex are Franklin Fearing, *Reflex Action* (Baltimore, 1930), and Georges Canguilhem, *La Formation du Concept de Réflexe aux XVIIe et XVIIIe Siècles* (Paris, 1955).

18. The pineal gland was so named by Galen because in the ox brain he was studying, it was shaped like a pine cone (Latin: *pinare* = pine cone). Vesalius in 1540, caught up in the Renaissance love of metaphor, called the pineal gland the cerebral penis, a notion that may have at least stressed its importance to Descartes and given him the absurd supposition of its motility. See *Vesalius' First Public Anatomy at Bologna 1540, An Eyewitness Report* by Baldasar Heseler, ed. by R. Eriksson (Uppsala & Stockholm, 1959). Its true function is still obscure, but it is believed to be an evolutionary vestige of an ancestral light-sensitive organ still present in some lizards. It probably is involved in regulating biological functions related to the amount of light. Its very high concentration of serotonin suggests that some important new discoveries may soon be made here, particularly in regard to insanity.

19. Descartes, *L'homme,* p. 347.

20. Nicolaus Steno, *Lecture on the Anatomy of the Brain* (1669), ed. by G. Scherz (Copenhagen, 1965). The great Bishop of Titopolis did not tackle the problem of animal motion himself, but he came to understand the nature of muscle better than anyone else of his century. He knew that if a muscle is cut up lengthwise by scissors in three or four bits, each bit may be made to contract, proving that the power of contraction lies in the muscular substance rather than in the whole muscle as a machine.

21. *Philosophical Trans. of the Royal Society* (1665-1667), p. 387.

22. *Ibid.,* pp. 353-358.

23. Mayow, *De Sal Nitro* (London, 1668), cited by Michael Foster, *Lectures on the History of Physiology* (Cambridge, 1924), p. 184.

24. Wilhelm Reich, *The Discovery of the Orgone: The Function of the Orgasm.* trans. by T. P. Wolfe (New York, 1961).

25. Jan Swammerdam, *The Book of Nature; or the History of Insects: reduced to distinct classes, confirmed by particular instances, displayed in the anatomical analyses of many species.* With life of the author, by Herman Boerhaave. Trans. from the Dutch and Latin original editions by T. Flloyd. Revised and improved by notes from Réamur and others, by John Hill (London, 1758).

26. As cited by Fearing, p. 37.

27. Thomas Willis, *The remaining Medical Works of that Famous and renowned Physician, Dr. Thomas Willis,* trans. by S. Pordage. V. Of Muscular Motion. VI. Of the Anatomy of the Brain. VII. Of the Description and Use of the Nerves (London, 1681).

28. Hall, "On the reflex function of the medulla oblongata and medulla spinalis," *Phil. Trans. Roy. Soc.* (1883), *123,* 635-665.

29. Borelli, *De Motu Animalium* (Rome, 1680-1681).

30. As cited by Fearing, p. 35. Claude and P. Perrault, *Oeuvres Diverses de Physique et de Méchanique* (Paris, 1761). The quotation is from his *Essai de Physique* (1680).

The Role of Psychology in the Nineteenth-Century Evolutionary Debate

ROBERT M. YOUNG

The history of psychology is a discipline whose relationship with psychology and with the history of science has yet to be defined. This paper is a case study in the relations between the history of psychology and an important issue in the mainstream of the history of science—the nineteenth-century debate on evolutionary theory. It was prepared as a talk for an audience of psychologists, and one of its aims is to suggest parallels between current debates on the relevance of psychology to society and an analogous debate that occurred in the eighteenth and nineteenth centuries.

I

I want to begin by considering the current debate about the relationship between academic psychology and wider issues concerning the nature of man and society. There is a great deal of soul-searching going on about the relevance of the behavioral and social sciences — in their experimental, theoretical, and applied aspects — to social, political, and ideological issues in the public domain. Alongside the publications in professional journals and the traditional forms of research and teaching, there is growing up a literature which charges the so-called objective, positivist, un-ideological behavioral and social sciences (along with psychiatry and psychotherapy) with irrelevance and/or strong ideological biases. More accurately, they are being charged with having the wrong ideological biases.[1] Others are attempting to draw on the biological and behavioral sciences as sources of extrapolation for generalizations about politics and the organization of society. Everyone will have his own list of such works, but the ones which my students are reading in lieu of the books assigned to them are R. D. Laing's *The Divided Self,* Lucien Goldmann's *The Human Sciences and Philosophy,* Herbert Marcuse's *Eros and Civilization* and *One-Dimensional Man,* Konrad Lorenz's *On Aggression,* and Desmond Morris' *The Naked Ape.* Some of the more intrepid ones have gone on to weightier books in the same unorthodox genre, for example, Arthur Koestler's *Beyond Reductionism* and C. D. Darlington's *The Evolution of Man and Society.* I don't suppose that many academic psychologists assign these books, and this helps to make one of my points in two ways. First, it is not immediately clear how they relate to our scientific work. Although it is fairly obvious that different ones relate in very different ways, it is surely a comment on academic psychology that these relationships are not explored in detail as a central aspect of our commitment to the subject. The second point provides the basis for most academic psychologists' failure to take on that task — that is, such works do not meet the accepted standards of scientific methodology. Having said that either explicitly or implicitly, most psychologists say no more. Professional responsibility ends there, or so it is said, and curiosity seldom takes us further.

Yet many of us get into psychology with the same wider issues in mind that such popular and extrapolating works explore. And many of us feel bitter that academic courses do not concern themselves with broad issues of human nature and society. Sometimes, of course, such courses are offered, but it is a rare psychologist who does not consider such courses as "service teaching," something rather far removed from his real commitment to research and, of course, students know this. One is left wondering what happened to the curiosity which might have taken us further. I think that there are two sorts of answers which apply to those who remain in academic psychology. Some find sufficient intellectual challenge within experimental psychology as currently practiced — the domains of perception, learning theory (especially in its more formal and mathematical branches), and physiological psychology are favourite havens. Most who take this path either develop a strong attitude of intolerance for such "muddled" and "wooly" issues or are left with a vague sense of nostalgia for these problems, coupled with a sense of impotence based on our inability to approach such issues with sufficient scientific rigor to make them intellectually rewarding. The other sort of answer involves making a greater or lesser sacrifice of scientific elegance, in turning to some branch of what we patronisingly call "applied psychology" — clinical, educational, ergonomic research; motivational research, mental testing, psychotherapy.

I am in no position to provide a panacea for these ills. Nor is my main purpose to increase our discomfort in a destructive spirit. Rather, I should like to provide a perspective on what I take to be some of the conceptual and methodological problems involved in the scientific investigation of human nature by considering earlier episodes in the debate on man's place in nature, debates that reveal an intimate union of psychological, biological, social, and ideological issues. My purpose in doing so is not to change the subject but to suggest that there is an important *critical* function for the history of psychology.

I am an historian of science and am preoccupied with the history of attempts to apply the methods and assumptions of science to the study of man and society. I hasten to add that I do history because I believe that our present predicament might be eased if we could gain greater perspective on the assumptions we make and on the ways in which the heritage of the past constrains our present thinking. We could then act on the basis of what we see. Similarly, the structure and the conceptual affinities of past controversies can perhaps help us to take a broader view of our own situation. Historical studies thereby become an analytic tool, not an antiquarian quest in search of who did what first or whether or not A is buried in B's grave.

The writing of the history of a subject at any point in time is highly constrained by contemporary conceptions of the subject itself. This is particularly true of the history of psychology, because its small number of practitioners is on the defensive. They feel themselves to be under attack from colleagues who wonder why they aren't doing experiments, and they also feel shunned by professional historians of science who do not see the relevance of the history of psychology to the mainstream of the history of science. If I were giving this whole paper on the historiography of psychology, I would try to point out in some detail the fundamental philosophical issues behind these reactions. Instead, I shall only say that they reflect the methodological and metaphysical insecurity of all three groups — the historians of psychology and of science, and the practicing experimentalists. It is therefore not surprising that the history of psychology is in a very primitive state and that its practitioners have, until very recently, tended to write synoptic surveys — *The History of Psychology from Plato to NATO* — to show that they have culture, or they search (I think vainly and irrelevantly) for the first truly scientific treatment of this or that problem.

II

In the space that remains I should like to address myself to the three issues I have raised by directing attention to the evolutionary debate in the late-eighteenth and nineteenth centuries. In doing this I hope to provide some evidence for the claim that there are intimate relations between psychological, social, philosophical, and theological issues, and thereby to show the importance of wider issues for the history of psychology. More importantly, I shall try to show the crucial role of the history of psychology *in* the mainstream of the history of science, considered in its social and political context.

At first glance this seems to be an easy task. Every schoolboy knows that the furor over evolution was largely due to the wider implications of the theory, i.e., that the theory of organic evolution implied that man was descended from the apes. Put slightly more formally, it meant that the origin of man occurred by means of the continuous operation of natural laws and not by special creation. This, in turn, implied that it was no longer possible to separate mind and culture from the domain of scientific laws. Man and all his works — body and mind, society and culture — became, in principle, part of the science of biology. The continuity of types was based on the continuity of natural causes, and discontinuities between body and mind and between nature and culture became untenable. God did not act by isolated interpositions, and moral responsibility no longer had a separate, divinely ordained basis in the freedom of the will.

Notice, however, that I have not suggested that discoveries in psychology were central to this set of issues. On the contrary, it is usually argued that it was the theory of evolution which gave psychology — especially comparative, developmental, and physiological psychology — a sound conceptual basis. Charles Darwin's theory was not derived from such findings. Rather, it was derived primarily from studies in geology, paleontology, zoogeography, theory of classification, the study of domesticated animals, and the practices of breeders. Once established, the theory transformed psychology. It is true that Darwin indulged in some speculations about psychology and mental inheritance as he was working out his evolutionary theory, that he made numerous notes on instinct, and that he wrote a short study in child development as well as two books that dealt with issues recognizably psychological: *The Descent of Man*[2] and *The Expression of the Emotions in Man and Animals*.[3] However, it is clear that these were not his central concerns. He considered *The Descent of Man* to be an unoriginal work, and he handed his notes on instincts and comparative psychology to George J. Romanes, who set out to do for the evolution of the mind what Darwin had done for the evolution of the body.[4]

If we look closely at the *Descent of Man,* we find Darwin accepting the *principles* which follow from evolutionary continuity. However, his examples are excessively anecdotal, and his categories of analysis are drawn from a pre-evolutionary psychological tradition. Here is a sample of his approach to the issues:

> It is, therefore, highly probable that with mankind the intellectual faculties have been mainly and gradually perfected through natural selection; and this conclusion is sufficient for our purpose. Undoubtedly it would be interesting to trace the development of each separate faculty from the state in which it exists in the lower animals to that which exists in man; but neither my ability nor knowledge permits the attempt.[5]

Darwin had taken the same, rather laconic, approach to the problem of instincts in *On the Origin of Species*.[6] This is slightly surprising, since he had been very aware of the importance of the problem of mind from the beginning of his researches. The following passages appear in his notebooks of 1837 and 1838, the period in which he was developing his conception of natural selection, but before he had the flash of insight which will be discussed below: "My theory would give zest to recent and fossil comparative anatomy; it would lead to the study of instincts, heredity, mind-heredity, whole [of] metaphysics." [7] In the same period he was also concerned with the origins and philosophical status of mind, and wrote: "Why is thought being a secretion of brain more wonderful than gravity a property of matter?" [8]

However, as I have said, he gave his notes on instinct and mind to G. J. Romanes, whom some believe to be the most important pioneer in comparative psychology. When Romanes asked Darwin's advice about the question of the origins of mind, Darwin was again rather casual, and his reply did not reveal the intensity of interest and the penetrating reasoning which characterized, say, his correspondence about plants:

> I have been accustomed to looking at the coming of the sense of pleasure and pain as one of the most important steps in the development of mind, and I should think it ought to be prominent in your table. The sort of progress which I have imagined is that a stimulus produced some effect at the point affected, and that the effect radiated at first in all directions, and then that certain definite advantageous lines of transmission were acquired, inducing definite reaction in certain lines. Such transmission afterwards became associated in some unknown way with pleasure or pain. These sensations led at first to all sorts of violent action, such as the wriggling of a worm, which was of some use. All the organs of sense would be at the same time excited. Afterwards definite lines of action would be found to be the most useful, and so would be practiced. But it is no use my giving you my crude notions.[9]

Darwin was, therefore, very diffident about psychology and characteristically deferred to Spencer, Romanes, and Huxley on psychological topics. Historians of psychology have, nevertheless, habitually attributed a great deal to Darwin's influence on the subject. My point is that, whatever the *implications* of his work for psychology and whatever the long-term influence of evolutionism on psychology, it is clear that the main sources of Darwin's theory were derived from the studies of a field naturalist and from geology. This was where his real interests lay and where he made his own contributions to the *findings,* as opposed to the theories and assumptions of science. He wrote twenty books, four of which were major *(Origin, Variation of Plants and Animals, Descent of Man, Expression of the Emotions),* of which only the last was primarily psychological. And even that was really only intended as an essay to be appended to *The Descent of Man* and was published separately because of the excessive length of the *Descent.*[10] By comparison, eight of his books were strictly about plants.

Having denigrated the significance of psychology in Darwin's work, I want to make one important exception: the influence of Malthus' *Essay on Population* on Darwin's ideas. This was a crucial influence, but in order to understand it, I must make a large detour that will introduce my main theme, i.e., the extremely intricate ways in which psychological ideas influenced the evolutionary debate, both implicitly and explicitly, in its details as well as in its very wide implications. I want to address mvself to this issue in two ways. The first is to stress the relative *isolation* of the internalist history of psychology in the nineteenth century from the mainstream of the great debate on man's place in nature, and the second is to go back and look again to see that at another level psychological theories were at the very heart of the debate, providing its most fundamental conceptions and touching on its widest implications for human nature and society and indeed for the philosophy of nature itself.

III

First, let us consider the isolation of the evolutionary debate from the internal history of psychology. If we recall what I said about the significance of the evolutionary debate for views of human nature, one would expect that the findings of psychologists would provide the data for a central area of contention. What is the evidence for mental determinism? How closely comparable are the behaviors of men and lower organisms? Is there a perfect correlation between the mind's activities and the physiology of the nervous system? What are the grounds for believing that criminals and lunatics have no control over their actions? All of these issues were being assiduously investigated and debated in the late eighteenth century and throughout the nineteenth. Surely these debates should be closely integrated with the evolutionary debate.

One might object that the general public was not expert enough to consider the detailed findings of psychologists, physiologists, and psychiatrists. This is an initially plausible hypothesis until we look at the astonishing level of sophistication of the public debate in the nineteenth-century periodicals on such abstruse issues as the details of geological stratification and natural history. The most prestigious of the periodicals were the three main quarterlies, and from the beginning the *Edinburgh Review* (1802), the *Quarterly Review* (1809), and the *Westminster Review* (1824) contained extended critical essays on nearly every significant work in geology and biology, written by the leading scientists, philosophers, and theologians of the period. Works on the philosophy of science and on natural theology received the same exhaustive treatment. The complex interrelations among geological, biological, and theological issues were also discussed at great length.

In the same period three main sorts of investigation were occurring in psychology.[11] The first concerned the laws of mind and centered on the concept of the association of ideas. The tradition of associationist psychology goes back to the work of David Hartley (1749) (to which I shall revert in the next section) and can be traced ultimately to the mainstream of the Scientific Revolution in the works of Newton and Locke.

The association of ideas was also a basic assumption of the epistemology and psychology of David Hume and had continental parallels in the work and influence of Condillac. In the nineteenth century there were extremely important writings in this tradition by Thomas Brown, James Mill, J. S. Mill, Alexander Bain, Herbert Spencer, and G. H. Lewes. The laws of mind, and their relations with the laws of nature, with society, and with education, were discussed at great length. These books were reviewed in the periodicals, but there is very little sustained treatment of them in connection with the evolutionary debate until well after 1860. Also, the context in which they were considered was neither primarily psychological or biological.

Similarly, beginning as early as 1811, there were important experiments on the structure and function of the central nervous system. By the early 1820s, the functional division of the spinal nerve roots was being investigated experimentally in Britain, France, and Germany. In the same period there were extensive experiments on the functions of the brain which might have given strong support to the antideterminists and antimaterialists in the evolutionary debate. Between 1822 and 1870 numerous experimental tests provided *no* evidence for localization of functions in the brain or for the production of purposive movements by artificial stimulation of the cerebral cortex, and the interpretation placed on these experiments was that they supported the autonomy of an indivisible mental substance and belief in free will. There were extensive debates on these findings in the physiological and clinical journals, but the issues found almost no expression in the general debate. This is all the more curious, since the evolutionary debate focussed on the structure of the brain after 1860, and the people conducting the public debate about evolution were also intimately involved in the physiological and medical debates. I am thinking particularly of Richard Owen and T. H. Huxley.

There were also heated controversies on the concept of reflex and on how far up the neuraxis automatic, reflex functions prevailed. Eminent physiologists differed on issues that were perfectly parallel to those in the mainstream of the general evolutionary debate. Thus, while evolutionists argued about whether or not the activities of animals and men were entirely determined by unchanging laws, the physiologists differed on whether or not the thinking part of the brain — the cerebral cortex — obeyed the same laws as the automatic, reflex functions of lower brain centers and the spinal cord. Once again, it was often the same people who took leading parts in both debates. William Carpenter and G. H. Lewes are notable examples.

Even when, in the 1840s, Thomas Laycock applied the reflex concept to all levels of the central nervous system and argued for complete continuity of function, he did not do so on the basis of the theory of evolution but, on the contrary, based his claims on the principle of continuity in the antievolutionary theory of the Great Chain of Being. He did this in spite of the fact that the general version of his theory was presented to the British

Association in 1844, the year of publication of a widely read and hotly debated argument in favor of evolution, *Vestiges of the Natural History of Creation.*[12]

Twenty-five years later, when the tide had turned, and it was demonstrated by experiment that movements which had hitherto been attributed to free will could be produced by localized electrical stimulation of the cerebral cortex, these findings might have been taken up by the evolutionists and determinists. They might have told the general public that thought and action were entirely functions of brain centers and that free will was thereby proven to be a chimera. But they didn't. This work was based on inferences drawn from experiments on dogs and monkeys, whose relevance for man was based on evolutionary theory, but the implications of the findings for man were not driven home in the general debate.

An indication of this isolation can be found in Darwin's *Descent of Man.* There was a section on the brain added to the second edition, which Darwin persuaded Huxley to write. Even so, the two editions of that work —1871 and 1874—appeared in the period of greatest discovery in the physiology of the cortex, and no whisper of these developments occurs in the book: the argument is conducted entirely in terms of comparative anatomy, without reference to physiology. The issue of comparative anatomical structures in the brain had preoccupied Huxley in the 1860s, in his debates with Owen on the brain.[13] It could, of course, be argued that Huxley was not *au fait* with developments in cerebral physiology. If so, he must have learned it fairly soon thereafter, since the Royal Society turned to him to act as referee for some very delicate issues raised by papers which David Ferrier submitted on the subject in the mid-1870s.[14] Yet neither his contribution to Darwin's book nor his popular essays draw on the findings and theories of psychologists and neurophysiologists. The same can be said of William Carpenter, who was the chief expositor of experimental physiology in Britain at the same time that he was one of the most active and respected interpreters of evolutionary theory.[15]

Having discussed the curious sequestration of associationism and neurophysiology — two approaches with evolutionary and determinist implications — I want to increase our bewilderment by briefly discussing the example of phrenology. In this case our problem is made worse by the fact that phrenology was one of the most popular and publicly controverted theories in the nineteenth century. Its alleged determinist, materialist, and atheist implications were grasped at the outset, and its adherents were regularly reviled in the main periodicals — for example, in the third number of the *Edinburgh Review,* again in 1815, and again and again. I know of only one extensive, balanced treatment of it — by Richard Chevenix in the *Foreign Quarterly Review* in 1828.[16] The same people who attacked uniformitarian geology and evolutionism sallied forth against the putative atheism and degradation of man which lay in the phrenological doctrines of Gall, Spurzheim, and their Scottish exponent and popularizer, George Combe. Phrenological works were in the library of every Mechanics

Institute, and by 1832 there were twenty-nine phrenological societies and numerous publications in Britain (with others in France and even more in America). Combe's *Constitution of Man* sold 50,000 copies between 1835 and 1838, 80,000 by 1847, and a total of over 100,000 by 1865. It is said that homes which contained only the Bible and *Pilgrim's Progress* chose Combe's *Constitution of Man* as their third book.[17] I shall argue below that phrenology played a central role in the development of evolutionary theories, but the close conceptual affinities between phrenology and the issues in the evolutionary debate were not a significant feature of the public debate. The condemnation of phrenology and that of uniformitarian geology and evolutionism went on side by side.

To complete our confusion, I should point out that these three themes in the history of psychology — associationism, neurophysiology, and phrenology — came together in the writings of Alexander Bain and that they were placed in the context of evolutionism by Herbert Spencer. In the crucial period of 1855-1859, when they were providing perfect ammunition for the wider debate, the connection was not widely grasped. When psychophysiology was placed on an experimental basis in the early 1870s by the findings of Fritsch and Hitzig and of Ferrier in their research on cerebral localization, these findings were available for the debate surrounding *The Descent of Man,* but they were not taken up.[18] When they were extended by physiologists and neurologists — especially John Hughlings Jackson — the failure of the evolutionists and anti-evolutionists to exploit them becomes astonishing.

IV

Having borne with me this far, you will have anticipated that I have been setting up an elaborate rhetorical question which I shall now proceed to answer. If so, you will be half-disappointed, and the half that I cannot explain is the most puzzling one. That is, it is easy to point out that the anti-evolutionists understandably did not want to conduct the debate on grounds which their whole position required them to deny *in principle* as long as they could hope to defeat the enemy on safer territory. For example, it was preferable to defeat the uniformitarians on the battlefield of the history of the earth. If this could be shown to be unexplainable without recourse to divine intervention, then the question of the vulnerability of man's special place in nature need never arise. Even Lyell's uniformitarian geology represented an outwork, protecting the central citadel of man's special nature. He was uniformitarian about the history of the earth, but denied biological evolution. For safety's sake he added that even if evolution was required to explain the history of the animal kingdom, to apply it also to man would stretch analogy beyond all reasonable bounds.[19]

This is not to say that psychological, physiological, and phrenological issues never got mentioned in the general debate. However, when they did come up, they were isolated from the mainstream of the debate and/or treated polemically. Those who were upholding the traditional picture of the order of nature and society were unwilling to dignify the sciences of mind and brain by debating their findings, when their whole position required them to deny that man's mind lay within the domain of science. This interpretation is given support by the appearance of *Mind,* the first professional journal in psychology and philosophy in any country. By the time it was founded — we would say, very tardily — in 1876, psychologists were fed up with being fobbed off. The journal was financed by Bain, and the first editor was his protégé, George Croom Robertson. In the prefatory remarks in the first issue, Robertson wrote:

> Even now the notion of a journal being founded to be taken up wholly with metaphysical subjects, as they are called, will little commend itself to those who are in the habit of declaring with great confidence that there can be no science in such matters, or to those who would only play with them now and again. . . . MIND intends to procure a decision on this question as to the scientific standing of psychology.[20]

This partially satisfactory explanation of why the defenders of man's special status were unwilling to debate the laws of mind and brain — because they denied the relevance of scientific methods and laws to higher functions — leaves us with the problem of why the *proponents* of evolutionism and of a science of man did not draw on the detailed findings of psychologists and neurophysiologists to bolster their own case. Since I simply don't know the answer to this at the straightforward level, I will spare you my paltry speculations on the subject while inviting you to look at the much more significant role which psychological theories played at a deeper level in the theories of the evolutionists.

Before doing so, however, I should add that psychology was in some respects in good company. While I cannot explain its isolation to my own satisfaction, I can remind you that the relevance of findings in one discipline to those in another can take time to dawn on very clever men — even to the men whom we see as most directly concerned with the integration of those sets of findings. In the nineteenth-century debate on man's place in nature there were relatively few articles which, as they say nowadays, got it together. I have found only one essay in the pre-1859 period which closely integrates the question of evolution with the question of the natural history of man, and that was written by a medical psychologist, Henry Holland, in the *Quarterly Review* in 1850.[21] For the most part, however, the debate on man's place in nature was not an integrated debate. It was, rather, a network, involving partial overlaps between issues that seem obviously to be related from the anachronistic vantage point of a current observer. There was uniformitarian geology, but its chief preoccupation was to combat catastrophism. Its use of paleontology was in that context.[22] Viewing paleontology from another perspective, it was closely integrated with the study of comparative anatomy under the in-

spiration of Cuvier. Richard Owen was called "the English Cuvier," but
it was not until the 1860s that debate centered on comparative anatomy
as applied to man, a debate in which the advocate of evolution, Huxley,
engaged the opponent, Owen. The quarrel was refereed by Lyell, who was
still six years away from accepting evolution.[23] Physical anthropology was
related to the problem of the antiquity of man, while its preoccupation
with skulls was strongly influenced by issues that had been raised by
phrenology.[24] But anthropology in general was concerned with issues
which it had inherited from speculative history and Utilitarianism. The
foundation of an Anthropological Society in 1863 was not a consequence
of evolutionism but a reflection of earlier preoccupations.[25] When an-
thropologists drew ideas from evolutionism, it was not a new inspiration,
but an alliance which served to obscure other, deeper problems in their
work.[26] The study of the geological evidences of the antiquity of man was
done for a variety of reasons, but the concentration on the issue in the
1860s was not in any simple sense seen as a consequence of Darwin's
theory. Finally, students of social development, like those in anthropology,
had preoccupations which owed more to questions that had faced the
Scottish Enlightenment and the Utilitarians, rather than to evolutionism.[27]
My point in parading these disciplines before you is to apply to the past a
truism of current intellectual life. Whatever an outsider may consider to
be the relevant conceptual affinities and common interests, different disciplines have their own preoccupations, and the relations between these
form a loose network of issues and interests, which does not conform to
any abstract pattern. Professionals, students, and laymen differed as much
then as they do now about the relevance of given issues. It could be argued
that our ability to see this clearly in examples drawn from the past might
help us to loosen our categories and perhaps recover some of our lost
curiosity.

The example of the geological evidence of the antiquity of man is
revealing.[28] What could be more central to the question of man's place in
nature? Many alleged fossil remains of man had been found in the
eighteenth century and again in the 1820s by William Buckland, the main
exponent in that period of the recent and special origin of man. These
were found in strata which also contained the remains of extinct animals,
but they were all explained away, and Buckland wrote confidently in 1836
that there was no convincing evidence of fossil human remains which were
laid down with the bones of extinct animals. Charles Lyell — Buckland's
geological opponent but a believer in the special creation of man — saw
some very convincing evidence in 1833 and wrote that the circumstances
of the remains were "far more difficult to get over than I have previously
heard of." As late as the 1855 edition of his *Principles of Geology*, he
remained unconvinced. However, as early as 1849, and again in 1857,
Boucher de Perthes had reported unequivocal evidence of fossil men
with extinct animals, but nobody was convinced, and I have seen no
report of these findings in the general debate at the time. Even Darwin

was forced to admit in 1863, "I am ashamed to think that I concluded the whole was rubbish."

However, in 1858, in Brixham Cave in South Devon near Torquay, some flint implements were found in direct association with bones of extinct animals from the Pleistocene. This was reported to the British Association in 1858, but there is no reference to these findings in Darwin's *Life and Letters*. There was another paper read to the Royal Society in May 1859, after the joint Darwin-Wallace paper to the Linnean Society in July 1858 in which they announced their theory of evolution by natural selection. This paper was concerned with additional findings in the Somme Valley. The debate was largely confined, however, to geologists and antiquaries. Lyell went to France to see for himself and confirmed the findings in his Presidential Address to the British Association in 1859. Once again, however, these startling confirmations of the worst fears of the anti-evolutionists did not appear in the reviews of Darwin's *Origin of Species* in 1860. Indeed, they were hardly mentioned at all in the public debate, until Lyell forcibly drew attention to them in 1863 in *The Geological Evidences of the Antiquity of Man;* and even he remained — as Darwin saw it — maddeningly uncommitted to their implications in support of evolution.[29] By 1871, the connection between the question of man's antiquity and acceptance of evolution was much clearer, and Darwin could allude to them rather complacently in the introduction to *The Descent of Man:* "The high antiquity of man has recently been demonstrated by the labours of a host of eminent men, beginning with M. Boucher de Perthes; and this is the indispensable basis for understanding his origin. I shall, therefore, take this conclusion for granted, and may refer my readers to the admirable treatises of Sir Charles Lyell, Sir John Lubbock, and others." [30] My point in giving this example is that, as with the study of psychology, neurophysiology, and phrenology, we can understand the failure of opponents of evolution to give publicity to such findings, but the tardy integration by the proponents of evolution is odd. In any given period, intellectual life is fragmented in ways that appear bizarre to those who have the benefit of hindsight.

V

I appreciate that the structure of this paper is maddeningly parenthetical and even recursive. I now want finally to make my positive case. I want to begin with a truism that is often forgotten by those who view the past through spectacles crafted in the workshops of current disciplinary boundaries: the river of nineteenth-century naturalism was fed by many streams.[31] The part of that river which interests us most is that which led to the interpretation of man in naturalistic terms. I have mentioned that evolutionary theory drew on geological, paleontological, natural historical, and breeders' interests and issues. But it also drew on Utilitarianism, associationism, phrenology, mesmerism, Owenite socialism, Positivism, and scientific historical criticism of the Bible. For present purposes I want to draw attention to the number of streams in that second list which are psychological. Indeed, we could extend it to include classical economics and the development of sociological and anthropological theory. I want to point out the specific role of psychology in evolutionary and social theories, but in order to do so we must look below the surface. Before Bain, psychology was not seen as a discipline in its own right. It was playing a broader social and intellectual role, and in the development of evolutionary theory its influence was more abstract. Thus, for example, important psychological works were seen in social, theological, ethical, educational, colonialist, and logical contexts. This is particularly true of associationist psychology in the writings of the Utilitarians or Philosophical Radicals.[32] Similarly, phrenology was propagated and well received as a platform for social, educational, and public health reforms. It was offered as the key to all philosophical and social problems — a panacea for all social ills. If we are to understand the role of psychology in the evolutionary debate, we must stop looking for it at the level which has been reviewed thus far in the argument. My point for the remainder of this paper is that psychological theories lay at the very basis of much of evolutionary theory. Indeed, it can be argued that in many respects evolutionary theory (as well as theories of progress, Utilitarianism, and social science) was *applied psychology*.

In order to see this, however, we must look again at certain key figures, not all of whom are usually regarded as psychologists. It is generally acknowledged that Descartes and Locke were figures in whose work there were important and intertwined strands of ontology, epistemology, physical science, theology, psychology, and (implicitly in Locke, explicitly in Descartes) physiology. But the effective beginning of the modern tradition in empiricist psychology is usually attributed to David Hartley's *Observations on Man, His Frame, His Duty and His Expectations,* which appeared in 1749.[33] Hume's work also contained very influential arguments about the association of ideas, and although he spelled out in detail some of the laws of association, he eschewed any speculation on the physical basis of the associative process. The association of ideas had been an afterthought in Locke's *Essay,* and although it was central to Hume's argument, it is still the case that he was preoccupied with epistemological and ethical issues. The same argument can be made about Hartley's *Observations,* since he was really most concerned with questions of natural theology, morality, and the afterlife. Nevertheless, in integrating arguments drawn from Locke, John Gay, and Newton, he went into great detail about the associative process in the primarily psychological context of learning and constantly related this to a theoretical framework based on vibrations in the brain. For present purposes, it was Hartley's formulation which was most influential in providing a mechanism for changing utilities and adaptations. His detailed theory allowed others to speculate on ordered change through experience in both the psychological and, by analogy, the somatic structural realms. His ideas were the fountainhead for the development of the associationist tradition in psychology, but they were also used in theories of progress and evolution. Thus, for example, Erasmus Darwin introduced the section on "Generation," in which he puts forth his theory of evolution in *Zoonomia* with the following passage:

> The ingenious Dr. Hartley in his work on man, and some other philosophers, have been of the opinion, that our immortal part acquires during this life certain habits of action or of sentiment, which become for ever indissoluble, continuing after death in a future state of existence; and add, that if these habits are of the malevolent kind, they must render the possessor miserable even in heaven. I would apply this ingenious idea to the generation or production of the embryon, or new animal, which partakes so much of the form and propensities of the parent.
>
> Owing to the imperfection of language, the offspring is termed a *new* animal, but is in truth a branch or elongation of the parent; since a part of the embryon-animal is, or was, a part of the parent; and therefore in strict language it cannot be said to be entirely *new* at the time of its production; and therefore it may retain some of the habits of the parent-system.
>
> At the earliest period of its existence the embryon, as secreted from the blood of the male, would seem to consist of a living filament with certain capabilities of irritation, sensation, volition, and association; and also with some acquired habits or propensities peculiar to the parent: the former of these are in common with other animals; the latter seem to distinguish or produce the kind of animal, whether man or quadruped, with the familiarity of feature or form of the parent.[34]

Erasmus Darwin has here adapted Hartley's argument and employed it as the basis for a theory of evolution. First, he has taken principles which Hartley had used to refer to the afterlife; he has secularized them and treated inheritance as an extended form of learning. In so doing, he treats the offspring, its inherited habits, and its bodily features as a prolongation of the acquired experiences of the parent. Associationist psychology, suitably extrapolated, becomes evolution. The other examples I shall cite are similar in using psychological theories as the basis for other sorts of theories, although there is space only to mention them.

Joseph Priestley also drew on Hartley's psychological theories in support of his necessitarianism and abrogated Hartley's vestigial mind-body dualism in support of his Unitarian materialist progressive philosophy of nature. This served as the foundation for his work in such diverse fields as theology, chemistry, and politics.[35] In the sphere of social theory, William Godwin, one of the founders of modern anarchism, based his theory of inevitable and indefinite human progress on Hartlean psychological mechanisms.[36] The writings of James and J. S. Mill, and the logical, educational, social, and political theories which they espoused, were also based on associationist principles.[37]

Looking across the Channel, the epistemological and psychological writings of Condillac also employed a sensationalist epistemology and an associationist mechanism.[38] These were taken up by Condorcet as the basis for his theory of human progress in the *Sketch for a Historical Picture of the Human Mind* (1795) in a way that parallels Godwin's use of associationism in England.[39] Paralleling Erasmus Darwin's evolutionism, one finds one aspect of Lamarck's evolutionary theory also dependent on the inheritance of characteristics that were acquired through the repeated strivings of individuals. This aspect was secondary in his theory to an inherent tendency to progress, but, as we shall see, some of his interpreters made it the primary factor.[40]

I have provided these examples of the influence of the psychological writings in the period before the nineteenth-century debate to show their fecundity in generating biological and social theories. It is an important task — one to which historians of psychology and of the other sciences have not begun to address themselves — to consider how many fundamental aspects of the so-called Scientific Revolution can be reinterpreted from the point of view of psychological theories. After all, the fundamental ontological, epistemological, and methodological shifts during the sixteenth and seventeenth centuries were, in large measure, concerned with problems of perception, purposiveness, and objectivity — topics that are central concerns of current psychology.[41]

But our main concern is with the nineteenth-century debate, and I want to address myself to the writings of the three main evolutionary theorists in Britain: Darwin, Wallace, and Spencer. In the crucial period in which he was formulating his theory, Charles Darwin needed a basis for making an analogy from the artificial selection of breeders to a natural process whose directionality did not depend on the intentions of a conscious selecting agent. How, to put it crudely, could *nature* select? [42] In providing an answer to this, Darwin drew on a theory which was rooted in associationist psychology but which was at two removes from the basic Hartlean doctrine. As a social doctrine, Utilitarianism depended on the associationist pleasure-pain theory of learning. In its economic form it required that men act in their rational self-interest, seeking the pleasures that flow from employment and avoiding the pains of poverty. The equilibrium and wealth of society depended on this mechanism. Pleasure and pain became the rewards and punishments of rational social and economic behavior. The system worked if there was enough to go around or if enough wealth could be created — if nature was bountiful enough and man industrious enough. Adam Smith tended to feel that they were.[43] Twenty years later, T. R. Malthus took the opposite view, putting a different face on social equilibrium and pointing out the checks on progress which, you will recall, was being advocated on the basis of parallel extrapolations from sensationalism and associationism by Godwin and Condorcet.[44] Malthus pointed out that nature was not bountiful enough, human industry was not inventive enough, and the sexual appetite was too strong. The conflict between the limits of nature and industry, on the one hand, and population growth, on the other, produced laws of struggle. He interpreted struggle as a benevolently designed cosmic learning theory:

I should be inclined . . . to consider the world and this life as the mighty process of God, not for the trial, but for the creation and formation of mind, a process necessary to awaken inert, chaotic matter into spirit, to sublimate the dust of the earth into soul, to elicit an etherial spark from the clod of clay. And in this view of the subject the various impressions and excitements which man receives through life may be considered as the forming hand of his Creator, acting by general laws, and awakening his sluggish existence, by the animated touches of the Divinity, into a capacity of superior enjoyment. The original sin of man is the torpor and corruption of the chaotic matter in which he may be said to be born.[45]

He continues:

The first great awakeners of the mind seem to be the wants of the body. They are the first stimulants that rouse the brain of infant man into sentient activity, and such seems to be the sluggishness of original matter that unless by a peculiar course of excitements other wants, equally powerful, are generated, these stimulants seem, even afterwards, to be necessary to continue that activity which was first awakened. . . . From all that experience has taught us concerning the structure of the human mind, if those stimulants to exertion, which arise from the wants of the body, were removed from the mass of mankind, we have much more reason to think that they would be sunk to the level of brutes, from a deficiency of excitements, then that they would be raised to the rank of philosophers by the possession of leisure. . . . Necessity has been with great truth called the mother of invention. . . .[46]

To furnish the most unremitting excitements of this kind, and to urge man to further the gracious designs of Providence, by the full cultivation of the earth, it has been ordained that population should increase much faster than food. . . . Strong and constantly operative as this stimulus is on man to urge him to the cultivation of the earth, if we still see that cultivation proceeds very slowly, we may fairly conclude that a less stimulus would have been insufficient. . . . Had population and food increased in the same ratio, it is probable that man might never have emerged from the savage state.[47]

The mechanism had produced progress, but the means were painful. The only hope of mitigating the resulting suffering was "moral restraint" from premature marriage, and Malthus did not put much faith in this partial palliative. I have quoted the rationale for his mechanism at length in order

to offer convincing evidence that his explanations of progress and the re-
straints on it were generalizations of the pleasure-pain theory of learning:
it caused progress, just as the survival or death of individuals constituted
the ultimate sanctions of the law of population. As I said above, Darwin
read Malthus' *Essay on Population* (in the sixth edition, where the arguments I have quoted are not offered in a summary form) at the crucial time
when he was looking for a basis for an analogy between artificial and
natural selection. Both his working notebooks and his retrospective accounts make it clear that the Malthusian population theory, when applied
to plants and animals (and, secondarily, to man), provided the concepts
of law and of natural pressure which Darwin required in order to formulate
the theory of evolution by natural selection.[48] He wrote to Wallace in 1859:

> You are right, that I came to the conclusion that selection was the
> principle of change from the study of domesticated productions; and
> then, reading Malthus, I saw at once how to apply this principle.
> Geographical distribution and geological relations of extinct to recent
> inhabitants of South America first led me to the subject: especially
> the case of the Galapagos Islands.[49]

The case of A. R. Wallace, the co-discoverer of the theory of evolution
by natural selection, was different in important respects. I only want to
make a few observations about it. He did not reach the theory by analogy
to artificial selection. Indeed, he denied the analogy.[50] However, Malthus'
conception of struggle also provided him with the key to the theory of
natural selection. In the cases of both Darwin and Wallace, the concepts
of species survival and extinction were explicit generalizations of the
Malthusian concepts of population survival and death, and these were
based on utilitarian concepts which, in turn, were derived from the association psychology. It is ironic that Wallace later claimed that the principle
of utility was a corollary of the concept of natural selection: "The utilitarian
hypothesis . . . is the theory of natural selection applied to the mind. . . ." [51]
I should perhaps add that in addition to the influence of Malthus and Lyell
on him, Wallace's naturalistic approach to man was derived from three
main sources: Robert Owen's socialism, Robert Chambers' *Vestiges of
Creation,* and George Combe's *Constitution of Man.* All three of these
drew on the principles of phrenology to support their biological approach
to human nature.[52]

If we turn to the writings of the third main evolutionist, Herbert
Spencer, we find a complicated situation which begins, for our purposes,
with his first book, *Social Statics* (1851).[53] His central purpose in that
book was to rebut moral and social theories based on Utilitarianism,
theories which, of course, depend on associationism. Spencer considered
the psychology of the Utilitarians to be too abstract, thereby paying insufficient attention to individual differences. Individualism was a central
belief of Spencer's, and in answering the Utilitarians he turned to a theory
which at once provided a sufficient number of variables to account for

individual differences and made the context for the study of man that of biological adaptations rather than mind in general. That theory was phrenology. But Spencer's individualism was coupled with another basic belief in social progress, and the faculty psychology of phrenology was a static one that allowed for only partial modifications as a result of experience. After all, phrenology had been derived by Gall in explicit reaction against naive sensationalism, and Gall had postulated innately given instincts as the basis for his faculties. Thus, Spencer's adaptive view of man and his organic view of society gave no promise of social progress. In search of this he turned to another psychological theory on biological form: Lamarckian evolution. Lamarck's theory, you will recall, had two aspects: an inherent tendency to progress in life, and perturbations of this due to the recalcitrance of the environment. The secondary factor led organisms to acquire structural modifications as a result of striving, and these were passed on to the next generation. I want to stress these two aspects because what most of us mean by "Lamarckian" evolution is the version of the theory which became popular once Spencer got through with it. He conflated the two aspects of Lamarck's doctrine and made the inheritance of acquired characteristics the mechanism of inevitable biological and human progress.

Notice that the "Lamarckian" aspect of Lamarckianism was derived from continental expressions of the associationist psychology — the tradition inspired by Condillac and united with biology and physiology by the French Idéologues. Spencer set aside his former belief in the faculty psychology of phrenology and adopted the associationist psychology as expounded by J. S. Mill in his *Logic*. He had developed a renewed interest in psychology through his friendship with G. H. Lewes, and when he decided to write a book on the subject, he drew on Mill's expressions of the Hartlean doctrine. The heart of Spencer's *Principles of Psychology* (1855) [54] was Part III, in which he extended learning by association from the experience of the individual to that of the race, and made this the basis for biological evolution. Two years later he presented a general theory of progress based on evolution, which was, in turn, an extrapolation from the inheritance of functionally produced modifications according to the mechanisms of associationist psychology. After publishing this essay, entitled "Progress: Its Law and Cause," [55] he further generalized his theory in *First Principles* (1862), and this contained the foundations for his synthetic philosophy as applied to psychology, education, sociology, and ethics.[56] It also provided the basis for much of later functionalist theory in psychology, sociology, and anthropology as well as for so-called Social Darwinism in political theory.[57] (It is worth adding parenthetically that it had important direct influences on neurology through the work of John Hughlings Jackson who, in turn, had an important influence on certain of the assumptions of Freud's psychoanalytic theory.) [58] My reason for reiterating the history of Spencer's intellectual development and some aspects of his influence is to draw your attention to its roots in two psychological theories: phrenology and associationism, placed in an evolutionary context and then reapplied to society in the form of the organic analogies which have been central to functionalist thought in the behavioral and social sciences. If there were space to pursue these issues further, we might explore the role of psychological theories in political and social thought — for example, in Walter Bagehot's conservative *Physics and Politics* and in John Dewey's liberal theories of industrial democracy.[59] But instead of pursuing the influence of psychological conceptions further outward into society, I would like to look briefly at a still deeper level of scientific thought.

VI

There is still another way in which psychological conceptions played an important part in the nineteenth-century debate. Once again, the issue is not straightforward. The domain of this influence was the philosophy of nature, with particular effect on the concepts of "cause" and "force." This aspect of the debate is very elusive, and most scholars have only seen one bit of it in the epistemological debate between William Whewell and J. S. Mill on induction.[60] This controversy, however, was only the tip of a very large iceberg that has been investigated by Dr. Roger Smith of the University of Lancaster. In an extremely interesting doctoral dissertation on "Physiological Psychology and the Philosophy of Nature in Mid-Nineteenth Century Britain," [61] he discusses a network of ideas and influences which involved debates on the role of touch in learning (going back to Berkeley), the organic sense (or "muscle sense"), the principle of the conservation of energy, and the concept of force itself. I am not competent to summarize his very illuminating findings, but it is clear from his research that a number of ideas were exploited in psychology, physiology, epistemology, and the philosophy of nature in an effort to overcome the problems raised by Cartesian mind-body dualism in the course of the period of the evolutionary debate. Putting the issues very crudely, there seem to have been two camps, one of which was phenomenalist in its approach and used a Humean conception of the association of ideas to argue that science can only be concerned with the constant conjunctions of phenomena. Phenomenalists argued that the concepts of cause and force were, as far as science was concerned, not amenable to further analysis. The other group, represented by some of the arguments of the Scottish School, by William Whewell, and by the later thought of A. R. Wallace, wanted to be anthropomorphic about nature and to project a dynamic view. Thus, they argued that the concept of cause referred to a power behind the phenomena, while the concept of force was not only derived by analogy from the concept of human intention but also implied will in nature. As Wallace said, "All Force is probably Will-Force." [62] Proponents of this view were very much in sympathy with spiritualism and other manifestations of alleged forces behind the phenomena of nature which might bridge the gaps between mind and body, human will and mechanism, dynamic nature and dead nature. I do not want to pursue this issue further except to say that Dr. Smith seems to me to have opened up a whole new dimension of research which promises to help to show the real connections among psychological, philosophical, scientific, social, and popular theories in the period. He has shown that below the surface of the histories of psychology, biology, and related disciplines, as hitherto written, lies a much more potentially illuminating field of research in which psychological ideas were fundamental.

I have tried to shed light on three roles for mind in the evolutionary debate. My first pass at the problem produced a puzzling set of negative findings. Issues that appear central from the point of view of hindsight play a surprisingly small role in the great debate on man's place in nature. The opponents of scientific naturalism about man were not prepared to discuss in detail what they were not prepared to concede in principle, while the proponents were working with a set of overlapping conceptions which only came into focus after evolutionism had gained the center of the debate and the burden of proof had shifted to the opponents. A second view of the same debate reveals that psychological conceptions played a central role in social theory and in the theoretical assumptions of the evolutionists and those who influenced them most. Thirdly, I briefly reported that at the level of the philosophies of nature which underlay the scientific ideas not only of psychologists but also of physiologists, evolutionists, and philosophers, psychological conceptions appear to be fundamental. It seems clear that in the nineteenth-century debate there was an intimate mixture of psychological, social-philosophical, biological, and theological issues. These were linked with basic beliefs about man, nature, and society which were themselves playing an important role in the period. Those of us who find ourselves cut off as professional psychologists or historians of psychology from the contemporary mainstream of social and political issues can perhaps learn something from the earlier debate. It is only by taking a narrow and superficial view of that debate that the isolation of psychology can be made to appear real. It wasn't actually so isolated. It was engaging in scientific, philosophical, theological, political, and ideological work.

It seems to me that the task of a critical history of psychology is to use historical research to help us to consider the work that our own research and theoretical conceptions are doing, to evaluate that work, and then to debate among ourselves and with our students and colleagues what work we think we ought to be doing. That, of course, is a political question, but if we ponder both the negative and positive roles of psychology in the evolutionary debate, we may begin to see that it has always been political. Conceptions of psychology lie at the center of debates on man's place in nature. Such debates, however, are at the same time fundamentally concerned with man's place in society and — overtly or covertly — with the putative desirability and possibility of alternative social structures.

Psychology is never sequestered. It is only that its students, teachers, and researchers are more or less self-conscious and critical about the actual roles which their theoretical and applied scientific activities are playing in the maintenance or transformation of conceptions of nature, human nature, and society.

NOTES

1. See David Ingleby, Ideology and the human sciences: Some comments on the role of reification in psychology and psychiatry, *The Human Context, 2,* (1970), 159-187; R. M. Young, Evolutionary biology and ideology: Then and now, *Science Studies, 1,* (1971), 177-206.
2. Charles Darwin, *The descent of man, and selection in relation to sex* (1871; 2nd ed. London: Murray, 1874).
3. Charles Darwin, *The expression of the emotions in man and animals* (London: Murray, 1872).
4. George J. Romanes, *Mental evolution in animals, with a posthumous essay on instinct by Charles Darwin* (London: Kegan Paul, Trench, 1883).
5. Darwin, *Descent of man,* pp 128-129.
6. Charles Darwin, *On the origin of species by means of natural selection, or the preservation of favoured races in the struggle for life* (London: Murray, 1859; facsimile reprint: N. Y.: Atheneum paperback, 1967), Chap. 7.
7. Francis Darwin (Ed.), *The life and letters of Charles Darwin,* 3 vols. (London: Murray, 1887). Vol. 2, p. 8.
8. Quoted in Sir Gavin de Beer, *Charles Darwin. Evolution by natural selection* (London: Nelson, 1963; also paperback), p. 108.
9. Francis Darwin (Ed.), *More letters of Charles Darwin,* 2 vols. (London: Murray, 1903). Vol. 2, pp. 51-52.
10. Darwin, *Descent of man,* pp. 3-4.
11. I have discussed the issues which are here considered only briefly in *Mind, brain and adaptation in the nineteenth century* (Oxford: Clarendon, 1970) and in outline in The functions of the brain: Gall to Ferrier (1808-1886), *Isis, 59,* (1968), 251-268.
12. Thomas Laycock, On the Reflex Functions of the Brain [read at York before the Medical Section of the British Association for the Advancement of Science on Sept. 28, 1844], *British & Foreign Medical Review, 19* (1845), 298-311; cf. his systematic treatise, *Mind and brain: Or the correlations of consciousness and organization,* 2 vols. (Edinburgh: Sutherland & Knox, 1860); [Robert Chambers], *Vestiges of the natural history of creation* (London: Churchill, 1844; facsimile reprint: N. Y.: Humanities Press, 1969). [Names in square brackets denote anonymous authorship.]
13. Thomas H. Huxley, *Man's place in nature* (1863; reprint: Ann Arbor, Michigan: Ann Arbor paperback, 1959); see especially pp. 133-138 for A succinct history of the controversy respecting the cerebral structure of man and the apes, which is not reprinted in the standard edition of Huxley's *Collected essays.*
14. George Rolleston *et al.,* Referees' reports on Ferrier, 1874, Archives of the Royal Society, RR. 7. 299-305, RR. 12. 103.
15. William B. Carpenter, *Nature and man. Essays scientific and philosophical* (London: Kegan Paul, Trench, 1888).
16. [Thomas Brown], Villers *sur une Nouvelle Theorie du Cerveau* . . . by Dr. Gall of Vienna, *Edinburgh Review, 2* (1803), 147-160; [John Gordon], The doctrines of Gall and Spurzheim, *ibid., 25* (1815), 227-268; [Francis Jeffrey],

Phrenology, *ibid.,* *44* (1826) 253-318, 515, and *45* (1826), 248-253; [Richard Chevenix], Gall and Spurzheim—Phrenology, *Foreign Quarterly Review,* 2 (1828), 1-59. Anyone who wishes to investigate the fine texture of the Victorian debate as understood in its contemporary context must rely on the indispensable key to the authorship of the (usually anonymous) essays in the main periodicals provided by the research of Walter E. Houghton (Ed.), *The Wellesley index to Victorian periodicals, 1824-1900,* of which Vol. I has so far appeared (London: Routledge, 1966).

17. [Chevenix], *op. cit.,* pp. 17-20; A. Macalister, Phrenology, in *The Encyclopedia Britannica,* 9th ed. (Edinburgh: Black, 1885), Vol. 17, p. 844; advertisement in *The Leader, 1* (1850), 24; George Combe, *The constitution of man considered in relation to external objects* (1828), 9th ed. (The Henderson Edition, Edinburgh: Maclachlan & Stewart, 1866), p. viii; J. D. Y. Peel, *Herbert Spencer. The evolution of a sociologist* (London: Heinemann, 1971), p. 11; Charles Gibbon, *The Life of George Combe,* 2 vols. (London: Macmillan, 1878).

18. [W. Boyd Dawkins], Darwin on the descent of man, *Edinburgh Review, 134* (1871), 195-235; [St. George J. Mivart], Darwin's *Descent of Man, Quarterly Review, 131* (1871), 47-90; Alvar Ellegard, *Darwin and the general reader. The reception of Darwin's theory of evolution in the British periodical press, 1859-1872* (Göteborg: Acta Universitatis Gothoburgensis, 1958), Chap. 14

19. Charles Lyell, *Principles of geology, being an attempt to explain the former changes of the earth's surface by reference to causes now in operation,* 3 vols. (London: Murray, 1830-1833), Vol. 1, p. 156.

20. John Croom Robertson, Prefatory words, *Mind, 1* (1876); cf. Alexander Bain & T. Whittaker (Eds.), *Philosophical remains of George Croom Robertson* (London: Williams & Norgate, 1894). The only document I have encountered in the mainstream of the evolutionary debate which makes anything like a serious attempt to integrate the implications of psychology with those of the general evolutionary theory is John Tyndall's notorious "Belfast Address" to the British Association in 1874, reprinted in his *Fragments of science,* 7th ed., 2 vols. (London: Longmans, Green, 1889), Vol. 2, pp. 135-201; cf. pp. 202-223. He draws primarily on the theories of Spencer, and although his address is a central document in the debate, it is usually considered to represent the final victory statement of the evolutionists. As such, it is consistent with my general thesis about the sequestration of psychology until after evolution had won the day.

21. [Henry Holland], Natural history of man, *Quarterly Review, 86* (1850), 1-40.

22. M. J. S. Rudwick, The strategy of Lyell's *Principles of Geology, Isis, 61* (1970), 5-33.

23. Charles Lyell, *The geological evidences of the antiquity of man, with remarks on the origin of species by variation* (London: Murray, 1863); Leonard G. Wilson (Ed.), *Sir Charles Lyell's scientific journals on the species question* (New Haven: Yale, 1970); cf. above, note 13.

24. James Hunt, On the localization of functions in the brain, with special reference to the faculty of language. *Anthropological Review, 6* (1868), 329-345, and 7 (1869), 100-116, 201-214.

25. John W. Burrow, Evolution and anthropology in the 1860's: The Anthropological Society of London, 1863-71, *Victorian Studies, 7* (1963), 137-154.

26. John W. Burrow, *Evolution and society. A study in Victorian social theory* (Cambridge, 1966; also paperback reprint).

27. *Ibid.*

28. I have drawn this example from Jacob W. Gruber, Brixham Cave and the antiquity of man, in M. E. Spiro (Ed.), *Context and meaning in cultural anthropology, in honor of A. I. Hallowell* (N. Y.: Free Press, 1965), pp. 373-402.

29. *Life and letters of Darwin, op. cit.,* Vol. 3, pp. 8-14.

30. *Ibid.*, pp. 15-16; *Descent of man, op. cit.*, p. 2.
31. For interpretation of the general shape of the evolutionary debate, See Walter F. Cannon, The basis of Darwin's achievement: A revaluation, *Victorian Studies, 5* (1961), 109-134; R. M. Young, The impact of Darwin on conventional thought, in Anthony Symondson (Ed.), *The Victorian crisis of faith* (London: S.P.C.K., 1970), pp. 13-35.
32. Elie Halévy, *The growth of philosophic radicalism*, trans. M. Morris, 2nd ed., corrected (London: Faber & Faber, 1952); Ernest Albee, *A history of English Utilitarianism* (1901: reprint: N. Y.: Collier paperback, 1962).
33. David Hartley, *Observations on man, his frame, his duty and his expectations*, 2 vols. (London: Leake & Frederick, 1749; reprint: Gainesville, Florida: Scholars' Facsimiles & Reprints, (1966); cf. excerpts in Richard J. Herrnstein & E. G. Boring (Eds.), *A source book in the history of psychology* (Cambridge: Harvard, 1965), pp. 279-283, 348-355. There are passages in this collection from the writings of nearly all the figures mentioned in this paper. See also R. M. Young, Association of ideas, in P. P. Wiener (Ed.), *Dictionary of the history of ideas* (N. Y.: Scribner's, in press) and David Hartley, in C. C. Gillispie (Ed.), *Dictionary of scientific biography* (N. Y.: Scribner's, in press).
34. Erasmus Darwin, *Zoonomia; or, the laws of organic life*, 2 vols. (Dublin: Byrne & Jones, 1794-1796), Vol. 1, pp. 524-525.
35. Joseph Priestley, *Hartley's theory of the human mind, on the principle of the association of ideas, with essays relating to the subject of it* (London: Johnson, 1775; 2nd ed., 1790); *The conclusions of . . . Dr. Hartley's observations on the nature, powers, and expectations of man; strikingly illustrated in the events of the present times, with notes and illustrations by the editor* (London, 1794); John A. Passmore, *Priestley's writings on philosophy, science and politics* (N. Y.: Collier paperback, 1965), pp. 9-10.
36. William Godwin, *Enquiry concerning political justice, and its influence on morals and happiness* (1793; 4th ed., 2 vols. London: Watson, 1842), Vol. 1, Chap. 9, especially p. 190 n. This explicit acknowledgement to Hartley does not appear in the more readily available edition edited and abridged by K. Codell Carter (Oxford: Clarendon paperback, 1971); George Woodcock, *Anarchism. A history of libertarian ideas and movements* (N. Y.: World, 1962; reprint: Harmondsworth: Penguin paperback, 1963 and 1970), Chap. 3, in which the author points out that Godwin's influence was most strongly felt in literature and in the development of socialist theory.
37. See above, note 32; [J. S. Mill], Bain's psychology, *Edinburgh Review, 110* (1859), 287-321.
38. Etienne Bonnot de Condillac, *Condillac's treatise on sensations,* trans. G. Carr (London: Favil, 1930).
39. Antoine-Nicolas de Condorcet, *Sketch for a historical picture of the progress of the human mind* (1795), trans. June Barraclough (London: Widenfeld & Nicolson, 1955); Alexandre Koyré, Condorcet, *Journal of the History of Ideas, 9* (1948), 131-152.
40. Jean-Baptiste de Lamarck, *Zoological philosophy. An exposition with regard to the natural history of animals* (1809), trans. H. Elliot (London: Macmillan, 1914; reprint: N. Y.: Hafner, 1963); W. M. Wheeler & T. Barbour (Eds.), *The Lamarck manuscripts at Harvard* (Cambridge: Harvard, 1933), showing Lamarck's abiding interest in psychology.
41. I have suggested other aspects of the desirability of integrating the history of psychology with the history of science in Scholarship and the history of the behavioural sciences, *History of Science, 5* (1966), 1-51, at pp. 18-25, and Animal soul, in P. Edwards (Ed.), *The Encyclopedia of philosophy* (N. Y.: Macmillan, 1967), Vol. 1, pp. 122-127.
42. R. M. Young, Darwin's metaphor: Does nature select?, *The Monist, 55* (1971).

43. Adam Smith, *An inquiry into the nature and causes of the wealth of nations* (1776; reprint: 2 vols., London: Dent, 1910). For analyses relating his arguments to associationism, see Leslie Stephen, *History of English thought in the eighteenth century* (1876; reprint: 2 vols., London: Hart-Davis, Harbinger paperback, 1962), Vol. 2, pp. 53-68; Halévy, *op. cit.* (note 32, pp. 16-18, 88-120); Sir Alexander Gray, *Adam Smith* (London: Historical Association, 1948 and 1968); cf. the editor's introduction by Andrew Skinner to the Pelican (abridged) edition of *The wealth of nations* (Harmondsworth:Penquin, 1970).

44. Thomas R. Malthus, *An essay on the principle of population as it affects the future improvement of society with remarks on the speculations of Mr. Godwin, M. Condorcet, and other writers* (London: Johnson, 1798; reprint: Ann Arbor, Michigan: Ann Arbor paperback, 1959, and Harmondsworth: Penguin paperback, 1970, with an excellent introduction by Anthony Flew).

45. *Ibid.* (Ann Arbor edition), pp. 123-124.

46. *Ibid,* pp. 124-125.

47. *Ibid,* pp. 126-127.

48. R. M. Young, Malthus and the evolutionists: The common context of biological and social theory, *Past & Present,* No. 43 (1969), 109-145.

49. *More letters of Darwin, op. cit.* (note 9), Vol. 1, pp. 118-119.

50. Alfred R. Wallace, On the tendency of varieties to depart indefinitely from the original type (1858), reprinted in Sir Gavin de Beer (Ed.), *Charles Darwin and Alfred Russel Wallace, evolution by natural selection* (Cambridge, 1958), pp. 275-277; A. R. Wallace, *Darwinism* (London: Macmillan, 1889), p. vi; cf. above, note 42.

51. A. R. Wallace, *Natural selection and tropical nature. Essays on descriptive and theoretical biology* (London: Macmillan, 1891), pp. 199-200.

52. On the influence of Owenite Socialism, see A. R. Wallace, *My life. A record of events and opinions,* 2 vols. (London: Chapman & Hall, 1905), Vol. 1, pp. 87, 91-105; Vol. 2, Chap. 24, and the appendix to *The wonderful century. Its successes and failures* (London: Swan Sonnenschein, 1898); on the influence of Chambers' *Vestiges,* see *My life,* Vol. 1, pp. 254-255; on the influence of Combe and phrenology, see *My life,* Vol. 1, pp. 234-235, and *The wonderful century,* Chap. 16. Wallace's beliefs in phrenology and socialism played important parts in his retreat from belief in the adequacy of natural selection to account for fundamental features of man's body and mind. See R. M. Young, "Non-scientific" factors in the Darwinian debate, in *Actes du XIIe Congrès International d'Histoire des Sciences* (Paris: Blanchard, 1971), tome 8, pp. 221-226. The influence of phrenology on Owenism is not straightforward. The phrenologists contributed the general orientation that men should be seen in intimate relationship with their environments, and this point of view was used to support innumerable movements and schemes for social improvement, including Owenism. On the other hand, even as modified by Spurzheim and Combe, Gall's theory did not allow sufficient scope for alteration of character as a result of alteration of external conditions. Thus, although the phrenologists provided a general warrant for seeing man in adaptive, biological terms, they clashed with the Owenites over the degree of improvement which changed social conditions could achieve. (George Combe visited New Lanark in 1820, and his brother, Abram, founded an Owenite community. Owenism was, of course, in full flower before phrenology became a popular movement in Britain, and George Combe was certainly influenced by Owen's environmentalism.) There is a systematic ambiguity between the fundamental assumptions of phrenology and the meliorist uses to which it was put. See J. F. C. Harrison, *Robert Owen and the Owenites in Britain and America* (London: Routledge & Kegan Paul, 1969), pp. 86-87, 239-240, where the uneasy relations are mentioned, although Harrison stresses the conflict at the expense of the common assumptions.

Chambers' debt to phrenology is unequivocal. See *Vestiges, op. cit.* (note 12), pp. 322-323, 324-360. Chambers' acknowledgment of his debt to Combe's *Constitution of man* is reprinted in the 12th edition of *Vestiges,* in which the authorship of the book is first acknowledged (Edinburgh: Chambers, 1884), pp. xxx, xvi.

53. The development and affiliations of Spencer's evolutionary theory are considered in detail in *Mind, brain and adaptation, op. cit.* (note 11), Chaps. 5-6; Malthus and the evolutionists, *op. cit.* (note 48), pp. 134-137; R. M. Young, The development of Herbert Spencer's concept of evolution, *Actes du XIe Congrès International d'Histoire des Sciences* (Warsaw: Ossolineum, 1967), Vol. 2, pp. 273-278.

54. Herbert Spencer, *Principles of psychology* (London: Longmans, 1855).

55. [Herbert Spencer], Progress: Its law and cause, *Westminster Review, 11* (1857), 445-485.

56. Herbert Spencer, *First principles* (London: Williams & Norgate, 1862).

57. J. D. Y. Peel's *Herbert Spencer. The evolution of a sociologist, op. cit.* (note 17), provides an excellent analysis of Spencer's work in its social and intellectual context, with an assessment of his influence. This should be complemented by the account given by Donald Macrae in his introduction to the Pelican edition of Spencer's *The man versus the state with four essays on politics and society* (Harmondsworth: Penguin, 1969), in which the essay, The social organism, is particularly relevant to the points being stressed here.

58. E. A. Stengel, A re-evaluation of Freud's book "On Aphasia": Its significance for psycho-analysis, *International Journal of Psycho-Analysis, 35* (1954), 85-89; Hughlings Jackson's influence on psychiatry, *British Journal of Psychiatry, 109* (1963), 348-355.

59. Walter Bagehot, *Physics and politics, or thoughts on the application of the principles of "natural selection" and "inheritance" to political society* (London: King, 1869); C. H. Driver, Walter Bagehot and the social psychologists; and The development of a psychological approach to politics in English speculation before 1869, in F. J. C. Hearnshaw (Ed.), *The social & political ideas of some representative thinkers of the Victorian age* (London: Harrap, 1933; reprint: London: Dawson, 1967), pp. 194-221, 251-271; John Dewey, *Human nature and conduct. An introduction to social psychology* (New York: Holt, 1922; reprint with new introduction, N. Y.: Random House, 1930); George R. Geiger, Dewey's social and political philosophy, in Paul A. Schilpp (Ed.), *The Philosophy of John Dewey* (1939; 2nd ed., N. Y.: Tudor, 1951), pp. 337-368.

60. E. W. Strong, William Whewell and John Stuart Mill: Their controversy about scientific knowledge, *Journal of the History of Ideas, 16* (1955), 209-231; A. Ellegard, The Darwinian theory and nineteenth-century philosophies of science, *ibid, 18* (1957), 362-393; Edward H. Madden (Ed.), *Theories of scientific method: The renaissance through the nineteenth century* (Seattle: Washington, 1960), Chaps. 10-11.

61. Doctoral dissertation, University of Cambridge, 1970.

62. A. R. Wallace. *Natural selection and tropical nature, op. cit.* (note 51), p. 211; cf. *Darwinism, op. cit.* (note 50), Chap. 15.

Dissociation Revisited

ERNEST R. HILGARD

Psychologists have a major interest in the manner in which a person controls his behavior and his cognitions. While some are satisfied to assign all of the control to the environment (Skinner, 1971), for most psychologists this is an unsatisfactory answer. There are too many problems of conflict, of indecision, of self-deception, on the one hand, and signs of courage and persistence toward deliberately set goals, on the other, for the multiple control mechanisms within the person to be ignored. After examining some ways of classifying and dichotomizing these control mechanisms, I wish to reexamine an earlier attempt to discuss some of these problems by way of the concept of dissociation.

THE CLASSIFICATION OF CONTROLS

There are numerous ways in which to provide an approach to the study of control mechanisms. Attribution theory, for example, attempts to determine the circumstances under which a person attributes his behavior to controls from within himself and outside himself (e.g., Kelley, 1967; Bem, 1970). Cognitive dissonance theory, and its relatives, explore evidence based on a struggle for consistency, as between belief and practice (Festinger, 1957; Abelson et al., 1968). In order to simplify my empirical references, I shall illustrate control processes chiefly in terms of the behavior and experience of hypnotized subjects.

The voluntary-involuntary distinction. Whenever words are taken from the common vocabulary to describe scientific phenomena, they have the advantage of familiarity of reference and connotation, but the difficulties of imprecision. The words "voluntary" and "involuntary" are such a pair of words. We know that operating a typewriter is a voluntary act, while sneezing from pepper in the nose is involuntary. But we also know that the skilled typist is carrying out much of the activity quite automatically, and that, if necessary, a person can withhold his sneeze. Even in our clearest examples we have some confusion between what is voluntary and what is involuntary.

In hypnosis, the distinction is sharpened, particularly in challenge items, when the subject is told that his arm has become stiff (presumably through involuntary processes) so that he cannot bend it, even if he tries (so that

205

voluntary and involuntary processes are in conflict). That there is conflict here is clear enough, but the nature of the conflict is not so clear. It does not suffice to say that it is a conflict between involuntary and voluntary processes because some voluntary acquiescence was involved in making the arm stiff in the first place. Because many subjects also say, "I could have bent it if I had wanted to," I did a small experiment a few years ago to determine how real this impression was. When the subject who normally passed challenge items (that is, did not bend his arm when told that he could not but should try) was told to try especially hard on a test item of his own choice, he made the choice (while under hypnosis) and did indeed try harder. Two results were very impressive: some subjects could not exert the effort even though they wished to; others appeared to be exerting tremendous effort, but were unsuccessful; and most of the subjects, even though ultimately successful in bending their arms (or breaking other similar suggestions), worked against resistance, so that, in winning voluntarily, they did not in fact "cancel" the effect of prior suggestions. Some sort of conflict persisted, but it is quite unclear that it is sufficiently explained as a conflict between voluntary and involuntary activity (Hilgard, 1963).

The conscious-subconscious distinction. Many practicing hypnotists find it convenient to set up a dichotomy between conscious and subconscious (or unconscious) controls over behavior. A familiar form is to use verbal responses as indicative of conscious controls and finger responses as indicative of subconscious controls. I know of no careful experimental analyses to determine just what is happening, but it is quite clear that the central neural controls of saying "yes" and "no" with the voice and signaling "yes" and "no" with selected fingers are not very different. Both are differentiated symbolic responses, including deliberate and automatic components. This does not mean that the responses of the two systems may not differ, because conflictual responses may be differentially reported; perhaps one response system captures one side of an ambivalent response, and the other system captures another side. However, two sides of a conflict may be represented within the verbal system itself, since both primary and secondary processes can appear within the free associations of the psychoanalytic patient.

The question, naively put, is this: Does hypnosis give ready access to subconscious processes? A naive answer is that it does, but a more sophisticated answer has to be more analytical about what is meant by subconscious processes, and what is meant by gaining access to them. Subconscious processes may become conscious, in which case access to them is by the same processes as access to other conscious processes. Does hypnosis make subconscious processes more readily become conscious? Or subconscious processes may have to be inferred from their derivatives. Truly unconscious processes always have to be inferred. By the role of hypnosis do we mean that it produces derivatives that can be used more efficiently than other available processes to infer subconscious or unconscious processes? When one asks these more searching questions, easy answers are not forthcoming.

Considered as control mechanisms, conscious and subconscious have some of the flavor of the voluntary and involuntary distinction. When we are conscious of what we are doing, we have a better opportunity of being planful, and hence of exerting voluntary control; when we are doing something for subconscious reasons, we do not know the whys of our behavior and hence are behaving in involuntary fashion. But the two sets of terms are by no means isomorphic. We may be fully conscious of what we are doing, even while carrying out an involuntary act — say, performing what is required to fulfill a posthypnotic suggestion under a sense of compulsion — or we may have a lapse of awareness while carrying on a voluntary act, such as driving an automobile.

As in the case of the voluntary-involuntary distinction, the conscious-subconscious distinction has some naturalistic validity, but gets us into trouble as we search more deeply.

The distinction between a normal and a regressed ego-state. Gill and Brenman (1959) were so impressed by the regressive nature of hypnosis that they subtitled their book on hypnosis "psychoanalytic studies in regression." This was done in the context of psychoanalytic ego theory, in which the normal ego has an integrative function in the control of behavior, and is, in their terms, regnant over other processes of control. By contrast, the ego under hypnosis is regressed to a more primitive structure, although the regnant ego may persist alongside it. Here, then, is another distinction, that between a normal ego and a regressed ego.

The concept of regression always has two aspects: one is that of an age-regression, in which the controls over behavior are those associated with those of early infancy — dependent, nonverbal, etc.; the other is a primitive or irrational quality which, while immature in some sense, is not necessarily childish. Because of the rich use of metaphor in psychoanalytic thinking, these two aspects are not sharply distinguished. Thus hallucinations, as in adult dreams or schizophrenic thinking, are defined as regressive, though the dream content may be far from childlike. In a more formal sense, the distinction is that between primary and secondary process thinking (Hilgard, 1962). Primary process thinking characterizes regressed states; secondary process thinking characterizes normally integrated ego-states.

When Orne described trance logic a few years ago (Orne, 1959), he gave some support to the primary process nature of hypnotic thinking, whereby ordinary contradictions were not troublesome; on the other hand, however, he showed also that the hypnotized subject was capable of orderly secondary process thinking in which the hypnotized subject reasoned out a method to test which of two perceived persons was the hallucinated one. Because the hypnotized subject can learn paired associates, pass intelligence tests, and do other tasks requiring ordinary responses to the environment, it does not seem quite right to classify it simply as a regressed state, without a number of qualifications.

It is evident that each of these distinctions (voluntary-involuntary, conscious-unconscious, normal and regressed ego-state) has validity, and can be used to describe some of the alterations of behavior and some of the conflicts within hypnosis. At the same time there is an incompleteness to each pair, to be supplemented either by further distinctions or by some alternative formulation.

THE HISTORICAL CONCEPT OF DISSOCIATION

My dissatisfaction with the prevalent terms for describing controls operating over human behavior generally, and more specifically within hypnosis, have led me to go back to the earlier attempts to deal with the same phenomena according to the concept of dissociation. Usually, when one goes back to an earlier concept, it is with a difference, and in implying some usefulness for the concept of dissociation I am not committing myself to the views of Pierre Janet or Morton Prince. Yet their views deserve some review.

Janet and his immediate followers. The beginnings of the concept of dissociation are commonly attributed to Pierre Janet in 1887. Although his first term was *désagrégation* in French, which might better be translated *disaggregation,* the term *dissociation* became accepted in English, as by James in his *Principles* (1890) and by Janet himself in his Harvard lectures, *The major symptoms of hysteria,* in 1907. Janet's interpretation is that systems of ideas are split off from the major personality and exist as a subordinate personality, unconscious but capable of becoming represented in consciousness through hypnosis.

William James was much impressed by Janet, and prior to 1889 entered into correspondence with him about dissociation. In this correspondence Janet admitted that dissociation need not be complete; for example, he felt that dissociated ideas might still affect the emotional life of the patient (James, 1890, II, footnote, p. 456).

The two American writers who did the most, for a time, to keep Janet's concept alive were Boris Sidis and Morton Prince. Boris Sidis edited a large book, *Psychopathological researches in mental dissociation* (1902). It is of some interest that Janet's name appears only once in the book, in connection with a case study; there is nothing in the book to indicate that dissociation is at all puzzling as a concept, although the whole book is devoted to its empirical elucidation. The unacknowledged debt to Janet is clear in the interchangeable use of the terms "disaggregation" and "dissociation," as the following quotation shows:

> The whole domain of the subconscious belongs to these stages of
> disaggregation in the course of the pathological process, such as the

phenomena of hypnosis, of somnambulism, of motor and sensory automatisms, of the so-called "hysterical" sensori-motor disturbances of various organs, the functions of which are found on examination in regions of the subconscious over which the personal consciousness has lost control by reason of neuron disaggregation or dissociation (Sidis, 1902, pp. x-xi).

Morton Prince continued the free use of the notion of dissociation, titling his book on the Beauchamp case (he always pronounced it "Beecham") *The dissociation of a personality* (1906).

His support of the notion of dissociation was somewhat guarded. He preferred the term "coconscious" to either subconscious or dissociation. His preference for "coconsciousness" arose because it makes clear that the ideas of which the subject is unaware are still active ones, and that unconscious cerebration is going on, as revealed, say, in automatic writing. Prince did not demand a complete dissociation, as the following quote indicates: "Certainly in many cases there is a halting flow of thought of the principal intelligence, indicating that the activity of the secondary intelligence tends to inhibit the untrammeled flow of the former" (Prince, 1929, p. 411).

The decline of dissociation. The notion of dissociation seemed so plausible, and the concept was used so widely, that it is difficult to see why it faded away as it did. I have done a hasty count of the references to dissociation in the index of *Psychological Abstracts*. In the first ten volumes, from 1927 through 1936, there were 20 abstracts indexed; in the next ten years a total of 8, then dropping to 2 and 3 in the next two decades. Of course there have been discussions of dissociation that do not get indexed, such as the very thoughtful (and favorable) discussion by Murphy (1947) in his chapter on multiple personality. Still, the failure to get into the titles of papers that are indexed is some indication of decline in prominence of the topic.

Decline of interest does not necessarily mean that a concept has been rejected as being inappropriate or wrong. If one were to look up *attention* he would find a similar decline, until a recent upturn.

What happened? One important historical fact is the upsurge of interest in psychoanalysis during these years. Just as there was a decline in interest in hypnosis during the heyday of psychoanalysis, so also there was a decline in non-Freudian concepts in studies of psychopathology; the competing concepts were more likely to be Pavlovian, or those of S-R learning theory. This is a plausible conjecture, and when highlights of the discussion of dissociation are examined during these years, the discussions usually relate dissociation to Freudian concepts.

One illustration is given by an important paper on the concept of dissociation by Bernard Hart in 1927. Hart is best known for his small book on the psychology of insanity, which went through many editions (Hart, 1912). It represented a kind of introduction to psychoanalytic concepts, such as the defense mechanisms. Hart was responsible for naming the mechanism of logic-tight compartments — "the right hand knoweth not what the left hand doeth" — which has implicit within it some sort of dissociation connotation. His 1927 paper was delivered as the presidential address before the Medical Section of the British Psychological Society. He accepted the general notion of dissociation while objecting to Janet's conception of a complete splitting of parts of the personality.

I quote him: "Instead of regarding dissociation as the splitting of conscious materials into separate masses, it must be regarded as an affair of gearing, the various elements of mental machinery being organized into different functional systems by the throwing in of the appropriate gear . . ." (Hart, 1929, p. 163). This use of an automobile analogy, with gear-shifting, is obviously a metaphor, and is rather incompletely explained.

Hart goes on to say that Freud's notion of the unconscious is an entirely different kind of analysis. "[The unconscious] is not itself a fact of consciousness and its existence cannot be demonstrated in the way in which the existence of Janet's dissociated streams can be demonstrated. . . . The subconscious of Janet is a description of phenomenal facts, while the unconscious of Freud is a conceptual construction, an imagined entity created in order to explain phenomenal facts" *(ibid., pp. 165-166)*.

Hart explains the lack of interest by psychoanalysts in dissociation on two grounds: (1) the psychoanalytic method is not one under which multiple personalities grow; (2) dissociative phenomena do not yield the dynamic interpretations that psychoanalysts seek. Hart's own position is as a mediator: he thinks analysts *ought* to take more note of dissociation and double personality.

It is important to remember that Hart was writing when all the principal characters were still alive and active: Janet, Morton Prince, Freud, and McDougall.

A second paper to which I should like to call attention appeared eleven years after that of Hart. It was by William McDougall, and was entitled "The relations between dissociation and repression" (1938). In this paper, published in the year of his death, he returned to some ideas presented in his *Outline of abnormal psychology* (1926) and attempted to refute some of the later criticisms by Lundholm (1933) and Pattie (1935). I do not propose to review the paper in detail, except to point out that Mc-Dougall felt that the basic cleavage was between Janet's doctrine of dissociation and Freud's doctrine of repression. He felt that he himself had developed a balanced position, with repression as a dynamic factor which, in many cases, prepares the way for and leads to (or causes) dissociation. Like Hart, he did not reject dissociation.

It appears that we cannot account for the lack of interest in dissociation as due to any concerted attack upon it, but rather to a gradual withdrawal of interest in the kinds of problems to which it was appropriate — by the analysts, who had a different language, and by the behaviorists, who had other things to think about.

Hull and Sears. To assert that S-R psychologists paid no attention to dissociation would be to overlook two important treatments in the 1930s.

In his work on hypnosis, Hull (1933) devoted a chapter to the dissociation hypothesis. After an introductory exposition of Janet's views, he proceeded to discuss in some detail the experiments of Prince (1909), Burnett (1925), and Barry, MacKinnon, and Murray (1931). The experiments of Messerschmidt (1927-1928) and of Mitchell (1932), having been done as part of his program of research, were of course also discussed, and led Hull to the conclusion that "whatever else so-called hypnotic dissociation may be, it is *not* a functional independence between two simultaneous mental processes" (Hull, 1933, p. 185). He ended his chapter with the expressed hope that "the near future will see a series of well-controlled, large-scale investigations which will completely remove the uncertainties which at present becloud this extremely important problem" (p. 191).

Sears (1936), who had done some hypnotic experimentation with Hull, wrote an important review of functional abnormalities of memory, making use of S-R concepts similar to those developed by Hull in his learning theories, but giving consideration to the broad range of phenomena of amnesia, and of such explanatory concepts as repression and dissociation. In his discussion of dissociation he did not attempt to cover again the ground that Hull had covered, but he treated Prince's theory more completely than Hull had done (Sears, 1936, pp. 263-269). He concluded, coherent with his own efforts at an S-R theory, that "if the theory of dissociation were to be completely restated in the stimulus-response idiom . . . there seems good reason for considering it a valuable hypothesis coordinate with the repression hypothesis as an explanation for amnesias of reproduction" (Sears, 1936, p. 269).

These invitations of Hull to further experimentation, and of Sears to theoretical restatement, had little effect in the following years. As previously noted, the directly relevant literature is scant, although references to dissociation occur frequently in the clinical literature, especially in relation to fugue states and multiple personality. Nagge (1935) reported results somewhat contradictory to those of Mitchell. Cass (1941), in a master's thesis published only in abstract, had some results encouraging further study. Takahashi's (1958) results were on the positive side, though not supporting a complete functional independence of "dissociated" activities. A somewhat tangential study was used by Rosenberg (1959) to argue against dissociation. In a theoretical paper, White and Shevach (1942) had dismissed dissociation as not sufficiently comprehensive to explain hypnosis; they preferred to use suggestion as a starting point.

To these must be added a doctoral dissertation completed in our laboratory (Stevenson, 1972). He used two simultaneous tasks similar to those used by Cass (1941): color naming as a "conscious" task, and a counting task in automatic writing as "subconscious" task, with appropriate waking controls and simulator controls. He found important evidence denying the functional independence of the tasks, and some evidence supporting a "repression" interpretation of the subconscious task. The repression interpretation arose because he was able to show that the counting task deteriorated through being kept out of awareness, *without* any interfering task to be performed by the subject. In other words, some kind of cognitive effort appeared to be needed to hold the task out of awareness, and this expenditure of effort interfered with performing the task. When a conscious interfering task was added, the performance further deteriorated. The simulators, who did not actually hold the task out of awareness, showed significantly less deterioration for the single task, and showed less deterioration also for the conscious task. (The more difficult the "subconscious" task, the more interference as a consequence of holding it out of awareness.)

Stevenson's results support all the earlier findings of a lack of functional independence between tasks, one of which is out of awareness, but add the important evidence on the cognitive cost of holding a task out of awareness.

A NEO-DISSOCIATION CONCEPT PERTINENT
TO CONTEMPORARY PSYCHOLOGY

Let us assume that we understand what we mean by ordinary control mechanisms, according to which we take care of our needs and behave in socially acceptable ways, knowing what we are about and making sensible choices. Let us call these control mechanisms *normal ego controls*. If they constituted the whole of psychology, we would not have any use for a concept like dissociation. However, if it turns out that there are processes carried on outside of such normal ego controls, and if, even occasionally, two systems of control appear to be operating simultaneously, then a concept such as dissociation is inviting. Because I do not wish to defend all that has been claimed for dissociation in the past, I prefer to state the case for a neo-dissociation concept — that is, one that has affiliations with the historical concept, but has been reformulated to account for what we now know. I believe that a neo-dissociation concept is pertinent for reasons specified in what follows:

1. *The human behavior and conscious control apparatus is not highly unified and integrated.* It is a *weak*, not a *strong* Gestalt. Although there is some motivational pull toward consistency and toward a sense of unity of the personality, as those studying cognitive dissonance point out, dissonance does in fact exist and persist between behavior systems of the person. Discrepancies exist between any two or any combination of the familiar tripartite division of feeling, thinking, and doing. The separation of feeling from thought and action has, in the extreme, given rise to the concept of schizophrenia, but there are schizoid trends in those not classified as psychotic.

2. *The stream of consciousness flows in more than one channel at a time, or, to put it differently, there are more than one concurrent streams.* It is quite clear that in order to carry on an intelligent conversation, several things must happen at once or in rapid alternation. You listen to what the other person is saying, while at the same time formulating a reply supporting or refuting what he is saying: you utter something in reply, but concurrently watch his face to see how effectively your point is getting across — that is, you operate a monitoring system as well as a talking system. One stream of self-talk runs along with the overt activity of talking and listening. Some of this has been commented on by Miller, Galanter, and Pribram (1960).

3. *Habitual control mechanisms can often operate in behavior with a minimum of conscious attention, freeing conscious processes to reflect other kinds of cerebration.* The driver of a car along the highway, if he is experienced and the highway is familiar, can react to traffic and follow signals while carrying on a spirited conversation with a passenger beside him. Only as traffic becomes more complex does he find the demand on his attention so severe as to interrupt his conversation.

4. *Under some circumstances, conscious processes take place that in their nature and sequence are relatively independent of normal ego control.* The night dream (which, if remembered, *is* conscious) is the most familiar example, although daydreams and fantasies may move off in similar directions.

Note that the four points I have made to support the need for a concept of dissociation are all from psychology generally, and not from hypnosis. Instead of requiring a concept of dissociation to explain hypnosis, I would turn the matter around and point out that a contribution of hypnosis may be to help us to understand the various dissociative processes that are, in fact, ubiquitous.

HYPNOTIC PHENOMENA AS ILLUSTRATIVE OF DISSOCIATION

Almost any hypnotic phenomena can be used to illustrate dissociation. I shall choose five: posthypnotic amnesia, posthypnotic automatic writing, age regression, positive hallucinations, and "challenge" motor items.

Posthypnotic amnesia. Posthypnotic amnesia supports McDougall's interpretation of the relation of repression-like processes to dissociation, for the memories that are temporarily unavailable are not actually destroyed. Because they exist but are unavailable, they illustrate a kind of dissociation.

Posthypnotic automatic writing. To the extent that automatic writing reveals a kind of cerebration going on independent of some other stream, it is one of the clearer representatives of dissociation. The dissociation need not be complete; the degree of interference between the simultanous tasks is subject to study.

Age regression. When a person under hypnosis is regressed to an earlier age and behaves as if at that age, there is commonly a split between the regressed system and an observing system that retains the normal age. The relation is very much that between two multiple personalities in which one shares the memories of the other, but the relation is not reciprocated. The two sets of controls are dissociated, even if incompletely; for example, there may be a strong compulsion to talk or otherwise behave like the regressed child, even though the observing ego is aware of what is happening.

Positive hallucinations. Positive hallucinations provide very interesting testing grounds for studying control processes. The hallucination itself, if it is of a perceptual quality, departs from normal ego control processes, which rely on environmental stimuli as the occasions for perception. The split in controls is well illustrated by those occasions on which the subject is told that he is hallucinating but continues to hallucinate. The major experience in our laboratory has been with the hallucinated light, in which the subject sees two lights where there is only one. When told that there is only one, this often does not reduce the hallucination, but it sets into motion discriminative processes by the observing ego, according to which the true and hallucinated lights are distinguished. For example, the hallucinated light may not be reflected in the polished surface of the box on which it is seen; hence it is recognized as the hallucination. Sometimes an error is made, as when the true light is inferred incorrectly from the position of the electrical wire entering the box. In any case, the control mechanism producing the visual hallucination differs from the mechanism seeking to decide which light is the true one and which is the hallucinated one. Something similar occurs in the lucid dream, in which the dreamer knows he is dreaming and attempts some sort of experiment within the dream to demonstrate that it is a dream (Green, 1968).

"Challenge" motor items. I previously referred to the challenge motor items, in which the subject is told to break a contraction or other suggested motor response, while given the contradictory suggestion that he will be unable to do it. Here is a conflict between two control mechanisms, the one producing the response and the one attempting to break it. While the conflict is dramatic within hypnosis, it is a kind of caricature of similar conflicts in daily life, such as the salted peanut phenomenon, in which the desire to stop eating is contradicted by the compulsion to continue doing what has been once begun.

These illustrations suffice to indicate what I am talking about when I say that hypnosis provides a promising set of phenomena for the study of dissociative processes.

ATTEMPTS TO EXPLAIN DISSOCIATIVE PHENOMENA

Even though the term "dissociation" has been out of favor, the kinds of controls and processes I have described as dissociative are sufficiently well recognized that a number of theories bear upon their explanation. The two main classes of theory are psychoanalysis and social learning theory, but there are also some commentaries that do not fit well into these two classes.

The most appropriate version of the psychoanalytic theory is that of Gill and Brenman (1959), whose particular solution, bearing on the dissociation problem, is to construe hypnosis as a type of regression in the service of the ego, that is, a partial regression, which is arrested as temporary ego structures are set up in hypnosis, subordinate to a regnant ego. While they give elaborate explanations according to a psychoanalytic model proposed by Rapaport and Gill (1959), the main proposal of the subordinate ego structures is very reminiscent of earlier conceptions of dissociated congeries of ideas. A related set of ideas coming from psychoanalysis, ideas that can bear upon multiple personalities and other forms of dissociation, derives from Erik Erikson, particularly his notion that as the child grows he must gradually integrate separate identifications into an achieved identity of his own. If these identifications remain separate, and in conflict, the result may very well be dissociative manifestations of one sort or another.

What I am saying is this: A dichotomous distinction between two levels of functioning, such as conscious vs. unconscious, or primary vs. secondary process, has not been found sufficient to account for the several control mechanisms operative at once in hypnosis. The concept of multiple subordinate egos, while acceptable, does not follow directly from the concept of regression, and when examined closely is simply another way of describing multiple cognitive structures, or multiple control systems, and is not in contradiction to a neo-dissociation interpretation.

Social learning theorists have not come to grips directly with the problem of dissociation, so far as I know, but it is not hard to see how they might go about it. Perhaps the nearest we come to this is the role theory of Sarbin and his associates (e.g., Sarbin and Vernon, 1968), for conflicting roles could easily result in dissociated controls, essentially in the form of habits of social behavior. An experimental paradigm can be provided by the work of Skinner, in which various systems of behavior in the pigeon have been shown to be independently conditioned through operant reinforcement. For example, pecking can be conditioned on one schedule and leg-lifting on another, apparently with little interference between them (Skinner, 1950). If independent habit systems can be set up in this way, it is as though separate controls operate within a common nervous system. This is the basic paradigm of dissociation. In man, the established habit systems that operate at a high degree of automaticity, with lapse of consciousness, may fit this pattern.

The double-bind hypothesis of Haley (1958) may be considered a commentary on the utility of a neo-dissociation standpoint. This proposes that the only way in which the subject can conform to the hypnotist's commands, e.g., to try to keep the eyes open while they are being closed to suggestion, is to dissociate the two controls: *I* am trying to keep my eyes open, but *they* are closing by themselves. This is the kind of interpretation a cognitive dissonance theorist might propose, but the reduction of dissonance comes about not through integration but through a splitting of controls. In general, little serious effort has been made to explain multiple personalities, which are the examples of dissociation *par excellence.*

There are occasional physiological explanations, of which one of the earliest is *diaschizis,* as proposed in 1902 by von Monakow and commented on favorably by Sherrington in 1906. While directed to other forms of dissociation, such as the symptoms of spinal shock, the explanation is based on "a loosening of nexus between the links of the neurone-chain composing the arc; a defect of transmission at the synapse" (Sherrington, 1906, p. 246). I doubt if this kind of explanation will prove of much help.

THE NATURE OF NEO-DISSOCIATION THEORY

While I am not prepared to propose a neo-dissociation theory in any detail at this time, something of the nature of a satisfactory theory can be indicated.

1. Neo-dissociation theory does not require a complete functional independence between structures that are considered to be dissociated. Hence all dissociation will be viewed as a matter of degree.

2. The concept of organized subordinate control structures is essential to a neo-dissociationist theory. This is what these theories have in common with Janet, who said at one point: "Things happen as if an idea, a partial system of thoughts, emancipated itself, became independent and developed itself on its own account" (Janet, 1920). Janet went too far, but a system of ideas must have a coherence, and some endurance through time, if even a partial independence of control structures is acknowledged. This is what is implied when Gill and Brenman (1959) refer to the somewhat autonomous ego structures that appear in the reorganization that takes place after the ego (in their view) has been fractionated through hypnotic induction.

3. Some kind of hierarchical system is implied, or there would not be as much coherence in normal behavior as we ordinarily find. Hence the interaction between dissociated systems will not be random, but will have an order that can be studied.

4. Hypnosis will have an appreciable effect upon the hierarchies of existing dissociated structures, and may create novel dissociations. This interpretation is suggested by Shor (1959) in describing the setting aside of ordinary reality orientation, and by Tart (1972) in his description of subsystems as reorganized in hypnosis.

5. Because neo-dissociation recognizes plural structures, it overcomes some of the difficulties in the attempt to describe hypnosis as a definable "state" of the organism. For example, a subject may come out of hypnosis with an arm paralyzed as a result of a posthypnotic suggestion. His whole

personality organization need not be that of deep hypnosis in order for the arm (as a symptom of dissociation) to remain out of ordinary control relationships.

6. The psychophysiology of dissociation is obscure, but nothing in neo-dissociation theory contradicts known psychophysiological facts or relationships. Murphy (1947) points out that Goldstein (1939) earlier noted that some processes can become "isolated" in diseases of the brain.

The question may be asked: Would a worked-out neo-dissociationist theory be a complete theory of hypnosis? The question is what President Franklin D. Roosevelt called too "iffy," and it would be arrogant to raise the hope that it might be a complete theory. Many detailed problems concerning the developmental aspects of hypnotic abilities, the nature of individual differences, and the social and environmental influences upon hypnotic behavior remain to be worked out at an empirical level. A coherent theory of the substructures in the control of human behavior, with varying degrees of awareness, as implied in neo-dissociation theory, could provide a coherent framework into which new knowledge could be fitted.

The problem of control mechanisms is a problem for psychology generally, for there is nothing more important than understanding the secrets of internal control and loss of control. While not a problem limited by any means to hypnotic phenomena, those of us working in the field of hypnosis have an unusually fertile opportunity to contribute through our studies to furthering the understanding of these neglected but important processes.

REFERENCES

Abelson, R. P., Aronson, E., McGuire, W. J., Newcomb, T. M., Rosenberg, M. J., & Tannenbaum, P. H. (Eds.), *Theories of cognitive consistency: A sourcebook*. Chicago: Rand McNally, 1968.

Barry, H., Jr., MacKinnon, D. W., & Murray, H. A. Studies in personality: A. Hypnotizability as a personality trait and its typological relations. *Human Biology*, 1930, *3*, 1-36.

Bem, D. J. *Beliefs, attitudes, and human affairs*. Belmont, California: Bruce/Cole, 1970.

Burnett, C. T. Splitting the mind. *Psychological Monographs*, 1925, *34*, No. 2.

Cass, W. A. An experimental investigation of the dissociation hypothesis utilizing a posthypnotic technique. *Psychological Bulletin*, 1941, *38*, 744.

Gill, M. & Brenman, M. *Hypnosis and related states: Psychoanalytic studies in regression*. New York: International Universities Press, 1959.

Goldstein, K. *The organism*. New York: American Book Company, 1939.

Green, C. *Lucid dreams*. Bristol, England: Western Printing Services, Ltd., 1968.

Haley, J. An interactional explanation of hypnosis. *American Journal of Clinical Hypnosis*, 1958, *1*, 41-57.

Hart, B. *The psychology of insanity*. Cambridge: Cambridge University Press, 1912.

Hart, B. The concept of dissociation. *British Journal of Medical Psychology*, 1927, *6*, 241-256.

Hart, B. *Psychopathology* (2nd ed.). Cambridge, England: Cambridge University Press, 1929.

Hilgard, E. R. Impulsive vs. realistic thinking: An examination of the distinction between primary and secondary processes in thought. *Psychological Bulletin,* 1962, *59,* 447-448.

Hilgard, E. R. Ability to resist suggestions within the hypnotic state. *Psychological Reports,* 1963, *12,* 3-13.

Hull, C. L. *Hypnosis and suggestibility.* New York: Appleton-Century-Crofts, 1933. (Paper edition, 1968).

Janet, P. L'Anesthésie systematisée et la dissociation des phénomènes psychologiques. *Revue Philosophique,* 1887, *23,* 449-472.

Janet, P. *The major symptoms of hysteria.* 1907. (2nd ed., New York: Holt, 1920).

Kelley, H. H. Attribution theory in social psychology. *Nebraska Symposium on Motivation,* 1967, *15,* 192-241.

Lundholm, H. Laboratory neuroses. *Character and Personality,* 1933, *2,* 127-133.

McDougall, W. *Outline of abnormal psychology.* New York: Scribner's, 1926.

McDougall, W. The relations between dissociation and repression. *British Journal of Medical Psychology,* 1938, *17,* 141-157.

Messerschmidt, R. A quantitative investigation of the alleged independent operation of conscious and subconscious processes. *Journal of Abnormal and Social Psychology,* 1927-28, *22,* 325-340.

Mitchell, M. B. Retroactive inhibition and hypnosis. *Journal of General Psychology,* 1932, *7,* 343-358.

Nagge, J. W. An experimental test of associative interference. *Journal of Experimental Psychology,* 1935, *18,* 663-682.

Orne, M. T. The nature of hypnosis: Artifact and essence. *Journal of Abnormal and Social Psychology,* 1959, *58,* 277-299.

Pattie, F. A. A report of attempts to produce uniocular blindness by hypnotic suggestion. *British Journal of Medical Psychology,* 1935, *15,* 230-241.

Prince, M. *The dissociation of a personality.* New York: Longmans, Green, 1906.

Prince, M. Experiments to determine co-conscious (subconscious) ideation. *Journal of Abnormal Psychology,* 1909, *3,* 33-42.

Prince, M. *Clinical and experimental studies in personality.* Cambridge, Massachusetts: Sci-art, 1929.

Rapaport, D. & Gill, M. M. The points of view and assumptions of metapsychology. *International Journal of Psychoanalysis,* 1959, *40,* 153-162.

Rosenberg, M. J. A disconfirmation of the descriptions of hypnosis as a dissociated state. *International Journal of Clinical and Experimental Hypnosis,* 1959, *7,* 187-204.

Sarbin, T. R. & Allen, V. L. Role theory. In G. Lindzey and E. Aronson. *Handbook of social psychology* (2nd ed.). Reading, Massachusetts: Addison-Wesley, 1968, Vol. 1, 488-567.

Sears, R. R. Functional abnormalities of memory with special reference to amnesia. *Psychological Bulletin,* 1936, *33,* 229-274.

Sherrington, C. S. *The integrative action of the nervous system.* New Haven: Yale University Press, 1906.

Shor, R. E. Hypnosis and the concept of general reality-orientation. *American Journal of Psychotherapy,* 1959, *13,* 582-602.

Sidis, B. (Ed.), *Psychopathological researches: Studies in mental dissociation.* New York: Stechert, 1902.

Skinner, B. F. Are theories of learning necessary? *Psychological Review,* 1950, *57,* 193-216.

Skinner, B. F. *Beyond freedom and dignity.* New York: Knopf, 1971.

Stevenson, J. H. The efftct of hypnotic and posthypnotic dissociation on the performance of interfering tasks. Unpublished doctoral dissertation, Stanford University, 1972.

Takahashi, R. An experimental examination of the dissociation hypothesis in hypnosis. *Journal of Clinical and Experimental Hypnosis,* 1958, *6,* 139-151.

Tart, C. T. Measuring the depth of an altered state of consciousness, with particular reference to self-report scales of hypnotic depth. In E. Fromm & R. E. Shor, *Hypnosis: Recent developments and perspectives.* Chicago: Aldine-Atherton, 1972.

White, R. W. & Shevach, B. J. Hypnosis and the concept of dissociation. *Journal of Abnormal and Social Psychology,* 1942, *37,* 309-328.

Hermann Ebbinghaus

Leo Postman

"Psychology has a long past, yet its real history is short." Since Ebbinghaus (1908) wrote the familiar opening sentence of his textbook (p. 3) some sixty years ago, the history of psychology has been rapidly gaining on its past. My purpose in this paper is to consider some of the ways in which Ebbinghaus added to the historical record and shaped the subsequent course of the discipline.

When we attempt to assess Ebbinghaus' role in the history of experimental psychology, our thoughts turn at once to his research on memory, his unique and pioneering contribution to the field. Before focusing on the impact of this classical study, however, I would like to consider the man and his work in broader perspective. The salient importance of his major research accomplishment should not lead us to neglect his wider influence on the intellectual climate of experimental psychology in its formative years. Here his contribution was not unique, and merged with that of others, but there is every reason to believe that it was considerable. And there are many indications in Ebbinghaus' own writings that for him the research on memory was primarily an example of a new scientific approach to the problems of psychology; it provided a concrete and compelling illustration of what the new psychology could and should do.

It is, of course, difficult to gauge the influence of one man on the cumulative history of ideas. Whether Ebbinghaus was a cause or a symptom of the developments of his times, the principles which guided him in his approach to theory and experimentation clearly reflect the gathering changes in psychological thought. Let me try to identify some of these guiding principles as they emerge from his writings.

The first guiding principle was the emancipation of experimental psychology from philosophy. Historically and institutionally, the new experimental psychology of the late nineteenth century had remained tied to philosophy. While psychology had, indeed, become experimental and borrowed freely from physiology, the preoccupation with the fundamental irreducible characteristics of mental processes remained, as witness the long controversy between content and act. Of the leading exponent of the new psychology, Boring (1950) says: "Wundt came by a rational philosopher's method to his convictions about experimental psychology. . . . He was an experimentalist; but his experimentalism was the by-product of his philosophical views" (p. 327). Ebbinghaus was far more ready to renounce,

This article, which has been abridged by the editors, appeared in its original form in the *American Psychologist*, 1968, *23*, 149-157.

or at least postpone indefinitely, philosophical speculation and to pursue a wholehearted empiricism. He came to this conviction at an early stage in his career. Two of the propositions which he defended in his doctoral examination were (1) that psychology in the widest sense belongs under philosophy in no more intimate way than natural philosophy (i.e., science) belongs there, and (2) that existing psychology consists more of logical abstractions and verbal classifications than of knowledge of the real elements of mind (cf. Shakow, 1930, p. 510; Woodworth, 1909, pp. 253 f.). He summarized his position in another well-known sentence in his textbook:

> When Weber in 1828 had the seemingly petty curiosity to want to know at what two distances apart two touches on the skin could be just perceived as two, and later with what accuracy he could distinguish between two weights laid on the hand, or how he could distinguish between the perception received through the muscles in lifting the weights and the perception received through the skin, his curiosity resulted in more real progress than all the combined distinctions, definitions and classifications of the time from Aristotle to Hobbes (1908, p. 17).

The future of psychology would depend on its ability to adopt the conceptions and methods of natural science. It was the power and promise of such an orientation that the work on memory was designed to illustrate.

The second guiding principle is emancipation from orthodox constraints on the scope of experimental inquiry. According to the prevailing doctrine, only those mental phenomena which were directly subject to physical influences were to be studied experimentally. As Wundt (1907) put it, "We cannot experiment on mind itself, but only upon its outworks, the organs of sense and movement which are functionally related to the mental processes" (p. 10). Understanding of the higher mental processes was to be gained by the historical method, by the insights of folk psychology. Ebbinghaus refused to be bound by such a priori constraints and preferred to be guided by the successes and failures of experimentation. Thus, in the preface to his treatise on memory he asks "those who are not already convinced a priori of the impossibility of such an attempt to postpone their decision about its practicability." He then proceeds to show that it is, indeed, possible to make reliable observations about memory which yield lawful relationships. The prohibition against the experimental study of the higher mental processes had been successfully challenged.

The third principle, which follows readily from the second, I should like to designate as methodological eclecticism, i.e., the adaptation of experimental and analytic procedures which traditionally belong to one substantive area to a new realm of inquiry. This is what Ebbinghaus did when he extended the basic logic of psychophysical measurement to the quantification of the degree of retention. Fechner had believed that the magnitude of sensations could not be measured directly. He set out, therefore, to measure it indirectly by determining the intensity of stimulation required to produce a change in sensation, i.e., a just noticeable difference. The number of just noticeable differences then provided an indirect measure of the magnitude of a sensation. Ebbinghaus confronted the parallel problem that the strength or vividness of a memory was apparently incapable of precise measurement. "By what possible means," he asked, "are we to measure numerically the mental processes which flit by so quickly and which on introspection are so hard to analyze?" (1913, pp. 7 f.) The logic of the solution in turn paralleled Fechner's — the strength of memory was to be measured indirectly, in terms of the number of repetitions required to relearn a given set of materials to the original level of mastery. There is, of course, an important difference between Fechner's and Ebbinghaus' method. In the measurement of sensation the critical psychological change is given in introspection; in the case of memory there is a criterion of performance, although Ebbinghaus included a feeling of subjective certainty in the definition of that criterion. But he was willing to relax, if not to abandon, reliance on introspection in the interest of achieving precision of measurement. Such transposition of the logic of measurement from one area of inquiry to another evidently requires more than an eclectic attitude; it must await a flash of insight on the part of an investigator facing an apparently intractable problem. But it will not occur unless there is a willingness to ignore barriers between traditional fields.

Fourth, there is Ebbinghaus' theoretical eclecticism, which goes hand in hand with his methodological eclecticism. Again this attitude is clearly apparent in his approach to memory. As we have seen, his formulation of the problems of measurement was derived from psychophysics, and his definition of a criterion of performance tempered by considerations of introspective validity. The questions to be asked about the conditions and characteristics of memory, however, were manifestly rooted in the tradition of British associationism. The choice of serially ordered discrete units for memorization reflects directly the analysis of the contents of mind into ideas that derive order and coherence from spatial and temporal contiguity. He took it for granted that the variable governing the strength of memory was frequency of repetition, for frequency had emerged as the dominant law of association.

Ebbinghaus did not, however, accept associationism as a comprehensive system of psychology. He saw as one of its major weaknesses the reliance on physical and chemical analogies. There was little merit for him in the mental mechanics of the early associationists and in Mill's mental chemistry, because such analyses failed to take cognizance of the organized nature of mental functioning. In the realm of higher mental processes, perhaps the most serious defect was the failure to provide an explanation of the phenomenon of attention. "The associationists," he said, "pass over this important fact either with complete silence or with a very insufficient treatment" (1908, p. 12). The proper orientation of psychology, he held, must be toward biology rather than physics and chemistry. Living organisms cannot be understood as aggregates of discrete and unrelated events, and no more can the functions of the mind: both must be viewed as unified systems. The biological point of view brings into focus the mental capacities essential for adaptation to the environment which must be assumed to be part of the organism's innate endowment. Thus, Ebbinghaus rejected empiricist explanations of the perception of space, time, and movement, and instead espoused a nativistic interpretation. He made his eclecticism explicit, seeing no contradiction between nativistic views of perception and associationistic accounts of the effects of experience (1895).

Like others at the turn of the century, Ebbinghaus anticipated some of the arguments for perceptual organization which a decade or so later would become the rallying cries of Gestalt psychology. He described as an attribute common to all sense impressions

the belonging together of sensations, the *unity in variety,* so to speak. The most striking example is the relationship of tones in harmony and melody. . . . We cannot explain this by reference to conscious agents mediating the effects. It is a fundamental attribute of each tonal combination, the conscious effect of our inherited nature. It is a property of sense, not of thought (1908, pp. 68 f.).

But he failed to pursue and press these arguments. He was neither a system builder nor a crusader, but a true eclectic.

The final principle to be mentioned is the reconciliation of pure and applied psychology. We find in Ebbinghaus' work a recognition of the fact that it is the problem and the method that count rather than the context in which the solution is pursued. His contribution to mental testing is a case in point. The story is well known. When the authorities of the city of Breslau were contemplating a change in the duration of school sessions, Ebbinghaus was appointed to a commission that was to consider the advisability of the new program. It would be useful for the work of the commission to have an instrument for measuring the mental capacity of schoolchildren. True to his faith in the possibilities of psychological measurement, Ebbinghaus set out to devise one — the completion test (1897), which introduced a method that was to become a standard ingredient of many subsequent tests of intelligence. The circumstances were very similar to those which led Binet to embark on his investigations. In the quantitative analysis of the higher mental processes, Ebbinghaus helped to lead the way in the classroom as well as the laboratory.

These, in broad and sketchy outline, were some of the attitudes and beliefs which Ebbinghaus expressed in his research and writing. He was a gentle but determined dissenter from both philosophical traditionalism and the orthodoxy of psychological schools. In his theoretical views he was a tolerant eclectic, motivated not by indecision or a spirit of compromise but by the conviction that the understanding of concrete phenomena must take precedence over the internal consistency of a doctrine. He had a great, almost romantic, faith in the promise held out by the methods of natural science for the growth of a scientific psychology. Above all he was an experimentalist and an innovator bent on substituting controlled measurement for speculation.

It was in this intellectual context that his studies of memory were undertaken. What has been their long-term significance for psychology? The major thesis of the research — that the experimental method can be successfully applied to the investigation of learning and memory — has so long been taken for granted that it has received the highest recognition possible by being absorbed into the mainstream of psychology. Many of his empirical findings have found confirmation, which serves to remind us that painstaking control and careful observation can sometimes compensate for a paucity of subjects and a lack of instrumentation. We need to think only of the length-difficulty relationship, the effects of overlearning on retention, and the first demonstration of the phenomenon of distribution of practice. When we examine his methods and his concepts of measurement, it soon becomes apparent, however, that they were not final solutions but points of departure, marking the beginning of a long line of development. Let me now consider briefly some of these methods and concepts. In doing so I shall emphasize the changes which have occurred in the intervening years. The lasting value of Ebbinghaus' contribution is not to be gauged by the extent to which his assumptions and procedures remained intact but by the developments that were stimulated in a growing and self-critical discipline.

The nonsense syllable. With respect to Ebbinghaus' original objectives, the choice of nonsense syllables as the learning materials in his experiments may fairly be characterized as a productive failure. Nonsense materials appeared to him to offer three advantages. First, they were relatively simple and relatively homogeneous, at least as compared to passages of prose and stanzas of poetry. But Ebbinghaus was quick to note that the homogeneity of the materials fell far short of expectations:

> These series exhibit very important and almost incomprehensible variations as to the ease or difficulty with which they are learned. . . . the predisposition, due to the influence of the mother tongue, for certain combinations of letters and syllables must be a very heterogeneous one (1885, trans. 1913, pp. 23-24).

Second, they provided an almost inexhaustible supply of comparable combinations composed of the same elements. Third, they permitted clearly defined variations in the amount of material.

What Ebbinghaus noted in passing has been established firmly through many years of work on the scaling of verbal units: Nonsense syllables are very heterogeneous indeed, and cover a remarkable range of meaningfulness. They represent greater variations in difficulty than can be obtained with any other kind of verbal material. It is true that the number of units can be specified unequivocally, but this is of little value if the units are not in fact comparable, and it can be done for other types of materials just as well. Last but not least, the nonsense syllable has turned out to be a verbal unit of very limited utility for the study of associative processes per se. This fact has been brought out by the distinction, in current analyses of verbal learning, between response learning and associative learning. If the responses to be learned are from outside the subject's verbal repertoire, they must become integrated units before they can enter into new associations (Underwood & Schulz, 1960). The lower the meaningfulness of the responses, the larger the proportion of the total learning time occupied by the integration phase. When we eliminate or minimize the response-learning stage by the use of familiar and available units, we can focus most directly on the course of associative learning.

For all these reasons, nonsense syllables failed to provide the advantages Ebbinghaus had hoped for. If he was mistaken in the reasons for his choice of materials, his error was productive because nonsense syllables have been an extremely useful device in the development of verbal learning, but precisely because they did not have the properties that Ebbinghaus had attributed to them. The heterogeneity of nonsense syllables with respect to scaled meaningfulness and the correlated differences in speed of learning called attention early to the powerful effects of language habits on the acquisition of new verbal materials. It is true that for a long time the influence of language habits was treated more as a source of error to be controlled than as a focus of experimental analysis. In recent years, however, there has been increasing emphasis on the systematic exploration of the role which preexisting language habits play in acquisition and retention. Thus, nonsense syllables were put to their full analytic use many years after their invention, whereas they were probably far from the best materials for much of the earlier work that was directed at the analysis of associative processes. This paradoxical trend illustrates, I believe, the risks of standardization. The innovations which Ebbinghaus introduced were accepted so rapidly and enthusiastically that they were soon treated as standard methods whose inherent limitations were slow to be questioned. The fact that nonsense syllables are far from homogeneous was recognized early; they continued to be used routinely because they were accepted as standard units for verbal experiments. As the body of knowledge based on nonsense-syllable learning grew, the pressure for comparability no doubt perpetuated the custom. Although this tradition has died hard, most investigators today will use nonsense materials only if they are interested in the special properties of such units.

Serial learning. In one of the earliest statements of the doctrine of association, in Hobbes's essay on human nature, there is a famous passage enunciating the principle that the coherence of ideas in the mind reflects the order of sensory impressions in the past:

> For example, from St. Andrew the mind runneth to St. Peter, because their names are read together; from St. Peter to stone, for the same cause; from stone to foundation, because we see them together; and for the same cause, from foundation to church, and from church to

people, and from people to tumult: and according to this example
the mind may run almost from anything to anything (cf. Rand, 1912,
p. 157).

The preservation, in the sequence of ideas, of the temporal order of past
experiences has from the beginning been at the heart of the associationistic
conception of memory, and this conception Ebbinghaus accepted without
reservation. Of the laws of association, he says:

> There is one which has never been disputed or doubted. . . . Ideas
> which have been developed simultaneously or in immediate succession
> in the same mind mutually reproduce each other, and do this with
> greater ease in the direction of the original succession and with a
> certainty proportional to the frequency with which they were together
> (1913, p. 90).

Thus, the serial task was an obvious choice for the experimental investigation of memory, for serial memorization would reflect directly the underlying process of successive association. Ebbinghaus' successors approached
the problems of learning and memory within the same theoretical framework and readily adopted serial learning as the standard laboratory procedure. Serial learning retained its fundamental status, providing as it were
the experimental realization of the mechanisms of association, even when
sequences of ideas were superseded by stimulus-response connections and
conditioned responses. Each item in the serial list was now seen as serving
the dual function of stimulus and response. Given this translation, it was
possible for Hull to use the serial task as the vehicle for the application of
the principles of classical conditioning to the analysis of verbal learning
(Hull, Hovland, Ross, Hall, Perkins & Fitch, 1940).

The adoption of the language and concepts of S-R theory brought to
the fore the distinction between the stimulus and response functions of
verbal units. Experimental analyses of verbal learning and memory leaned
more and more heavily on principles derived from classical conditioning,
such as stimulus and response generalization, differentiation, and extinction.
With the change in theoretical orientation, the serial task, which does not
permit independent manipulation of stimulus and response variables, lost
much of its analytic usefulness. Other paradigms which had a more direct
bearing on the current theoretical constructs came into increasing use,
notably the paired-associate task which does permit a sharp distinction
between stimulus and response functions. But like the nonsense syllable,
the serial task tended to linger on and was used in the investigation of
problems in which the separation of stimulus and response functions was to
prove essential. Some of the early work on negative transfer and interference is a case in point (cf. McGeoch, 1942, pp. 490 ff.). The risks of
standardization again become apparent.

Criterion measures. For Ebbinghaus, the criterion of perfect recitation
was the stable end point to which his measuring operations were anchored.
The amount of time required to reach the criterion gauged the difficulty of

a task, and the amount of time to relearn to criterion indicated the extent of forgetting. As was noted earlier, the defining characteristics of the criterion were errorless performance and a feeling of subjective certainty. With the trend toward objective measurement, the subjective component of the definition dropped out; time or trials to a fixed criterion of performance was universally adopted as a measure of the speed of learning. The logic of the fixed criterion was extended to other levels of performance, and the work required to proceed from one criterion to the next provided a standard measure for charting the course of acquisition (Melton, 1936). As criterion measures came into general use, their inherent limitations became progressively apparent. In spite of their limitations, criterion measures remain very useful for certain purposes, particularly for assessing differences in the difficulty of materials and in the ability of subjects. However, they have long since lost their unique status because other measures, notably the probability of recall after a given amount of practice, have proved to be more sensitive and more general in their application.

The saving method, which provided Ebbinghaus with a purchase on the measurement of forgetting, is rarely used in contemporary studies. It is, of course, closely tied to the logic of criterial measurement and hence suffers from all the limitations of the latter. There are additional difficulties, specific to the problem of retention. Thus the saving method has been applied with decreasing frequency. It was an important first step in the measurement of retention, but a first step only.

The temporal course of forgetting. Based as it was on the saving scores of a highly experienced subject, Ebbinghaus' famous forgetting curve turned out to be a very special function. This would not have surprised Ebbinghaus. In presenting his findings he said, with characteristic caution: "Considering the special, individual and uncertain character of our numerical results, no one will desire at once to know what 'law' is revealed in them" (1913, p. 77). The curve drops precipitously to less than 60 percent retention within 20 minutes and more slowly thereafter to about 34 percent after 24 hours, and to 21 percent after a month. We know that the extremely rapid rate of forgetting was undoubtedly caused by massive proactive interference from the many lists Ebbinghaus had learned previously. A naïve college subject may be expected to retain about 80 percent after 24 hours. The powerful proactive effects of prior experimental tasks were not recognized fully for many years; we owe their conclusive demonstration to Underwood's insightful analysis in 1957. We are once more reminded of the potentially far-reaching consequences of standardization. Counterbalanced experiments in which each subject was tested under all experimental conditions were for a long time standard practice in verbal learning laboratories. They had the advantage not only of economy but also of yielding data of low variability, but the results proved to have limited generality. Today prior experience is more likely to be treated as a manipulated variable than as a constant parameter of all experimental observations.

However much the numerical values of forgetting curves were to change, what is of greater significance is the steady evolution of systematic approaches to memory since Ebbinghaus first set out to plot his curve. Ebbinghaus decided to chart the temporal course of retention because he had concluded that the many speculative accounts of the memory process were totally devoid of any foundation in fact. The time had come to set speculation aside and to gather some empirical facts about forgetting. "By the help of our method we have a possibility of indirectly approaching the problem . . . in a small and definitely limited sphere, and, by means of keeping aloof for a while from any theory, perhaps of constructing one" (1913, p. 65).

His assessment of future trends proved to be substantially correct. Once methods of measuring retention had become available, it was inevitable that they would soon be put to use in the service of theoretical analysis. The moment of aloofness from theory for which Ebbinghaus called was short, but he used it well to build a bridge from speculation to experimental analysis.

How can we summarize the "fate" of Ebbinghaus' concepts and methods? The basic principle he sought to establish — that human learning and memory can be studied by the experimental method — has surely been vindicated many times over. As I have suggested earlier, an equally great measure of his success is provided by the rapid and continuing evolution of both methods and concepts which by now has carried us far outside the carefully defined boundaries within which he chose to work. Many of his procedures may by now be obsolescent, but there is a clear line of continuity between his early breakthroughs and the sophisticated methodology of the present day. And with the removal of subject-matter barriers we are drawing closer to the realization of the historical goal of a unified discipline devoted to the experimental analysis of the higher mental processes.

This is the goal which Ebbinghaus envisioned for the future when he inscribed on the title page of his treatise on memory the motto, "From the most ancient subject we shall produce the newest science." He is one of those who made it possible for experimental psychology to honor this promise.

REFERENCES

Boring, E. G. *A history of experimental psychology.* (2nd ed.) New York: Appleton-Century-Crofts, 1950.

Ebbinghaus, H. *Über das Gedächtnis: Untersuchungen zur experimentellen Psychologie.* Leipzig: Duncker & Humblot, 1885. (Trans. by H. A. Ruger & C. E. Bussenius as *Memory: A contribution to experimental psychology.* New York: Teachers College, Columbia University, 1913.)

Ebbinghaus, H. Über erklärende und beschreibende Psychologie *Zeitschrift für Psychologie,* 1895, *9,* 161-205.

Ebbinghaus, H. Über eine neue Methode zur Prüfung geistiger Fähigkeiten und ihre Anwendung bei Schulkindern. *Zeitschrift für Psychologie,* 1897, *13,* 401-459.

Ebbinghaus, H. *Abriss der Psychologie.* Leipzig: Veit, 1908. (Trans. by M. Meyer as *Psychology: An elementary textbook.* Boston: Heath, 1908.)

Hull, C. L., Hovland, C. I., Ross, R. T., Hall, M., Perkins, D. T., & Fitch, F. B. *Mathematico-deductive theory of rote learning.* New Haven: Yale University Press, 1940.

McGeoch, J. A. *The psychology of human learning.* New York: Longmans Green, 1942.

Melton, A. W. The end-spurt in memorization curves as an artifact of the averaging of individual curves. *Psychological Monographs,* 1936, *47,* (2, Whole No. 212), 119-134.

Rand, B. *The classical psychologists.* Boston: Houghton Mifflin, 1912.

Shakow, D., Hermann Ebbinghaus. *American Journal of Psychology,* 1930, *62,* 505-518.

Underwood, B. J. Interference and forgetting. *Psychological Review,* 1957, *64,* 49-60.

Underwood, B. J., & Schulz, R. W. *Meaningfulness and verbal learning.* Philadelphia: Lippincott, 1960.

Woodworth, R. S. Hermann Ebbinghaus. *Journal of Philosophy, Psychology and Scientific Method,* 1909, *6,* 253-256.

Wundt, W. *Lectures on human and animal psychology.* (Trans. from 2nd German ed. by J. E. Creighton & E. B. Titchener.) New York: Macmillan, 1907.

E. L. Thorndike:
The Psychologist as Professional
Man of Science

GERALDINE JONCICH CLIFFORD

During the celebration of Thorndike's twenty-fifth year at Teachers College, Columbia psychologist James McKeen Cattell (1926) quoted William James to the effect that E. L. Thorndike, more than anyone else he knew, had that objectivity essential to scientific work. And the introduction that James wrote for Thorndike's *The Elements of Psychology* (1905) seemed to Cornell psychologist E. B. Titchener (1905) to be so extreme in its "unstinted praise" that he even questioned its tastefulness in his review of the book written for the prestigious British journal, *Mind* — a review so sarcastic that Cattell protested to the editors of *Mind*.[1]

Whether or not James' assessment is overly generous and uncritical in Thorndike's case, remains an open question. What appears a clear and indisputable fact is that James was expressing a judgment of Thorndike — one focusing upon his taste and temperament for scientific work — that precisely matched Thorndike's own self-image. Over his entire career Thorndike tried to guide his behavior by the "scientist" model, because this is what he wanted most to be, this is what he was convinced he could be, and this is what he thought he was.

As a professional man, Thorndike can be said to have occupied two other chairs: one is, of course, the psychologist's; he was also the educationist, concerned with professionalizing teaching and school management. Nevertheless, his position as professional scientist was the more important to him. It overrode both others because it incorporated both, while connecting him with a whole system of scientific expertise and its high prestige. There are innumerable indications of Thorndike's preference, but only one will be mentioned here. Note the character of Thorndike's response to Titchener's attack upon *The Elements of Psychology*. To Titchener's warning that his book would receive harsh words, Thorndike replied in July 1905:[2]

> I do, of course, regret if I have fallen in your estimation with respect to accuracy of scholarship. However I cherish hopes of rising again if

This article, which has been abridged by the editors, appeared in its original form in the *American Psychologist*, 1968, *23*, 434-446.

you will read my *"Measurements of Twins"* (to be out soon) which is 75 pages of solid accuracy and of which there were 40 pages more accurate still but too expensive to print. I confess to two points of view, — practical expediency in books for beginners and the limit of exactitude in contributions to my equals and superiors.

When the review finally appeared in the October 1905 issue of *Mind,* Thorndike wrote to Titchener his objections to the assault upon his scientific reputation.

Titchener's reply failed to assuage Thorndike's hurt and he wrote a final time, closing with a pious withdrawal to the scientific ethic of impersonality:

> I would rather make a million errors in names, dates, references and the like than make such insinuations as you made unless I knew absolutely that the impression they would leave was in exact accord with the fact. Nor would I make them unless there was some clear benefit to the science.
>
> However in my view of life it is all a small matter. The best thing about scientific work is that it may be impersonal. I do the best I can and if you think I misuse my time and effort so much the worse for me if you are right, and for you, if you are wrong. . . .
>
> Yours truly
Edward L. Thorndike

Obviously, science is not an impersonal activity; what Thorndike was expressing was an ethic and ideology enjoying wide acceptance among his professional associates. It is inconceivable, then, that a Thorndike would ever echo Freud's self-description (Jones, 1961): "I am not really a man of science, not an observer, not an experimenter, and not a thinker. I am nothing but by temperament a conquistador — an adventurer" (p. xi).

In an autobiographical sketch (Murchison, 1930), Thorndike attempted to adumbrate the more potent environmental forces operating upon him. He listed "home life with parents of superior intelligence and idealism," college and university study, colleagues eminent in psychology and other fields, and "the great body of published work in science. The last is of course the most important." "Though an investigator rather than a scholar, I have probably spent well over 20,000 hours in reading and studying scientific books and journals" (Jonçich, 1962, p. 33). As a scientist, however, the psychologist must first publish and only secondarily read, and Thorndike's own bibliography numbers over 500 items.

To recapitulate, there is in Thorndike that certainty that he (like any trained investigator of human behavior) has as his major professional identification that of scientist *sui generis,* and that his primary reference group is the whole community of science. The explanation of this certainty inheres, it seems, in the greater (and, by today's standards, remarkable) cohesiveness of the scientific community in the late nineteenth century—when Thorndike left Wesleyan University a graduate in the classics and opted for science by selecting psychology at Harvard and Columbia.[3] To sketch out an account that will explain this communality of science—using Thorndike for illustration—is the aim of the rest of this article. The responsible factors, in ascending order of importance, are (1) personalistic and sociological characteristics held in common by Thorndike's generation of scientists; (2) the recency and incompleteness of American science's attempts to professionalize itself; (3) the dominance of positivism; and (4) the messianic zeal of the "sciences of human nature," and especially of psychology.

PERSONAL AND BACKGROUND CHARACTERISTICS

In 1927, E. K. Strong asked Thorndike to take his Strong Vocational Interest Blank. His profile of scores showed a marked interest in the quantitative, a manipulative interest in ideas, a rather small interest in people, and a very low concern with objects. He shared most of the characteristics which Strong and later testers found associated with careers in mathematics and accounting, science and engineering. Had personality inventories been more widely applied to his generation, it seems more than likely that such a temperamental characteristic as Thorndike's preference for solitary work would have been found to have marked the whole scientific community then, as it does today. Lacking the evidence, however, we turn to factors of background — to find that psychologists typically shared common origins and a body of common experiences with the generality of other scientists.

Thorndike's may be called the "transitional generation" of men of science; they were the accommodation group, forced to adjust to an America in flux and tending to make similar decisions along similar career lines. They contrast significantly with scientists born before 1865 or so, men whose backgrounds and range of choices better describe them as the "security generation."

American science before the Civil War was peopled with amateurs and generalists, typically of the patrician class and overwhelmingly from New England. Even the young men joining Henry Rowland in creating the physics department at the new, innovative Johns Hopkins University were raised in comfort — the sons of well-to-do businessmen, prosperous farmers and lawyers, ministers of the older respectable Protestant denominations. They represented clerical and commercial New England, Yankee stock, a society that was passing away. They attended tiny, sectarian, static (even decadent) colleges, where it was an oddity if any of the professors wrote books; in a few cases they supplemented this with study in Germany or France. The technological boom following the Civil War carried virtually no concomitant emphasis on the basic sciences. In 1850, Harvard, the nation's best and strongest educational institution, had no laboratories for teachers or students in chemistry, not a single piece of apparatus, not even any lectures in the subject since Harvard's sole chemistry instructor had been hanged for murder the previous year (Beardsley, 1964). Columbia in the 1870s gave a little laboratory experience only in chemistry and then only to engineering students. When Michael Pupin left Columbia for graduate study in Europe's great centers of physics, he did so without any laboratory training behind him.

To contrast this earlier generation with the one coming immediately after Thorndike's is to suggest the magnitude of the challenge, and the exhilarating sense of opportunity, faced by his generation of transition. Later scientists may be termed the "generation of ambition," representing a markedly upward-mobile social group and magnetized by engineering. Thus, physicists embarking on careers in 1910 and after came less often from the homes of lawyers and ministers than from those of small businessmen and farmers, schoolteachers and white-collar workers; the rise in technical enrollments in public institutions and in the aggrandizing private universities evidences the fact that the middle class, the traditionally opportunity-minded class, was now using the nation's colleges.[4] As part of the shift to middle western origins, these scientists typically were public school, not private academy, products, whose collegiate educations — in state universities, technical schools, the weaker colleges — were succeeded, nearly invariably, by doctoral study in an American university. No longer was expensive foreign study necessary, since domestic programs multiplied with specialization, diversity, and the elective system, while the force of institutional imitation pushed even reluctant college administrations closer to the mainstream of a now securely technocratic society.

In 1884, Reverend Thorndike moved his family, including 10-year-old Edward, to Lowell, Massachusetts. For a community of 60,000 people, there were 30 churches, but it was the factory chimney, not the steeple, that dominated the Lowell skyline. Most scientists of Thorndike's generation still came from northeastern America, but their boyhoods were spent in similar mill-town surroundings, for when Thorndike entered college New England alone led every country in the world in the per capita value of its manufactures. Like his fellows in science, Thorndike was of Yankee stock, but the decline of the "old-English" strain was obvious, for the cities and mill towns attracted huge numbers of immigrants. In 1800, Everett's population was 90 percent of English ancestry; by Thorndike's time 25 percent were immigrants and another 25 percent were the children of immigrants.

Such population diversity, plus the secularizing influence of an urbanizing, industrializing economy, meant a less fundamentalistic, less secure Protestantism. This consequence was directly pertinent to our population of scientists, for the striking fact is that a clergyman's household, combined with a New England setting, was the best predictor of a future career in science. Indeed, among Americans born around 1870, as was Thorndike, the proportion which became notable and who were sons of clergymen was twice as large as the combined total coming from all the other professions.

Thorndike's was a day when organized religion was nonetheless steadily losing stature in the nation's social and intellectual life, when theology (like medicine) was becoming a specialized study and not a part of general education, when science was usurping its place in academic disputations and attracting college graduates away from ministerial careers. This was not, however, a day of atheism; most academic scientists of Thorndike's generation — while rejecting their fathers' careers and liberalizing their own confessional associations — were apparently quite sincere in professing Christianity *and* the new biology, geology, physics, psychology. Thorndike was atypical here because his conversion to science was preceded by his adopting an exclusively naturalistic view of man; he once called agnostics, like himself, "conscientious objectors to immortality." Yet, like certain other wayward sons of the clergy, he (guiltily perhaps) infused his work with messianic fervor, so that science itself took on a crusadelike character. Moreover, in contending that agnostic scientists usually rate very highly for their private and public virtues, Thorndike was expressing the common tendency of nineteenth-century science to moralize about its advancement. Indeed, there has been a pronounced tendency in America to moralize all activities, all knowledge! "The proper study of nature begets devout affection [and] a true naturalist cannot be a bad man," one reads in *Knickerbocker* magazine in 1845. Similarly, General Francis A. Walker, President of M.I.T., told a gathering in 1893 that the scientific men of America were surpassed, if indeed approached, by no other group in their "sincerity, simplicity, fidelity and generosity of character, in nobility of aims and earnestness of effort" (p. 20).

In Thorndike's youth, interest in science was so intense that *Popular Science Monthly* was an outstanding success in the magazine field, and the sale of Herbert Spencer's books in the United States exceeded 300,000 copies. Yet, while the *Atlantic Monthly* was telling its readers, in 1898, that "America has become a nation of science," Thorndike's generation of future scientists attended schools and colleges grossly deficient in science education. Had it not been for a handful of ambitious graduate schools, the doing of American science — as opposed to its dissemination — would have been delayed even more. Although historians of science disagree as to how poor American science actually was before 1900, scientists contemporary with Thorndike have described the available training as seriously retarded (Jonçich, 1966). Only at the university level were matters much improved. While Charles Judd was convinced enough of the still-present advantage of a German doctorate to borrow the fare from his hometown minister, students who chose Hopkins, Clark, Cornell, Chicago, or (like Thorndike) Harvard and Columbia were exposing themselves to Americanized versions of a German university — and with every expectation of adequate preparation.

Students in the physical and social sciences now accounted for a full half of American graduate enrollments. At Teachers College, Thorndike succeeded in teasing and prying — from an administration reluctant to support such "academical" pursuits — a succession of teaching and research assistants, research courses, and, finally, even a research institute in which he secluded himself for twenty years. He was securely within that first generation of academic science in the modern era.

THE PROFESSIONALIZATION OF SCIENCE

A common characteristic of turn-of-the-century science in America was its heavy academic involvement. Government science was small, and industrial laboratories were still in the future. Full-time research was more rare in the United States than in Europe; Germany, in 1913, had six times as many research men in proportion to population as did the United States. In 1910, Cattell calculated that barely 1,000 Americans were occupied with serious research, and then, on the average, for only half-time.

Academe was, moreover, a setting where generalists and generalism had long reigned, where the standard of the broadly learned scholar hung on into the modern age of specialism. Since the typical college remained small —about 150 students—the philosopher-generalist had an employment advantage over the psychologist-specialist. For example, he would teach more subjects and rarely hounded the president for research time, laboratory space, costly equipment. Small wonder that, in 1898, Thorndike contemplated medical studies, or even a second doctorate in psychology. For months his only offer of employment was from the Oshkosh (Wisconsin) State Normal School, and Teachers College would not even accept his offer to teach there at half pay!

With academic specialization still only emergent, conglomerate and ill-defined departments abounded — prolonging, however, the opportunity for intellectual communion among the disciplines. Thorndike took his own doctorate in Columbia's Department of Philosophy, Psychology, Anthropology, and Education. And it was via anthropology, for example, that psychologists first entered membership in the National Academy of Sciences.

Before scientists cut themselves off from one another by specialization, priority went to cutting themselves off from the public; that is, the first order of business was banding together to effect the tardy professionalization of science writ large. To become professionalized meant the erection of various barriers against amateurs, the untrained, the unorthodox, the exotic, the "merely interested."

One such structure was the degree barrier. University expansion—greatly facilitated by the benefactions of businessmen and by institutional competition — permitted formal graduate training in the sciences to become widespread enough to assist in the exclusion process. In fact, by the time the

American Psychological Association celebrated its twenty-fifth anniversary, psychology had exceeded all the other sciences in the proportion of its members holding doctorates — 84 percent (Cattell, 1917).

When a body of knowledge becomes esoteric, that is, unavailable to the general scholar, its possessors are isolated by a second barrier: the barrier of unintelligibility (Daniels, 1965). Before the Civil War, science principally meant astronomy, agronomy, and medicine, and was part of the general stock of knowledge; by 1860, however, chemistry, geology, and the natural history fields had advanced enough to wrest away the designation of "science," while proceeding into esoterica too rapidly to be captured by nonprofessionals. For a while popularizers pretended to bridge the widening chasm between the common man and the now uncommon knowledge, but by 1915 the once prosperous *Popular Science Monthly* was dropped by its publisher of forty-two years, in significant contrast to Cattell's other journal, *Science,* successful because its content was almost wholly professional.

Although the charter members of the American Psychological Association, founded in 1892, contained a goodly number of philosophers, the situation soon changed, and psychology's future as a science, empirical and experimental, was loudly trumpeted within this professional association. For this, James McKeen Cattell — Thorndike's mentor and colleague at Columbia — was in large measure responsible; no one else as vigorously boosted psychology, meanwhile reiterating its connections with the whole of science. Cattell was proud to have been the world's first (1888) to be titled "professor of psychology." His laboratory at the University of Pennsylvania was reportedly the first to conduct research while teaching experimental methods systematically to undergraduates. Between 1891 and 1917 Cattell built the nation's largest Ph.D. program at Columbia, himself supervising some 50 dissertations. He was the first psychologist elected to the National Academy of Sciences, in 1901, preceding even William James. Cattell was of that small group which established the American Psychological Association; he was its President in 1895, and edited *Psychological Review.* He induced the New York Academy of Sciences to establish a section for anthropology and psychology — where Thorndike first reported his findings from "Animal Intelligence" and several other critical researches, including the famous 1901 studies of transfer of training.

In 1900, Thorndike was assisting Cattell in the editorship of *Popular Science Monthly* and *Science* when he met biologist Jacques Loeb at the Marine Biological Laboratory at Woods Hole. As Thorndike recorded it, "Loeb . . . told me I was a damned fool, that I was spoiling myself and ought to be shut up and kept at research work." He decided that Loeb was "largely right," and dropped this sideline; nevertheless, even this brief editorial experience only reinforced Thorndike's sense of familiarity with, and participation in, the totality of American science.

Thorndike was much less the committee man, the organizational figure, than was Cattell; despite this, he also became conspicuous in scientific circles. He was the first of the younger experimental psychologists to be elected (1917) to the National Academy of Sciences and attended its sessions fairly often. Like the Academy's membership, the leadership of AAAS has been dominated by chemistry, physics, astronomy, and geology; half of its presidents to date have come from these fields. Still, in 1934 Thorndike was chosen President of AAAS; except for economist W. C. Mitchell in 1938, no other social scientist headed this professional organization for the whole body of scientists since Thorndike's tenure, until Don Price became President in 1966.

POSITIVISM—A COMMON MENTAL SET

In common with every working scientist, Thorndike constructed his experimental situations according to his own theoretical postulates; when possessed of even a rudimentary theory, he tried to test the predictions emanating from that theory. It is such choices of experimental situation that decrease the probability that one theorist will directly test the major premises of another's theory.[5] The collecting and interpreting enterprise itself, however, must conform to certain expectations held in common with other scientists, for science is in part an attitude of mind shared by all its practitioners — even when they are ill-put or loath to articulate it.

Speaking of their college days together, Thorndike's long-time friend and associate, Robert S. Woodworth (Murchison, 1932), said of him, "His sane positivism was a very salutary influence for a somewhat speculative individual like myself . . ." (p. 366). The modifier "sane" conforms to Thorndike's own self-perception of his moderate, "common-sensical" intellectual approach in the quest for natural laws. In 1941, in recommending Thorndike for the William James Lectureship, Edwin G. Boring[6] was impressed with his continued mental vigor, and described Thorndike's latest research as "a very elementary positivism but a very interesting approach in the way it works out." The modifier here, "elementary," undoubtedly reflects the progress of philosophical sophistication about scientific method over the intervening forty-five years.

Even before his conversion to psychology, Thorndike was victim of the optimistic and widespread assumptions of nineteenth-century positivism. Even his college literary exercises revealed a hard tone, a disdain for the sentimental, a total confidence in dispassionate analysis ("the emotionally indifferent attitude of the scientific observer," he called it), the surety of the existence of "truth" and its ineluctable serviceability. Nature is, above all, he wrote in his first article addressed to teachers (Thorndike, 1899), *"a thing to study, to know about, to see through"* (p. 61). He abhorred vagueness, and for indeterminacy he substituted positivism: things do not happen by mere chance in human life any more than in the fall of an apple or an eclipse of the moon; behind the seemingly endless variety of human affairs there are invariably acting laws which make possible the advance of human control by reason.

That knowledge is power, that truth can be known, that facts can be trusted — these approached copybook maxims in Thorndike's youth, and such ideas no less distinguished those inducted into science in its perhaps most optimistic age. Facts were considered prepotent, and fact-finding the essence of all scientific endeavors. This applied as well to the social sciences. In a college essay on the moral force of the realist school of fiction writing, Thorndike [7] opined: "Truth is only truth, I think, [and] knowledge of any fact, no matter how vile, cannot but be morally helpful if it is true in the perspective and import given to it." "Look and see" was his advice to all other investigators of animal intelligence. While he considered that school visitations (for the purpose of marrying theory to practice or for the demonstration of already known psychological principles) were a tedious, inefficient, and unnecessary expenditure of the time of an educational psychologist, he was willing even to go into a schoolroom if the purpose was collecting facts for science.

Academic circles in the late nineteenth century were strangers to scientific relativism. Instead, knowledge was considered something firm, and in all the disciplines the emphasis was upon the never again to be repeated, upon the definitive study. It is *not* that Thorndike craved certainty. The immaturity of science, even of parts of the "hard sciences," was an accepted — and acceptable — proposition. But that indeterminacy is an ultimate barrier of nature against science was not yet proposed and would never be tolerated by many of his age; that all the psychologist's concepts, as well as the physicist's time and space, probably apply only to the unsophisticated, commonplace experiences of daily life requires a philosophical reorientation too radical for a generation of positivists. What Thorndike accepted about the introspectionist — that is, his uncontrollable, unintentional, but inevitable distortion of the psychological data he reports —cannot be true of the behaviorist.

The perfect model of the certain, nearly finished (i.e., perfectly polished) science of Thorndike's day was physics: it was preeminently experimental, devoted to the collection of physical facts and the testing of hypotheses. All its great discoveries were presumed made, and its remaining task centered upon the making of measurements of already known phenomena and their statement in forms precise to the sixth decimal point (Kevles, 1964). Roentgen's animating report in 1895 of the X-ray did not end the impress of physics upon the whole scientific community, for physics stood best for the widespread faith in quantification. Clerk Maxwell had expressed it well: "We owe all the great advances in knowledge to those who endeavor to find out how much there is of anything." So did Lord Kelvin: "One's knowledge of science begins when he can measure what he is speaking about, and express it in numbers." How redolent of Thorndike's these words are, and where Thorndike thought himself most deficient was in his meager mathematical training.

The year Thorndike spent at Columbia University (1897-98) was its first year at the new Morningside Heights campus; no longer was the President's house home to both Pupin's electrical laboratory (in its cellar) and Cattell's laboratory (in its attic). Yet that spatial juxtaposition of physics and psychology had been an apt symbolization of a compatible methodological and conceptual "togetherness" — call it "reductionism" if you will — so evident in the 1890s. The laboratory was the destination of virtually every aspiring young scientist of the later nineteenth century. Botanists left their fields, even their herbaria, for the laboratory's dyes and microscopes. Many a psychologist developed his aggressively mechanical and materialistic visages in Germany's psychophysical and physiological centers. Albion Small (Small and Vincent, 1894) declared laboratory discipline essential to social science, calling research experience in physics, chemistry, and biology "ideal preparation for sociological research . . ." (p. 24).

When American students made "experiment" synonymous with "scientific," this was methodological reductionism; in conceiving of "mental atoms," the "conservation of psychic energy," or "the natural selection of cultures," this was theoretical or conceptual reductionism (Wolman, 1965). Reducing (i.e., taking over) Galileo's theory of falling bodies into Newton's theory of gravitation and mechanics was an early example entirely within the field of physics. More obvious and controversial is reductionism across the sciences — treating metabolic processes or the emotions entirely as chemistry, for instance. Breakthroughs in one science often precipitate or speed reductionism. Thus, chemistry assaulted the not so ancient distinction between organic and inorganic because chemical synthesis seemed to drive vitalism out of biology and physiology. Even the radical reductionist — accepting an identity of the subject matter as he does — leaves separate spheres for the different sciences, however, and John B. Watson distinguished between psychology and physiology by giving the former the organism's functions as a whole to deal with, and the latter its separated functions.

The science toward which most others gravitated was physics. Despite the power of physics, however, it is also necessary to recall that each science responded to the others' revolutions. Even before Darwin, for instance, there was sizable interest in all the sciences in the origins of matter. Franz Boas, who taught statistics to Thorndike, began as a physicist, proceeded to geography, and settled in anthropology; his reasons for abandoning physics were similar to the botanist's who left morphology for plant life history. Nicholas Murray Butler was largely correct in claiming that every strain of nineteenth-century thought had been cross-fertilized by the doctrine of evolution. Impersonal evolutionary forces and environmental adaptation furnished historiography with alternatives to catastrophic and heroic explanation. And conservatives and liberals alike rushed to buoy their political and economic preferences with Darwinism.

The circle of the earth is long since complete, but in the presence of each man is an unexplored world — his own mind. There is no mental geography describing the contents of the mind, still less is there a mental mechanics demonstrating necessary relations of thought. Yet the mind is the beginning and the end of science. Physical science is possible because the mind observes and arranges, and physical science has worth because it satisfies mental needs (Cattell, 1893, p. 779).

Such comfortable and familiar allusions as "mental geography" and "mental mechanics" came naturally to Cattell's pen. As the twentieth century advanced, however, they would become anathema to many behavioral scientists. Quantum mechanics, probabilistic physics, and the rediscovery of Mendel and the new genetics made nature appear more complex, even mysterious. "The range of the measurable is *not* the range of the knowable" — this was sociologist Robert A. MacIver's challenge to Thorndike across the Columbia campus. Pitirim Sorokin (1943) was a particularly acicular commentator upon such borrowings as "social distance" and "organizational equilibrium"; he held up for ridicule A. P. Weiss' definition of consciousness as "an electron-proton aggregation" (Sorokin, 1943, p. 27). In a similar manner, some social psychologists became wary of what seemed a psychobiologic dominance; they protested that special social-psychological laws preclude dependence upon generalizations drawn from individual behavioral systems. It was now heard that the social sciences are the sciences of culture, not of nature. By the time that Thorndike's mammoth *Human Nature and the Social Order* appeared in 1940, his was too simplistic and atomistic, too unified an application to interest most other social scientists.

The multiplication of "schools" and theories was fragmenting psychology also. Nevertheless Wolman (1965) may be correct that, even in 1965, at base most psychologists hope for the eventual reduction of psychological processes to the physicochemical sciences. At any rate, this seems true of Thorndike. He was early convinced of the unity of nature and that psychology must attain the certainty and exactness of the physical sciences, and could not do so without resting upon their foundations. In the last month of his life he said that he still wanted most in his lifetime to see demonstrated the fruitfulness, for the social arts and sciences, of the exacting sort of scientific procedures found in his youth only in the physical sciences.

THE MESSIANIC CHARACTER OF THE "NEW PSYCHOLOGY"

In his presidential address to the American Psychological Association in 1937, California's E. C. Tolman (1938) declared that — given psychology's inability even to predict the direction a rat would turn in a maze— he considered his science unready to furnish guidelines for human behavior. Thorndike's perceptions of both the possibilities and the actual achievements of psychology were considerably more immodest than Tolman's; he never lost much of that optimism, buoyancy, and sense of mission evident in the "new psychology" of the 1890s.

Fully accepting Karl Pearson's (1892) proposition, in *The Grammar of Science,* that science, rightly understood, is competent to solve all problems, Thorndike was understandably impatient with the backwardness of psychological knowledge, although not with its new aims. In a graduate seminar paper Thorndike noted with indignation:[8]

> [Descartes'] physiological theories have all been sloughed off by science long ago. No one ever quotes him as an authority in morphology or physiology. . . . Yet his theory of the nature of the mind is still upheld by not a few, and the differences between his doctrines of imagination, memory, and of the emotions, and those of many present-day psychology books are comparatively unimportant.

Not that this deplorable situation was all grim, however: a good opportunity for iconoclasm was made available, and Thorndike got much sheer delight from it in his early, "assertive years." [9] Of his thesis he wrote to his future wife, "It is fun to write all the stuff up and smite all the hoary scientists hip and thigh. I shall be jumped on unmercifully when the thing gets printed, if I ever raise the cash to print it."

Years later, when Thorndike himself was older and mellower and successful, he chided John B. Watson a little for that same mixture of scientific evangelism and iconoclastic sarcasm which colored his own beginnings: In a review of *Behavior,* Thorndike (1915) wrote: "For students of objective behavior to regard themselves as martyrs, heroes or prophets is now unnecessary" (p. 466).

The new psychology meant, in part, the eschewing of "armchair speculation," a cleaving from the humanities, a rejecting of philosophy. At times the philosophers seemed to assist the process. It was a philosopher who inducted Judd, Thorndike, Freeman, and W. F. Dearborn into psychology. And Princeton's philosopher President, James McCosh, presumably an unregenerate conservative, wrote to James Mark Baldwin (1926) in Leipzig in 1884: "You may tell Professor Wundt that his works are known in this college to our best students . . . [and that] two years ago we had a Wundt Club which met to read the Mental Physiology" (pp. 199-200). From but four independent psychology departments in American universities in 1904, there were 34 a decade later.

The number of psychological laboratories increased rapidly. Between 1874 and 1904, 54 were established in North America. Even Titchener's group, espousing the unpopular method of introspection as a unique psychological tool and in self-imposed structuralist isolation from the main body of American psychologists, counted itself within the new psychology for its devotion to the laboratory. Cornell offered probably the nation's most stringent training, cultivated a highly technical vocabulary, conducted elaborately controlled investigations. Such among Titchener's students as Carl Seashore (Murchison, 1930b) thought Titchener's four-volume *Experimental Psychology* "the highest embodiment of the idea of intensive, fundamental drill exercises" (p. 262) and lamented when such stylized training and laboratory formalism fell away.

The new psychology had its skeptics, of course, including William James, America's best known philosopher and psychologist. Dispatching a copy of his *Measurements* to James, Thorndike warned him:[10]

> I am sending you a dreadful book which I have written, which is no end scientific but devoid of any spark of human interest. You must make all your research men read it, but never look within its covers yourself. The figures and curves and formulae would drive you mad.

James' response was cordial, tactful, affectionate:

> I open your new book with full feelings of awe and admiration for your unexampled energy. It was just the thing I hoped for when I was teaching psychology and wondered why no one wrote it. And now you are the man to have done it. I should think it would immediately be translated.
>
> I am glad I have graduated from the necessity of using that kind of thing any longer. I shall stick to "qualitative" work as more congruous with old age. Nothing like metaphysics for people in their dotage.

Thorndike well knew that his teacher thought America was already oversupplied with psychological laboratories, and that James doubted even the credibility of the "exact" sciences. James preferred, instead, "non-systems" — in an eternally pluralistic, liberal, permissive, open universe. Thorndike revered him above all other men, but the younger psychologists were so anxious to give scientific status to their work that James seemed an "irritating impressionist." Thorndike's own tolerance of James did not extend to G. Stanley Hall, however, and he never criticized or satirized anyone as severely as he did Hall. The possibility that the pseudo-scientific pretensions of the child-study movement might be mistaken for educational psychology was too horrible to contemplate.

Hugo Münsterberg typified a different kind of skeptic. He dichotomized the art and the science of education, for instance, and doubted applied psychology's worth (especially for education). But Thorndike (1898b) answered: "Many things have been declared out of court . . . which the widening researches of matter-of-fact men have triumphantly reinstated" (p. 646). In 1918, speaking as a Vice-President of AAAS, Thorndike (1919) described applied psychology as "much more than cleverness and common sense. . . . It is scientific work, research on problems of human nature complicated by conditions of the shop or school or army, restricted by time and labor cost and directed by imperative needs. The secret of success in applied psychology or human engineering is [he concluded] *to be rigorously scientific*" (p. 60).

To explain the difficulties of behavioral research, Thorndike (1935) once used this illustration: "*Science* cannot roll identical villages down a depression again and again to test the laws of economics as *it* rolls ivory balls down an inclined plane to test the uniformity of the laws of motion" (p. 228). Such difficulties were not totally unappreciated in the larger scientific community either. It seemed to one American physicist (Crew, 1934) that "to tell the truth about an experiment in physics is child's play, compared with telling the truth about a man" (p. 331). Another observed that "physics is the simplest of all sciences, for the reason that all the rest are *physics-plus* . . ." (p. 23).[11]

Nevertheless, American psychology continued to be extremely active— and in the name of science. By 1913, *Who's Who in Science* (published in England) reported the United States was the most productive nation in psychological research, with 84 of the world's leading investigators (sur- passing the combined totals of Germany, England, and France). Only here, among all the sciences, was America the world's leader. In 1931, at an international gathering of psychologists and educators, it was frequently remarked that America virtually owned psychometrics. As Thorndike (Monroe, 1931) protested to that assemblage, however, "it would be more in the interests of science and of our comfort" if standardized tests were *not* called "American examinations," since *"science is certainly not national and the only claim of Americans busy in that line is that they are trying to be scientific"* (p. 262, italics added).

As for himself, among all the congratulations showered upon him with his election to the presidency of the American Association for the Ad- vancement of Science, none must have pleased Thorndike more than those words in the *New York Times* (January 13, 1934) editorial that said simply, "But first and last, he is a scientist."

NOTES

1. Cattell to the editors, undated. Copy in unpublished Thorndike papers (not indexed), Montrose, New York.
2. Thorndike's replies to Titchener are located and indexed in the Titchener Papers, Cornell University, Ithaca, New York.
3. Just how much separatism has developed in this century is suggested in Higham (1966).
4. See Kevles (1964), Veysey (1965), and Visher (1939).
5. Because Thorndike believed learning to be grounded in trial-and-error behavior, he adopted puzzle-box techniques; because of his associationist theory, he em- ployed word tests of paired associates. Where Thorndike constructed experi- mental situations to secure random responses, Köhler devised his to secure evidence of insight.
6. E. G. Boring, personal communication to Gordon Allport, May 2, 1941. Archives of the Psychology Department, Harvard University.
7. Student essays, in the collection of the Eclectic Society, Wesleyan University, Middletown, Connecticut.
8. "The Psychology of Descartes," 1898. In unpublished Thorndike papers, Mont- rose, New York.
9. E. L. Thorndike, personal communications to Elizabeth Moulton, February 26, 1898; March 12, 1898: January 6, 1899. In unpublished Thorndike papers, Montrose, New York.

10. E. L. Thorndike, personal communication to W. James, September 28, 1904. In Thorndike file, James Papers, Houghton Library, Harvard University. James' response (dated October 6, 1904) in unpublished Thorndike papers, Montrose, New York.
11. Daniel F. Comstock, "Autobiographical Notes." In Comstock Papers, Library, American Institute of Physics, New York City.

REFERENCES

Baldwin, J. M. *Between two wars*. Vol. I. Boston: Stratford, 1926.
Beardsley, E. H. The rise of the American chemistry profession, 1850-1900. *University of Florida Monographs in Social Sciences*, No. 23, 1964.
Cattell, J. McK. The progress of psychology. *Popular Science Monthly*, 1893, *43*, 779-785.
Cattell, J. McK. Our psychological association and research. *Science*, 1917, *45*, 275-284.
Cattell, J. McK. Thorndike as colleague and friend. *Teachers College Record*, 1926, *27*, 461-465.
Crew, H. *Thomas Corwin Mendenhall*. Biographical Memoir, National Academy of Sciences, 1934.
Daniels, G. The process of professionalization in American science: The emergent period, 1820-1860. Paper presented at the meeting of the History of Science Society, San Francisco, December 1965.
Higham, J. The schism in American scholarship. *American Historical Review*, 1966, *72*, 1-21.
Jonçich, G. (Ed.) *Psychology and the science of education: Selected writings of Edward L. Thorndike*. New York: Teachers College, 1962.
Jonçich, G. Scientists and the schools of the nineteenth century: The case of American physicists. *American Quarterly*, 1966, *18*, 667-685.
Jones, E. *The life and work of Sigmund Freud*. (Abridged ed., by L. Trilling & S. Marcus) New York: Basic Books, 1961.
Kevles, D. J. The study of physics in America, 1865-1916. Unpublished doctoral dissertation, Princeton University, 1964.
Monroe, P. (Ed.) *Conference on examinations*. New York: Teachers College, 1931.
Murchison, C. (Ed.) *A history of psychology in autobiography*. Worcester, Mass.: Clark University Press, Vol. 1, 1930a; Vol. 2, 1932; Vol. 3, 1936.
Murchison, C. (Ed.) *Psychologies of 1930*. Worcester, Mass.: Clark University Press, 1930. (b)
Pearson, K. *The grammar of science*. New York: Scribners, 1892.
Small, A. W., & Vincent, G. E. *An introduction to the study of sociology*. New York: American Book, 1894.
Sorokin, P. A. *Sociocultural causality, space, time*. Durham: Duke University Press, 1943.
Thorndike, E. L. Animal intelligence. *Psychological Review Monographs*, No. 2, 1898. (a)
Thorndike, E. L. What is a physical fact? *Psychological Review*, 1898, *5*, 645-650. (b)
Thorndike, E. L. Sentimentality in science teaching. *Educational Review*, 1899, *17*, 57-64.
Tharndike, E. L. *The elements of psychology*. New York: A. G. Seiler, 1905.
Thorndike, E. L. Review of Watson's "Behaviorism." *Journal of Animal Behavior*, 1915, *5*, 462-470.
Thorndike, E. L. Scientific personnel work in the army. *Science*, 1919, *49*, 53-61.

Thorndike, E. L. The paradox of science. *Proceedings of the American Philosophical Society,* 1935, *75,* 287-294.

Titchener, E. B. Review of Thorndike's "The Elements of Psychology." *Mind,* 1905, *56,* 552-554.

Tolman, E. C. The determiners of behavior at a choice point. *Psychological Review,* 1938, *45,* 1-35.

Veysey, L. R. *The emergence of the American university.* Chicago: University of Chicago Press, 1965.

Visher, S. Distribution of the psychologists starred in the six editions of "American Men of Science." *American Journal of Psychology,* 1939, *52,* 278-292.

Walker, F. *Formal opening of the engineering and physics building.* Montreal: McGill University Press, 1893.

Wolman, B. (Ed.) *Scientific psychology.* New York: Basic Books, 1965.

OF THEORIES
AND THEORISTS:

OCCASIONAL PAPERS
BY EDNA HEIDBREDER

Freud and Psychology

EDNA HEIDBREDER

The death of Sigmund Freud [1] has reminded the world anew of his extraordinary role in the broadening and deepening of psychological inquiry. Yet his influence on psychology was a very small part of the total effect he produced on the intellectual life of his age. In some of the arts, in literature especially, the impress of his teachings is one of the distinctive marks of the day. In the social sciences, too, notably in anthropology and sociology, the signs of his influence are unmistakable and familiar. In psychiatry, as everyone knows, he effected a revolution. Problems of ethics and esthetics have been reviewed in the light of his theories, and the implications of his doctrines have by no means escaped the attention of students of philosophy and religion. Even such impersonal disciplines as logic, mathematics, and the physical sciences take on, as human enterprises, a special significance when seen from his point of view. But most remarkable of all is his effect on the thought of everyday life. Much of the Freudian terminology has found its way into common speech; and a general, though vague, notion of his interpretation of human nature is part and parcel of the common thought of the age.

It would be a mistake to regard Freud's influence on psychology as constituting a problem essentially different from that of his influence on any other field. For it was not as a psychologist that Freud influenced psychology. Neither was it as a man of letters that he influenced literature, nor as an anthropologist that he influenced anthropology. In every case his action was that of a force from without. Even psychiatry is no exception to the rule, for it was not by working in the professional tradition that he exerted his influence on his own profession. His development in psychiatry was always outside the regular line of professional advancement, and when eventually he was recognized by fellow psychiatrists in Zurich, the main direction of his thought had been definitely and firmly set. He had even acquired a group of disciples in Vienna and elsewhere, and the time had passed, if indeed it had ever existed, when Freud could be absorbed by a professional group as a member on an equal footing with other members.

His capacity for maintaining a course of action without the support and encouragement of his profession was an essential factor in his achievement. Whatever else his teachings may be, they are those of a man working at his own task in his own way. Nothing in his career is more remarkable than the complete trust he placed in his own perceptions. As one reads his comments on those who did not wholly agree with him, one is struck by the fact that it apparently did not occur to him that divergences from his own opinion might be anything but errors [2] — errors due to an inability, temperamental or otherwise, to understand and accept what he so plainly saw to be true. In marked contrast to his repeatedly demonstrated readiness to change his theories when his own observations and reflections required it, was his resentment of changes suggested by others, especially those who had once been his followers. Apparently he could accept the contributions of disciples while they remained disciples; but the give and take between colleagues on terms of equality seems to have been foreign to his nature.

Without his independence of professional support and professional conventions, Freud could not have accomplished his task. Without it, he could never have maintained the novel and difficult direction of attention that gave his contributions their distinctive character. For the uniqueness of his achievement was determined by the fact that he saw human beings neither as common sense saw them nor as they appeared to the eyes of any existing profession. He addressed himself to problems of human nature which were not quite the problems anyone else had seen; his interest was attracted by a field of observation not exactly that which anyone else had explored or even clearly noted; and he gradually evolved a conceptual system which, derived from his personal observation in his special field, came nowhere near engaging smoothly with the accepted conceptions of any professional group. In a sense, of course, Freud was working on an age-old problem, that of inner conflict. In a narrower and more professional sense he was observing the material every psychiatrist must perforce observe. But his attention was caught by occurrences and connections no one else had made focal and steadily regarded, and in reflecting on them he made explicit and welded into a connected (though not closely articulated) system, facts and relationships which others had overlooked or had only dimly sensed or had noted and reported as fragmentary observations.

Perhaps Freud's most striking intellectual characteristic is his utter absorption in the class of facts he had set himself to understand. At any rate, it was this absorption, unhampered as well as unsupported by professional tradition, that gave his theory both its strangeness and its scope— on the one hand, putting it out of line with the intellectual mores of the day, and, on the other, by keeping it close to the concrete and the actual, making it relevant to a wide range of human interests. Freud's disregard of the accepted rules of science and scholarship is notorious. Using the special tools of no profession or craft, he had recourse to a method more akin to common observation and common sense than to the specialized techniques of any of the established intellectual disciplines. Fundamentally his observations were like those involved in the social perceptions and judgments of everyday life — more sensitive and more shrewd, of course, and inevitably marked by his personal preoccupations — but dependent nevertheless on the ordinary operations of social intelligence. It is interesting that his special method uses the commonest mode of social communication. Psychoanalysis is carried on by means of talk, conversation. Indeed, much of the strength of Freud's theories and practices lies in the fact that his methods were *un*technical and *un*specialized, and therefore kept him close to the familiar actualities of common life and common sense.

Yet it would be manifestly absurd to identify Freud's theories with the insights of common sense. Rather, they were the outcome of explorations into the subsoil of common sense; and if for this reason they are relevant to the whole range of human endeavor, they are for the same reason difficult to place with reference to existing bodies of knowledge and modes of procedure, not excluding those of common sense. It is extraordinarily difficult to describe Freud's method in any but negative terms. Perhaps the nearest approach to a positive description may be found in Emerson's phrase, "man thinking." "Thinking in unhabitual ways" is another phrase that suggests itself as appropriate, especially when it is recalled that Freud's inquiries have been directed toward the very facts concerning which conventional modes of thought have been most subject to the pressure of habit and custom. Freud's task required the difficult and delicate adjustment of focusing just off the usual fixation point; of maintaining a line of regard almost coinciding with, yet always distinct from, the one favored by habit and common practice. Furthermore, his observations were a personal enterprise, one in which he neither utilized, nor indeed felt the need for, the safeguards which the sciences find indispensable.

No psychologist need be told that this mode of observation was not one approved by the psychology of Freud's day. It is a commonplace that when psychology emerged as a science, its goal and direction, along with its method and assumptions, were determined by the physical sciences of the nineteenth century. No more impersonal psychology has ever existed than that which developed in the first psychological laboratories. There is a sense in which its special method, introspection, represents the height of objectivity and detachment, requiring as it does the observation of events defined as available only in immediate experience, with the same disregard for personal values and implications demanded of an experimenter observing any event — say, a falling body — in the external world. The introspection of the early laboratories was not self-exploration, and insofar as psychoanalysis was precisely self-exploration for the person analyzed, it ran directly counter to the approved methods of the psychology of the time. It would be difficult to find a task in sharper contrast with that of the "observer" in a psychological laboratory than that required of a patient undergoing psychoanalysis.

This difference in method and outlook becomes especially significant when one considers how closely Freud's career coincides in time with the rise and development of psychology as an experimental science. Freud was born in 1856, four years before the publication of Fechner's *Elements of Psychophysics,* the book commonly regarded as the first achievement of a definitely experimental psychology. By the time he had reached university age, the early classics in psychology had been written. During his own student days at Vienna, Wundt's famous laboratory was opened at Leipzig, and in the decade of the eighties — the formative period of his professional life — such notable pioneer studies in psychology were appearing as Galton's researches on imagery and association, Ebbinghaus' monograph on memory, and the contributions of James and Lange to the theory of the emotions now known by their names. The list might be extended, but it has gone far enough to exhibit in an account of Freud's work the character of "not belonging." Yet imagery and association, memory and emotion, are processes of vital importance to the Freudian theories and to the success of psychoanalysis as therapy.

The fact is that Freud's interests were so completely outside the psychology pursued by professional psychologists that he was altogether unaffected by their activities. To be sure, there was a time when he acknowledged the usefulness of the free association experiment which Jung introduced from the psychological laboratory. But in his *History of the Psychoanalytic Movement,*[3] written after the break with Jung, his comment on this importation is entirely unenthusiastic and constitutes the only reference to experimental psychology in the entire account. It is interesting, too, that the five lectures entitled *The Origin and Development of Psychoanalysis,*[4] given at Clark University at the invitation of G. Stanley Hall, likewise contain only one reference to a psychological study; a reference, moreover, which seems an expression of courtesy rather than of an interest in the findings of psychologists. Freud's indifference, furthermore, persisted throughout his career. It remained completely unaltered when psychology itself changed, partly by enlarging its field and including problems similar to his own. The mere suggestion that his attitude might have been otherwise is slightly absurd. It is interesting, nevertheless, as additional evidence of his extraordinary absorption, that a whole new intellectual movement arose and developed in a field presumably related to his own without arousing his curiosity or even attracting his serious attention.

It is interesting, too, that psychology did not meet indifference with indifference, but paid far more heed to Freud than to most of its own workers. Why, then, did Freud, who had no interest in psychology, become one of the most potent influences in the psychology of his day?

An obvious answer, and one that is less trivial than it seems, is that psychologists would have been blind and deaf to what was going on in the world about them if they had not noticed the tremendous stir Freud was creating concerning topics presumably within their own field.

Many psychologists, of course, are almost that. In other words, many of them are almost as absorbed in their special problems as Freud was in his, and some of the problems are such that they can be profitably investigated without reference to the teachings of Freud. It is well to recognize that this is the case. If psychology is defined as the work psychologists are doing, it becomes a mere matter of empirical fact that there are portions of psychology which have been as unaffected by Freud, as Freud's teachings have been unaffected by psychology.[5] This means, among other things, that the subject matter of psychology is not limited to problems of personal adjustment. It is well that this point be explicitly stated since it is one that most psychoanalysts and some psychologists seem to find either inconceivable or incredible. Yet in the *difference* between the tasks of psychologists and psychoanalysts lies the reason for their different attitudes toward each other. Psychoanalysts, whose activities and thoughts are centered about a special problem that is both practical and pressing, can afford to work at this problem with little concern for what most psychologists are doing. Psychologists, however, undertaking a more detached but more comprehensive survey of human nature, find it impossible not to listen to Freud. Even the most specialized workers find it hard to be unaware of the total field of which their problems are a part. They can therefore be only "almost" as absorbed in a special problem as Freud. Psychologists know, too, that the field Freud explored is one in which their own efforts have been most fruitless. It is interesting to find a symposium on Freud's concepts which includes among its participants a number of psychologists whose chief contributions and characteristic interests are elsewhere.[6] Psychologists do not find it possible to ignore Freud and his theories, as Freud and his followers have found it possible to ignore psychology. Psychology, aiming at comprehensiveness, is aware of incompleteness.

A sense of the incompleteness of psychology, however, does not explain the positive appeal of Freud's teachings. Not everything that promises to deepen and vitalize psychological knowledge [7] gains from psychologists the respectful hearing they have given this theory, based on methods and conceptions so different from their own.

There is no escaping the fact that the Freudian theories found their way into psychology without the backing of accepted, or acceptable, scientific evidence. They entered with no support but that of common knowledge about human nature, knowledge neither more nor less accessible to psychologists than to anyone else. There is a sense in which Freud's teachings were unfamiliar to few, in which despite their boldness and originality, they were often heard even at first with something like recognition. To be sure, Freud's theories were considered bizarre. No one had seen exactly what Freud had seen, and no one had seen all that Freud had seen; yet many had noticed something sufficiently similar to arouse their willingness and eagerness to listen to his interpretations. It is this obscure relevance to common knowledge that made Freud's teachings credible, though not always acceptable, to the man in the street; and it is in his role as man in the street, not on the basis of his special knowledge, that a psychologist pays attention to Freud.

But more than vague relevance to common knowledge was needed to give Freud's theories the importance they attained. An essential part of Freud's contribution is the form in which he presented his teachings, a form which made statable for open and public discussion events that occurred in hidden private worlds. In brief, he invented a mythology and a terminology. By the liberal use of analogy and metaphor he constructed a world of symbols well adapted to the human propensity for thinking in terms of concrete situations: a world not of abstractions, difficult to conceive and attend to, but of picturable persons and objects and places, as easy to think and talk about as the world of a novel or drama, and somewhat similar in its appeal to human interest. By reference to this world, layman and scientist alike found it possible to formulate the problems of depth psychology. It is profoundly significant that the Freudian terminology has been widely adopted, and that even among psychologists who find Freud's explanations worthless, there are many who find his terminology indispensable. Whether the terminology would have become current without the mythology is a question. The mingling of the two is now a *fait accompli,* and a source both of strength and of confusion in the Freudian system.

It is a source of strength because, as has just been suggested, it takes advantage of the mode of thought which human beings find easiest and most effective. By using a terminology which externalizes inner conflicts, by presenting them imaginatively as if they were situations like those encountered in the external world, Freud did much toward placing the emotional entanglements of human beings in a context in which they could be looked at objectively and recognized as problems for scientific investigation. The confusion arises from the fact that the device is not only helpful but dangerous, offering as it does an ever-present temptation to reification. Imagined objects and situations may all too readily be thought of as actually existing. Furthermore, when used as symbols, they involve the risk of surrounding the concept with irrelevant implications. They place before the reader more than is there in order to make him see that something is there. The question then rises: Can the excess, which is merely arbitrary and may therefore be misleading, be effectually cleared away or at least rendered harmless? Can products of the imagination be transformed into scientific concepts?

Murray's *Explorations in Personality* [8] is an attempt to come to terms with this problem by one whose main interests are in clinical rather than in academic psychology. But academic psychologists are concerned with a problem similar in general outline. Among these are men of such different interests and academic backgrounds as Tolman, Lewin, and G. W. Allport —all far more impressed than Freud by the requirements of science, but all finding the conventional systems of psychology inadequate to the problems with which they deal. Thus, from within academic psychology itself there has come a demand for concepts suitable to dynamic problems. Perhaps not the least of Freud's achievements is the impetus he has given to a movement in which he seems to have had no interest whatsoever, a movement toward a revision of the theoretical framework of academic psychology for the accommodation of problems in dynamics.

But while gaining attention for some aspects of human nature, Freud needlessly thrust others into the background. Absorbed in the psychology of the primal urges, he paid little attention to the implications of the fact that the human animal is capable of intelligent action. Yet one of the conspicuous differences between human beings and other animals is the greater extent to which the human species employs the mode of adaptation called intelligence. No other species develops arts, sciences, and philosophies; no other species produces and destroys civilizations. To ignore such conspicuous differentiae of a species is as one-sided and unrealistic as to ignore those characteristics which place it in the same class with other animals.

Of course Freud did not ignore the intellectual processes completely; but in comparison with the nonrational urges, they seemed to him unimportant. It is significant that he never worked out a very clear position with respect to the intellectual processes. At first he rather vaguely regarded them as associated with the ego, admitting that there was much in the ego that he did not understand. Thus he conceived of the ego as more or less effectively opposing the libido, and at the same time he thought of the intellectual processes as subservient to the libido. He regarded rationalization and autistic thinking as typical intellectual activities. It is unfortunate and somewhat strange that the intellectual operations as such did not arouse his curiosity, for the very occurrence of such practices as rationalization and day-dreaming suggests that intellectual activities are not incapable of imposing their own conditions. Does not rationalization suggest that there are intellectual demands which must be satisfied, even when the main object of the intellectual activity is to serve the nonrational impulses? And is not some explanation required for the fact that imperious primal urges can be satisfied, even temporarily and partially, by such flimsy stuff as daydreams? At any rate, a field of inquiry is indicated concerning lines of relationship between cognitive activities and the primal urges.

As a matter of fact, a recognition of something of the sort is implied in the direction Freud's own thought has taken. In his later theories he posited, largely as a result of a study of the ego trends, a far greater complexity of organization, a far more intricate system of interrelationships among the parts of the personality, than that pictured in the simple opposition of ego and libido. The old theory seemed inadequate to the complexities of a creature capable of going beyond the pleasure principle. In consequence, Freud developed the concept of an elaborate organization consisting of the ego, super ego, and id. The new theory, while keeping the emphasis unmistakably on nonrational urges, nevertheless definitely recognized in the cognitive and intellectual processes distinctive and essential and complicating factors involved in the production of conflicts and in the formation of the personality. It also recognized strong alliances as well as bitter conflicts between the rational and nonrational components of human nature.

It is impossible, of course, to foresee the lasting outcome of Freud's system, but the general character of his contribution is easily discernible. Like Copernicus and Darwin — the comparison has become inevitable —

he put the facts of common observation in a setting which profoundly altered their meaning, and which introduced into both science and common knowledge radically new perspectives. But unlike Copernicus and Darwin, Freud presented his theories in a form unsuitable to scientific verification and use. The situation abounds in difficulties and recalls the half-despairing advice given by William James in another connection: "The only thing then is to use as much sagacity as you possess and to be as candid as you can." [9]

NOTES

1. Freud died in London on September 23, 1939.
2. There are illustrations of this attitude scattered throughout Freud's works. They are especially numerous in his History of the psychoanalytic movement (translated by A. A. Brill), *Nerv. & Ment. Dis. Monogr. Series*, No. 25, 1916, 1-58.
3. *Op. cit.*, p. 20.
4. S. Freud. The origin and development of psychoanalysis (translated by H. W. Chase, revised by Freud), *Amer. J. Psychol.*, 1910, *21*, 181-218. The reference to a psychological investigation occurs on p. 208. The study referred to is "A Preliminary Study of the Emotion of Love between the Sexes," by Sanford Bell, which appeared in the *Amer. J. Psychol.*, 1902, *13*, 325-354.
5. Any issue of the *Psychological Abstracts* may be referred to as evidence on this point.
6. Contributions of Freudism to psychology, *Psychol. Rev.*, 1924, *21*, 175-218. The participants are L. L. Thurstone, J. H. Leuba, K. S. Lashley and J. Jastrow.
7. An interesting comparison, one that would reveal some of the basic assumptions of psychology, might be made between the attitudes of psychology toward psychoanalysis and toward E. S. P.
8. H. A. Murray, *Explorations in personality*. New York, London: Oxford University Press, 1938.
9. W. James, *The principles of psychology*, Vol I. New York: Henry Holt and Co., 1890, p. 92.

Lewin's Principles of Topological Psychology

EDNA HEIDBREDER

It may be assumed that anyone who is seriously interested in psychology as a science is familiar with the salient features of Lewin's thought. In his separate papers on special topics and in the collected papers called *A Dynamic Theory of Personality,* he has introduced his concepts to the psychological public and has shown how they can be put to work in particular situations. In *The Principles of Topological Psychology* he undertakes a different task. Here he sets forth the foundational notions of his system with the primary purpose of exhibiting the conceptional structure he proposes for the science as a whole, of revealing the theoretical framework within which he prepares to deal with all psychological materials, and of clarifying the relations of psychology to physiology and to physics. To be sure, the book does not give a complete account of Lewin's system; vector psychology is not included. But it is abundantly clear from *Topological Psychology* alone that he is proposing a revision of psychological thinking which radically affects the practices of experimental investigation, and indeed the very manner in which the subject matter of psychology is conceived.

And yet, in a sense, Lewin does not present a system at all, certainly not a system as that term is commonly understood. What he does present is primarily a conceptual tool, but one by means of which he hopes to give psychology the unity, coherence, and articulation that system-makers regularly try to achieve.

In a letter to Köhler that constitutes the preface to the book, Lewin writes:

> I remember the moment when — more than ten years ago — it occurred to me that the figures on the blackboard which were to

This a greatly shortened and somewhat revised form of the "Special review" of Kurt Lewin's *The Principles of Topological Psychology* (Trans. by Fritz and Grace Heider. New York, McGraw-Hill Book Co., 1936, pp. xv + 231.), published in the *Psychological Bulletin,* 1937, *34*, 584-604. The reduction in length is due chiefly to omissions, and the revisions chiefly to changes attendant upon those omissions. An effort has been made, despite these alterations, to keep the presentation and evaluation of the book as they were in the original review—i.e., to keep them unaffected by developments in theoretical psychology which have occurred since the review was written.

illustrate some problems for a group in psychology might after all be not merely illustrations but representations of real concepts. . . . I began studying topology and making use of its concepts, which soon appeared to me particularly fitted to the specific problems of psychology (p. vii).

These sentences briefly present the core of Lewin's conception: the use of mathematical concepts that are spatial rather than metrical and quantitative. As mathematical, they possess the logical rigor that characterizes mathematics generally; as spatial, they have a special suitability, Lewin believes, to the empirical subject matter of psychology, particularly to those problems of motivation and action which have come to be called dynamic. With the help of topology, he maintains, a system can be achieved which is "oriented in two directions, namely, toward theoretical connectedness and toward concreteness . . . equally suitable for the representation of general laws and of the characteristics of the individual case" (p. 5). He is here recommending what, in an earlier publication, he called "Galilean" as opposed to "Aristotelian" thought, contrasting the "constructive" procedures of post-Galilean physics with the "speculative" and "classificatory" methods of ancient and mediaeval natural philosophy. He believes that psychologists can now work with intellectual constructs which they clearly recognize as such; that the development of topology has enabled them to do so; and that by using and developing concepts which topology has constructed, they can produce a science of psychology as different from the psychologies of current systems as modern physics is from the pre-Galilean systems of natural philosophy.

It is important to notice that the space to which Lewin refers is neither that of ordinary perception, nor that of three-dimensional Euclidean geometry, nor that of physical science, the only empirical space commonly treated in a scientific as contrasted with a metaphysical way. Mathematical space is by no means limited to space that can be visualized. Mathematical space can be developed from different fundamental relationships, one of which — it is not hard to see why a Gestaltist finds it significant — is the whole-part relationship. By means of certain series of inclusion, it is possible to characterize the concept of a point and also the concept of a surrounding, and on that basis to construct a topological space in which mathematical relationships can be dealt with without recourse to measurement; in which a drop of water and the earth are fully equivalent, as are also a sphere and a cube; in which only certain relationships and the possibilities of certain relationships are relevant. Besides, a highly developed branch of mathematics has grown up about the concept of connectedness. It deals with such matters as separated and connected spaces, different kinds of connectedness, regions, boundaries, and cuts. Even problems of dimension can be treated on the basis of topological concepts without recourse to measurement.

An example of the use of topological concepts is given in the following passage. Here the author shows how, in an individual, concrete case, psychological events can be coordinated with and represented by topological concepts such as paths, boundaries, and regions.

The vocational goal of a sixteen-year-old boy is to become a physician. The "path" to his goal leads through definite stages: college-entrance examinations, college, medical school, internship, establishing a practice. . . . When he passes his college entrance examinations he has made a "step forward" on the way to his goal. This movement is certainly not a bodily one. Nevertheless it is real locomotion, a real change of position. . . . The reality of the change in his position becomes clear when one considers that many things are now within his reach which were not before. . . . His social position too is changed: he can play on the football team, go to dances, etc. His examinations therefore had for him the character of a boundary between two distinct regions. He had to cross the boundary if he wished to go from one region to the other (p. 48).

In a similar manner, by the use of topological concepts, it is possible to represent any psychological event as a function of a given situation, the situation including both the person and the environment. The basic formula is $B = f(S)$ where B stands for behavior and S for situation; or, more fully, $B = f(P,E)$ with P standing for person and E for environment. The whole situation is the life space, the totality of facts that determine the behavior of an individual at a given moment. The life space can always be represented as finitely structured, and thus as representing the totality of possible events.

This representation, it need hardly be said, is not limited to that of physical space as determined by physical science. It also includes quasi-physical facts — i.e., facts of the physical world as they affect the individual at the moment under consideration, but only to the extent and only in the manner in which they affect him, regardless of whether or not the way in which they do so, and thus figure in the life space, corresponds to the facts determined by physical science. Similarly the representation includes quasi-social and quasi-conceptual situations, not as they are determined by the relevant sciences, but as they affect the person and the environment included in the life space represented. Furthermore, the life space includes only those facts — physical, social, and conceptual — that are relevant to the situation considered; it is not necessary, for example, in the case just quoted, to take into account the total state of the physical universe. It is important, too, that the person included in the life space can also be represented as structured, and that regions, boundaries, and connections within the person can also be represented by topological concepts.

Finally, it must be understood that this treatment of the life space must take into account the special, concrete nature of the particular situation; otherwise a full understanding of the P and E in the formula would be impossible. In Lewin's thinking, the individual case is always completely lawful; or, to state the same point in another way, a scientific law is absolutely without exception. The f in the formula represents a functional relationship, an exceptionless psychological law. But knowledge of psychological laws is not enough. "Even if all the laws of psychology were known, one could make a prediction about the behavior of a man, only if in addition to the laws the special nature of the particular situation were known" (p. 11). In other words, no conceptual treatment can be effective which does not take into account the general law and the individual case, thus giving psychology both the theoretical connectedness and the concreteness previously mentioned. That the concepts of topology can do precisely this is the theme developed throughout the book, and the concept of the life space, which is the central construct of topological psychology, is the example *par excellence* of this mode of thinking. It is a construct in which the individual case and the general law meet, in which any supposed opposition between them is overcome. Repeatedly Lewin insists that the single case must be treated as completely lawful, never as an event which, in this or that selected respect, is merely an instance of a general law — certainly never as an event that can be swept aside as merely an exception to the rule.

No one who is acquainted with the compactness of Lewin's literary style will expect an adequate summary of his system in a review. It seems possible, however, to indicate something of its tone and content by considering with some care the way in which its author deals with certain persistent misinterpretations to which he believes his writings have been subjected.

One of these concerns the drawings by which he represents the conceptual structure of the life space in given situations. These have sometimes been discussed as if they were intended as schematic visual pictures, as illustrative devices which serve as visual aids to exposition, and thus as descriptive rather than explanatory in function. To Lewin, this treatment completely misses the point of topological psychology. Illustrative drawings, he admits, have their legitimate uses, but the drawings he presents have a very different function. They are not offered as visually picturing the life space even in a severely schematic form. Instead, they are seriously intended as representations of its conceptual structure; and to fail to take them as such is to fail to understand the strict and direct conceptual treatment of psychological materials which topological psychology proposes and which is its basic *raison d'être*. The actual drawings or diagrams used are of secondary importance; they may even be misleading if interpreted in terms of the usual metrical geometry. They neither are nor pretend to be pictorially faithful to perceptually observable situations. On the contrary, it is their function to represent conceptual structures, to represent "mathematical concepts [which] 'picture' the dynamic properties of the situation only in the sense in which concepts represent facts" (p. 78). It is the gist of Lewin's contention concerning the drawings by which he represents the topological structure of a situation, that they should be taken no less seriously than is mathematical representation in physics, and that "mathematical concepts are distinguished from other means of representation . . . in that they belong to a system of concepts which are related to each other in a univocal way. The scope and unambiguousness of these relationships are what makes the coordination of mathematical systems to real facts so fruitful for investigation" (p. 78).

Lewin finds another and somewhat similar misinterpretation in the treatment of explanations as involving the use of models. In this connection he explicitly states that he has "intentionally avoided the use of any model of a physical or of a non-physical nature" (p. 78). He believes that a model, like an illustration, always contains something arbitrary, something superfluous, irrelevant, and inapplicable to the situation to which it refers. "One uses it," he says, "like an illustration only insofar as the analogy holds, really only as long as it is convenient" (p. 79). In contrast, if a fact is represented by a concept, all the consequences of the concept must be acknowledged. Any science, psychology or any other, "will obtain the real benefit of the application of mathematical concepts only if it uses them in an absolutely binding way" (p. 79).

Lewin discusses at some length the use of physical and physiological models in psychology. Many psychologists, he notes, turn to physiological models in the hope of giving definiteness and concreteness to psychological explanations — a practice which he regards as all too likely to create the impression that in moving from psychological facts to physiological explanations, one is moving from a lesser to a higher degree of reality. His main objection to physiological models is that they are unnecessary, and that some of them are essentially duplications in physiological terms of the psychological facts they are supposed to explain.

As a case in point he cites a theory authored by a fellow-Gestaltist—Köhler's theory of neural activity. This theory, he insists, is grounded in psychological findings. It was through psychological, not physiological, facts that Köhler became convinced that a new theory of neural activity was necessary — facts obtained by psychological methods in psychological research, his own and that of others. And it was just these psychological facts, Lewin maintains, that led to a reexamination of accepted physiological teachings. In constructing his theory, to be sure, Köhler considered physical and physiological as well as psychological evidence. But Lewin makes much of the point that it was the psychological facts which gave rise to the theory and that Köhler himself offered it as essentially required by those facts. To Lewin, however, the theory is, from the standpoint of psychology, unnecessary; the psychological facts need no physiological explanation to support them. They can and should be accepted in their own right, and they can and should be explained, not by a detour into physiology and physics but by direct coordination with the appropriate mathematical concepts. Valuable as Köhler's theory may be on other grounds — in its implications for neurophysiology, for example — it has no place in the kind of psychology proposed by Lewin. That psychology has no need for physiological or physical models to which psychological facts may or must be referred for explanation.

"By the way," Lewin writes in the previously mentioned letter to Köhler, "I have tried my best to destroy the myth that Gestaltists do not attack each other" (p. viii). Koffka also comes in for a certain amount of attack: he too is criticized for his treatment of the relation of psychological to physical and physiological facts, especially in his distinction between the behavioral and the geographical environment. Lewin objects to this treatment partly because it assumes that psychological experience is immediately given, whereas physical (and hence physiological) facts are merely inferred, and partly because it also assumes that all explanations — all "conditional-genetic factors," in Lewin's terminology — must be found in the physical world. Lewin formulates his position on this problem in one of the most characteristic passages in the book:

> The objects of all empirical sciences, including the objects of physics, can be experienced no less directly than those of psychology. This direct experience concerns first of all the appearance of objects—i.e., their phenomenal properties. In order to understand causal relationships, one has to proceed to the conditional-genetic properties. But this progression to deeper levels takes place *within one and the same field of science.* The conditional-genetic factors of a piece of iron that physics finds, remain properties of *this same piece of iron which one perceives directly and uses,* however far the concepts of physics may progress and however indirect physical methods may be. Otherwise the scientific analysis would be meaningless both from a practical and from a theoretical point of view (pp. 20-21; italics added).

A belief in the close connection between percept and concept in science, and in the concreteness of the reality with which scientific theory deals, could hardly be stated more plainly.

It is this procedure, this constructive progression, that Lewin proposes to follow in psychological research. The starting point is the phenomenal fact, the situation as it appears to ordinary observation. But in order to understand the phenomenal fact, one must progress to its conditional genetic properties, constructing appropriate concepts as physics does, which may be many abstractions removed from the phenomenon itself, but must nevertheless retain their connection with it. If psychology pursues this course, it will not have to move into another science—physiology or any other—in order to explain its empirical materials. It will explain those materials by conceptualizing them directly, by providing a conceptual framework with reference to which the empirical features of a psychological situation can be brought into order and in that sense explained.

This mode of explanation, Lewin believes, is the object of still another common misinterpretation of his system. Some of his critics say that the procedure just outlined gives no explanation at all; that the representations he offers as explanations merely describe the situation that constitutes the problem, indicating the pattern of relationships it involves, but adding nothing that can be considered a solution to the problem it presents. For example — so the objections go — Lewin often speaks of "deriving" from his representation some event which is in that sense predicted and may subsequently be observed to occur. But if the representation takes into account, as an adequate representation must, all the relevant laws and all the relevant facts of the concrete situation, then the event in question is in some sense already included in the representation, and its derivation follows in a self-evident fashion. In other words, its derivation and even its occurrence add nothing to the knowledge already at hand, the knowledge that made the representation possible in the first place.

Lewin cheerfully admits that his representation does not explain if by "explanation" is meant the disclosure of something *behind* the event to be explained, something which can be intellectually isolated and identified as its cause. To one who holds fast to this notion of causality, any explanation in terms of patterns of relationship which hold within the materials to be explained is sure to be disappointing. But the very point of Lewin's argument, and of his whole approach to psychological problems, is that this notion of causality is no longer tenable, that its inadequacy has been revealed by the course and development of natural science since the time of Galileo. Scientists no longer try to explain an event by looking for some as yet undetected entity behind it; instead, they try to explain it by constructing a system of relationships that holds among the objects and events that constitute the situation in which the event occurs. If something more is expected, if such explanations seem somehow to evade the issue, the reason lies, Lewin believes, in a not yet complete adjustment to the post-Galilean ways of thinking in science.

To the criticism that his derivations are self-evident, Lewin replies that it is precisely the purpose of scientific inquiry to produce a conceptual structure from which the derived events are indeed self-evident. To achieve this goal in psychology in representing a single case — and the importance of the single case must not be forgotten — all the laws and all the facts relevant to that case would have to be known and included in the representation. No one knows better than Lewin how far that goal is from attainment, and that the path to it is beset with difficulties, some of which cannot be foreseen. He says, to quote again from his illuminating letter to Köhler:

> As we do not yet have the knowledge of facts which really suffices to determine this system of concepts and as, on the other hand, this knowledge of "facts" cannot be acquired without developing this system of concepts, there seems to be only one way open: to proceed slowly, by tentative steps, to make decisions rather reluctantly, to keep in view always the whole field of psychology, and to stay in closest contact with the actual work of psychological research (p. viii).

From comments such as these—from criticisms and replies to criticisms, as well as from positive statements—the main outlines of topological psychology become discernible. But two questions remain which are central to the enterprise and which must be faced although they lead to a state of affairs that yields no decisive answers. (1) On what grounds are topological concepts offered as especially suitable to the problems of psychology? (2) Are topological concepts in fact practicable as conceptual tools? Are they actually helpful in the initiation and conduct of productive research?

Concerning the first of these questions, Lewin reminds the reader that from the standpoint of mathematics there is no impropriety in applying topological concepts to psychological materials; that to the mathematician the nature of the field in which a mathematical system is used is wholly a matter of indifference; more specifically, that "the nature of the things whose system constitutes a mathematical space is entirely irrelevant for modern mathematics. It does not matter whether one thinks of them as physical objects, temperatures, numbers, colors, events, or anything else" (p. 52). The question then is one of the suitability to each other of topological concepts and the empirical subject matter of psychology. Can topology supply the appropriate concepts? And do psychological materials lend themselves to topological treatment?

On these matters Lewin speaks as a thoroughgoing Gestaltist. The pivotal construct of his system is that of the life space, and he conceives the life space as an out-and-out Gestalt; as a whole, no part of which is unaffected by the whole and no part of which can change without affecting the whole. From this point of view he accepts as entirely suitable to psychological materials the whole-part relationship and the relationship of interconnectedness as they have been developed in topology. He admits, to be sure, that topology does not as yet provide all the concepts psychology needs, but he believes that, so far as mathematics is concerned, there will be no difficulty in developing the appropriate concepts.

He also discusses certain characteristics of psychological materials which, according to some critics, make psychological situations unamenable to topological treatment. One of these is the instability of psychological situations; but, according to Lewin, even if all psychological situations displayed this characteristic — though as a matter of fact not all of them do — their instability would constitute no obstacle to topological treatment, since in the application of mathematics it is altogether irrelevant whether a given situation represents a section through an event that occurs with great rapidity or through a relatively constant situation. A more serious criticism is that indeterminacy of psychological situations may be an obstacle to topological treatment. A child's perceptual field, for example, may be so undeveloped and unstructured as not to permit the application of even the simplest concepts of parts and connectedness. To this criticism Lewin replies in his role as a convinced Gestaltist:

> It seems to me that one of the most important general characteristics
> of the psychological life space is that it is not infinitely structured, but

that it is always structured only to a certain degree. . . . For the present discussion of topological questions it suffices to say that the life space is to a certain extent structured. At least there is a certain topological structuring of the environment in nearly all situations with which psychology deals, and no doubt there is always some structuring of the person. This supplies the empirical premise for the application of topological concepts to the life space (pp. 61-62).

This statement is essentially the declaration of a basic conviction. In effect, Lewin is here saying that psychological situations, as he perceives them and believes them to be, are such as to be amenable to topological treatment, and that he accepts this conviction as part of the basis of his proposed intellectual enterprise.

The second question is one that cannot possibly be answered by examining the system itself. In the long run its practical effectiveness, it fruitfulness in the production of knowledge, must be found in the outcome of the actual investigations to which it gives rise. Lewin is of course aware of this fact, and it is one of the merits of *The Principles of Topological Psychology,* the purpose of which is to present the system as such, that its author does not stop with the presentation of the principles themselves. In the second half of the book he devotes chapter after chapter to working out in detail the topological representations of specific psychological problems. Here he definitely undertakes the task of showing how topological concepts can be coordinated with empirical materials and put to work in the investigation of particular psychological problems. He does not, to be sure, discuss actual experiments. But it must not be forgotten that topological psychology is by no means lacking in accompanying experimental research. During an exciting decade in Berlin, Lewin and his students were actively engaged in research along the lines of the developing system— research in which refreshingly novel and ingenious approaches were devised to problems of action and motivation — for example, those concerning levels of aspiration and the resumption of and memory for unfinished tasks. Yet it is no answer to the question concerning the fruitfulness of a system to point to a body of research which it has presumably generated. The relation between a system and its accompanying research is often far from obvious. A great deal of analysis may be required, both of the system and of the research, before one can say of an experiment, or of a body of experiments, to what extent it was determined by the system, by the systematist, or by the experimenter who adopted the system.

What, then, does topological psychology have to offer? Primarily a conceptual tool which Lewin hopes and believes will open the entire field of psychology to the kind of scientific inquiry which has produced modern physical science, as contrasted with the treatment of the problems of the physical world which characterized ancient times and the Middle Ages. Perhaps it should again be explicitly stated that throughout his book Lewin speaks as a Gestaltist; that he offers topological concepts as effective means primarily of extending the scope of Gestalt psychology beyond the field in which it took its rise — that of perception and closely related processes. It is interesting that nowhere in *Topological Psychology* does he argue in behalf of Gestalt psychology. When he argues, it is in behalf of topological concepts as suitable for psychological research conducted in the spirit of Gestalt psychology. Essentially his topological psychology is a conceptual reconstruction of Gestalt psychology, offered as capable of strengthening and tightening its theoretical structure and enlarging its theoretical range.

The sheer originality of Lewin's conceptual scheme has made it the object of widespread interest and, like most innovations with far-reaching implications, it has received adverse criticism as well as favorable attention. Some of his critics have seriously questioned the soundness of his analysis of the methods and intellectual attitudes on the basis of which he contrasts Aristotelian and Galilean modes of thought. And many critics have found in his discussions of the use of quantitative measures in psychology — in his disparaging references to "unreal averages," for example, as contrasted with the intellectual "constructs" he proposes — a failure to understand quantitative measures and statistical procedures as they are actually used and interpreted in contemporary psychology. At present the status of topological psychology is that of a challenging and challenged attempt to reconceptualize the subject matter of psychology.

It is in fact one of several such attempts which together constitute a movement that may well turn out to be the most important line of activity now occurring in psychology. Among them are such various intellectual ventures as those presented in Boring's *Physical Dimensions of Consciousness,* Tolman's *Purposive Behavior in Animals and Men,* Hull's developing theory of learning in terms of S-R conditioning, and, in a different vein, the several theories of mental organization associated with research on factor analysis. The variety and the very occurrence of these attempts indicate that all is not well with the theoretical structure of psychology as a science; that no comprehensive conceptual scheme has yet been devised which is adequate to the scientific investigation of the problems in which psychologists are actually interested and are actually at work. In a sense, all these attempts, despite differences and even clashes among them, may be regarded as cooperating in a common enterprise: that of conceptualizing the empirical subject matter of psychology in such a way as to make it accessible and amenable to scientific investigation, as scientific investigation has come to be understood since the revolutionary changes that occurred in physics during the early years of the twentieth century. From this point of view, topological psychology takes its place as a bold and active participant in that enterprise.

William McDougall
and Social Psychology

EDNA HEIDBREDER

No one could be even slightly acquainted with McDougall's role in contemporary psychology without realizing the impossibility of making him the hero of the usual laudatory obituary essay. Yet the materials for such an essay are abundantly supplied by his career. Even in a limited portion of his work, that devoted to social psychology, the occasions for eulogy are plentiful and in some cases striking.[1]

It would be easy to dwell on the fact that he brought to social psychology an exceptionally rich and varied experience — that he had enjoyed a brilliant career as a student of the physical and biological sciences and had read in the social sciences both widely and critically. It would be easy, too, to stress the fact that he had acquired firsthand knowledge of cultures other than his own — that he had been a member of the famous Cambridge Anthropological Expedition to the Torres Straits; that he had assisted Dr. Charles Hose in his extensive study of the natives of Borneo; and that he had seen with his own eyes the civilizations of China, Java, and India. It could be pointed out that, as a member of the expedition to the Torres Straits, he had been one of the pioneers in studying primitive peoples by the methods of experimental psychology; and that in *The Pagan Tribes of Borneo*,[2] a joint publication with Dr. Hose, he had put forward, as one of the many hypotheses he contributed to that book, an interpretation of one of the religions of Borneo which may be regarded as an independent anticipation, within its restricted field, of Eliot Smith's theory of the diffusion of cultural elements. It would also be possible to emphasize his achievements in experimental and physiological psychology, and to call attention to the fact that it was his work in this field, particularly in vision, attention, and the general functioning of the brain, that led to his election as a Fellow of the Royal Society.

It would be difficult to overemphasize the influence of his *Social Psychology*. The barest account of his career could hardly avoid stating, as a mere matter of record, that the basic theory of the book not only became a major issue in psychology but gave rise to reverberations which, spreading beyond the borders of psychology, definitely affected the treatment the topic has received ever since. *The Group Mind*, though far less influential than *Social Psychology* and far less generally acceptable, might be described as a challenging presentation of a controversial subject; and his numerous papers on special topics in social psychology might be brought forward as evidence of his unflagging and widely ranging interest in the field. It would be possible, too, to trace the theories he first set forth in his *Social Psychology* as he developed them in the other problems that subsequently engaged his interest — in abnormal psychology and in psychology in general. It would be more to the point, in an essay on his work in social psychology, to show that his influence is discernible in some of the movements especially characteristic of the social psychology of the present —in the emphasis on the importance of conation and motivation; in the steadily increasing interest in larger formations like sentiments, attitudes, and whole personalities; and above all in the deliberate search for dynamic explanations. It would even be possible, in conformity with a prevalent convention, to make a count of the references to his work in the writings of his contemporaries, and to plot their distribution with reference to different points of view and fields of interest, in a manner too familiar to need description. With or without such data — for the point is too obvious to require their support — McDougall could be presented as a dominant figure in the psychology of his day.

But any such treatment, though true in itself, would completely miss the special quality of his influence. For the plain fact is that to many of his fellow psychologists, McDougall stood outside the pale of scientific respectability. In America he was widely regarded as an anachronism and a menace; his name became almost synonymous with theories and practices regarded by most American psychologists as remnants of exploded but still dangerous superstitions — with animism, vitalism, and teleology; with nativism in the discredited form of Lamarckism; and with shady ventures into psychical research and extrasensory perception. He became something of a stereotype to the psychological public, and it has long been possible to express an attitude toward a topic, and to some extent to indicate its theoretical connections, by associating it with McDougall's name. Perhaps more than any other one individual, McDougall became a symbol of what American psychology has most heartily set itself against.

It is obvious, however, that no one becomes a symbol and a stereotype without reason, and to follow the course of events that gave McDougall this status is one way of understanding his significance in psychology. It began, insofar as it is possible to fix a beginning, in the publication of his *Social Psychology*. His autobiography contains an enlightening passage about the origin of this book:

> Lecturing one day in 1906, I found myself making the sweeping assertion that the energy displayed in every human activity might in principle be traced to some inborn disposition or instinct. When I returned home I reflected that this was a very sweeping generalization, not to be found in any of the books; and that if it was true it was very important. I set to work to apply the principle in detail, becoming

more and more convinced both of its truth and of its importance; and my *Social Psychology* emerged.[3]

Coming in this way, the idea was probably a more complete expression of its author's thought than a more deliberately constructed theory would have been. At any rate, it set the direction of his intellectual life. It is no exaggeration to say that the rest of his work in psychology was devoted mainly to developing and defending the thesis he first stated in *Social Psychology*.

The influence of the book was due largely to its promise of a psychology which, by penetrating to the springs of action, would engage with the realities of concrete situations. McDougall permitted and even encouraged his readers to use their commonsense ways of thinking about people; to regard them as living individuals striving toward goals in a world where desire, foresight, and effort were really effective. He believed that the conventional, experimental psychology of the day was sterile and incomplete — that it had nothing to offer to the pressing problems of human existence as they present themselves in their immediate complexity. In its stead he proposed a psychology that was dynamic rather than merely descriptive, concerned with the actual situations of daily life rather than with the pared-down abstractions of the laboratory, occupied with units which today would be called molar, and perhaps configurational, as opposed to the molecular and atomistic. A return to common sense is often an attempt to get a fresh view of the problem itself, especially of aspects habitually neglected. It was decidedly so in McDougall's case. By turning to whole concrete situations and by seeking the springs of action, he hoped to produce a psychology that was genuinely relevant to human life and genuinely and explicitly causal.

Naturally his claims were not taken at their face value; naturally, too, the immediate object of criticism was the specific doctrine of the book, the role of innate dispositions. A conspicuous outcome was the famous instinct controversy which reached its height (as a controversy) in the nineteen-twenties. Since, like many controversies, it involved more than the points at issue, it gave rise to distortion and confusion.

For one thing, a vague impression was created that McDougall, in insisting on the basic importance of innate dispositions, was *for* the instincts indiscriminately and at all costs. It was not often remembered that his doctrine was, among other things, an attack upon the uncritical use of the term *instinct*. Some of the most vigorous pages of *Social Psychology* are devoted to this attack, and to an attempt to give an exact, and, it is especially to be noted, a restricted meaning to the term. By limiting its use to native reactions, by setting up definite criteria, and by describing a definite pattern of organization, he gave the term a more precise meaning than had ever before been in general use in psychology.

An appeal to nativism, however, has always had a way of arousing suspicion in a psychology striving to be scientific. To many, a native reaction has the look of something "given," perhaps to be accepted without further investigation, perhaps even to be regarded as unknowable. And science and the unknowable are traditional enemies, whether a situation is unknowable because of insuperable practical difficulties or (if there is any difference) because of its intrinsic nature. It is possible, on the other hand, that in spite of the inconvenience to science, some reactions, even those involving complex organization, may, as a matter of fact, be native. The acceptance of inconvenient facts, even of limits of knowledge, is as much a part of the scientific discipline as the attempt to press inquiry as far as possible. Actually, however, the native need not be a stopping point in investigation. There are ways of investigating heredity and maturation which have proved at least as successful as investigations of learning and of environmental influences.

Another source of opposition not purely evidential was the feeling that if a trait is native it cannot be changed. The whole question — "Can human nature be altered?" — was thus brought into the discussion, along with its many practical implications. In the thinking of those who consider social and political changes desirable and vastly important, this issue was especially prominent. Again it is possible that this matter is independent of human wishes; that just as there may be limits to man's knowledge, so too there may be limits to his control of nature, perhaps even, or especially, of his own. And again it is possible that native tendencies do not imply unalterable modes of behavior. This stand, as a matter of fact, is the one that McDougall took. He clearly stated and even emphasized the ways in which native tendencies undergo change and development. Both through their cognitive inlets and through their motor expressions, the instincts and native tendencies are, in his opinion, subject to enormous modification.

To raise these considerations, however, is not to defend McDougall's position. To make them explicit — for they are familiar enough — is rather to suggest reasons for the deep antagonism he aroused. It is also to suggest the ways in which McDougall's ideas differed from those commonly attached to the symbol and the stereotype. The most unflattering features of the stereotype and the most objectionable meanings of the symbol were determined, however, by issues far more fundamental and even more emotionally loaded than the nature-nurture problem and the question of the immutability or modifiability of human nature. His theory of purposive striving implied teleology. Through the clash of his theory with mechanism and through his insistence on psychical causation, he touched upon the basic problem of what constitutes scientific explanation.

It was through its involvement in this fundamental issue that *Social Psychology* got so completely out of hand as actually to change the course of its author's life. McDougall somewhere calls attention to the fact that the full title of this book — almost never used — is *An Introduction to Social Psychology*. His intention was to make it propaedeutic to a series of volumes on social psychology which he hoped would be his masterpiece. But instead of leading to a life-work devoted to social psychology specifically, the book became the starting point of an inquiry affecting psychology in general. It is significant that his next book on psychology was not one of the projected series. It was *Body and Mind,* to which, in what he called a spirit of defiance, he attached the subtitle *A History and Defense of Animism.*[4]

Of course McDougall had always known that his views required a revision of current notions of causality — in particular, that they required an acceptance of psychic causation. His dissatisfaction with mechanism was among the deepest determinants of his own beliefs. As nearly as can be ascertained, he made two demands on causal explanation. One was the cognitive demand that it be genuinely intelligible; the other was the practical demand that it be dynamically effective; and to his mind the mechanistic conception satisfied neither. His own theory was stated with characteristic clarity and vigor. That the concept of causation itself be admitted, he always emphatically insisted. "Science must hold fast to causation," he said in one of his later expositions, "if not to strict determination. Psychical events, though teleological, have their conditions and their causal antecedents."[5] He further demanded psychic causation. There is a point, he insisted, where desire and foresight and conscious direction enter the psychological situation; and they are not merely present, they are among the factors that determine events. McDougall regarded the occurrence of goal-seeking behavior as the most obvious matter of fact, inexplicable without psychic causation. Causation in this form seemed to him not only dynamic but intelligibly dynamic, evidently because he thought of human beings as familiar with its workings in their own inner experience. The system of psychology he built upon this notion therefore emphasized purposive striving as a causative factor — not supernatural but not reducible to mechanistic principles — a causative factor that makes psychology an autonomous science, free to take account of its material in all its specificity, not bound by the principles of physical science no matter how effective they have proved in their own field.

The mind-body problem, however, was not in and of itself his major concern. That he insisted on no one solution to it is both curious and significant. Provided only that psychic causation was recognized, he did not care greatly how the psycho-physical relation was conceived. He did not even care whether it was conceived monistically or dualistically. Recognizing a general preference for monism,[6] he obligingly pointed out two ways in which monism and psychic causation could be made compatible. Psychic monism was offered as an obvious possibility, and emergence was recommended as a conception that many scientists were finding satisfactory. He himself had put forward a theory of emergence early in his career, but had abandoned it as not sufficiently radical. Later he adopted a theory of psychological monadism, admitting that it gave rise to many difficulties, but saying in effect that the same was true of all theories on the mind-body problem. His willingness to allow for differences of opinion in this respect is in strange contrast with his strict insistence that psychic causation itself be recognized.

But these developments of his theory are chronologically out of order. *Body and Mind* was written while its author still had hopes of producing as his major contribution a series of volumes on social psychology. *The Group Mind* was intended as the first volume in the series. Once again McDougall chose a title deliberately calculated to antagonize, in this case one that might easily be misleading. For by this phrase he intended no ghostly social oversoul. The group mind he referred to was neither "a unitary consciousness of the society over and above that of the individuals comprised within it" [7] nor "a super-individual and semi-divine person before whom all men must bow down." [8] It was a system of relationships which today would be called a configuration, an outcome of the fact that "a society when it enjoys a long life and becomes highly organized, acquires a structure and qualities which are largely independent of the qualities of the individuals who enter into its composition and take part for a brief time in its life." [9] Never influential, the book aroused little interest. Its reception was such that the projected volumes on social psychology were never written and its author's hope of producing a masterpiece in that field perished.

From this point on, McDougall's chief activities were not in social psychology. To be sure, he never ceased to be interested in its problems; they formed the subject matter of many of those writings in which, following the tradition of British scholars, he addressed himself not to his professional associates only but to the reading public in general.[10] But the main line of his thinking took a different direction. Instead of building a social psychology on the foundations he had laid, he turned to the examination of the foundations themselves; as if, thwarted in his original plan, he was prompted to test the validity of his principles both by applying them in other fields and by following out their theoretical implications. His work in abnormal psychology, in general psychology, and in the development of his theoretical position may be regarded in this light. So also may his interest in psychical research, in extrasensory perception, and in his Lamarckian experiments. It was as if the theory he proposed in *Social Psychology* carried implications so far-reaching and so unexpectedly disturbing that, in their light, his original plan became inappropriate and in a sense even impossible. Unless he wished to ignore rather than to meet the opposition he aroused — and it was hardly in his nature to ignore opposition — he was compelled, instead of writing a social psychology, to develop and justify his basic conceptions.

As his views developed, he used the word *hormic* to characterize his psychology. He made use of this word not only to emphasize the conative aspects of mental life, but also to distinguish his own view of motivation from that of the hedonists. For McDougall, purposive striving was literally goal seeking, an activity directed specifically toward an object or situation

—not toward pleasure and away from pain in themselves. Pleasure and pain might be important in influencing the means toward an end, but they were not in themselves the ends sought or avoided. This part of his theory has received less attention than it deserves; it is not so promptly associated with his name as are some of his other contentions. It is interesting, however, that an essential part of his teaching was the conception of psychological processes as directed toward objects — a conception prominent in various enterprises today, in social psychology and in psychology generally.

It is significant that in developing his theoretical conceptions, McDougall never lost sight of the concrete situations which always, in his eyes, gave them their significance. His fundamental interest was in "the art and theory of the internal life of man," an art and theory which in his opinion were woefully lacking in "a foundation of a scientific knowledge of man." [11] "If I thought that psychology were incapable of furnishing the required foundation," he said, "I should not regard it as of much interest." [11] Grounded in a concern for the actualities of human experience, his interest in the theoretical basis of psychology was compelling. Every topic he considered had its place in a conceptual system in which the entire field of psychology was represented. Indeed, a large part of his importance, certainly an essential part, lay in his relation to psychological theory. It is a commonplace today that the concepts of causation and explanation, not in psychology merely but in science in general, are undergoing a critical and perhaps revolutionary revision; much of the scientific work now going forward reveals the need for new concepts which, while retaining the thoroughgoing naturalism proper to science, do full justice to the data of empirical observation. It is probable that McDougall's place in the history of psychology will be in the neighborhood of this movement. The chances are that he will be remembered as a man sufficiently insistent on the special character of psychological facts as he saw them to demand that accepted principles of explanation be adjusted to receive them.

Yet it is difficult to describe his contribution in this field. It was neither creative nor critical in the full sense of those terms. McDougall came nowhere near working out a new concept of causation or of scientific explanation. In rejecting mechanism he simply swung to the other extreme, adopting the theories conventionally opposed to it, apparently without feeling the need of a radically different way of conceiving the whole situation. That mechanism was *not* the answer seemed uppermost in his mind. On the other hand, his contribution was not essentially critical. It was critical in the sense of asserting that there were inadequacies in accepted assumptions, but the criticism consisted less in diagnosing the precise nature of those difficulties than in communicating a sense of acute disharmony between the proffered explanations and the psychological facts as he saw them. The point he refused to yield was the special character of the observed facts. That the theory be adjusted to accommodate the facts was his ever-recurring demand.

This attitude gives the clue to his true originality; he had a lively and extraordinarily obstinate sense of the presence of a problem. He flatly refused to say that there was no problem when he was sure that one was staring him in the face. To him the facts of goal seeking were both obvious and important, and the facile formula "If all the facts were known . . ." was a futile evasion. It is this stubborn sense of a problem — not his solution, not even his way of conceiving it — that constitutes his service to psychology. His work was never a contented recording of facts for their own sake; his intellect was always avid of explanation. Neither was he satisfied with the detached speculation of pure theory; his sense for concrete reality was too acute and too insistent. By communicating his discomfort at an unresolved situation, he awakened in others an active and often indignant awareness of the problems he considered crucial.

The antagonism he aroused was an essential part of his influence. Its strength was due in part to the magnitude of the issues he raised, but in part also to his combative style in argument. In none of his activities was his temperament negligible. He described himself as arrogant; no one could deny that he was forthright and courageous. Perhaps it was his temperament that impelled him to attack major problems; certainly a temperamental urge to take sides decisively was not without influence in determining his theoretical position. His example, however, has not led others to take sides. In social psychology and in psychology in general, the problems he pushed to the fore do not today demand an alignment for or against his position. These problems are now being conceived in ways to which the basic terms of his own formulations are irrelevant. But the decisiveness with which he treated them, and the very opposition he aroused, have led others to attack them with fresh conceptions. To solve the problems he raised was not McDougall's role in psychology. His achievement was to bring them to light in a manner so disturbing as to force them upon the attention of a generation of psychologists trained to ignore them.

NOTES

1. To place this limited portion of his work in its setting, the reader is referred to McDougall's autobiography. In this account of his life, he expresses his attitude toward many of the major problems of psychology and, in a restrained, considered, never very hopeful manner, his estimate of his own work. The autobiography also gives the events, places, dates, academic positions, personal and professional associations with reference to which his activities in social psychology may be placed biographically and historically. William McDougall, in C. Murchison (Ed.), *History of psychology in autobiography*. Worcester, Mass.: Clark University Press. Vol. I, 191-223.

2. This book was written thirteen years after McDougall's experiences in Borneo, at a time when his interests had become definitely settled upon psychology. C. Hose and Wm. McDougall, *The pagan tribes of Borneo* (2 vols.). New York: Macmillan, 1912.

3. William McDougall, In C. Murchison (Ed.), *op. cit.*, 208.

4. Wm. McDougall, *Body and mind.* New York: Macmillan, 1911.
5. Wm. McDougall, The hormic psychology. In C. Murchison (Ed.), *Psychologies of 1930.* Worcester, Mass.: Clark University Press, 1930, pp. 9-10.
6. *Ibid.,* 7-8.
7. Wm. McDougall, *The group mind.* New York: Putnam, 1920, 12.
8. *Ibid.,* xii.
9. *Ibid.,* 12.
10. Among these writings are: *National welfare and decay,* London: Methuen, 1921; *Ethics and some modern world problems,* New York: Putnam, 1924; *The indestructible union,* Boston: Little, Brown, 1925; *The American Nation: Its problems and psychology,* (Eng. ed. of the title preceding), London: Allen & Unwin, 1926; *Character and the conduct of life,* London: Methuen, 1927; *Janus: The conquest of war,* New York: Dutton, 1927; *Religion and the sciences of life,* Durham, N. C.: Duke University Press, 1934. He also contributed many articles on topics in social psychology to British and American periodicals.
11. William McDougall, in C. Murchison (Ed.), *op. cit.,* 221.

Functionalism

EDNA HEIDBREDER

According to a stereotype not uncommon among American psychologists, functionalism,[1] as it developed in the United States, was important chiefly and perhaps solely as a movement that helped psychologists in this country to make the transition from psychology as a science of consciousness to psychology as a science of behavior. Like other stereotypes, this one is an oversimplification, but there is something to be said in its favor.

Functionalism *did* make its appearance as a psychology of protest. Its leaders *did* oppose the school that was then the establishment in American psychology: the classical experimentalists, essentially Wundtian in outlook, who saw as their basic and immediate scientific task the introspective analysis of conscious experiences under experimentally controlled conditions. These were the psychologists who, during the ensuing controversy, came to be called structuralists. And the functionalists *did* place more emphasis on the study of behavior than the classical experimentalists had accorded it. Without denying introspection a legitimate and useful role, the functionalists in their own researches drew heavily on behavioral data. Influenced as they were by the Darwinian theory, they undertook investigations that required that most, and in some cases all, of the empirical data be obtained from the study of behavior — researches in developmental psychology, in educational and other forms of applied psychology, and in animal psychology, to mention a few examples.[2] And it was through his work in animal psychology, in the stronghold of functionalism at the University of Chicago, that Watson began to develop what may be called classical American behaviorism, thus taking the first steps that led to the rise of the school that succeeded structuralism as the establishment. The functionalists themselves never became, and had no ambition to become, the establishment. In opposing structuralism, they were not even trying to set up a rival school, though for a time, in defending and maintaining their own position, they had something of the character of a school thrust upon them. But theirs was not the kind of school — insofar as it was a school — of which establishments are made.[3] And behaviorism plainly was.

Thus the stereotype is useful in placing functionalism in its immediate historical setting, and also in indicating the central importance, at the time to which it refers, of the question: What shall we accept as the subject matter of psychology if we are to treat psychology as a science?

But the stereotype *is* an oversimplification, and one that may easily be misleading. It is misleading if it suggests that the subject matter of psychology, as the functionalists treated it, can be adequately described merely by saying that it included both experience and behavior. It is misleading too, and seriously so, if it suggests that the central issue with which the functionalists were concerned was the question: consciousness or behavior, one or both? That question did not become an issue in American psychology until the rise of classical behaviorism; and both before and after that momentous event, the main concern of the functionalists lay elsewhere. It lay in treating psychological processes as *functions,* as Titchener (1898, 1899) clearly perceived when he gave functionalism its name, and in placing them in the context of the Darwinian theory. Whether psychological processes are conscious or occur without consciousness; whether empirical data concerning them are obtainable from conscious experience, from behavior, or from both; whether the answers to these questions vary from one process to another and from situation to situation — all these matters the functionalists considered important, but of secondary importance as compared with their basic and positive proposal that the subject matter of psychology be conceptualized as functions.[4] But the stereotype, focused as it is on the consciousness-behavior issue, creates a perspective in which that basic and positive issue is likely to be lost or greatly obscured.

Another point easily lost or obscured in that perspective is the essential basis of the functionalists' protest against structuralism: the very protest that launched functionalism as a definite movement. That protest was made against the restrictions on psychological *inquiry* which the classical experimentalists were trying to impose; it was not made, in principle, against the kind of research they were actively pursuing in their laboratories. The functionalists, in fact, took over many of the methods and accepted many of the findings of the classical experimental school. They did not, it must be remembered, reject introspection as a scientific method. Nor did they deny that conscious experiences can be studied experimentally, though they were less than enthusiastic about the trend of the structuralists' research toward increasingly minute dissections of such experiences. What they did find objectionable, and flatly unacceptable, was that the structuralists had conceived the subject matter and methods of psychology in a way that ruled out as unsuitable for strictly scientific research, in a strictly scientific psychology, questions concerning activities and situations which by criteria other than those decreed by their school — by the criteria of educated common sense, if you will — would be considered both psychological and important. Characteristic of the excluded questions were those concerning the actual doings of people in the actual situations they met in their actual lives, questions which to the functionalists had important psychological aspects, both theoretical and practical. The functionalists refused to disregard such questions or to postpone them indefinitely.[5] They considered the grounds on which they were urged to do so arbitrary and doctrinaire.

Instead, they reconceptualized the subject matter of psychology. They did not merely add behavior to conscious experience as a major source of empirical data, though of course they did that. Their essential innovation consisted in taking a different conceptual approach to the problems of psychology, in placing its subject matter in a different conceptual perspective.

In the Darwinian theory they found a conceptual framework which had a definite place for the kinds of activities they considered it important to investigate. And in the concept of function they found a straightforward way of treating psychological processes as natural events in the natural world, specifically by including them among those activities which, like respiration, digestion, reproduction and the rest, are means by which living organisms and species are maintained in an environment on which they are dependent. Within that broadly biological framework, they treated psychological processes as functions in the sense — or rather in the two main senses [6] — in which biologists commonly use the word "function": (1) as *activities* (functions of living organisms or parts of living organisms), and as (2) *utilities* (functions of such activities); i.e., as effects of such activities which typically and in the long run presumably are or have been advantageous to the maintenance of life in the kinds of organisms in which they occur. Carr's treatment of the adaptive act and Woodworth's several versions of the S-O-R formula are well-known examples of the way in which the concept of function has been put to work in psychology.[7]

In taking this stand, in refusing to give up questions they considered important, in adopting a conceptual scheme that accommodated those questions, the functionalists were in fact identifying the subject matter of psychology on grounds not essentially methodological, i.e., on grounds not critically weighted by methodological considerations. In this respect they differed from both structuralists and classical behaviorists. In each of those schools the subject matter had been selected chiefly because of its suitability, according to that school, to scientific investigation, specifically because it lent itself to scientific *observation*. Each school in its own day and in its own way made much of the point that its subject matter was *observable* and that, properly observed, under suitably controlled conditions, it would yield data that met the criteria of scientific acceptability. The two schools were remarkably similar in this respect. In asking: What shall we accept as the subject matter of psychology?, both seemed to be asking: What shall we as psychologists *observe* when we make our investigations? From what sources shall we obtain the empirical data without which no field of inquiry — psychology or any other — can be or become a natural science? Both schools seemed to assume, and here too they were remarkably similar, that, given a scientifically observable subject matter, psychologists could make their discipline a science if only they investigated it according to the accepted rules and standards of science; and they seemed to have little doubt, if any, that those rules and standards were thoroughly understood and securely established.[8] Accordingly, both schools seemed satisfied that they had identified their subject matter when they had identified the observable materials which were the sources of their empirical data.

Implicit in the action taken by the functionalists is a different interpretation of the question: What shall we accept as the subject matter of psychology? They asked not only: What shall we as psychologists observe when we make our investigations? but also: About what shall we as psychologists ask our questions? Like anyone who treats psychology as a natural science, they were of course acutely interested in identifying suitable sources of empirical data relevant to the questions they put in their investigations. But it was their attitude toward the questions themselves that determined their course of action. They insisted on accepting, as genuinely psychological, certain questions which, as they immediately present themselves in advance of investigation (and quite apart from the questioner's views on reductionism), concern topics that cannot be specifically and exhaustively characterized with reference to the observable materials from which psychologists obtain their data. Among these, for example, are perception and learning, topics with which structuralists and behaviorists respectively were especially concerned in some of their major research.[9]

From what sources do such questions, such topics, arise? From the prescientifically organized knowledge which, for lack of a better name, may be called the commonsense knowledge of the culture in which psychology arose, developed, and changed, and is still developing and changing. There is an important sense in which psychologists, like natural scientists generally, do not initially select their own subject matter. They begin by accepting it as it has been prescientifically selected and conceptualized in the commonsense knowledge of the culture in which they operate; although, as they operate, they may depart widely from the knowledge with which they began: extending, refining, and altering it, sometimes in a manner that is radically revolutionary. Eventually the knowledge so gained modifies the body of commonsense knowledge which, though strongly resistant to change, nevertheless changes continually.

We know all too little about commonsense knowledge; especially, despite important pioneer work in the field,[10] about its beginnings in the first year or two of life when it becomes a part, largely implicit, of a person's basic psychological makeup, and thus a part of his way of perceiving and otherwise knowing his world, evaluating it, and behaving in it. But we do know that the commonsense knowledge that has become a part of our culture contains a roughly delimited domain, selected and organized prescientifically, which, when it becomes a field of scientific inquiry, is generally accepted as the domain of psychology and as including the empirical materials with which psychology as a science must come to terms. Among such materials are processes like perceiving, learning, and growing angry or afraid; such achievements as the execution of a skill or the solution of a problem; and such dispositions as intellectual capacities and abilities, persistent motives, and traits of personality. Commonsense knowledge of this domain is, of course, subject to the limitations, inconsistencies, and obscurities, to the implicit assumptions, downright errors, and other faults that characterize common sense generally. In a sense it is the enemy — the obstructionist to be overcome. But for all its faults, it has the virtue which, in this domain as elsewhere, is for commonsense knowledge its essential reason for being. Over a considerable range it is effective in practice, sufficiently so to become deeply and firmly entrenched both in the individual and in the culture. Such knowledge is an indispensable basis for the *questions* that give rise to genuinely scientific inquiry.[11] It is involved both implicitly and explicitly in such questions. It has become a part of the questioner, and a part of his way of perceiving and otherwise knowing the materials with which his questions are concerned.

Without such knowledge, no one can ask or even understand a psychological question, to say nothing of answering it. It is the kind of knowledge which seems simply "there" when one becomes reflective and questioning; the kind of knowledge which is a precondition of becoming reflective and questioning at all. A beginning student in psychology does not have to learn from scratch what is meant by such terms as "perception" and "learning," "intellectual ability" and "trait of personality." To be sure, he cannot define them satisfactorily, and he cannot satisfactorily specify the kinds of situations to which he habitually and confidently applies them. And neither can his instructor. What the student does learn, and what his instructor has learned, is to reconceptualize, in the ways currently regarded as important in psychology, especially those currently involved in its ongoing research, the materials he has already conceptualized as part of his commonsense knowledge.

And a comparable reconceptualization must occur in the psychological enterprise as a whole — as it must occur in the development of any natural science — if it is to achieve the kind of knowledge and to practice the kind of research which over the years have come to be expected of a well-established, productive scientific discipline. A comparable reconceptualization must occur, but one that is more thoroughgoing and comprehensive and more nearly acceptable to all competent psychologists than any now available to students, to their instructors, or to psychologists generally. For no such reconceptualization has occurred in psychology, or, if it has, it has not been recognized and accepted as such. Psychologists have succeeded, in some cases brilliantly, in effectively reconceptualizing one or another portion of their domain. But they have produced no achievement which, in the manner of Newton's in physics and Darwin's in biology, has given psychology a conceptual scheme with reference to which, over a considerable period of time, all or nearly all of its available knowledge could be integrated, its ongoing research directed and to some degree coordinated, and its workers united into a single group sharing, despite diverse interests and specialized practices, a common outlook on their common domain.[12]

One way of looking at schools of psychology is to regard each of them as proposing some conceptual scheme, some reconceptualization of the subject matter of psychology, which it offers as a means of bringing about such a state of affairs in psychology. How are the functionalists to be characterized from this point of view?

Chiefly, I suggest, by their serious regard for what they considered the materials-to-be-conceptualized; by their insistence on questions that kept them in touch with what, to them, were the empirical actualities with which psychologists must come to terms, both in their research and in their conceptual treatment: the empirical materials already conceptualized in commonsense knowledge and requiring reconceptualization and further investigation. The functionalists criticized both schools which were for a time their rivals, as failing to do full justice to such materials. It has already been noted that they found structuralism arbitrary and doctrinaire in its prohibitions and exclusions. Classical behaviorism, too, they regarded as arbitrary and doctrinaire in its quite different prohibitions and exclusions. Significantly, however, they found behaviorism more congenial than structuralism. For the behaviorists were willing and eager to undertake the problems the functionalists considered important, insisting that all of them could be investigated by investigating behavior. The functionalists, of course, had no objection to the study of behavior. What they questioned was whether all the problems the behaviorists were willing to undertake could be, and in fact had been, stated without implicit references to conscious experience.

It is hardly necessary to say that the functionalists, by adopting and adapting the framework of the Darwinian theory, did not provide psychology with a carefully elaborated conceptual scheme which ordered its available knowledge within a single well-structured system, and united all psychologists into a band of brothers working harmoniously within the guidelines of that system. It is unlikely that this is what they were trying to do. And if, as just suggested, it is characteristic of schools to make such an attempt, this is one of the several respects in which the functionalists did not constitute a typical school.

Certainly the functionalists proposed no sharply outlined, closely articulated system or theory of psychology. Their reconceptualization was essentially a reorientation, one that placed the subject matter of psychology in an enlarged and altered setting. The reorientation, it should be noted, was a genuine innovation. Classical experimental psychology, without rejecting Darwinism, had been relatively unaffected by it. To be sure, this "new" psychology, centered in Germany in the nineteenth century, had developed in close association with the "new" physiology of the time. But that physiology was physical rather than biological in its orientation — physical in that the avowed aim of some of its most influential leaders was that of accounting for physiological structures and functions in terms of physics and chemistry.[13] Accordingly, classical experimental psychology, looking to physiology for its explanations, was itself oriented toward the physical sciences.

In any case the new setting in which the functionalists placed the subject matter of psychology quickly proved to be strongly directive. It immediately suggested lines of inquiry like developmental and comparative psychology, and gave a strong impetus to the study of individual differences. It also suggested means of investigation like the use of nonhuman animals as experimental materials, and the need in certain problems for broad-range, long-term studies requiring the use of large numbers of human beings — in many cases, children — as subjects. It was in studies suggested by this setting that learning emerged as a highly significant psychological process, and motivation as a factor to be reckoned with in learning. In this setting, too, the social environment began very early to receive serious attention as among the important determinants of the psychological makeup of human beings.[14] Soon the general orientation, and many of its attendant interests and practices, became firmly established in American psychology, not as the special concerns of any one group or school, but as obviously having a place in the pursuits proper to psychology. Before long they were quite simply taken for granted. When this happened, the functionalists appropriately ceased to be a school insofar as they had ever been one. They had won acceptance for a kind of inquiry and for a conceptual perspective that no longer needed the support of a school.

NOTES

1. The word "functionalism" refers in this paper to a movement in American psychology. It is not here used, as it sometimes is, in the broad sense that includes, among other movements, the Act Psychologies of Austria and Germany, and the British researches, stimulated in part by the Darwinian theory, in animal psychology and in anthropology.

2. The functionalists, of course, did not *introduce* the study of behavior into psychology as a method of scientific investigation. From the first, the classical experimentalists had sought relevant behavioral data, e.g., in the reaction-time experiment which they used extensively as one of their standard procedures. But to them behavioral data were valuable as empirical evidence relevant to their subject matter, consciousness, itself directly observable only introspectively.

3. For a time, largely because of Titchener's opposition—published (1898, 1899) and unpublished—the movement led by Dewey, Angell, and later by Carr at Chicago, required and received the support of staunch adherents who formed something very like a school. But psychologists with leanings toward functionalism as a point of view do not as a rule found schools, though they may exert a distinctive influence on sizable groups of followers. Among the older generation of American psychologists who are sometimes classified as functionalists—a classification that for obvious reasons is not easy to make—there are, in addition to the three just mentioned, James, Hall, Baldwin, Cattell, Woodworth, and Thorndike. All of these have been influential; none has

founded a school; and none has been the center of a school founded by others upon his teachings. They have been leaders of thought without being founders of schools. These and related points are discussed more or less explicitly in several chapters on functionalism (Boring, 1950; Heidbreder, 1933; Hilgard & Bower, 1966; Marx & Hillix, 1963; Woodworth & Sheehan, 1964).

4. The classic statements of early functionalism are those of Dewey (1896) and Angell (1907). Watson (1913, 1936) vigorously rejected functionalism along with structuralism, regarding it as by no means a helpful transition from structuralism to behaviorism, but as a confused compromise between the two. Yet his behaviorism, upon becoming dominant in American psychology, was a large factor in creating the atmosphere and in establishing the perspective within which functionalism, seen in retrospect, took on the appearance of a transitional movement. It is this retrospective view which the stereotype represents.

5. One line taken by the structuralists, notably by Titchener (1898, 1899), was that in the *new* science of psychology, it was of the utmost importance to determine, first, the basic structure of its subject matter: the elementary constituents of consciousness and their modes of entering into blends, complexes, compounds, and the like. The argument was that to study functions without the restraining prior knowledge of the basic psychological structures involved, was to risk falling into faculty psychology, teleology, and other modes of thought inimical to a truly scientific psychology.

6. It has become customary to refer to a third, the mathematical sense, as characteristic of the way in which the functionalists use the term 'function.' But the use of mathematical functions is so prevalent in psychological research, that it can hardly be called characteristic of any one group or school. In any case, in the initial and distinctive position taken by the functionalists, the use of mathematical functions was not the point at issue. Later, after functionalism had become a going enterprise, Carr (1930) called attention to the mathematical sense as a way of meeting criticisms raised by Ruckmick (1913) concerning the ambiguity of the term 'function' as used in psychological textbooks. Discussions of the mathematical sense of 'function' in relation to the views and practices of functionalists occur in chapters on functionalism in Heidbreder, 1933; Hilgard and Bower, 1966; Marx and Hillix, 1963; Woodworth and Sheehan, 1964.

7. Carr's treatment of the adaptive act is presented in Chapter IV (1925). Woodworth's use of the S-O-R schema is so pervasive in his writings that the selection of specific references is not easy. Phases of its development can be traced through the four editions of his introductory text (1921; 1929; 1934; 1940). An important discussion of the role of O in the schema occurs in 1937.

8. The emphasis placed by both schools on having an *observable* subject matter stems largely from their conviction that the emancipation of psychology from speculative philosophy, and indeed the very possibility of pursuing psychology as a natural science, depended on their having such a subject matter. Their rather unquestioning attitude toward the currently accepted rules and standards of science is hardly surprising. Psychology as a science arose during the latter half of the nineteenth century, when "the scientific movement" was achieving impressive successes, and before the revolution in physics had led to a general reexamination of the conceptual framework within which the scientific enterprise operates. It is especially noteworthy, in this connection, that some of the main roots of the new science of psychology lay in the new developments in physiology, especially in sense physiology, and that the brilliant achievements of nineteenth-century physiology were largely unaffected by the researches in physics which led to the revolution in physical science. The logical and methodological implications of this revolution for science generally did not receive serious consideration in American psychology until about 1930, when oper-

ationism and logical positivism began to be influential, most conspicuously, but not solely, in the learning theories of the neobehaviorists.

9. In a significant passage, Hilgard and Bower (1966, pp. 2-6) discuss the point that no satisfactory definition of learning is now available, and make the further point that controversies about learning arise "over fact and interpretation, not over definition" and that "occasional confusions over definition . . . may usually be resolved by resort to pointing, to denotation." The implication is that psychologists can identify, and agree in identifying, actual cases of learning, and can and do conduct research which they agree is research on learning, without being able to define learning satisfactorily or to specify satisfactorily the situations in which they agree that learning has occurred. Similar considerations hold for perception, which is at least as hard as learning to define and to identify by specifying the conditions of its occurrence.

10. Especially relevant to the present discussion is the work of Piaget (1926, 1952), according to whom the child during the first eighteen months of life comes increasingly to behave as if he were dealing with enduring objects, existing independently of himself in an independently existing environment that is spatially, temporally, and causally organized. It is possible to interpret Piaget's account as indicating that during this early period of his life, the child, in his sensory and motor engagements with his surroundings, is laying the foundations of the naive realism which is the implicit metaphysics of common sense, and which in a normal person is so deeply and firmly established that it operates all his life as a part of his commonsense knowledge in his ordinary dealings with his environment. And even when, in some scientific or other intellectual enterprise, it becomes necessary for him to depart from his commonsense knowledge, he, or someone else, is likely to discover that he is in fact still unwittingly operating with some irrelevant or damaging portion of it.

11. This is not to say that psychology as a science arose directly and solely as a development of commonsense knowledge. Historically, psychology as a science, especially as an experimental science, began in and took its departure from other sciences, notably physiology (cf. note 8). But it must not be forgotten that the conceptualization of certain events as sensing, perceiving, discriminating, and the like, had been achieved in commonsense knowledge long before physiologists and other scientists began investigations bearing on such events; that physiology, for example, became one of the immediate sources of scientific psychology, precisely because its work on sense organs, reaction-times, and other structures and processes afforded promising means of investigating empirical materials prescientifically conceptualized and prescientifically regarded as psychological.

12. This paragraph, as must be evident to many readers, has been written with Kuhn's (1962) concept of paradigm in mind. In it I have attributed to the kind of reconceptualization and conceptual scheme under discussion some of the effects Kuhn attributes to paradigms—or rather to those paradigms which he regards as *first* integrating their respective disciplines and converting them into mature sciences. However, my terms "reconceptualization" and "conceptual scheme" are not intended as synonyms for Kuhn's term "paradigm," which is more inclusive in its coverage. Without unreservedly accepting Kuhn's concept of paradigm and his discussion of it, I believe that in presenting his case for it he has made an important contribution to the psychology of cognition. In my opinion, he has placed in a revealing context the role and vicissitudes of complex cognitive structures, not only as they occur in science, but also, at least by implication, as they occur in prescientific and extrascientific commonsense knowledge.

13. The commitment of eminent leaders to this program—"The Helmholtz program"—is discussed in Chapter III in Shakow & Rapaport, 1964, and pp.

91-94 of this volume [*Schools of psychology*: *A symposium,* ed. by David L. Krantz. New York: Appleton-Century-Crofts, 1969].
14. One of the first functionalists to enter this field was George H. Mead, a friend and associate of Dewey at Chicago. It is interesting to note the recent revival of interest, among social psychologists, in Mead's work. Some of his influential publications have been collected and edited by Strauss (1964).

REFERENCES

Angell, J. R. The province of functional psychology *Psychological Review,* 1907, *14*, 61-91.
Boring, E. G. *A history of experimental psychology.* (2nd ed.) New York: Appleton-Century-Crofts, 1950.
Carr, H. A. *Psychology*: *A study of mental activity.* New York: Longmans, 1925.
Carr, H. A. Functionalism. In C. Murchison (Ed.), *Psychologies of 1930,* Worcester, Mass.: Clark University Press, 1930.
Dewey, J. The reflex arc concept in psychology. *Psychological Review,* 1896, *8*, 357-370.
Heidbreder, E. *Seven psychologies.* New York: Appleton-Century-Crofts, 1933.
Hilgard, E. R., & Bower, G. H. *Theories of learning.* (3rd ed.) New York: Appleton-Century-Crofts, 1966.
Kuhn, T. S. *The structure of scientific revolutions.* Chicago: The University of Chicago Press, 1962.
Marx, M. H., & Hillix, W. A. *Systems and theories in psychology.* New York: McGraw-Hill, 1963.
Piaget, J. *The child's conception of the world,* 1926. Trans. by A. and J. Tomlinson. New York: Harcourt, Brace and World, 1929.
Piaget, J. *The origins of intelligence in children,* 1936. Trans. by M. Cooke. New York: International Universities Press, 1952.
Ruckmick, C. A. The use of the term *Function* in English textbooks of psychology. *American Journal of Psychology,* 1913, *29*, 99-123.
Shakow, D., & Rapaport, D. The influence of Freud on American psychology. *Psychological Issues,* New York: International Universities Press, 1964. Vol. IV (1 Monogr. 13).
Strauss, A. (Ed.) *George Herbert Mead on social psychology.* Chicago: Phoenix Books, The University of Chicago Press, 1964.
Titchener, E. B. The postulates of a structural psychology. *Philosophical Review,* 1898, *7*, 449-465.
Titchener, E. B. Structural and functional psychology. *Philosophical Review,* 1899, *8*, 290-299.
Watson, J. B. Psychology as the behaviorist views it. *Psychological Review,* 1913, *20*, 158-177.
Watson, J. B. Autobiography. In C. Murchison (Ed.), *A history of psychology in autobiography.* Worcester, Mass.: Clark University Press, 1936. III, 271-281.
Woodworth, R. S. *Psychology.* New York: Henry Holt, 1921, 1929, 1934, 1940.
Woodworth, R. S. Situation-and-goal-set. *American Journal of Psychology,* 1937, *50*, 130-140,
Woodworth, R. S., & Sheehan, M. R. *Contemporary schools of psychology.* (3rd ed.) New York: Ronald Press, 1964.

Robert Sessions Woodworth
1869-1962

EDNA HEIDBREDER

Robert Sessions Woodworth died on July 4, 1962, at the age of ninety-three. His life included over sixty years of sustained, absorbed inquiry into psychological problems.

A major trend in his thinking was his persistent effort to conceptualize the subject matter of psychology in such a way as to make it amenable, without oversimplification, to scientific research. One outcome of this endeavor was his interpretation of the relation between psychology and physiology. Early in his career, while working in both fields, he gradually became convinced that in their different accounts of an event — say, hearing a tone — the physiologist and the psychologist are describing the same identical process; that what the physiologist describes as occurring in the receptors and nervous system is the very process which the subject describes as hearing a tone and which the psychologist describes, perhaps as assignable to a point on a scale of loudness, perhaps as containing "beats." Similarly, in describing behavior — say, a conditioned response — the two investigators give different descriptions of the same identical process. They use different techniques in their research and they report at different levels of description. Characteristically, but not invariably, the physiologist describes in greater detail, the psychologist in greater breadth. Both descriptions are necessary; neither can be substituted for the other; at each level of inquiry facts are disclosed which at the other are unobservable.

In this conception Woodworth seems to have achieved his basic orientation to his life-work. It enabled him to treat the subject matter of psychology, whether observed introspectively or otherwise, as consisting of natural events in the natural world, and to see psychology as having, like physiology or any of the other natural sciences, its special function in their common enterprise. He first presented this view in a public lecture in 1908, and he subsequently stated it in several of his writings, including his last book.

Unless this basic orientation is taken into account — and it is often overlooked — Woodworth's treatment of some important problems may easily be misinterpreted. Woodworth is sometimes described as being "on the fence," as being so acutely aware of the complexities of a controversial issue as to be unwilling or unable to stand decisively for either side. He did not, in fact, join either side in the battle between Watsonian behaviorists and Titchenerian introspectionists. Yet he neither avoided nor evaded the issue. He met it by stating and defending a definite position of his own. From his point of view — essentially that indicated above — both sides made unnecessary and unwarranted exclusions; neither side admitted all the relevant empirical data obtainable. Characteristically, he stuck to the facts of the case as he saw and understood them — as he did on other occasions when his interpretation of a situation cut across the lines drawn by some controversy then in progress. On those occasions, too, some of his fellow psychologists saw his treatment of the situation as unclear and indecisive.

In coming to terms more specifically with the subject matter of psychology, Woodworth adopted first the *S-R,* then successive versions and various forms of the *S-O-R* formula. These he regarded as statements of psychology's essential task: that of accounting for the give and take between the organism and its physical and social environment. Psychological processes, he maintained, are characteristically directed toward an objective environment; they are essentially an organism's ways of dealing with such an environment. They include, in addition to motor behavior, such activities as perceiving and learning. Perceiving the environment, for example, consists in dealing with it by transforming — or better, translating — sensory input from it into information about it, thus acquainting the organism with objective things, events, and situations in an objective world. Learning, too, is a way of dealing with the environment. It consists largely in object-learning and place-learning, kinds of learning that are intimately involved in motor learning. Furthermore, these motor, perceptual, and other ways of dealing with the environment require no motivation from sources outside themselves. Their activity is not dependent, directly or indirectly, on primary organic needs. They can and often do run on their own drive.

This is substantially the position Woodworth took in *Dynamic Psychology* (1918), in opposing McDougall's theory of the instincts. In "Reenforcement of Perception" (1946) he presented perception as a motivated process, treating it as motivated intrinsically, as positively reinforced by its own successful outcome, and as not requiring reinforcement through any drive other than its own. In *Dynamics of Behavior* (1958) he took a further step: here again he treated motor, perceptual, and other ways of dealing with the environment as intrinsically motivated; but in addition he maintained that the tendency to deal with the environment is the primary and all-pervasive motivation of behavior. Though the give and take between organism and environment is often directly or indirectly motivated by basic biological needs, the processes that constitute it do not require such motivation. They occur with it or without it, whereas they are themselves indispensable to the successful execution of behavior that is driven directly or indirectly by primary needs.

No one believed more strongly than Woodworth that any theory, to be scientifically acceptable, must engage with the relevant facts. His two editions of *Experimental Psychology* (1938, 1954), the second with Schlosberg, indicate not only his respect for experimental findings but also his comprehensive, detailed, and critical knowledge of them. And going beyond experimental psychology in the strict sense of that term, he kept in touch, to an impressive degree, with developments in psychology generally. His extraordinary knowledge of psychological research was an integral part of his theoretical thinking, a fact clearly evident in both editions of *Contemporary Schools of Psychology* (1931, 1948). His own experimental investigations, some of them conducted with colleagues, included research on voluntary movement, imageless thought, "racial" differences, transfer, and association. In addition, during the First World War, he prepared a *Personal Data Sheet* designed to screen out recruits whose precarious mental health might make them unfit for military service. Some of these studies were pioneering ventures into fields later developed by other investigators.

Many honors came Woodworth's way. Only one will be mentioned here. In 1956, six weeks before his eighty-seventh birthday, he received the first Gold Medal of the American Psychological Foundation. The citation referred to his "distinguished and continuous service to scholarship." It soon became evident that his distinguished service had not ceased. Two years later he published *Dynamics of Behavior,* the book in which he presented his soberly challenging interpretation of perception, learning, and motivation.

Bibliography of the Published
Writings of Edna Heidbreder

An experimental study of thinking. *Archives of Psychology*, 1924, *11*, 1-65.

Thinking as an instinct. *Psychological Review*, 1926, *33*, 279-297.

Measuring introversion and extroversion. *Journal of Abnormal and Social Psychology*, 1926, *21*, 120-134.

Intelligence and the height-weight ratio. *Journal of Applied Psychology*, 1926, *10*, 52-62.

Reasons used in solving problems. *Journal of Experimental Psychology*, 1927, *10*, 397-414.

Introversion and extroversion in men and women. *Journal of Abnormal and Social Psychology*, 1927, *22*, 52-61.

The normal inferiority complex. *Journal of Abnormal and Social Psychology*, 1927, *22*, 243-258.

Problem solving in children and adults. *Journal of Genetic Psychology*, 1928, *35*, 522-545.

Self ratings and preferences. *Journal of Abnormal and Social Psychology*, 1930, *25*, 62-74.

(With D. G. Patterson, R. M. Elliott, L. D. Anderson, & H. A. Toops.) *Minnesota Mechanical Ability Tests*. Minneapolis: University of Minnesota Press, 1930.

Minnesota personal traits rating scales test blank. Chicago: Stoelting, 1931.

(With G. Holmes.) A statistical study of a new type of objective examination question. *Journal of Educational Research*, 1931, *24*, 286-292.

Seven Psychologies. New York: Century, 1933.

A study of the evolution of concepts. *Psychological Bulletin*, 1934, *31*, 673. (Abstract.)

Thinking. In C. Skinner (Ed.), *Readings in Psychology*. New York: Farrar and Rinehart, 1935.

Language and concepts. *Psychological Bulletin*, 1936, *33*, 724. (Abstract.)

William McDougall and social psychology. *Journal of Abnormal and Social Psychology*, 1939, *34*, 150-160.

Freud and psychology. *Psychological Review*, 1940, *47*, 185-195.

Perceptual and intellectual factors in the production of concepts. *Psychological Bulletin*, 1942, *39*, 497-498. (Abstract.)

(With H. Peak.) Tentative suggestions on undergraduate training for women in the emergency. In S. H. Britt (Ed.), Psychology and the war. *Psychological Bulletin*, 1942, *39*, 369-410.

Adjustments of the College Curriculum to Wartime Conditions and Needs.
Report No. 1: Psychology. Washington, D. C.: U. S. Office of Education, 1943.

The orientation of college women toward war needs. *Journal of Consulting Psychology,* 1943, *7,* 289-295.

Toward a dynamic psychology of cognition. *Psychological Review,* 1945, *52,* 1-22.

The attainment of concepts — a psychological interpretation. *Transactions of the New York Academy of Sciences,* 1945, *7,* 171-188.

Psychology of thinking. *Encyclopedia Brittanica,* 1946.

The attainment of concepts: I. Terminology and methodology. *Journal of General Psychology,* 1946, *35,* 173-189.

The attainment of concepts: II. The problem. *Journal of General Psychology,* 1946, *35,* 191-223.

The attainment of concepts: III. The process. *Journal of Psychology,* 1947, *24,* 93-138.

(With M. L. Bensley and M. Ivy.) The attainment of concepts: IV. Regularities and levels. *Journal of Psychology,* 1948, *25,* 279-329.

(With P. Overstreet.) The attainment of concepts: V. Critical features and contexts. *Journal of Psychology,* 1948, *26,* 45-69.

The attainment of concepts: VI. Exploratory experiments on conceptualization at perceptual levels. *Journal of Psychology,* 1948, *26,* 193-216.

Studying human thinking. In T. G. Andrews (Ed.), *Methods of Psychology.* New York: Wiley, 1948.

The attainment of concepts: VII. Conceptual achievements during card-sorting. *Journal of Psychology,* 1949, *27,* 3-39.

The attainment of concepts: VIII. The conceptualization of verbally indicated instances. *Journal of Psychology,* 1949, *27,* 263-309.

Experiments by Dattman and Israel on the attainment of concepts. *Journal of Psychology,* 1952, *34,* 115-136.

Stimulus discriminability and concept-attainment: A question arising from Baum's experiment. *Journal of Psychology,* 1955, *39,* 341-350.

(With C. Zimmerman.) The attainment of concepts: IX. Semantic efficiency and concept-attainment. *Journal of Psychology,* 1955, *40,* 325-335.

Woodworth and Whorf on the role of language in thinking. In G. H. Seward and J. P. Seward (Eds.), *Current Psychological Issues: Essays in Honor of Robert S. Woodworth.* New York: Holt, 1958.

Robert Sessions Woodworth, 1869-1962. *British Journal of Psychology,* 1963, *54,* 199-200.

Preface to A. H. Kidd and J. L. Rivoire (Eds.), *Perceptual Development in Children.* New York: International Universities Press, 1966, viii-ix.

Functionalism. In D. L. Krantz (Ed.), *Schools of Psychology: A Symposium.* New York: Appleton-Century-Crofts, 1969.

Mary Whiton Calkins. *Journal of the History of the Behavioral Sciences,* 1972, *8,* 56-68.

REVIEWS

J. W. Bridges. Psychology, Normal and Abnormal. *Journal of Abnormal and Social Psychology,* 1932, *27,* 95-96.

Glenn D. Higginson. Fields of Psychology. *Journal of Abnormal and Social Psychology,* 1932, *27,* 96-97.

W. B. Pillsbury. An Elementary Psychology of the Abnormal. *Journal of Abnormal and Social Psychology,* 1933, *28,* 96-97.

Douglas Fryer. The Measurement of Interests. *Journal of Abnormal and Social Psychology,* 1933, *28,* 319-321.

S. Freud. New Introductory Lectures on Psycho-Analysis. *Journal of Abnormal and Social Psychology,* 1934, *29,* 106-109.

Karin Stephen. Psychoanalysis and Medicine. *Journal of Abnormal and Social Psychology,* 1934, *29,* 235-236.

C. Burt, E. Jones, E. Miller, & W. Moodie. How the Mind Works. *Journal of Abnormal and Social Psychology,* 1935, *30,* 129-131.

M. Krout. Major Aspects of Personality. *Journal of Abnormal and Social Psychology,* 1935, *30,* 131-133.

George Hartmann. Gestalt Psychology. *Psychological Bulletin,* 1936, *33,* 541-544.

Kurt Lewin. Principles of Topological Psychology. *Psychological Bulletin,* 1937, *34,* 584-604.

E. I. Adamson. So You're Going to a Psychiatrist. *Journal of Abnormal and Social Psychology,* 1937, *31,* 494.

T. A. Ross. Prognosis in the Neuroses. *Journal of Abnormal and Social Psychology,* 1937, *32,* 244-246.

A Symposium on the Relation Between the Individual and the Group, American Journal of Sociology, 1939, *44,* No. 6. *Journal of Abnormal and Social Psychology,* 1939, *34,* 550-551.

G. Zilboorg & G. W. Henry. A History of Medical Psychology. *Journal of Abnormal and Social Psychology,* 1942, *37,* 416-417.

A. S. Porterfield. Creative Factors in Scientific Research. *Journal of Abnormal and Social Psychology,* 1942, *37,* 574-575.

E. J. Kahn. The Army Life. *Journal of Abnormal and Social Psychology, Clinical Supplement,* 1943, *38,* 195-197.

K. Goldstein. Aftereffects of Brain Injuries in War. *Journal of Abnormal and Social Psychology,* 1943, *38,* 407-408.

C. P. Oberndorf. The Psychiatric Novels of Oliver Wendell Holmes. *Journal of Abnormal and Social Psychology,* 1944, *39,* 271-275.

Gardner Murphy (Ed.), Human Nature and Enduring Peace. *Journal of Abnormal and Social Psychology,* 1946, *41,* 237-238.

E. B. Hunt. Concept Learning: An Information Processing Problem. *Contemporary Psychology,* 1964, *9,* 40-41.

J. C. Flugel & D. J. West. A Hundred Years of Psychology. Also: L. S. Hearnshaw. A Short History of British Psychology. *Contemporary Psychology,* 1965, *10,* 385-387.

SOURCES IN THE HISTORY
OF PSYCHOLOGY

Annotated Bibliographic Sources in the History of Psychology

RICHARD A. BAGG

The burgeoning body of reference material useful in the history of psychology has greatly facilitated research in this area. This appendix does not presume to provide an exhaustive compilation of even the most significant sources in the field. However, an acquaintance with the international references cited will provide a foundation and a fruitful starting point for study in the modern history of psychology and related areas.

A word about style is appropriate. If the particular source has an author or editor, the latter is specified by "Ed.," unless there have been changes in editorship, in which case the designation "various" is adopted. The original publication date, where applicable, appears in parentheses.

Due to the limitation of space, it was decided that two categories of references would be designated in depth: bibliographic and biographic sources. Several major categories were not included, such as the dictionaries of psychological terminology, encyclopedias, handbooks, and textbooks. In evaluating a source, one must consider the number of volumes against the breadth of coverage.

A. BIBLIOGRAPHIC SOURCES

American bibliography. C. Evans. (12 vols.) New York: Peter Smith, 1941-1942 (1903-1934).

Covers the period from 1639 to 1799. The preface states that it is "a chronological dictionary of all books, pamphlets and periodical publications printed in the United States of America from the genesis of printing in 1639 down to and including the year 1820 with bibliographical and biographical notes." Although the preface states the intent to complete the work to 1820, the author never finished. It has a subject, author, and publisher's index.

L'année psychologique. (70 vols. plus) (Vols. 1-49, Liechtenstein: Kraus Reprint, 1970) Paris: Presses Universitaires de France, 1951–.

Every volume includes a section entitled Table Bibliographique (1894-1904) or Analyses Bibliographiques (1905——), which lists the major journal articles and books published that year in psychology. English and German citations are frequent. After 1905, the cited material was abstracted; previous to that time, the materials were merely listed.

Annual review of psychology. Various. (22 vols. plus) Menasha, Wis.: Banta, 1950–.

This represents a survey of the most important literature published in the field of psychology. Not all topics are surveyed each year, but an attempt is made to survey certain areas on a regularly scheduled basis; for example, a review of the contemporary literature in perception will be included every second year. The intent is not only to present an abstract of the material, but also to give evaluative consideration to the topics selected for review. A carefully selected bibliography which forms the basis for the review follows each chapter.

Author index to Psychological index (1894-1935) and Psychological abstracts (1927-1958). (5 vols.) Boston: Hall, 1960.

This is exclusively an author index, in which all published works by an individual from 1894 to 1958 are cited. In case of joint authorship, only the primary author is credited. Supplementary volumes follow which attempt to bring the series up to date. Also included in the series is a *Cumulated subject index to Psychological abstracts (1927-1960)* with supplementary volumes.

Bibliographic index. Various. (9 vols. plus) New York: Wilson, 1945–.

This source is a bibliography of bibliographies that have appeared in both books and journals, many of which are in foreign languages. It surveys over 1,700 periodicals covering many fields of knowledge. It spans the period from 1937 to the present, and the index is alphabetized by subject only. As of 1966, only those bibliographies with 40 or more titles are included.

Bibliographie der deutschen Zeitschriftenliteratur. (1896-1964) (128 vols.) New York: Kraus Reprint, 1961-1964.

This reference to German sources (not books) dating back to 1861 provides an extensive author and subject index. The subject index is rather broad; abbreviated titles are listed with the author's name following. Journal titles are also abbreviated, and a reference table for these truncations is provided. The author index lists those subjects upon which an individual has written that year; this necessitates finding the key word within the name of the article within the subject category. Though initially difficult to master, this source provides valuable and extensive reference material covering all fields of knowledge. These volumes form a companion series to the *Bibliographie der fremdsprachigen Zeitschriftenliteratur.* This series became part of the *Internationale Bibliographie der Zeitschriftenliteratur* in 1965.

Bibliographie der fremdsprachigen Zeitschriftenliteratur. (1911-1964) (51 vols.) New York: Kraus Reprint, 1961-1964.

These are companion volumes to the *Bibliographie der deutschen Zeitschriftenliteratur* and provide references on other than German periodicals, such as those from the United States, France, England, and Italy, covering all fields of knowledge. As of 1965, this source has been incorporated into the *Internationale Bibliographie der Zeitschriftenliteratur.*

Bibliographie der psychologischen Literatur der sozialistischen Länder. (1961-1966) Berlin: Volk und Wissen Volkseigener Verlag, 1965-1969.

This is a bibliography of the psychological literature of the socialist countries, including East Germany, Bulgaria, Russia, Rumania, Hungary, and neighboring countries. The bibliography is in the native language, i.e., German, Russian. There are no English translations. Inclusive volumes, so far, cover 1961-1966.

Bibliography of philosophy, psychology, and cognate subjects. Ed. by B. Rand. In J. M. Baldwin (Ed.), *Dictionary of philosophy and psychology.* Vol. 3, New York: Macmillan, 1905.

Lists bibliographic sources for the history of philosophy, systematic philosophy, logic, esthetics, philosophy of religion, ethics, and psychology. Also gives primary and secondary sources for most prominent philosophers.

British Museum: general catalogue of printed books. (263 vols.) London: The Trustees of the British Museum, 1965-1966.

This source cites the contents of the British Museum Library, alphabetically by author, from the fifteenth century to 1955. Several supplements update the material. An attempt has been made to cite most works with which an individual has been associated, whether his function be that of author, editor, or contributor. Also provided are secondary sources. This source is marred somewhat by its neglect, in many instances, to provide the name of the publisher.

Bücher-Lexicon. Ed. by C. G. Kayser. (36 vols.) Graz: Akademische Druck, 1961-1962.

An extensive bibliographic source arranged by author and covering the period from 1750 to 1910. This source provides title, date, and place of publication for major books and periodicals. In addition to the German references, some Swiss and Austrian publications are cited. It is essentially a bookdealer's catalog and lists major works published in the German-speaking countries.

A catalog of books represented by Library of Congress printed cards. (167 vols.) Ann Arbor, Mich.: Edwards, 1942-1946.

This catalog, which forms a series, represents, alphabetically by author, a listing of books in the Library of Congress. Two supplements followed: 1942-1948 (42 vols.) and 1948-1952 (23 vols.) In 1956 *The Library of*

Congress catalog — books: authors changed to include titles reported to the National Union catalog, and thus the title became *The National Union catalog, a cumulative author list.* Reflecting this alteration, several supplements were published. *The National Union catalog* is now being published; it contains all pre-1956 imprints. This includes the works cited above and is representative of the Library of Congress printed cards and, in addition, books held by participating libraries. *The National Union catalog* is the superior source when checking for date or place of publication. But this catalog has printed only A through Ferguut in 169 volumes. For information following this part of the alphabet, the other catalogs should be consulted.

Catalogue général des livres imprimés de la Bibliothèque Nationale. (206 vols. plus) Vols. 1-80, Paris: Catin. Paris: Imprimerie Nationale, 1924–.

This, as yet uncompleted (A to Véron), bibliographic reference lists books alphabetically by author. Though predominantly French, reference is also made to books published in English, German, and several other languages. The latter volumes list books published up to 1960. A supplement to include books after 1960 has been published.

Catalogue of scientific papers compiled by the Royal Society of London 1800-1900. (19 vols.) New York: Kraus Reprint, 1965 (1867-1925).

This catalog is representative of scientific works from journals and periodicals, not including books, for the nineteenth century, listed alphabetically by author. In many cases, biographies and secondary works are presented in a section prior to the listing of the author's work. In rare instances, it lists works previous to 1800.

Deutsches Bücherverzeichnis. (38 vols.) (Vols. 1-22, Leipzig: Verlag des Börsenvereins der Deutschen Buchhändler.) Leipzig: Verlag für Buch– und Bibliothekswesen, 1916–.

A bibliography of books published in the German language in Germany, Switzerland, and Austria. Successor to *Kaysers Bücher-Lexicon*. This reference publishes two volumes every five years, an author and subject index. The volumes cover the period from 1911 to the present.

Eminent contributors to psychology. Vol I. *A bibliography of primary references.* Vol. II. *A bibliography of secondary references.* Ed. by R. I. Watson. New York: Springer Publishing Co. (In press.)

Listing over 500 deceased psychologists who worked during the modern period, this is a selected bibliography of primary and secondary references, in two volumes. Biographies and other bibliographies are cited. In all, about 50,000 references are provided.

The encyclopedia of philosophy. Ed. by P. Edwards *et al.* (8 vols.) New York: Macmillan, 1967.

Defines philosophical terms and includes many influential persons in the field. Bibliographies following biographic material make reference to the individual's work and indicate secondary sources. As this work is encyclopedic in nature, it improves upon Baldwin's *Dictionary.*

The English catalog of books. (20 vols. plus) London: Publishers Circular et al., 1864–.
Covering the period from 1801 to the present, this source makes reference to works published in the United Kingdom. For some years, the subject index is a distinct volume, while other years include author, subject, and title headings within the same volume.

La France littéraire ou Dictionnaire bibliographique. Ed. By J. M. Querard. (12 vols.) Paris: Maisonneuve & Larose, 1827-1864 (reprinted 1964).
This source compiles a bibliography of French writers and persons who wrote in French during the eighteenth and nineteenth centuries. It provides a listing of books, including those translated into French, by author. A companion series, *La littérature française contemporaine,* is listed below.

Gesamtverzeichnis der deutschsprachigen psychologischen Literatur der Jahre 1942 bis 1960. Ed. by A. Wellek. Göttingen: Verlag für Psychologie, 1965.
A sourcebook which lists German, Swiss, and Austrian psychological literature for the years indicated. Provides references to both books and journal articles. Materials are listed chronologically within subdivisions of psychology.

Index-Catalogue of the Library of the Surgeon General's Office. (58 vols.) United States Army: Army Medical Library, 1880-1955.
This source, making reference to books, periodicals, and pamphlets, has an extensive subject and author index. Virtually every field of medicine and related areas is covered.

Index medicus. (Vol. 1–) Washington, National Library of Medicine, 1960–.
The most comprehensive index to the literature of medicine in the world. Subject and author indices are provided for several thousand journals. Translations of non-English materials are given. Areas of interest include psychology and psychiatry. Three series of the earlier *Index medicus* were published from 1879 to 1927. This was then incorporated into the *Quarterly cumulative index medicus,* published from 1927 to 1956, and the *Current list of medical literature,* published from 1950 to 1959. The *Cumulated index medicus* (1960–) compiles annually what the *Index medicus* attempts monthly.

The index of psychoanalytic writings. Ed. by A. Grinstein. (9 vols.) New York: International Universities Press, 1956-1966.

This reference attempts to list by subject and author all psychoanalytic works published between 1900 and 1960. The references are cited in both language of origin and English. Also included in this source are the titles appearing in an earlier work by J. Rickman, *Index Psychoanalyticus, 1893-1926.*

International bibliography of the social sciences. London: Tavistock; Chicago: Aldine, 1951–.

A series of references which include Anthropology (1955–, 14 vols. plus), Economics (1952–, 17 vols. plus), Political Science (1952–, 17 vols. plus) and Sociology (1951–, 18 vols. plus). These sources have an exhaustive list of books and journal articles published in many languages of the respective fields. References are indexed by subject and author.

International encyclopedia of the social sciences. Ed. by D. L. Sills. (17 vols.) New York: Macmillan, 1968.

Written by social scientists, this source defines terms related to all branches of the social sciences. In addition, it provides fairly complete biographies of persons who have helped shape their respective fields. Extensive bibliographies follow not only the biographies, but also the terminology. The fields surveyed include anthropology, economics, geography, history, law, political science, psychiatry, psychology, sociology, and statistics.

Internationale Bibliographie der Zeitschriftenliteratur. Ed. by O. Zeller. Osnabrück: Felix Dietrich Verlag, 1965–.

Over 7,600 periodicals are consulted for inclusion in this combined version of the *Bibliographie der deutschen Zeitschriftenliteratur* and the *Bibliographie der fremdsprachigen Zeitschriftenliteratur.* Both author and subject indices are provided; the latter topic headings appear in German with French and English equivalents. Virtually every field of knowledge is covered.

ISIS (official Journal of the History of Science Society) (60 vols. plus) London: Dawson & Sons *et al.,* 1914–.

Ninety-five critical bibliographies have been published to date in the journal, *ISIS.* The comprehensive bibliographies make reference to the history of science and its cultural influences, including a modest selection of references to psychology. Not only does it cover books, but pertinent journal articles are also cited.

Die Literatur der Psychiatrie, Neurologie und Psychologie von 1459-1799. Ed. by H. Laehr. (3 vols. in 4) Berlin: Reimer, 1900.

Covers the subject fields indicated in the title for books published during the period 1459-1799. Periodicals were not surveyed, and of the books listed, only the titles are cited; there are no annotations or abstracts.

La littérature française contemporaine. Ed. by J. M. Querard, L. F. Bourquelot, & C. Louandre. (6 vols.) Paris: Maisonneuve & Larose, 1842-1857 (reprinted 1965).

This reference provides an alphabetical listing, by author, of books by French authors, persons who wrote in French and works translated into French in the nineteenth century.

Manuel de bibliographie philosophique. Ed. by G. Varet. (2 vols.) Paris: Presses Universitaires de France, 1956.

This source addresses itself to ancient, medieval, and modern philosophy. It is essentially a bibliographic source, listing both books and journal articles. All publications appear in the language of origin.

Poole's Index to periodical literature (1802-1906). (6 vols. in 7) New York: Peter Smith, 1938.

Surveying 105 years, this index lists important nontechnical English and American periodicals. It is a subject index; authors' names appear as subject entries occasionally, but to find the works of a given individual, one must begin with a topic.

Psychological abstracts. (44 vols. plus) Lancaster, Pa., and Washington, D.C.: The American Psychological Association, 1927–.

Published monthly, this reference attempts to abstract all psychological materials that are published. Offering a complete subject and author index, it is the definitive source for the psychologist.

The psychological index. Various. (42 vols.) (Vols. 1-11, New York: Macmillan; Vols. 12-18, Baltimore, Md.: Review) Princeton, N. J.: Psychological Review, 1895-1935.

This reference is a compilation, by subject, of all known psychological and cognate material published during the years cited. Each volume, containing journal articles and published books, includes an index of authors. It should be noted that while this reference provides a definitive listing of psychological research, it does not attempt to abstract the cited material. A duplicate volume of this series appears in the *Author index to Psychological index (1894-1935) and Psychological abstracts (1927-1958.)*

The psychological register. Ed. by C. A. Murchison. Vol 3. Worcester, Mass.: Clark University Press, 1932.

Important psychologists, living in 1931, arranged by country, are cited with brief biographies and very extensive bibliographies. Note that Volume 3 is specified. Volume 1, intending to include psychologists then deceased, was never issued; Volume 2 was a preliminary run of the contents of the

third volume and, when found to be inadequate, was superseded by the
specified volume.

Readers' Guide to periodical literature. (29 vols. plus) New York and
Minneapolis: Wilson, 1905–.

This indexes most of the United States periodicals since 1900. Topics
may be looked up under title, author, or subject heading. It is a consoli-
dation of a cumulative index to a selected list of periodicals and a readers'
guide to periodical literature. This guide is a successor to *Poole's Index.*

B. BIOGRAPHIC SOURCES

Allgemeine deutsche Biographie. (56 vols.) Leipzig: Duncker & Humblot,
1875-1912.

This source, covering the period from the earliest accounts to 1900,
is the German counterpart to the American source called *The dictionary
of American biography.*

Asimov's Biographical encyclopedia of science and technology. I. Asimov.
Garden City, N. Y.: Doubleday, 1964.

Chronologically arranged, this source includes biographies for more
than 1,000 scientists from the Greek period to the present, and includes
both an author and subject index.

A biographical dictionary of scientists. Ed. by T. I. Williams. New York:
Wiley, 1969.

This source is a compilation of biographies of deceased persons who
have made significant contributions to the field of science; their selection
is not limited by nationality or temporal period. Individuals chosen represent such fields as mathematics, medicine, and science in general.
Several secondary references follow each biography.

Biographical memoirs: National Academy of Sciences. (41 vols. plus)
New York: Columbia University Press, 1877–.

Designed to present in-depth monographic biographies for all members
of the National Academy of Sciences whose subject areas cover virtually
every field of science. The lengthy bibliographies, chronologically arranged,
follow the exhaustive biographies.

Chamber's biographical dictionary. Ed. by J. O. Thorne. New York: St.
Martin's Press, 1962 (1897).

This source gives a very short summary of the biography with the
intent to clothe "the bare facts with human interest and critical observation" (p. iv). In many instances, title and date of publication are provided.
An attempt is made to include all "established notabilities" in all fields.

Dictionary of American biography. Various. (21 vols.) New York: Scribner's, 1928-1935.

Three significant factors make an individual eligible for inclusion in this biography: he must be deceased, he must have lived in the United States at some time in his life, and he must have made a contribution to the American way of life. References pertaining to each individual cited are listed at the end of each biographical statement. A description of the subject's personality and unique achievements is included.

The dictionary of national biography. Ed. by L. Stephen & S. Lee. (22 vols.) London: Oxford University Press, 1959-1965. (1885-1901).

This source has as its subject Englishmen and persons who have lived in the colonies. Its selections date from early times to 1900; supplementary volumes attempt to update the reference. Articles included are signed and may be depended upon to be accurate and scholarly.

A dictionary of universal biography. A. M. Hyamson (2nd ed.) New York: Dutton, 1951 (1916).

This source limits its biographical data to birth and death date of individuals cited and to mention of professional status, i.e., Irish Baptist Minister. Its value lies in its key to references, which provides an indication as to where a biography can be found.

The encyclopedia of philosophy. See bibliographic section.

The general biographical dictionary. Ed. by A. Chalmers. (32 vols., new ed.) London: J. Nichols & Son, 1812-1917.

This reference contains "an historical and critical account of the lives and writings of the most eminent persons in every nation; particularly the British and Irish; from the earliest accounts to the present time" (p. iii).

Die grossen Deutschen. Ed. by H. Heimpel, T. Heuss, & B. Reifenberg. (5 vols.) Berlin: Im Propylaen-Verlag, bei Ullstein, 1960-1961 (1935-1937).

Chronologically arranged, this biographical source cites significant German persons from 672 to date.

A history of psychology in autobiography. Various. (5 vols.) (Vols. 1-3, Worcester, Mass.: Clark University Press) New York: Appleton-Century-Crofts, 1930-1967.

Using as its criteria for selection those persons, American or foreign, who have notably influenced American psychology, and who, by virtue of their age (60 or over), have achieved a considerable perspective on their work, eminent psychologists are invited to submit autobiographical statements. In earlier volumes, emphasis was placed on the motivational intent of the author. Since this time, however, due to the inadequacy of self-reported motivations, the emphasis has been switched to the depiction of major factors and influences in the intellectual life history of the individual along with the standard autobiographical data.

International encyclopedia of the social sciences. See bibliographic section.

The national cyclopedia of American biography. (51 vols.) New York: White, 1898-1969.

This source attempts to trace American history through biographies of the most significant men who helped found, settle, and establish America. Supplements update the original volumes. Bibliographies are not included.

Neue deutsche Biographie. (8 vols.) Berlin: Duncker & Humblot, 1953-1969.

This source cites significant individuals who have died since the printing of the *Allgemeine deutsche Biographie* and also those who were overlooked in the original publication. References are provided at the end of the biographies.

The New York Times obituary index, 1858-1968. New York: The New York Times, 1970.

Occasionally useful; it provides biographies, albeit obituaries, of psychologists on whom biographies are otherwise unavailable. The volume makes reference to the location of the obituary in the New York Times newspaper.

Nouvelle biographie générale. (46 vols. in 23) Copenhagen: Rosenkilde & Bagger, 1963-1969 (1857-1866).

This source attempts to provide biographical data on eminent men, not exclusively French, from the ancient period to 1850-1860. Bibliographic references and secondary sources are provided for most individuals cited.

The author acknowledges the help of Professor Robert I. Watson of the University of New Hampshire, without whose assistance this project could not have been accomplished.

Name Index

Page numbers within entries in this index are arranged in the following order: (1) substantive discussion in text or notes, (2) incidental mention in text, (3) mention in notes, (4) mention as references in text.

Title Index

Subject Index

Page numbers within entries in this index are arranged so that numbers referring to substantive discussions in text precede those referring to incidental mentions.